STRATEGY & MARKETING

A CASE APPROACH

Kenneth Simmonds (Editor)

London Business School

Philip Allan

First published 1982 by
PHILIP ALLAN PUBLISHERS LIMITED
MARKET PLACE
DEDDINGTON
OXFORD OX5 4SE

British Library Cataloguing in Publication Data
Strategy and marketing.
   1. Marketing — Case studies
   I. Simmonds — Kenneth
   658.8'00722   HF5415

   ISBN 0-86003-516-6
   ISBN 0-86003-615-4 Pbk

Set in Compugraphic Paladium 11/12 by MHL Typesetting Limited, Coventry
Printed in Great Britain by Hartnoll Print Limited, Bodmin, Cornwall

Contents

Preface

Strategy and marketing go hand in hand. Although strategy has been given more attention recently than in the past, marketing was never intended to be studied as a tactical field divorced from its strategic implications. As a wise man once said, 'If you do not know where you are going, any direction will get you there'. And it is the strategy component of marketing that is concerned with direction. It is concerned with those core actions for any business which determine the direction it moves within its marketplace and are the essential cause of improvement or reversal in performance.

In choosing these core actions the strategically-aware marketer must decide not only the particular grouping of customers that are the target of his actions, but also allow for the actions of competitors. He must evaluate the opponents' competitive positions and likely moves and even the probable effects of his own moves on those positions.

Design of the Casebook This casebook has been developed to meet the need for a comprehensive set of case materials on strategy and marketing from which instructors might design their own case courses. Different students and different instructors will have a wide range of different needs and interests and there has been a demand for a case text with sufficient coverage to enable selection. This text has, therefore, included cases both old and new, long and short, strategic and functional, quantitative and verbal, consumer and industrial, national and international, for goods and services, and for discussion and role playing. Furthermore, while the case collection covers predominantly UK situations, there are cases set in over a dozen countries including the USA, Canada, Holland, Sweden, France, Italy, Indonesia, Hong Kong, Kuwait, Australia and Latin America. The text is divided into four parts:

> Strategic Marketing
> Market Assessment and Measurement
> Marketing Mix Decisions
> Managing Marketing Within the Organisation

Part A concentrates on the core of strategic actions for the business. The initial set of cases build an appreciation of workable marketing strategies through examination of situations in which the strategy is clearly open to question. Then follows a set of cases in which direct competitor reaction is likely and in which the success of any strategy will depend on the ways in which competitors react. Four more advanced cases examine the shaping of an international strategy where the market characteristics and competition can differ from country to country. Finally, this part of the book includes a few cases on corporate strategy, in which decisions need to reflect the long-term market mission of the enterprise, its financial structure and viability and the adjustment of emphasis among different businesses.

Part B of the text is directed at the assessment of markets viewed as a collection of buyers and consumers. Cases in this part open up discussion of underlying buyer motivation and the ways in which marketing actions appeal to such motivations. A particular effort has also been made to include cases which require assessment of the common sources of market data and the use and interpretation of statistical measurements. Courses with a market research bias are likely to draw heavily on this part.

Part C, entitled 'Marketing Mix Decisions', divides marketing into four areas of decision making and action: product, distribution, pricing and promotion. The cases in this part are those which would normally form the basis of a functional marketing course. Many instructors may decide in fact to start with cases from this part because the ramifications of the decisions are generally more constrained. I have endeavoured under each section to start with a short case that raises the major issues and then progress to more advanced cases.

Part D is concerned with what an organisation should expect of those in marketing functions and the management that will be required to achieve those expectations. The first set of cases deals with a firm's perception of its responsibility towards customers and the wider public with respect to products and marketing practices. Another set looks at sales management from a marketing viewpoint. It is the task of the marketing function to analyse whether sales effort should be expanded or contracted, upgraded or downgraded, split or amalgamated, and these cases introduce discussion on ways in which such analyses may be made. Lastly, there is a set of cases on making marketing happen. The conclusions emerging from discussion of these cases will depend very much on the standards discussants have developed for the level of performance of a marketing organisation.

In the final analysis, any classification of cases is highly subjective. Each case is a full problem with many facets and most could be classified under numerous different headings. Instructors, moreover, should develop their own course designs and may consider a quite different sequence of problems appropriate. For example, progression from relatively simple situations with one major action to be decided, through to complex situations requiring a sophisticated treatment, can be a very effective learning pattern. Detailed guidance for the instructor concerning the use of each case is set out in *The Instructor's Manual* (Philip Allan 1982).

Case Discussion

Case discussion plays a role in extending marketing skill that is difficult to fill with direct lecturing or worked examples. Marketing skill is essentially one of diagnosis. It is not an ability to apply a standard set of theories, nor deploy a collection of 'modern business techniques'. It is a skill in reasoning from the market situation back to a strategy for success, bearing in mind opposing forces of direct and indirect competition. Case discussion forces students to develop this skill, by making their diagnoses explicit and defending their reasoning against each other and the instructor.

Just any set of marketing cases will not do. Cases should contain enough data for students to carry through a reasonable diagnosis and argue their proposals on the basis of the facts of the situation and reasonable projections of buyer and competitor reactions to change. Examples that follow a situation chronologically right through to its final outcome, or 'success' stories that include no basis for evaluation of alternatives, generally miss the point of case learning.

All the cases in this text have been chosen carefully to meet the demands of business school teaching. They have been included only if they are of a level that challenges keen business minds and provides some excitement in group discussion. This does not mean, however, that all the intricacies of a case are immediately evident. What may on the surface appear quite simple and straightforward will, with some thought, disclose problems requiring considerable marketing competence in their full diagnosis and solution.

Acknowledgments

Case-writers from all around the world have contributed to this text. Authors of the individual cases are acknowledged on the front page of each case, and shown in the Table of Contents, except for those cases written entirely by myself. For those who would like to know a little more than the names of case-writers, however, a brief biography of each contributor is included after the next section.

I should like to express my personal thanks to all those who have contributed cases.* Good case writing is a demanding and time-consuming task quite definitely under-recognised for the work involved. A good case can require as much effort as a publication in an academic journal. Furthermore, good case writing is the mark of a good teacher. In particular, I wish to thank Philip Law, Robin Wensley, Jules Goddard, Paddy Barwise and Shiv Mathur who have provided so much help in the development of marketing case teaching at the London Business School. I also wish to acknowledge the contributions of the many organisations and individuals who have made it possible to report case situations. It takes men of some calibre to permit their own actions and inaction to be written up and subjected to the critical eye of thousands of students. Finally, but not least, I want to record my appreciation to Sally Mitchell who has been the production manager and the entire factory in making this text a reality.

Kenneth Simmonds
July 1981

TO THE STUDENT:
Learning Through Case Analysis

The purpose of this book is to provide a comprehensive set of case problems against which you will sharpen your marketing skill through individual preparation and group discussion. The cases are designed to cover a range of marketing situations that it would take many years to encounter in actual business practice.

In each case, you are placed in the role of the decision maker and expected to reason through to a preferred set of actions. The greater the amount of preparation you put into the case and the more you are prepared to participate in class discussion, the more you are likely to develop your own skills. Other class participants and the instructor will fill the role of critics and competitors showing up any flaws in your reasoning or interpretation of case facts and offering alternative prescriptions to fit the situation.

You will miss much of the opportunity for developing your own skills if you rely on other people for your ideas and reasoning. Force yourself to read a case thoroughly, specify the problems, identify alternative ways of handling the problems, and reason through as to which seems most appropriate. Keep on asking yourself, 'Why?' until you are persuaded by your own answers. Also think about how your conclusions would be implemented. Suggestions are frequently ruled out because there is no reasonable way of achieving them. Rather detailed description of how you would implement your conclusions is often needed. It makes little sense to advance generalities such as 'increase marketing emphasis', 'more sales effort', or 'lower prices'.

At the end of the day, many business decisions hinge on their incremental costs and revenues. Not only may these be difficult to identify, but the difference between profit or loss may be a very small percentage. Do not avoid quantifying actions. Wherever possible have a clear idea of how much you would spend and to what effect.

In many of the cases the obvious problems and decision alternatives are not the most important. The diagnosis of the decision maker in the case, for example, may focus on the symptoms and not the disease. In studying each case you should be prepared to dig deeply and uncover facts that are not spelt out directly. Question opinions, analysis and decisions presented by those in the case and even evaluate hard data against its source and any other data presented in the case.

Some of the cases require you to assess results produced using a particular quantitative technique, some require you to build a model, and many require you to read financial figures. If you do not understand the technique or figures involved, it is up to you to go to an appropriate text to cover the gap in your knowledge. Just because the casebook focuses on marketing does not provide an excuse for inadequate understanding of some other aspect basic to the case.

Finally, use your imagination and creativity. Business is not a discipline achieved through the application of basic principles or fundamental laws. Like any form of strategy, it requires flair in a very complex situation.

In the class discussion sessions be prepared both to participate and listen. Other participants will almost always have strong and well-argued suggestions that differ from yours. Attempts to make reasoned comparisons will build your own skills. Unwillingness to do so will hinder everybody's learning.

Practice in presenting your recommendations can provide valuable experience for later management situations. Be prepared to state your recommendations simply and clearly and support them with the most important elements of your reasoning. Remember, too, that a large proportion of your audience will be strongly committed to other courses of action, so endeavour to indicate the relative undesirability of these in support of your own conclusions. Avoid wasting time and interest by repeating facts from the case that the others have all read.

Do not expect the instructor to carry the class discussion or necessarily provide his own best solution. Of course, he will push the class to consider important aspects that may have been overlooked or make calculations that have been omitted or made incorrectly, but he is not there to do your learning for you. He may tell you at the end of the case discussion what actually happened in the real-world situation, but do not place too much emphasis on this. Marketing skill is not a question of guessing what actually happened, but of reasoning through a 'best' solution at a given point in time.

Contributors

Patrick Barwise is Senior Research Officer in Marketing and Business Policy at London Business School. His M.A. from Oxford was taken in engineering science with economics and he also holds the London Business School M.Sc. in business. Prior to joining London Business School in 1976, he worked for IBM as a systems engineer, for Pentos, and for Graphic Systems Ltd as Marketing Manager. Paddy's main research interests are in television viewing behaviour and in making written information more usable.

Dean Berry is Professor of Business, London Business School. Dean graduated in English literature from Dartmouth College, completed an M.B.A. degree at Indiana University and a Ph.D. in administration and psychology from University of Michigan. He was Associate Professor at Wharton School, University of Pennsylvania before coming to London in 1966 as Fulbright Lecturer and Professor of Organisational Behaviour. From 1971 to 1976, he was Dean of INSEAD (European Institute of Business Administration, France), followed by two years as a Visiting Professor, first at Harvard Business School and then at the School of Organisation and Management, Yale University. Dean specialises in strategic management and organisational problems and is a founder partner of Strategy Research Associates. He has served on the boards of The European Foundation of Management Education, Euroforum in Madrid and The Jerusalem Institute of Management.

Jean François Communaux is Directeur de la Recherche, ESCAE, Montpellier, France where he teaches Marketing and Statistics. He graduated from the Institut d'Etudes Politiques de Paris and has attended International Teachers Programmes at London Business School and Harvard Business School. Prior to his teaching career, he worked in marketing research for Singer and as Marketing Manager for Zanussi-Zoppas. Jean has a special interest in social marketing and telecommunications marketing.

José Ramon De La Torre is Associate Professor in Business Environment at INSEAD, Fontainebleau. Previously he was Assistant Professor of International Business at Georgia State University, and Visiting Professor at INCAE, Managua, Nicaragua, and at University del Valle, Cali, Colombia. Born in Cuba, José received a B.Sc. degree in aerospace engineering and an M.B.A. degree from Pennsylvania State University and a D.B.A. in international business from Harvard Business School.

V. Baxter English is Marketing Planning Executive for Davy Corporation. He took his M.A. Degree at Cambridge, and worked in a number of different capacities for Boots Pure Drug Company, becoming a director of Boots the Chemists in 1964. He joined the Manchester Business School as a Senior Lecturer in 1966 and became Director of Studies for Senior Executive Courses in 1967. After close involvement with Davy-Ashmore as a Consultant, he joined that company (now Davy Corporation) in 1971, while remaining as a Visiting Lecturer at Manchester Business School.

Martin Flash is a consultant with Strategy Research Associates Ltd and is carrying out research in company strategy at London Business School. He graduated in civil engineering from Imperial College, London, studied industrial management at Cambridge University and also completed the INSEAD M.B.A. Martin worked in South Africa for Murray & Roberts as a site manager, for seven years in various design and management posts with the international consultants Ove Arup and Partners, and as Divisional Manager for Simon Solitec (France). He has also worked in France as a researcher for INSEAD.

Kate Gillespie received a B.A. in Near Eastern Studies from Radcliffe and an M.B.A. from the University of Virginia. She is currently Assistant Professor of International Business, University of South Carolina and completing a Ph.D. in international business at London Business School. Earlier, she worked as a research associate for three years writing international business cases for IMEDE, the Harvard Business School in Vevey, Switzerland, and for the Iran Center for Management Studies. She has also studied in Cairo and specialises in Middle East business issues.

Jules Goddard received his M.A. in geography at Oxford, an M.B.A. from Wharton School, University of Pennsylvania and his Ph.D. from London Business School. Specialising in advertising, Jules worked with Ogilvy and Mather in New York and London and is currently a permanent consultant to J. Walter Thompson Co Ltd and Lecturer in Marketing at London Business School. Prior to his present appointment, Jules was founder and managing director of a building firm in the Dordogne and Reader in Marketing at Thames Polytechnic.

Warren Keegan is Professor of International Business Policy at the George Washington University and currently on leave as Visiting Professor of Marketing, New York University. He holds B.Sc. and M.Sc. degrees from the University of Kansas and M.B.A. and D.B.A. degrees from Harvard Business School. Warren was previously Associate Professor at City College of New York and at Columbia Business School and has taught at INSEAD, IMEDE, Hawaii, and many other universities around the world. He is a former MIT Fellow in Africa, serving as Assistant Secretary, Ministry of Development Planning, Dar es Salaam, Tanzania, and a consultant with Arthur D. Little, Inc and The Boston Consulting Group. Warren's special interest is international marketing and he is author of a standard text in this field.

Philip Law is Senior Lecturer in Marketing at London Business School and Director of the London Executive Programme. Educated in chemical engineering at Cambridge University and in business administration at Manchester Business School, he spent many years as an executive with Shell. He is a chartered engineer and a member of the Institution of Chemical Engineers. Since joining London Business School in 1969 he has lectured widely around the world on university and company executive programmes. Philip has a special interest in the teaching of business administration and was for several years Director of the International Teachers Programme.

William Massy is Vice-President for Business and Finance and Professor of Business Administration at Stanford University. He was previously Vice-Provost for Research at Stanford where he has taught marketing since 1962 following a teaching appointment at Massachusetts Institute of Technology. He received a B.S. degree from Yale and M.S. and Ph.D. degrees from MIT. Bill Massy's major interest has been in the quantitative aspects of marketing and he has published many articles in the Journal of Marketing Research.

Shiv Mathur is Midland Bank Research Fellow at City University Business School, London. He received a B.Tech. degree from the Indian Institute of Technology and an M.Sc. degree from London Business School where he is completing his Ph.D. Shiv held appointments with Pilkingtons India in marketing and corporate planning before joining London Business School as a Research Officer in 1974. He has taken a special interest in the management of multinational corporations and capital goods marketing.

Robert Mills graduated in economics from Cambridge and worked for five years in marketing positions with Robert Bosch Ltd. He completed the M.Sc. in business studies at London Business School in 1977 and is Assignment Manager for the Tube Investments Group Consultancy service.

David Montgomery is Professor of Marketing and Management Science at Stanford Business School. He completed a B.S. degree at Stanford in 1960 and also holds Stanford M.B.A., M.S. and Ph.D. degrees. He has been on the Stanford faculty since 1970 and prior to that time was an Assistant Professor at MIT and Senior Research Associate at the Marketing Science Institute. He has published widely mainly in marketing strategy, market measurement and marketing information systems. David is a Principal of MAC Inc Management Consultants.

Kin-Chok Mun is Professor of Marketing and International Business and Dean of Business at The Chinese University of Hong Kong. He has spent a year at London Business School and was also Associate Professor at Nanyang University, Singapore. Born in Shanghai, Kin-Chok holds the degrees of Diplom-Volkswirt and Dr. Rer.Pol. (1967) from the University of Freiburg, West Germany. His current special interest lies in business developments on the Chinese mainland.

Hugh Murray is Midland Bank Professor of Export Management & International Business, City University, London. He received his B.A., M.A. and Ph.D. from the University of Liverpool. He has held appointments as Lecturer in Marketing at The Chinese University of Hong Kong and London Business School, where he directed the London Executive Programme, and taught on a regular basis for business schools in Germany, Portugal and Japan. Prior to his academic career, Hugh worked as an Assistant Manager with Attwoods Marketing, Assistant General Manager for Newcastle Chronicle & Journal Ltd, Marketing Manager for Liverpool Daily Post & Echo Ltd, Marketing Director for Letraset Ltd, and as Managing Director for Transprint Ltd and Graphic Systems Ltd.

Kenneth Simmonds is Professor of Marketing and International Business at London Business School. He received B.Com. and M.Com. degrees from the University of New Zealand, a Ph.D. from the London School of Economics and a D.B.A. from Harvard Business School. Ken joined the London faculty in 1969, as Chairman of the Marketing area, after holding the first chair in marketing at Manchester Business School, and establishing marketing at Cranfield. He was previously Assistant Professor in international business at Indiana University and in 1974—75 was Ford Foundation Visiting Professor of International Business at the University of Chicago. He has run advanced management programmes for some 50 multinational corporations, and advised as a strategy consultant internationally. Ken started work in 1950, becoming a chartered accountant, cost and management accountant and chartered company secretary, and moved through various commercial positions before transferring to the United States in 1959. He has subsequently been a consultant with Arthur D. Little Inc and Harbridge House Inc and a director of several corporations in Britain, including Redpath Dorman Long. His special research interests lie in industrial and international marketing strategies.

Ralph Sorenson is President of Babson College. Prior to this he was Associate Professor at Harvard Business School where he headed the first-year marketing programme and also led the advisory group that set up the Asian Institute of Management in the Philippines. Earlier, he was a research associate at IMEDE and a marketing executive at Nestlé Alimentana in Switzerland. Bud received his Bachelor's degree from Amherst College and M.B.A. and D.B.A. degrees from Harvard Business School.

Michael Thorpe is a graduate in production engineering and management from the University of Nottingham and received the M.Sc. from London Business School.

He worked for five years as a manufacturing and production engineer with GEC-Elliott and Smiths Industries and is a Chartered Engineer and Member of the Institution of Production Engineers. Since 1977 he has been a director of McAlpine, Thorpe and Warrier, international management consultants.

Charles Weinberg is Professor of Marketing at the University of British Columbia. He received his Sc.B. from Brown University in applied mathematics, an M.B.A. degree from Harvard Business School, and his Ph.D. from Columbia University. Prior to his appointment in Vancouver, he was Associate Professor at Stanford, Lecturer at London Business School and Assistant Professor at New York University. Professor Weinberg has taken a special interest in the use of analytical techniques and model building in solving marketing problems, and has also published two books on marketing in public and non-profit organisations.

Robin Wensley has been Lecturer in Marketing at London Business School since 1974. He previously worked with Rank Hovis McDougall as a brand manager, with Tube Investments Ltd as an internal consultant, and with Ashridge Management College as Deputy Director of Studies in Marketing. He has recently returned from a year as Visiting Associate Professor of Marketing, Graduate School of Management, University of California, Los Angeles, and has been active as a marketing consultant. His special academic interest is in market share strategy. Robin holds the B.A. (natural sciences) from Cambridge, the M.Sc. (business studies) from London and a Ph.D. also from London.

Ulrich Wiechmann is Associate Professor at Harvard Business School currently teaching the Harvard International Senior Managers Programme in Vevey, Switzerland, as well as at Harvard in Boston. He received his Master's degree at Mannheim University, Germany, and Doctorate from Harvard Business School. Before joining the Harvard faculty, Ulrich worked in Germany and Great Britain in marketing, shipping and merchant banking and at the Institute of Marketing at Mannheim where he carried out management consulting and marketing productivity studies. He has published widely on marketing and international management and is the author of many international teaching cases. Ulrich has organised management development programmes for many corporations in the US and Europe and also taught for business schools in France, Israel and Japan. He is a faculty associate of Management Analysis Center Inc.

The Mareketyng Mans Tayl
(apologies to Prof. J.R.C. Chaucer)

A marektyng man was wyth us ther
Untydy dresst wyth shaggy her
Brown baggy sweater, unpressed trews
For any taylor he was bad news.
From eek student, he asked each tyme
1 page, 10 page, yt was a crime.
Yn mareketyng lectures he bygan
With wycked subtyltee to scan
Our weaknesses, and flaws, and quyrks
Destroyed our faith, and damned our wyrkes.
He made fact, out of rumour
Marektyng fools ye consumer
Tho hys technyches have many a name
Hys vyew of the world remayns the same
Eech man is a vayne and greedy snob
And yf t'were false, he would be out of a job
How trew, methinks, but what kind of man
Wyll choos hys job wher he kan
Exployt folkes common faults? In hys soule
A hoste of gymmycks fills the hole.
Hys holy writ was participation
Hys class has cerbal constipation
A wel-payed hacke I wolde assess
A B-school rebel ruined by success

PART A
Strategic Marketing

Strategic actions are those which have a significant impact upon the market position of a firm relative to its competition. Strategic marketing is concerned with identifying those actions, predicting their effects and planning them to maximise the firm's objectives.

This case was prepared by Kenneth Simmonds of the London Business School.
© *Kenneth Simmonds, 1981.*

CASE A1
The Mousetrap

The following advertisement appeared on 13th April, 1977, in the *Arab Times*, an English language newspaper published in Kuwait.

NEW SCIENTIFIC DEVICE FOR KILLING MICE

A new and advanced technology for killing mice and rats by electric sound waves.

For stores, poultry farms and other places.

NOTE : The device kills mice and rats ONLY. Tel : 447326

Kuwait's population was 950,000, of which some 450,000 were Kuwaitis and the daily circulation of the *Arab Times* was 20,000. The advertising rate in the six-page broadsheet was 4 Kuwait Dinars per cm./col. — making the cost of the advertisement 40 KD or approximately £80.00. What is your assessment of the marketing strategy adopted by the distributor?

This case was prepared by Kenneth Simmonds of the London Business School. © Kenneth Simmonds revised 1981.

CASE A2
Spanline Engineering

George Kent was introduced to Michael Burton, the majority owner and managing director of Spanline Engineering Ltd of Manchester, at a neighbourhood party and their conversation drifted into a discussion of the design and layout of advertising campaigns. On learning that George was a marketing consultant and adviser to some well-known national corporations, Mr Burton asked him if he would visit his works the following week and give him an opinion on his new advertising proposals.

Michael Burton had started Spanline Engineering on a shoestring some seven years earlier when the light engineering firm for which he was Works Manager was taken over by a foreign producer who closed the works and replaced the manufacture with imports. Michael had been able to purchase some of the machinery at throw-out prices and hand-pick a team from the 600 men who were being laid-off. Initially he had concentrated on precision machining of light mechanical parts for machinery manufacturers on a jobbing basis, but later added a range of chain hoists of his own design. These had been very successful, with their sales growing until they now represented nearly 50% of Spanline's output.

Spanline hoists were made in three lifting capacities of 5 cwt, 10 cwt, and 1 ton, and consisted basically of a lifting block with an electrically driven sprocket that engaged the links of the lifting chain. Chain hoists of this type were officially designated as Class I cranes and appropriate for light use of up to 6 hours per day with continual lifts of up to 20 minutes. Heavier use would be likely to damage the hoist. Chain hoists were used widely in garages and workshops for loading machinery and on loading docks. Mr Burton claimed that the Spanline models had no particularly outstanding features, but they worked efficiently and there had been very few complaints. Although Spanline hoist blocks were larger and heavier than other makes and might last longer than the average hoist life of about 5 years, competitors emphasised lighter weights as a prime sales feature. Despite this, Burton felt that the larger block looked more significant and professional when installed.

The first large order for Spanline hoists came from Century Steel, a firm specialising in supplies for smaller steel fabricators and constructors. In addition to its main line of steel blocks and erection equipment, Century supplied tanks, boilers, cranes and other equipment to its customers from a network of depots throughout Britain. Century's initial order was for 500 hoists marked with their Century brand, and this had been followed with orders that grew each year, then settled down to about 2,700 a year.

From time to time over the years, Michael Burton and Eric Davis, his Sales Director, had also called on most of the large engineering plants and engineering supply houses in the North. Orders were sporadic from these sources, but totalled around 600 annually. Several large orders for Spanline hoists had also come from tenders to the Ministry of Public Works and to large industrial developments, but open invitations to bid were limited. Representatives for the various makes of cranes frequently visited purchasers before invitations to bid were issued and influenced them to limit the subsequent invitations to a few suppliers.

Two years ago Spanline had moved into a new factory built to accommodate up to 110 men, and was currently operating at about 75% of this capacity. Over the past year growth had been minimal, however, and Michael Burton and Eric Davis had finally taken a careful look at their work opportunities and decided to place more emphasis on hoist production. According to their calculations, hoists were their most profitable activity. The retail prices for the 5 cwt, 10 cwt and 1 ton sizes were £180, £255 and £330 plus VAT respectively. A 17½% discount was allowed to Century Steel and most other customers and this left Spanline with an average net revenue of just over £210 per hoist, of which 55% represented materials, 20% direct labour and 25% contribution to overheads and profit. Spanline purchased castings, bearings, gears, motors, chains and electrical control gear, and then carried out the machining assembling and finishing.

Michael Burton thought there were around a dozen crane producers in the country and knew that the Spanline production must not be enough to cover more than a small share of the national market. Compared with what he knew of the prices of competitors, moreover, Spanline's prices were among the lowest. There was thus plenty of scope for expansion, and after several long discussions Burton and Davis decided to mount an aggressive advertising campaign to extend Spanline's share of the market. Together they visited a London advertising agency, recommended to them by one of their friends, which undertook to draw up a proposal for them, and Eric Davis also undertook to recruit a representative to help him on the sales side.

Most of the prospects for this sales representative post came through leads from Davis' wide contacts in local engineering circles. He finally chose Albert Wisdom, aged 45, who had come up from the shop floor of one of the largest manufacturers of heavy cranes and then spent ten years in their design office with responsibility for adapting basic crane designs to individual customer requirements. As Davis told Michael Burton, Wisdom knew all there was to be known about cranes. Wisdom was appointed on a good fixed salary of £9,000 with a company car, and Mr Davis indicated that he would be allocated a grouping of industries for which he would be solely responsible. In this way he could built up expertise in the particular requirements of different industries.

Eric Davis planned to retain some customer industries himself and also to cover the customers for whom jobbing work would continue. Eric had joined Michael Burton from the same firm when Spanline was founded and held 10% of the shares. In his previous post he had been customer service engineer, responsible for liaison between manufacturers and the works and had provided many of the initial contacts for Spanline jobbing work.

When the draft proposal for the advertising scheme arrived from the agency, Burton and Davis were impressed with the professional way in which it was drawn up. In brief, it proposed a campaign focusing on the Spanline brand name built into a new symbol of similar shape to the hoist block. The supporting copy emphasised the reliability and general all-purpose value of Spanline hoists. The agency recommended that the annual appropriation be set at £30,000 in order to make a significant impression on the market, and that it be allocated to handling and equipment journals. They proposed the schedule of journals set out in Exhibit 1.

Exhibit 1 *Proposed Advertising Schedule*

Journal	Circulation	Frequency	Proposed Annual Insertions	Page Size of Insertions	Additional Colour	Rate £	Annual Appropriation £
Materials Handling News	20,000	Monthly	12	Full	1	492	5,904
Mechanical Handling	6,918	Monthly	6	½	—	156	936
Freight Management	20,367	Monthly	12	½	—	216	2,592
Storage & Handling Equipment News	24,972	Monthly	12	½	—	252	3,024
Industrial Equipment News	33,807	Twice Monthly	12	Full	1	744	8,928
Factory Equipment News	26,000	Twice Monthly	12	Full	—	606	7,272
							28,656

Average Monthly Readership 128,000
Cost Efficiency = £18.9 per 1,000 readers per month

This advertising appropriation was a large sum for Spanline and Michael Burton found himself postponing a formal letter to the agency. It was not that Spanline lacked funds, as can be seen from the previous year's annual accounts in Exhibit 2, but rather it was due to Burton's unfamiliarity with advertising. Consequently, during his conversation with George Kent about this time, he decided to place the proposal in front of George for a second expert opinion.

Exhibit 2 *Spanline Engineering Ltd   Previous Year's Annual Accounts*

Profit and Loss Account
(all entries net of VAT)

Sales		1,422,000
Labour	288,000	
Materials	660,000	
Work in Progress Variation	114,000	
Direct Cost		1,062,000
Gross Margin		360,000
Variable Factory Expense	171,000	
Fixed Factory Expense	57,000	
Selling, Administrative and		
Interest Expense	48,000	
Directors' Remuneration	33,000	
Total Expense		309,000
		51,000
Taxation		21,000
Net Profit		30,000

Balance Sheet end of year

Sundry Debtors	159,000	
Materials	75,000	
Work in Progress	153,000	
Current Assets		387,000
Bank Overdraft	72,000	
Sundry Creditors	138,000	
Provision for Taxation	21,000	
Current Liabilities		231,000
Net Working Capital		156,000
Buildings	195,000	
Plant and Machinery	69,000	
Fixed Assets		264,000
		420,000
Long-Term Loan (secured)		135,000
Shareholders' Funds		285,000

This case was prepared by Kenneth Simmonds and Robin Wensley of the London Business School, with the co-operation of Vogue management, as a basis for class discussion rather than to illustrate either effective or ineffective handling of a business situation.
© *Kenneth Simmonds, 1976*

CASE A3
Vogue Bathrooms

The management of Glynwed Bathroom and Kitchen Products Ltd, trading as Vogue Bathrooms, was concerned in late 1975 with deciding whether to commit the firm to sizeable investment in modernising its plant. Vogue was the dominant producer of cast-iron baths in the United Kingdom and management believed that a failure to improve the enamel finish of Vogue baths would lead to a loss of the premium image for cast-iron over plastic and a more rapid decline in market share and sales. Moreover, with new plant it would be possible to reduce the gauge, and hence the weight, of the cast-iron baths and make some improvement in the plant working conditions. The production process for cast-iron baths was basically the same as it had been 100 years earlier with a little automation added. The bath was cast in a mould, then spray enamelled and baked. Dust from the foundry sand and a great deal of noise and heat combined to make an unpleasant work environment.

Vogue could continue to produce for another ten years without modernising its two existing casting and enamelling plants which had been built in the late 1950s. Nevertheless, management considered that it should make the investment decision urgently because sales of plastic baths seemed to be gaining at the expense of cast-iron ones at an increasing rate. As a precaution against building too much capacity, however, the Managing Director proposed to ask professional consultants to prepare a report on the rate at which buyers could be expected to switch across to plastic baths. The cost of new plant would involve a net investment of around £2 million after allowing for Government investment grants and depreciation allowances.

Vogue's Facilities and Profitability

Glynwed Bathroom and Kitchen Products Ltd, (Vogue), was a fully-owned subsidiary of Glynwed Ltd, a manufacturing group principally concerned with components for the building industry. Vogue had been acquired by the Glynwed group in 1969, and its headquarters were located in Bilston in the West Midlands.

Until 1974 Vogue operated three plants with a total capacity of about 370,000 cast-iron baths per annum:

Plant	Capacity
Bilston, West Midlands	130,000
Falkirk, Scotland	110,000
Greenford, London	130,000

At the end of 1974, however, the Greenford plant had been closed. The major United Kingdom recession had led to a steady decrease in demand for cast-iron baths from an annual rate of around 500,000 per year reached in mid-1973, to 350,000 in mid-1974. Vogue's inventory had risen to 45,000 units with no further storage possible at the plants. Moreover, there were strong indications that the decline would continue for some time and no sources predicted growth in the house building sector until late 1976. Vogue management reacted by closing the Greenford plant and putting the others on short-time working. Greenford was the plant with the highest wage and overhead costs and its closure, though costing £600,000, saved an estimated £150,000 in annual fixed costs and avoided losses from under-capacity operation in the short term.

With the difficult market conditions Vogue had recorded losses for 1973 and 1974. Directly variable costs represented 84% of total costs and only when volume was maintained at a constantly high level were the fixed costs covered. For 1975, however, Vogue expected to break-even at a sales level of £6.3 million as shown in Exhibit 1. This represented production of 190,000 baths as detailed in Exhibit 2. The order book was much healthier and delivery had risen to seven weeks on the average, although much shorter for the standard white models.

Both the Bilston and Falkirk plants had been designed to produce large quantities of standard white baths, which were acceptable to the market in the 1950s and 1960s, but by 1975 were bought by only 25% of the market. Fashion shapes requiring grip handles and a wider range of colours slowed down the production rate in both of Vogue's plants and increased the average cost of the baths produced. In 1975, standard factory costs varied from £21 for Vogue's basic white 'Vogue 60' model at the bottom of its line, through to £29 for its middle-of-the-line 'Caribbean 1700' model (either white or coloured), and up to £39 for its extra-wide, super-luxury 'Florida 1700'. Four years earlier, however, the basic white 'Vogue 60' had cost only £8 to produce.

Competing Bath Materials

Bath production in the United Kingdom was divided between steel, plastic and cast-iron as shown in Exhibit 3.

(i) Steel baths represented about 30% of the UK market by number in mid-1975, although slightly lower in share when measured by value. Baths were pressed from mild steel mainly of thin gauge (about 2 millimetre) and then enamelled. With these thin pressings the enamel chipped easily, leading to high losses in transit. Moreover, the baths were not as rigid as for cast-iron and sounded 'tinny'. Over the previous two years, thicker steel baths had begun to appear on the UK market — first 2.5 mm and subsequently 3.5 mm. The enamel chipped less readily and the difference in mass and rigidity between steel and cast-iron was greatly reduced. Vogue management expected that heavy gauge baths would provide very severe competition for standard cast-iron baths, particularly in the contract field. In European countries, steel already took a much larger market share — 40% in France, 50% in Italy and 65% in Germany. One drawback to steel was the limitation to its shaping. Only rectangular shapes were possible and there were limitations to other styling features imposed by the pressing process and the cost of dies. In variable cost, however, steel baths undercut even plastic baths.

(ii) Plastic baths were taking 40% of the market in mid-1975, a percentage that had grown from under 15% in 1970. Plastic baths were mainly vacuum formed from 'Perspex', an acrylic sheet produced and promoted by Imperial Chemical Industries Ltd. A small proportion of 'plastic baths', however, were made entirely from fibre-glass (Glass Reinforced Polyester). These were usually very large baths of unusual shapes — such as sunken round baths and corner baths. Perspex could be moulded in different thicknesses, but standardisation had taken place around two thicknesses of 3 mm and 8 mm. The bulk of the sales were at the low end of the market in 3 mm Perspex, with Glass Reinforced Polyester sprayed on underneath. Perspex was relatively easily shaped by a vacuum forming process with few limits to the range of shapes. Though not as solid and stable as cast-iron, the frames attached as plastic baths were installed had been improved to give a reasonable stability. Handling costs were low due to the light weight. A plastic bath weighed about 30 lbs against the normal 250 lbs of a cast-iron bath.

ICI had readily made Perspex available in a wide range of colour matches. Apparently there was no difficulty in adjusting the tint to get the required match, nor in producing a wider range of colours. While plastic did not chip readily like enamel, it could scratch and lose its sheen and the thinner mouldings had been known to bend out of shape with very hot water. On the other hand, scratches could be rubbed out with a mild abrasive because the colour went right through the material. The Plastics Bath Information Bureau claimed that the surface could be repolished with any liquid metal polish and that even major accidents like allowing a cigarette to burn out on the edge of a bath and produce a yellowish scar could be easily remedied. They claimed that wire wool would eliminate the blister and the

Exhibit 1 *Vogue's Expected Performance for 1975*

		£m.
Sales		6.30
Cost of Sales		
Materials — Direct	2.30	
Indirect	1.00	
Labour — Direct	0.60	
Indirect	0.70	
Wage Ancillary	0.25	
Factory Overheads (Rent, rates, depreciation, insurance etc.)	0.25	
Scrappage Sales	(0.10)	
		5.00
Gross Margin		1.30
Expenses		
Administrative Expenses — Vogue	0.40	
Glynwed	0.15	
Selling Expenses	0.15	
Distribution Expenses	0.33	
Rebates and Cash Discounts	0.27	
		1.30
Net Profit before Tax		

Exhibit 2 *Vogue Estimated Unit Sales 1975 ('000s of baths)*

	White	Colour	
Standard Range			
Vogue 54	2.0	—	
Vogue 60	13.1	0.7	
Vogue 66	65.2	25.0	
Atlanta 1700	11.0	—	
Vogue 72	1.6	0.6	
Atlanta 60S	7.6	—	
Vogue 60 Twingrip	1.4	0.4	
Vogue 66 Twingrip	10.9	11.7	
Vogue 72 Twingrip	0.6	0.7	
Luxury Range			
Harmony 66	1.7	6.9	
Caribbean 1700	2.0	15.6	
Caribbean 1800	0.1	0.4	
Mayfair 1700	0.7	5.9	
Mayfair 1800	0.3	1.4	
Super-Luxury Range			
Elysian 1840	—	0.3	
Florida 1700	0.2	1.9	
Bahama Corner Bath		0.1	
Total	118.4	71.6	190.0

Exhibit 3   *United Kingdom Bath Production by Material of Manufacture ('000s of baths)*

	1973	1974	1975
Cast-iron	454	340	226
Plastic	320	306	291
Steel	274	198	213
	1,048	844	730

yellow stain and that the liquid metal polish would put back the sparkle. Plastic was resistant to acids and alkalis, but could be attacked by acetone (nail polish remover) and would also burn in the event of a fire. However, plastic would not rust or corrode.

(iii) Cast-iron baths represented the remaining 30% of the market in mid-1975. This estimate showed a substantial fall from cast-iron's 60% share of the market in 1970. The glazed porcelain finish of a cast-iron bath was extremely durable and reglazing was possible. Around a general rectangular shape there was considerably more flexibility in developing luxury shapes in cast-iron than in steel. Sides, edges and corners could be rounded, bevelled and indented in a great many ways. But the sides had to slope away from the base to facilitate the bath's removal from the mould, and it was difficult and expensive to match in enamel some of the deeper shades of pottery, especially deep red.

Vogue's castings had a gauge of about 6 mm and with new plant it was considered likely that this gauge could be reduced by up to 30%. Size was limited to castings 1800 mm by 850 mm due to casting box limits. Anything larger in cast-iron, however, would have been very costly to handle because of the weight.

Market Segments and Competing Materials

Demand for baths was traditionally forecast separately for three segments — public new housing; private new housing; and modernisation, replacement and community. This last segment was really made up of three quite separate elements, but figures were not available separately. Past sales and the most recent forecasts for these segments are shown in Exhibit 4.

Periodically, Vogue's marketing staff estimated the number of baths of each material purchased in each of the three segments. The last attempt had been made in July 1974 and the figures are shown in Exhibit 5. In support of their projection of the material allocation by segments for 1978, the marketing unit made these comments:

1) 'Plastic baths, mainly of the cheap composite type, are believed to have increased their share of new public building. By 1978, their lead is expected to be overtaken by steel baths through severe price competition, and cast-iron is expected to have virtually disappeared from this segment.'

Exhibit 4   *United Kingdom Bath Market Forecast by Market Segment ('000s of baths)*

	Actual		Forecast		
	1973	1974	1975	1976	1977
New Housing — Public	114	135	151	161	170
— Private	190	143	149	154	160
Modernisation, Replacement and Community	744	566	430	410	470
	1,048	844	730	725	800

Exhibit 5 *Estimated Bath Material Shares by Market Segment ('000s of baths)*

		1970	1974	1978
New Housing — Public	Cast-iron	108	35	5
	Plastic	30	40	25
	Steel	50	35	100
		188	110	130
New Housing — Private	Cast-iron	124	35	60
	Plastic	30	60	100
	Steel	20	25	60
		174	120	220
Modernisation, Replacement and Community	Cast-iron	245	270	250
	Plastic	56	180	260
	Steel	116	180	190
		417	630	700
Total	Cast-iron	477	340	315
	Plastic	116	280	385
	Steel	186	240	350
		779	860	1,050

2) 'The greatest growth in new private building is expected to be in plastic bath models which offer a colour range and shapes at lower prices than cast-iron. Steel is expected to increase its share of this segment, possibly to the same level as cast-iron, because heavy gauge steel baths in colours will be available for installation by the private builder at lower prices than cast-iron.'

3) 'The great majority of the private replacement and modernisation markets are expected to be retained by cast-iron through 1978. However, the share of plastic baths will grow for replacement markets as more expensive models are introduced. The steel share in this sector will be concentrated mainly in community building, renovations of hospitals, hotels and council housing.'

Customer Attitudes Towards Different Bath Materials

In 1973 Vogue had commissioned a qualitative study of consumer attitudes towards baths by a commercial research firm. The research was carried out from June to October 1973 and involved firstly a series of twelve in-depth interviews with men, women and couples in London and Cheshire who had acquired a new bath within the previous three years. These were followed by six group discussions. Each group discussion included a mixture of couples who had and had not chosen baths within the previous three years, including at least one couple who had bought a plastic bath. All interviewees were drawn equally from age groups 20 to 39 and 40 to 55, and two discussions were held in each of Chorley (North of England), Edinburgh (Scotland) and Colchester (South of England). The ratio of cast-iron to plastic purchasers among the interviewees was two to one. Extracts from the report describing attitudes towards different bath materials are set out below and details concerning bath purchasing generally are included in Appendix A:

As far as materials were concerned, most of the sample considered they were traditionalists and preferred cast-iron. This material for baths was proven, lasted 30—70 years, was strong, sturdy, did not break, even if it chipped, was easy to clean, was more sensible with children and could be re-enamelled.

On the other hand, cast-iron was very heavy to transport and a 'do-it-yourself' man had to think twice about installing one upstairs unless he had help with the labouring.

Cast-iron was considered to be more expensive than other bath materials, because of the raw materials involved.

Not everyone was aware of the manufacture of baths in plastics, although the majority had heard of them even if they thought they had not seen one. Few were sure exactly what materials plastic baths were made from and called them variously and most frequently plastic, fibre glass and perspex and less frequently acrylic and nylon.

A number of the sample had actually considered plastic baths before making up their minds and not bought them; others had tried to find out from unbiased sources about plastic baths, been unsuccessful and decided to stick to cast-iron. Showrooms were accused of either trying to sell one kind or the other, but not supplying the potential purchasers with all the pros and cons of each type. For example, in one group in Chorley, a couple in the group said they had been really put off buying a plastic bath by showroom staff, while another couple had been told, by the same showroom, they only had plastic baths. In London one lady had been told the shop did not sell cast-iron any more, that they were too difficult to fix, were not being manufactured and were not safe with children.

To say the least, there was an amount of confusion and lack of correct information about plastic baths. The general criticisms were as follows:

(a)   Plastic baths had not been manufactured long enough to be as well-proven as cast-iron. They were not as strong, tough or durable as iron.

(b)   They were too light to be used as baths. The plastic moved when a person plus water were in it as the weight of the person and the water was greater than that of the bath:

> 'It's easier to fix a fibre glass one yourself, but you need a deal more fixing points. There's flexibility with fibre glass and movement is the drawback . . . they have to be strengthened underneath. The feeling in a plastic one is that you are going to topple over because of the movement. So it's no good for elderly people who are unsteady.'

> 'That *does* worry me — being rather heavy — they seem to be too light to hold my weight.'

(c)   They were not safe for children because of the movement, particularly if the children were rather boisterous when in the bath:

> 'Children are not good with plastic baths . . . not the same durability as cast-iron, swings when you get in — not the same rigidity, it's supposed to be fixed to the wall in a certain way, but it never happens with a cast-iron bath.'

> 'My husband felt, especially with two young children, that perspex gives a bit and we thought, if they were jumping up and down, we'd be better off with a cast-iron one — especially as everyone will be standing in the one spot when we are having showers.'

(d)   When they came away from the walls where they were fixed because of movement, they had to be replugged and rescrewed back. Some of those who had purchased plastic baths were not happy with their baths because either the baths themselves or the walls they were fixed to had cracked:

> 'We tiled up to the bath and it's splitting and slipping from them. It wouldn't happen to cast-iron — it's strong and solid. Perhaps the perspex ones are prone to poor installations — I don't know.'

(e)   Plastic baths were thought to burn into holes with cigarette ash and were cracked or pierced by sharp objects accidentally dropped in them (e.g. by a shattered glass bottle). Women were worried that their hair lacquer, nail varnish remover, hair colourant, or some medicines might harm the surface if accidentally splashed on such a bath.

(f)   Plastic baths were thought to lose their 'sheen' and 'lustre' after 6 months, 'with the hot water — as plastic reacts to temperature changes'. Purchasers stated that they scratched easily and were not easy to clean, so the surface lost its shine very soon (even with detergents and liquid abrasives). One explained:

'The family did not wipe it round enough at the shower end and a deposit seems to have accumulated. One end will be stained and I don't know what to use to clean it any more.'

(g) With the plastic bath one sometimes had a plumbing problem in connecting the waste to the existing piping. A couple of men had experienced or had heard that the plastic baths were prone to cracking at the waste.

On the positive side, there were fewer perceived advantages. These were that plastic baths were cheaper in cost, lighter in weight and lighter, therefore, for a DIY man to install; and they were of bright colours, with a smoother, shinier and more even surface finish than cast-iron baths. In the Colchester hard water area, the women thought plastic baths were easier to clean and this, apparently, had been one of the showrooms' 'selling points'. Some plastic bath purchasers felt the plastic bath was maligned by narrow thinking and rumour and that, at any event, in 10—15 years time raw materials would have become so scarce that no cast-iron baths would be available any more.

Those who had bought plastic baths did so for economy, colour and design, 'without even thinking', for their brightness and finish and apparent ease of fixture, on the advice of plumber or showroom assistant. Some had been swayed by the argument (even where price was not of importance) that plastic baths were safer where children were concerned, as it did not hurt them so much if by any chance they fell in the bath. The main selling points were that they were warmer, both initially to touch and when in the bath; that they retained the heat in the water longer than cast-iron, and consequently, that they were cheaper to run in terms of hot water than cast-iron.

Those with friends who had plastic baths were impressed and could not find fault with them on the whole in reality. The cast-iron die-hards still stated that they would not expect the plastic models to last the 'lifetime' that the cast-iron units would, but that they would probably last 10—12 years.

Hardly anyone was aware of the manufacture of *steel baths*. Those who were tended to be connected with the building/plumbing trade in some way. Steel baths were thought to be cold, shiny, 'stainless steel' by most of the women, but some of the men pointed out that they were more noisy and tinny sounding than cast-iron, and that the enamel was more likely to chip than on cast-iron. A few hazarded guesses that they were cheaper to buy than cast-iron, although one could only tell the difference by tapping them in the showroom for their sound.

However, two male interviewees had bought steel baths as they were cheaper than cast-iron and easier to carry up the stairs for installing themselves, but they had found that, like plastic, they also 'moved' when one got in and out and while actually bathing.

Vogue's Associates   Glynwed management was well aware of the threats to Vogue's cast-iron production from competing materials. They had therefore taken steps to set up production of both steel and plastic baths. Under the 'Leisure' brand name, a separate Glynwed subsidiary manufactured pressed steel baths, shower cubicles, vanity basins and units, and sinks of various descriptions. Production was approximately 20,000 baths per annum in two styles. The Vega 66 in 2mm steel was priced for quantities over 45 at £18.50 in white and £21.00 in colours. The Vega 1700 in 2.5 mm steel was priced at £23.90 in white with sur-charges of £2.15 and £4.25 for different colour groups. Vogue's sales force in certain areas had for several years represented this line to the outlets they called on.

The Glynwed move into plastic bath production was more recent. Production had just started in mid-1975. Spurred on by the high growth rate for plastic baths in 1973 and 1974 and the major emphasis placed on plastic baths by the Carron Company, who had always been the major cast-iron competitor, Glynwed drew on Vogue's expertise to draw up plans for a significant plastics operation with an eventual annual capacity of 75,000 baths.

The new unit was set up as Jupiter Plastics operating under Glynwed Plastics Ltd — a Glynwed division quite distinct from Glynwed Bathroom and Kitchen Products Ltd. Distribution was confined to builders' merchants, but a separate salesforce was hired to give plastic baths undivided attention. By mid-1975 six styles had been launched. At the bottom of the range was the Palermo with a list price of £22.50, followed by the California at £28.75. The remaining models went up in price steps until the Seychelles was reached at the top of the range with a list price of £150.00. The Seychelles had a modernistic design almost twice the width of the lowest priced styles.

Vogue's Competition

The only significant United Kingdom competition to Vogue remaining in cast-iron production was the Carron Company with a capacity of about 60,000 units per annum. Carron themselves were the leading UK producers of plastic baths in 1974 and had placed increased emphasis on plastics. Vogue saw no likelihood of any other firm entering cast-iron production on any scale, even should they themselves decide not to modernise.

In addition to Glynwed's 'Leisure' line there were only two United Kingdom manufacturers of steel baths. Carron also had a steel bath unit and so did Curran, part of the Reed International Group. Combined output of these two competitors was about 150,000 per annum. There were several European manufacturers with much higher volume production in steel than any of the United Kingdom manufacturers and competition on a cut-price base was currently being felt from them. Material and labour cost advantages, however, probably contributed more to this competition than economies from high volume. High volume production was achieved by the German firms where steel baths were the rule, yet Spain seemed to be the most competitive source of imports. In the first six months of 1975 imports fell slightly compared with 1974, but rose from 14% to 28% of the steel bath demand which was recording at an annual rate of 200,000 units. United Kingdom production for export also dropped from 64,000 in the first six months of 1974 to 28,000 in the first six months of 1975. Curran had introduced heavier gauge 3.5 mm steel in early 1975 aiming at the cast-iron market. To match this move Vogue had entered into negotiations with a West German supplier for heavier gauge baths, and supplies would commence in 1976.

As opposed to cast-iron and steel, the number of competitive manufacturers of plastic baths was large. There were about 30 firms involved and the range of a dozen included ten or more styles. Vacuum forming equipment was easily acquired, so investment in production facilities was not a barrier to entry. At the end of 1975, plastic bath manufacturers were suffering from a drastic surplus of capacity as evidenced by the ease with which an offer of delivery within a week could be obtained — even when stocks of the manufactured baths were not held.

Bathroom Pottery Suppliers

While some firms had recently begun merchandising plastic basins and plastic cisterns for toilets, almost all washbasins, toilets and bidets were of pottery. The pottery firms held the lead in introduction of new colours. At the impending 1975 Building Exhibition, for example, Vogue management expected there would be three new hard colours in pottery introduced by each of the three main manufacturers — possibly nine colours in all. It would be over to Vogue to react by introducing matching bath shades if it thought the sales would justify the cost.

Vogue had not been able to arrange for supply of an exclusive Vogue range of pottery from any manufacturer. However, in an implied threat to UK pottery suppliers as to where Vogue could turn if forced to by attempts to design Vogue out of bath markets via pottery colour changes, Vogue had just imported several sets of French pottery for the impending exhibition.

There were seven pottery manufacturing firms in the United Kingdom. By 1975 all had their own plastic bath manufacture and five were associated with major groups producing components for the building industry. In order of size of output these firms were as follows:

Armitage Shanks   Glynwed made an attempt to take this independent firm over in

1973, but the bid was dropped when a reference was made to the Monopolies Commission.

Ideal Standard   This was the UK subsidiary of the large US corporation. Glynwed had purchased Ideal's cast-iron capacity some years previously and had continued to supply them with their bath range in custom colours which they merchandised.

Twyfords   Twyfords was the object of a bid by Glynwed in August 1971, but the firm went instead to Reed International who were also strong in building materials though not in bathroom furnishings. Twyfords' management claimed that a merger with Glynwed would hamper Twyfords in winning a larger share of the sanitaryware market. Twyfords had since acquired Curran Engineering, manufacturing both steel and plastic baths.

Royal Doulton   The Doulton group was extensive and had taken over Peerless Plastics, a major plastic bath manufacturer. Although to date this firm had not come up with any major innovations, Vogue viewed Doulton as a slumbering giant who could awaken at any moment.

The remaining pottery manufacturers were Outram, a member of the 'Ladyship' group, Shires, a member of the Chloride group and Balterley of Stoke. This last firm was a private venture started about two years previously on a green field site by an experienced small producer who after merging his firm with a larger group did not agree with subsequent policies. Vogue executives estimated that manufacture of pottery could be made profitable at 250,000 pieces per annum, the equivalent of say 60,000 bathroom suites, but with the declining Vogue output they were not prepared to initiate a proposal for investment to the Glynwed group board.

Cost Movements for Competing Materials

Vogue's management did not think it possible to make sensible projections of cost increases for cast-iron, steel or plastic materials over any length of time. They were inclined to believe that the margin between the cost of acrylic and cast-iron materials would not change much for a while, but that labour content in the casting and enamelling would ultimately mean greater overall cost increases. Imperial Chemical Industries had had the United Kingdom market for acrylic to itself up until about five years previously when Rohm entered from Germany. More recently, Swedlow International had also entered from America. Their quality was slightly lower than that of ICI, but so were their prices. There was one other very small UK manufacturer.

It was believed that for a number of years ICI did not increase the price of acrylic sheet for baths in line with cost increases. ICI had apparently decided to keep prices down in order to establish a greater usage. Prices of acrylic for other uses had increased faster. Over the previous 12 months, however, prices for bath acrylic had been raised substantially (62% for white and 40% for colours). Unless competition from continental manufacturers forced ICI to keep prices down, it was thought that increases in the future would be of the order of 15—20% annually, although little was known of the economics of ICI production.

From Jupiter management Vogue had established that production cost for plastic baths varied mainly with the quantity and quality of the acrylic used. Although Jupiter's output was so far quite small, the unit received the maximum discount from ICI for large quantity purchasers, so the bulk of the competitors were supplied at similar prices. Costs for Jupiter's standard shaped baths were as follows:

	£
Acrylic sheet, resin, glass fibre	10—15
Frame, hand grips etc.	4—8
Reject allowance	1
Direct labour	1
Overhead 500% on labour	5

Vogue's Outlets

The traditional outlets for baths were builders' merchants. Vogue supplied its baths through members of the British Federation of Builders' Merchants of which there were 3,000, the majority of whom handled cast-iron baths. Many were extremely small and of the 2,400 supplied by Vogue, fewer than 700 had reasonable showrooms. Only forty or fifty of the largest dealt in steel baths.

The merchant usually added 65% to 75% to his works purchase price for showroom sales to individuals, but out of this he would pass 10% to 20% of his selling price on to the plumber. Builders installing a number of baths received a larger discount, but would not be supplied from the merchant's stock. The merchant would quote a price for delivery ex-works with his own margin depending on the size of the contract. His margin could vary from $1\frac{1}{4}$% for a large contract to 10% for a few baths.

Vogue estimated that builders' merchants had carried about one month's supply of cast-iron baths in early 1974, but had subsequently begun to destock, thus multiplying the market fall-off at the factory level.

The largest chains of builders' merchants were the Tilling Group, United Builders' Merchants and the Sankey Group. Of the three, the most creative in bath merchandising had been UBM. In 1973 they developed a concept of 'Home Plan' presentation of a full bathroom suite in a limited range of styles and colours. Purchasers of Home Plan were promised 6 weeks' delivery instead of the more usual 6 months at that time. A lot of sales resulted, but only 30 of the planned 100 showrooms were running by mid-1975. UBM had recently discussed with Vogue the possibility of obtaining its own brand, but had not pursued the idea. As opposed to UBM, the Tilling Group with a larger unit sales volume had consistently emphasised the low end of the market, selling 70% in standard white baths.

Home improvement centres, bathroom centres, and even bathroom boutiques were beginning to find a place in bath purchasing. Unlike builders' merchants, these outlets were found alongside other retail stores and sometimes in a prime site in the centre of the High Street. They tended to stock a wider range of plastic baths. Firms supplying these outlets usually also supplied builders' merchants, but Vogue was reluctant to make any major steps into new outlets for fear of upsetting the Federation of Builders' Merchants who were responsible for much of Glynwed's other sales. Among the builders' merchants, the fifth in size had moved into the High Street with Do-It-Yourself centres and also into cash-and-carry. Most innovation, however, had come from other types of outlet.

Vogue's marketing director believed that bathroom display centres would expand in numbers and that department stores would devote more attention to bathroom displays. Higher class stores such as Harrods, Heals and Debenhams were particularly moving in this direction and there were already about 50 specialist bathroom display centres. In Manchester, Elegant Bathroom's had established a 4-floor bathroom display store near Piccadilly Gardens selling direct to the public. This was the only outlet buying directly from Vogue. But, like the other centres, it also bought from builders' merchants who acted as factors.

Vogue's Range, Colour and Pricing Policies

The Vogue range was divided into three groupings of standard, luxury and super-luxury baths. There were nine models in the standard group, five in the luxury group, and three in the super-luxury group as listed in Exhibit 6. Prices were quoted for quantities of any models in any one order of 50 units or above, 25 to 49 units or below 25 units. For models in the standard range price per unit rose approximately 10% below 50 units and below 25 units a further 20%. For the luxury range the steps were smaller and uneven, but averaged around $7\frac{1}{2}$% for each step. Price did not change at all for quantity in the super-luxury range.

All prices were subject to a $2\frac{1}{2}$% cash discount if payment was received by the end of the following month. Discounts were also given on standard baths according to the annual volume of the builders' merchant. These discounts had been matched by Carron Company. Numbers of merchants receiving these volume discounts were as follows:

Discount on List Price	Number of Merchants	1974 Unit Sales		
		Standard	Luxury	Total
$7\frac{1}{2}\%$	3	60000	13000	73000
5%	1			
$2\frac{1}{2}\%$	14	60000	13000	73000
$1\frac{1}{4}\%$	18			
		120000	26000	146000

The cheapest bath had a basic list price excluding VAT of £30.55 for 50 or more units of the standard white Vogue 60, 66 or Atlanta 1700 styles as shown in Exhibit 6. The style numbers referred to lengths in inches or millimetres. Prices then rose for size, style or colour variations. For pricing purposes colours were classed as Groups 1, 2 and 3, and Penthouse, as follows:

Group 1	Primrose	*Group 3*	Wychelm
	Pink		Autumn
	Turquoise		Flamingo
	Sky Blue		
Group 2	Pampas	*Penthouse*	Beige
	Sun King		Night Blue
	Avocado		Tan
	Honeysuckle		Deep Turquoise Green
			Dark Plum

Exhibit 6   *Prices of the Vogue Range August 1975*

	Prices for 50 or more units or any quantity for super-luxury		
Standard Range	White £	Group 1 £	Group 2 £
Vogue 54	38.50	—	—
Vogue 60	30.55	33.65	—
Vogue 66	30.55	33.65	38.75
Atlanta 1700	30.55	—	—
Vogue 72	38.20	42.20	48.45
Atlanta 60S	36.70	—	—
Vogue 60 Twingrip	38.50	42.25	46.45
Vogue 66 Twingrip	38.50	42.80	46.45
Vogue 72 Twingrip	45.45	50.00	55.00
Luxury Range	White and Group 1 Colours £	Groups 2 and 3 £	
Harmony 66	50.10	54.50	
Caribbean 1700	45.45	48.25	
Caribbean 1800	60.85	65.35	
Mayfair 1700	59.15	63.85	
Mayfair 1800	75.65	81.80	
Super Luxury Range	White and Groups 1–3 £	Penthouse £	
Elysian 1840	271.60	361.10	
Florida 1700	69.75	110.00	
Bahama Corner Bath (Plastic)	166.95	—	

Over the previous three years Carron had led Vogue in price increases, because unlike Vogue they were below the size of company required to gain prior approval from the government for price increases. Nevertheless, Vogue marketing staff felt a continual pressure from the financial side to increase prices to cover the escalating labour, material and overhead costs, hence increases had been instituted approximately every three months, roughly doubling prices over three years. The most recent price increase in August 1975 raised the level 13% above that ruling at the beginning of the year.

Vogue's Sales and Promotion Activity

Vogue operated a regional sales organisation calling principally on builders' merchants. These were fourteen area representatives with northern and southern regional sales managers reporting to one sales administrator. The area representative endeavoured to influence the display policy of the merchants and in doing so called on the services of Vogue's two merchandisers who designed and set up display bathrooms. Each of these merchandisers set up between 20 and 30 outlet displays a year, as well as playing a major role in Vogue's displays at shows and exhibitions. Work done for an outlet in setting up displays was charged at cost and sales representatives had generally used the argument of higher turnover to justify better display. Reply coupons requesting further information received from the public as the result of advertising campaigns had also been used in the past by the sales force as levers for expanding the display of cast-iron baths in an outlet. A substantial amount of time of the salesforce was concerned with complaints and replacements, despite the development of a separate complaints department. Vogue's spending on its salesforce was running at an annual rate of £100,000 and the complaints section cost around £30,000. The sales representatives were mainly in their mid-50's and generally well-known in their areas. There had been no recent sales training as most were experienced salesmen inherited with the takeover, but one particularly good salesman operating in the West Country was being used extensively for arranging and managing exhibitions. Salesmen were paid fixed salaries and a proposed move to a commission basis had been generally opposed by the salesmen in late 1973.

Expansion of cast-iron display had been the principal objective of the sales staff over the preceding eighteen months and by August 1975 there were some 400 outlets with 2 to 3 cast-iron baths on display. In 1973, with shortage of cast-iron capacity during the building boom, delivery rose to three months or more and many outlets sold their display models. It was found during 1974, when the position reversed, that showrooms had either replaced their displays or else had installed plastic baths.

During 1973 Vogue had been the top spender on advertising baths in the United Kingdom, with budget around £40,000. A similar budget for 1974 was curtailed as demand dropped off. At that point Carron came in with a massive £40,000 campaign, but dropped out again in 1975. Vogue had spent only £6,500 up to August 1975, representing a one-third share of a joint promotion with Ideal Standard and Pilkington on Ideal's Penthouse suite. This appeared in April and May with one insertion in each of *Daily Telegraph, Observer Magazine, Good Housekeeping* and *House and Garden*.

Vogue's promotional literature was limited to one brochure of 6 pages illustrating the Vogue range ('How to Get Into Vogue') and to single sheets for each model setting out measurements and specifications for builders and installers. Approximately 200,000 of the brochures were distributed in a year at a cost of under £10,000 and the single sheets were available widely throughout the building and associated industries. At one time a prestige handout entitled the 'Good Bath Book' was made available to selected outlets, but this had been discontinued.

APPENDIX A
Customer Attitudes
Towards Bath Purchases
(Extracted from 1973
Consumer Attitude
Report)

'In most cases the decision to purchase was a joint one, and in some it was really a wearing away process by the wife, until the husband agreed. In some cases, the wife chose the colour, in most it was a joint decision, but the wife collected the information in brochure form and made the first visit to the showroom. The husband meanwhile dealt with the plumber, obtained estimates, and enquired about materials and about fitting a bathroom oneself.

The *reasons for purchase* were many, but fell into three main types:

necessity
replacement after time or breakage
the need for change or modernisation

Within these main types, the following reasons occurred:

(a) Some younger respondents had bought an old house without a bathroom and were converting it bit by bit.

(b) Some older informants had not had a bathroom and were encouraged by local Council grants to make the decision to complete a bathroom, irrespective of whether, in the end, they made use of such a grant.

(c) When people moved into a brand new house they had to purchase a new suite. In many cases, however, the purchase was made without reference to the house buyer. One couple in Cheshire, for example, bought a new house from plans and didn't even think of asking what kind of bathroom it would be, the colour of the suite or style. They were a little disappointed when they moved in to find it was a standard and uninteresting suite, in white.

(d) A few people had to buy a new bath or bathroom item because of breakage and either decided on one item or a whole new suite. Others renewed as they moved into another house with a bath which was very stained or when their own one had become stained.

(e) Five in the sample built extensions or converted a small room or recess to complete a bathroom or second bathroom. These operations were often undertaken at a time in their lives when they felt they could afford to do so, or needed to do so for convenience.

(f) Some of the older couples changed their suites in order to modernise or take advantage of a coloured suite and to take advantage of modern design improvements, such as hand rails, low sides, etc.

(g) One or two couples had to put a new bathroom in as a Building Society mortgage stipulation.

(h) A few informants had rebuilt their bathrooms as they were too small and had increased the accessories to include a shower unit or a bidet.

Various stimuli acted as catalysts to the decision at a particular time. The tiling needed doing as the tiles looked 'shabby — so we decided on a new bath as the tiles would show up the bath . . . no, we had already had a new basin (white)'. In addition, a modernised, bright bathroom was seen to be a good house selling point.

Some of the women with young children had become very concerned about a cracked lavatory pan, chipped bath or basin and hated old taps, which dripped, had lost their chrome and were difficult to clean. These had suggested change under the aegis of hygiene for the sake of the children.

A good suite was expected to last 'a lifetime' — 20—30 years or more, or until one got 'fed up' with it in the meantime. But durability and cost were not the only reasons why renewal was such an occasional thing. Most of the sample felt a new bathroom installation was such a great inconvenience and created such a mess that 'it wasn't worth it' unless one was changing house; added to which many people thought one of the biggest provisos was finding a good and reliable plumber.

Few of the sample had merely bought a new bath, but where this was so, it was because of mishap to this one item of the suite, or because other items were in very good condition. To the large majority, a bathroom suite was perceived to be rather like other suites of household furniture, and one renewed the suite not individual items. A very good reason for this was put forth by most respondents, that one had, or had heard of people having, difficulty in matching colours, particularly over time: another reason cited was that all advertising had seemed to be for whole suites, to make a bathroom new, modern and luxurious.

There were various complaints that some things were very difficult to colour match, for example, lavatory seats to the pan, soap holders and grouting to the tiles and bath, tiles and bath, and shower curtains.

Taps and accessories were too expensive to renew frequently and so they tended to be replaced at the time of the bathroom suite, or a new bath. Some informants thought they could not put new taps on old equipment as the plumbing materials had changed over the years (the size of bore, for example) and that basins and baths could be cracked trying to change the appliances.

Once the decision had been taken, activity started in terms of finding out as much as possible about baths, plumbers, showrooms, delivery, etc. The DIY men consulted friends, workmates, neighbours about the plumbing, materials, work involved etc, while non-DIY men and the women consulted plumbers or architects, builders, etc. Only one older couple left the decision entirely to the plumber to choose and replace a white bath with another. The rest sought plumbing advice (but did not necessarily take it) and planned with the man when to start the work, how much it would cost and an idea of how much time and inconvenience was involved.

The next step seemed to be to consult brochures and home-making books and magazines, to get an impression of the range of bathroom equipment, designs, colours, materials and prices. Non-purchasers considered they would choose on colour, cost and style. However, some female informants in the sample felt cost was not as important as overall effect. This attitude depended almost entirely on economic status, e.g.:

> "Did we really think about cost? ('I did', said her husband) — no we didn't. We came in here, looked around and said yes, that's the sort of bath we like, and you didn't say anything about cost and the builder then said he could get one for half the price, and we said no, we like that design and that colour."

Informants studied and discussed the suites between themselves and then, in nearly all cases, both husband and wife had gone to one or more showrooms. Nobody felt the choice should be left to what one saw in the brochures and some couples had changed their minds about colour or design once they had seen the actual items:

> "I'm not keen on just leaflets — as when you look at it, it's not at all like the picture — so we went off ours completely. We may have been able to order it, but I think you need to *see* it and feel it."

> "In the brochures everything looks big, spacious, comfortable and you go and look at it and you find you hadn't noticed that there was a rough edge here and that sort of thing. And it looks more realistic in the showroom, although even that is a bigger space than you've got at home."

The wider the choice, the more the informants liked it, and those who could only choose between two models of a bath were rather disappointed.

There were a number of *restraints on choice*, which respondents became familiar with either from plumbers or at the showrooms. Although a few men had taken their plumber or architect with them to the showroom, the majority leant very heavily on the showroom staff's opinions and knowledge. The Colchester showroom, in particular, was highly praised for its helpful and knowledgeable staff and for the totally relaxed, undemanding, yet efficient atmosphere. The showroom was also the best equipped of the three and had an extensive range of styles, colours, taps, shower units, curtains, screens, accessories, and a 'luxury' Victorian bathroom suite. The Edinburgh showroom was smaller, but again its staff were considered to be most courteous and helpful. In Chorley, however, disgruntled informants talked about the lackadaisical attitude of the assistants, their lack of technical and range information and what seemed a lack of interest and motivation to sell or provide service.

A bathroom suite was a large outlay for most people, particularly if new plumbing was involved and they, therefore, wished to find out as much about it as they could before they purchased. Most people considered they only bought one or two such items in their lifetimes and so they had to gain as much information as they could in order to make sensible choices.

The DIY men sometimes required technical information and fitting instructions, which they found were readily obtainable from DIY shops. Women wanted to know particularly about safety, cleaning the bath, the using of additives, whether the materials would crack and so on.

The informants themselves felt the first consideration in choice was colour, then design and materials, then price or a mixture of the former two with the latter (depending on circumstances). Constraints on choice were presented in most cases by the size of the bathroom or the area in which the bath could fit. Thus, although larger, longer, wider baths were the most desirable, the sample had to buy smaller, narrower baths than ideal in order to fit them into allotted space. Further constraints were imposed in some cases by the plumbing, where a purchaser had required taps which fitted, say, on the side and the plumber had advised against this, or where a shower was not possible seemingly because of lack of water pressure.

The colour choice seemed to be subject to personal preference, providing it was seen to be *warm* by the beholder:

"We chose the pampas for its colour. I like browns and mucky colours — you are not as limited for choice of decor, towels etc. The bathroom doesn't look cold nor does the 'loo'. Bathrooms can be so stark — my husband is not a fussy type of person . . . so it's plain, and the tiffany lampshade is my bit of 'frill' — the bathroom should be fitted out like a room I think, like in the brochures . . . not a room to put the bath and tiles in."

White bathrooms were not only considered to look cold to most, but were psychologically lower in temperature than coloured ones:

"The coloured ones look warm and the colour is most restful. You don't see the condensation either."

White was only chosen where the bath itself was all that was required, where economy was the main priority, or where the couple felt white suites were preferable so that one could add colour and pattern to the room by furnishings. Coloured suites were required to colour-match well and to be warm looking, bright and clean. Although a number of the sample had pink, blue, primrose or lilac bathroom suites, the deeper, non-pastel shades tended to be preferred, or the more unusual colours, such as avocado, sun king, pampas, turquoise, honeysuckle, orchid, wine red, deep blues, greens and browns, purple and orange. Younger people and those with more dynamic general attitudes tended to like the modern colours rather than the pastels. Ideally, most of the sample would aspire to blacks, navy, dark blue, dark green, wine, purple and other strong colours for their suites, but felt they would overpower their small bathrooms. Some of the women felt darker colours might show up dirt, soap marks and talcum powder and look perpetually 'scruffy'.

Most of the sample considered blue, as well as white, to be cold in colour; while some thought green and primrose were also cold, others did not. Pastel shades were considered 'nondescript' nowadays and difficult in terms of matching furnishings and towels, while colours like avocado were described as 'softly relaxing colour, warm and cosy, and it looks lovely with a variety of coloured towels'. The marbled effect baths were described as looking dirty, and as if the scum had not been washed out, or the items were cracked.

Nearly all the informants who had bought new bathrooms pointed out that one of the major factors in choice was one totally outside their control. This was *delivery*. Once having made their decision on style, colour, size and price range, and returning to the showroom or informing the plumber, they were then tremendously disappointed to be confronted with delays of anything up to a year or more. Those with white suites did not have this problem. Only a few had been lucky enough to order coloured baths (in pastel shades) which had been in stock and delivered almost immediately. Some of these, even so, had to wait a very long time for panels.

One man pointed out that it was because a pigment making factory in Wales had burnt down, so that the pigment for the coloured suites had been long delayed. The rest felt it was utterly dishonest for showrooms and advertising to create a demand which they could not meet. A number in the sample had spent a lot of time and money in really scouring showrooms and merchants for many miles around in order to avoid installation delays.

The purchasers had been extremely disappointed to find that after having come to their initial decision to go ahead with the bathroom and then to have spent a lot of time and effort choosing the desired suite, that they were then forced to wait for unreasonable periods for the items. Most people claimed to have 'booked' a plumber or decorator and then faced the delay. Those who, for example, were having several plumbing jobs done simultaneously chose something else, which was in stock. Some couples had had to change their minds over colour or design four times because it was necessary to have the suite quickly. Others decided to 'stick it out' and wait for what they wanted.

Among those who were lucky enough to have their suites delivered promptly were a number who had to send pieces back or suffer chips, bad surfaces, wrong handles, etc. or wait another 6 months or more for the replacement. One or two had been delivered complete in the wrong suite colour; another had pieces which did not match, another had the wrong size delivered and three had handles fitted in the wrong way round — 'there being no room to get your fingers round'.

This case was prepared by Jules Goddard of the London Business School.
© *Jules Goddard, 1980.*

Case A4
John D. Wood

"Dr Quine?"

"Yes, speaking."

"Good morning, Dr Quine. It's Robert — Robert Rorty. You may not remember me . . . I graduated in 1977 . . ."

"Robert! Of course I remember you. How could I ever forget you! How *are* you? What are you up to these days . . .?"

"Well, in a sense this is what I'm 'phoning you about. I'm in a bit of a fix. I've just taken a job with John D. Wood, the estate agents. As advertising director. I know next to nothing about property. You may remember that when I left L.B.S. I took a job with Phillips . . ."

"Oh yes, the auctioneers."

"Yes. I worked with them till just a month ago. Setting up their publicity department and trying to build a bigger name for them."

"Well, you seem to have succeeded. You've put them on the map. It's not just Sotheby's and Christie's now — it's Phillips' as well. I suppose you now want to do the same thing for John D. Wood?"

"Well, I'm not sure. You see, John D. Wood is pretty well-known. It has 5 offices in London and many branches in the country, particularly the south of England and now in the West Country. And it advertises every week in the quality Sundays and, of course, in *Country Life*. In the residential market, we're the fifth biggest."

"Who's bigger?"

"Knight, Frank & Rutley. Easily the biggest. With Savills, Strutt and Parker, and Chestertons between them and us."

"So how can I help?"

"Well, why don't we have croissants and coffee in Serafino's in Mount Street tomorrow morning at nine? Perhaps you could help open my mind to the possibilities of the job. At the moment, I feel I'm in danger of sinking without trace."

"My fees are exorbitant, Robert, even for John D. Rockefeller! I'll see you at nine. Till then, Robert, goodbye."

"Goodbye Patrick"

Patrick Quine, Lecturer in Marketing at London Business School, put down the 'phone, leant back in his chair and gazed out of the window, admiring Robert's nerve at fixing a breakfast appointment at 24 hours' notice. The M.Sc. Programme can't be all bad, Patrick mused, if graduates have such little respect for the value of a professor's time.

His mind then turned to the issue at hand. What *should* John D. Wood do with someone of Robert's talent? What should *Robert* do with an estate agent of John D. Wood's standing? Improve the advertising? How, for heavens sake? Or were there deeper, more strategic problems and opportunities?

Patrick wandered into his secretary's immaculate office to get some coffee.

"Sally, what would *you* do if you were an estate agent?"

"How do you mean?"

"Oh, never mind! But if you're not busy, could you get hold of a selection of estate agency ads from a recent *Sunday Times* and *Country Life*. You know the sort, 'A most attractive listed period house in lovely elevated rural position, with superb detached triple garage and studio flat over.'"

By 10 o'clock, Sally had gathered a selection of recent advertisements for the five leading estate agents. These were John D. Wood's:

JOHN D WOOD

FINAL REMINDER AUCTION SALE ON 19TH MAY, ACACIA ROAD, ST. JOHN'S WOOD, NW8

EXCEPTIONAL DOUBLE FRONTED DETACHED HOUSE, CARRIAGE DRIVE, SOUTH FACING GARDEN, 8 BEDROOMS, 5 BATHROOMS, 2/3 RECEPTION ROOMS (DRAWING ROOM 40ft. x 18ft.), RECEPTION HALL, DOMESTIC QUARTERS, DOUBLE GARAGE. EYRE ESTATE LEASE.

103 PARKWAY, REGENT'S PARK, N.W.1. 01-267 3267

BRYANSTON MEWS WEST, W1 £117,500
Attractive modern house off Bryanston Square, built some 15 years ago to a high specification with spacious accommodation in a quiet residential location. 3 bedrooms, bathroom, double reception room, kitchen, double garage. CH. Lease 105 years.

EATON MEWS SOUTH, SW1 £157,500
Bright modern South facing mews house, specially designed for present owner, with good sized first floor reception room in quiet mews close to Eaton Square. 4 beds., 2 baths., 2 recep. rms., kitchen, cloakrm., garage. CH. Lease 38½ yrs.

ST. JOHN'S HOUSE, SMITH SQUARE, SW1 £152,500
Very spacious light and bright maisonette ideal as family accommodation for M.P. etc. 3 mins. walk from Houses of Parliament. 7 beds., 2 baths., 2 recep. rms., large kitchen. CH. Porter. Lease 40 years.

EATON PLACE, SW1 £55,000
A delightful quiet 2nd floor flat in good decorative condition in well converted period property in heart of Belgravia. Double bedroom, bathroom, reception room, kitchen, CH. Lift, caretaker. Lease 33 yrs.

23 BERKELEY SQUARE, MAYFAIR, W.1. 01-629 9050

MALLORD STREET, SW3 £167,500
Just in the market a low built family house on ground, first & second floors only with a south facing garden and garage. 5/6 bedrooms, 2 bathrooms, drawing room, dining room, study, nursery, kitchen. Garage. Gas CH. F'hold.

CHELSEA GREEN, SW3 £145,000
An attractive freehold house on ground & 2 upper floors with a sunny roof terrace with an open aspect to the south and west. 3/4 bedrooms, 2 bathrooms (1 en suite). Drawing rm., dining rm., study, fitted kitchen. Gas C.H. F'hold.

SOUTH KENSINGTON, SW7 £129,500
A superb small house with a sunny garden facing west & a garage. 3 bedrooms, bathroom, cloakroom, attractive drawing rm., dining rm., excellent fitted kitchen & full CH. Ready for immediate occupation. Freehold.

HURLINGHAM, SW6 £145,000
A most attractive and well modernised family house with a 50ft. garden facing south-west. 6 bedrooms, 3 new bathrms., drawing rm., dining room, study, superb fitted kitchen and breakfast room, cloakroom. Full gas CH. Freehold.

FIRST FLOOR OVERLOOKING GARDENS, SW3 £130,000
Elegant flat with superb entertaining space in good decorative order. 4 bedrooms, 2 baths. (1 en suite), drawing room, dining room, very large hall, fitted kitchen, lift. Caretaker. Ind. gas CH. Recommended. 65 years.

CRANMER COURT, SW3 £175,000
Seventh floor flat of exceptional light & space in this prime block 5 minutes from Sloane Sq. & Sth. Kensington. 4/5 bedrooms, 2 bathrooms, sep. w.c., drawing room, dining room, study/bed., 5, large kitchen. Lift, C.H. C.H.W. Porter. 92 years.

REDCLIFFE SQUARE, SW10 £65,000
Attractive second floor flat with impressive views over square gardens & gardens of The Little Boltons. 3 bedrms., bathroom, large reception room, kitchen. Entryphone, use of square gardens, very low outgoings. 55 years.

HARCOURT TERRACE, SW10 £85,000
Ground floor flat which has been modernised and redecorated in this very popular and attractive street of period houses. 2 bedrooms, bathroom, reception room, bathroom, Ind. CH & HW. Very low outgoings. 71 years.

9/11 CALE STREET, CHELSEA, S.W.3. 01-352 1484/7701

HEREFORD ROAD, W2 £135,000
An early Victorian family house of great character. Recently modernised and in good order. 3 reception rooms, large kitchen, 4 bedrooms, 2 bathrooms, cloakroom, utility room. Delightful garden. CH.

BOLINGBROKE ROAD, W14 £67,500
A robust and spacious Edwardian house, well maintained, with 2 high ceilinged reception rooms, 4 bedrooms, kit., bathroom. Large area in basement ideal for playroom opening on to a good sized garden.

LEDBURY ROAD, W.11 £33,000
Attractive newly decorated first floor flat just north of Notting Hill. L shaped reception, kitchen, double bedroom, bath., low outgoings. New fitted carpets. 97 years.

CHENISTON GARDENS, W8 £72,500
Light & cheerful 2nd & 3rd floor maisonette. Good reception room (19ft. x 19ft.), kitchen, cloak., 3 bedrooms, bath. Quiet position just south of Kensington High Street. 90 years.

ABBOTSBURY ROAD, W14 £157,500
Holland Park entrance yards away, in exceptionally good order, this 4 bedroom, 2 bathroom house has a playroom, super kitchen & large dining room all on the ground floor opening into a delightful sunny garden. CH. 80 years.

HILLGATE PLACE, W8 £110,000
South facing sun terrace amongst flowering cherry trees, a super principal bed and bath en suite, 2 good recep rms. and a big well fitted kit. 2 more beds and bath. Good order. CH.

WEST KENSINGTON COURT, W14 £49,500
A cheerful ground & first floor maisonette with a well proportioned drawing room in excellent decorative order. 3 bedrooms, bathroom, kitchen, porter, CH. 95 years.

GLOUCESTER TERRACE, W2 £45,000
On the 3rd floor of a well modernised period house a 2 bedrm. flat in good order with a 21ft. x 15ft. recep. rm. Balcony. Lift. CH. 92 years.

162 KENSINGTON CHURCH STREET, W.8. 01-727 0705

ROWENA CRESCENT, SW11 £47,250
Fully modernised and well decorated Victorian terraced house in this popular quiet road close to Battersea Park Road. Double recep. 25ft. x 13ft., kit./breakfast rm., 3 beds., bath. Garden. Gas CH.

ADJACENT TO BATTERSEA PARK, SW11 £105,000
Superb family house in excellent condition with spacious, well arranged accommodation in a quiet road within minutes of the Park, and extremely close to Chelsea. Dbl. recep. rm., dining rm., 5 beds., 2 baths., kit. Sunny gdn. Gas CH.

ROSENAU CRESCENT, SW11 £85,000
Fully modernised Victorian terraced house in superb decorative order close to Battersea Park with an elegant drawing rm., 27ft. x 13ft., skilfully designed fully fitted kitchen/dining rm., 2 baths. Cellar. Gas CH. Garden 21ft. x 18ft.

URSULA STREET, SW11 £67,500
Situated in this very popular residential area close to Battersea Park, an extremely well decorated house benefitting from a large double recep. rm. 26ft. x 13ft., french windows lead to a large west facing gdn. 3 beds., bath., dbl. recep. rm., kit./bfast rm. Front/rear gdn., car port. Gas CH.

01 BATTERSEA PARK ROAD, S.W.11. 01-228 0174

JOHN D WOOD

SOUTH NORFOLK
Diss 9 miles. Norwich 15 miles.
Ipswich 30 miles. London 115 miles.

TO BE LET UNFURNISHED—A CHARMING COUNTRY HOUSE, QUIETLY SITUATED OVERLOOKING FARMLAND.
Entrance hall, hall, dining room, kitchen/breakfast room, rear lobby, utility room, small annexe room. 4 bedrooms, 1 small bedroom, bathroom. Garage. Small Garden. Swimming Pool. Well situated with fast road and rail links to London. Ideal for Company Executive or Private Residential Use.
Berkeley Square Office (Ref. AHBS)
23 BERKELEY SQUARE, LONDON W1X 6AL.
01-629 9050 Telex 21242

From: *The Sunday Times*

COUNTRY LIFE—NOVEMBER 27, 1980   *SUPPLEMENT—9*

JOHN D WOOD
In The West Country

John D. Wood are pleased to announce the formation of a
West Country Partnership with Gribble, Booth & Taylor, who have
eleven offices in Devon and Somerset.
The new Partnership will be

JOHN D. WOOD, GRIBBLE, BOOTH & TAYLOR

The local partner is Patrick Sellar,
who will be dealing with prime
Country properties and estates in
The West Country.

The new partnership will be at
61 East Street, Taunton, Somerset;
Telephone: Taunton 78111/2.

23 BERKELEY SQUARE, LONDON W1X 6AL. 01-629 9050
TELEX 21242

Also in The City of London, Chelsea, Kensington, Regents Park,
Southampton, Edinburgh, Harpenden, Winchester, Battersea and Paris.

Martin & Pole, John D. Wood **are in the Thames Valley**

1   *100 Great Advertisements*, edited by Barry Day; Times Newspapers, Mirror Group Newspapers, Campaign, 1978.

"What do you think of them, Sally?"

"A bit plonky, aren't they? And they're all the same as their competitors."

"Do you remember those marvellous Roy Brooks ads? Brilliantly written. There's one in this book[1] . . . yes, here it is:

ROY BROOKS ADVERTISEMENT

> **£5,995 FHLD! Broken-down Battersea Bargain. Erected at end of long reign of increasingly warped moral & aesthetic values it's what you expect -- hideous; redeemed only by the integrity of the plebs who built it—well. Originally a one skiv Victorian lower-middle class fmly res. it'll probably be snapped up by one of the new Communications Elite, who'll tart it up & flog it for 15 thou. 3 normal-sized bedrms & a 4th for an undemanding dwarf lodger, Bathrm. Big dble drawing rm. B'fast rm & kit. Nature has fought back in the gdn--& won. Call Sun 3-5 at 21 Surrey Lane, S.W.11. then Brooks.**

. . . they don't make them like that any more, do they?"

Patrick's coffee was now cold. Sally stoically went to make him another cup. He now remembered having recently filed a press cutting on American plans to bring franchising into the real estate market in Britain. He retrieved it. It was from 'Marketing Week' on August 28, 1980:

Franchising comes to UK real estate

By Hugh Tompson

First it was take-away food, then it was money shops and now the American franchise machine is about to hit another great British institution — the estate agent. In October, Realty World will begin its television launch in the Granada area. If that succeeds, the Realty bandwagon will roll into the Yorkshire and Southern areas.

Tom Collins, who hails from Michigan but has been a successful corporate insurance salesman for eight years, has researched the prospects for over a year. "As the property market goes down, our timing becomes even better", he says. "For right now, estate agents have time to listen and are worried about the future. Franchising is the answer."

Estate agencies' real costs are in promotion and office management. Franchising will offer the individual estate agent the lowest cost per thousand advertising tool, television. As well a packaged and taught management system.

In the States, 40 per cent of all homes are bought and sold through franchises, as are 30 per cent of all retail goods. It has been estimated that in five years the top ten real estate franchises will have completely sown up the market. Century 21 is the market leader, with 7500 outlets, and seven year old Realty World is one of the next biggest, with 2800 offices in North America. They are expanding at a rate of 60 a month.

Tom Harris is leading the Realty team in the UK. Already, a training school has been set up in Leeds and "various parties are talking seriously. We will offer a better service with computer matching, eventual nationwide coverage and a one-year guarantee on all our houses, covering everything including the plumbing and wiring," Harris says. "In America, Realty goes further and offers a surveying, finance and insurance package."

"We are only interested in successful agents, ones with a share of the market to build on and protect. And they are the ones who are most interested in us. They didn't get successful by being blind to new ideas," says Harris. The company hopes to launch with 40—50 outlets.

Already, large estate agency chains such as Fox and Sons in the South West, Whitgates in Yorkshire and Mann and Co. have shown the smaller estate agents the marketing power and consumer confidence which can derive from being part of a larger group. But a spokesman from the RICS the main professional body for British estage agents, says: "I can't see it working. Commission in the States is 10 per cent, while here it is only one-to-three per cent. The cake isn't big enough to cut up. Selling houses is not like selling hamburgers. A completely different and individual service is necessary."

Replies Tom Collins: "If the commission was higher then agents wouldn't need us. The big image, the projection, brings customers to the customers. Although we demand certain standards the agent keeps his individuality. Its not a case of wall to wall Realty."

In America, even legal services are being franchised. And in Britain it is accepted that in banking, another serious service area, the large image is the most successful. Overheads, if nothing else, will force the paper-intensive agents to look to ways of plugging into bigger computerised systems.

Other American franchises with equally high hopes have come to Britain (Orange Julius and Dunkin Donuts, for example) and failed. It has not always been the story of the triumphant McDonalds gravy train.

"Per capita, there are five times more estate agents in the States," says Tom Harris. "The competition demands franchises. Because there are less market tools being used in Britain — billboards, press and television — we expect our units to be much more profitable." Realty World is also looking at South America, Mexico and Japan.

The introduction of franchising, Realty hopes, will raise the ante for would-be estate agents and thereby help protect the franchises. In America, they pay between $7000 and $12000 for the privilege.

Universal McCann were chosen as the agency to run the Granada launch. "In advertising, all that matters is the lift-off the launch gives. It's immaterial what the product or the industry is," says Harris. "One sure thing in franchising is that if you are the first to successfully launch, then no-one ever catches you up."

On re-reading this article, Patrick became convinced that the estate agency business was ripe for structural change. He reflected that it was one of the only service industries in Britain to have gone through the '70's unscathed by the kind of dramatic changes that had hit retailing, banking, restaurants, cinemas, and many other services.

2 *Charges, Costs and Margins of Estate Agents,* Price Commission, Cmnd. 7647, HMSO, August 1979.

Excited, but not convinced that franchising was the answer, Patrick walked down to the library to see what he could find on the economics of the estate agencies. In no time he found himself browsing through a 1979 Price Commission report on the industry.[2] He soon realised that this was what he was looking for. It was broken down into nine main sections:

1. The Market
2. Consumer Attitudes
3. Competition
4. Services Provided by Estate Agents
5. Methods of Charges
6. Levels of Charges
7. Estate Agency in Other Countries
8. Comparison of Sole Agency and Multiple Agency
9. Profitability

In Patrick's view, the most relevant findings in each of these nine sections were as follows:

1. The Market

1. Estate agents operate mainly in the market for second-hand houses which has three principal characteristics — long-run growth, uneven flow of business in the short term and rising prices.

2. In the long term, estate agents are operating in a growing market. As a proportion of all dwellings in England and Wales, owner-occupier dwellings have increased from about 10 per cent in 1914 to over 55 per cent. Between 1951 and 1976 the number of owner-occupied dwellings rose by 156 per cent. Similarly, the number of second-hand houses coming on to the market each year throughout Great Britain, rose from 685,000 in 1971 to 710,000 in 1976. Further growth to 790,000 by 1981 and 860,000 by 1986 is expected.

3.   The underlying growth in the market is overlaid, in the short term, by considerable fluctuation in the volume of transactions. One reason for this is a seasonal pattern, under which house sales often dip in the first quarter of the year. The second and more important reason is a cyclical variation: for much of the time there is either a buyer's market or a seller's market but, at certain points, a substantial supply of houses for sale is matched by demand and a surge in transactions occurs. These peak periods, which bring high income to most estate agents, typically last only a number of months.

4.   The incomes of estate agents are directly affected by movement in house prices as well as by fluctuations in the volume of house transactions. This is because most estate agents adopt some form of *ad valorem* charging, so that as house prices rise the fees charged by estate agents also rise.

5.   There appears to be a long-term tendency for house prices to rise in relation to the general price level. In the short term, however, there are considerable fluctuations in the relationship between house prices and retail prices. For example. over the 10-year period 1969—78 house prices increased by 233 per cent and retail prices by 187 per cent, but between 1973 and 1978 retail prices rose by 111 per cent compared with a 52 per cent increase in house prices.

6.   There is no reason to believe that estate agents have any effect on the general level of house prices in the long term, although they may affect the speed with which prices adjust to a new, stable level after a change. The sharp increase in house prices in 1972 to 1974 was not a purely speculative boom engineered by estate agents, but was caused mainly by increased personal disposable income.

7.   We estimate that, at the present time, there are about 6,600 firms of estate agents with some 11,500 branches in England and Wales and that estate agents as a whole have about 70 per cent of the market for housing transactions. Most other house sales are accounted for by the do-it-yourself vendor, with the commonest method of finding a buyer being personal contact or newspaper advertisement.

8.   There are two main forms of estate agency; sole agency and multiple agency, and the country is sharply divided (by a line between the Severn and the Wash) according to the relative importance of each of them.

9.   *Sole Agency*: the vendor places the property for sale with one firm of estate agents, with or without a sole agency agreement under which the vendor undertakes (usually for a specified period) not to instruct any other agent to sell the same property. The vendor is not liable to pay commission if he sells the property privately, unless he has also granted *sole selling rights* to the agent, in which case commission is payable however the property is sold.

10.   *Multiple Agency*: the vendor places the property for sale with two or more agents separately and the whole of the commission is payable to whichever agent effects the sale, the others receiving nothing. If, meanwhile, the vendor sells the property privately, he is not normally liable to pay commission to any of the estate agents instructed.

11.   There are two other relatively unimportant methods of estate agency. *Joint Sole Agency*: the vendor instructs two principal agents to act for him in co-operation with each other. The fee, which can be more than the fee payable to a single agent, is shared between them. *Sub-Agency*: normally the vendor places the property with one (principal) agent, who appoints one or more sub-agents to co-operate with him. If a sub-agent is instrumental in effecting a sale, he shares the commission with the principal agent in proportions agreed between them.

13.   The largest organisations representing the interests of estate agents are:

The Royal Institution of Chartered Surveyors (RICS)
The Incorporated Society of Valuers and Auctioneers (ISVA)
The National Association of Estate Agents (NAEA).

For membership of the RICS and the ISVA, it is necessary to pass prescribed examinations. All three associations require members to have a degree of practical experience. The majority of practising estate agents are members of one or more of these organisations, which all have rules of conduct which reflect an awareness of the need to maintain high standards of behaviour in business dealings.

14.   In addition to the three main ones, there are several much smaller associations: nevertheless a large number of practising estate agents do not belong to any representative body.

15.   Sales of domestic (residential) property provide the major source of income of estate agents (nearly 60 per cent of total income in our sample), but some agents handle commercial property also and many provide a variety of other services such as structural surveys and valuations, property management, auction sales, letting, planning and development, compulsory acquisitions and architectural design services.

2.   Consumer Attitudes
(amplified in Exhibit 1)

16.   Our consumer survey showed about three-quarters of buyers and sellers operated through estate agents. The majority of buyers and sellers said they were likely to use estate agents again. Further questioning of sellers, who pay the estate agents' fees, showed that over 70 per cent were satisfied with various aspects of the services they received, except with regard to the value for money obtained, with which only 45 per cent were satisfied.

17.   Estate agents were thought to play an important role in recommending prices, but a lesser role in advising on the acceptance of an offer. It was apparent that the property-selling public is not very well-informed on the length of time needed to sell property — either to the 'acceptance of offer' stage or to the point when contracts are exchanged.

18.   The main services estate agents provided were seen as preparing descriptions of properties, advising on prices and the dissemination of this information to prospective buyers by various methods. Only a small proportion of purchasers were actually accompanied by estate agents when viewing properties, or were provided with additional advice.

19.   The great majority of sellers had the terms of business explained by their agents and three-quarters were finally charged as quoted, most of the remainder receiving no quote. The majority were charged a percentage fee which ranged from under 1 per cent to over 3 per cent of the selling price. If no sale was effected through the agent most clients expected to pay no fee, but 27 per cent expected to pay an expense of some kind. More surprisingly, 12 per cent of buyers were charged a fee by their agents although most did not know what this charge represented.

3.   Competition

20.   In 1969 the Monopolies Commission established that, in over 90 per cent of cases, estate agents charged the scales of fees laid down by national or local associations. The Commission made recommendations which led to the discontinuance of such scale charges, with the intention of encouraging price competition. Recognising that many agents would not easily set aside a long tradition, the Commission looked to new entrants to provide competition and warned against the creation of institutional restraints on entry.

21.   It is relatively easy to set up in business as an estate agent. There is no regulation of numbers of estate agents or of their qualifications and initial capital requirements remain modest. We estimate that about 20 per cent of estate agents now in business started during the past five years. Building up a secure position in a local market is, however, a more difficult matter. The reputation of existing agents makes it difficult for newcomers to attract vendors and the cyclical pattern of house sales also inhibits successful entry.

22.   Our study suggested that there has been an increase in the number of offices or branches in the last decade. Some of these are a result of established firms opening new branches, or experienced employees or partners leaving existing agencies and setting up in business for themselves. Far more effective in terms of increasing local competition are entirely new firms which bring professional marketing skills into estate agency. Commercially orientated new entrants actively seek vendors, using more aggressive sales techniques which are often contrary to the spirit, if not the letter, of national professional and local association rules. Since rules apply only to members of the professional associations, these practices are spreading and successful entry is becoming easier.

23.   Competition between agents takes three main forms: fees, promotion techniques and service. The first of these is not very common. Usually we found that each local market has its fee norm which is effectively a maximum and, where competition is weak, a minimum. Where competition does occur, fees are frequently subject to negotiation. Some firms under-cut the local norm and this is a fairly common tactic for new entrants. Competition on promotional techniques is more widespread. In areas where traditional estate agency practice prevails, agents normally compete only on service.

24.   Although common scale charges have been discontinued, competition between many estate agents is still influenced by the terms of membership of the national and local associations to which they belong. There is a clear distinction between the rules of the ISVA and the RICS on the one hand and those of the other representative bodies. The former can be divided into two groups: those providing a measure of consumer protection and those which affect competition (such as rules on advertising, soliciting and supplanting).

25.   Thirty-four local associations have agreements registered with the Office of Fair Trading. Many of their terms are similar to, or taken verbatim from, the rules of the ISVA or RICS. (A number of other unregistered local agreements exist.) Examination of the registered agreements suggests greater attempt to regulate competition than is contained in the rules of the national associations; e.g. by restrictions on charging, advertising, supplanting, canvassing, co-operation with other agents and restraints on opening hours.

26.   There is, however, little doubt that competition in estate agency has increased during the present decade, since the 1970 Order[1] against common scale charges and the growth of commercially orientated firms. But the degree of change and consequently the current strength of competition varies widely from one local market to another.

1   The Restriction on Agreements (Estate Agents) Order 1970; SI No. 1696 (1970).

4.   Services Provided

27.   Over the UK as a whole, we did not find much variation in the type of service given by estate agents. Except in Northern Ireland and, to a lesser extent in Scotland, most agents confirm in writing their own terms of business and the instructions received from a vendor. The great majority, throughout the UK, inspect a property and take details of its description and measurements. Most agents include a photograph of the property in the details provided for purchasers, although this service is notably less common in London than elsewhere.

28.   Most agents advise on the method of sale and on the asking price, but by no means all are prepared to show potential purchasers around a property. Arranging appointments to view and handling negotiations are services normally available from the bulk of agents, although sole agents are less likely to arrange viewing appointments than those operating on a multiple basis.

29.   Except in Greater London and, to a lesser extent in Scotland, local press advertising is usual. National advertising is significant only in London and in Scotland, where advertisements by agents in the Scottish national press are fairly prevalent. 'For Sale' boards are a common feature in some regions, but not in others.

30.   Most estate agents send lists of individual schedules of properties to potential purchasers, although this service is less common in Scotland and Northern Ireland. Window display of property is a normal feature of the services provided, but again is less frequent in Scotland than elsewhere.

31.   Assistance to purchasers consists mainly of advice on such matters as mortgage facilities, a suitable solicitor and insurance problems. Very few agents are instructed to find a property.

5.   Methods of Charging

32.   Nearly all estate agents (95 per cent) throughout the UK use a method of charging which is directly related to the selling price of the house — *ad valorem* fees. There are two main forms: a simple *ad valorem* fee (e.g. 2 per cent of the selling price) and a tapered *ad valorem* fee (e.g. 2.5 per cent of the first £10,000 and 2 per cent of the excess over that figure). The permutations of percentages and cash bands in tapered tariffs can vary considerably. The remaining 5 per cent of agents use one of a variety of

methods which include a fixed fee, a mixture of fixed fee and *ad valorem* charge and, in a few cases, the agent has no 'normal' charge but negotiates each fee separately.

33.   Over the UK as a whole the proportions of agents using simple and tapered *ad valorem* charges are about 55 per cent and 40 per cent respectively, and these proportions do not vary a great deal in most regions. However, in Greater London and Scotland, around 90 per cent use simple *ad valorem* and in Northern Ireland 96 per cent use a tapered tariff. In the northern sector of the country (including Northern Ireland) advertising is charged for separately in most cases, whereas in the southern sector the fee is usually all-inclusive.

34.   When a vendor agrees to give his agent sole selling rights it means the agent's fees and expenses are payable even if the property is sold privately. In other cases, the vendor may have to meet the agent's expenses only. This arrangement is a lot more common in the north than in the south, where the great majority of agents operate on the basis of 'no sale no fee'.

6.   Levels of Charges

35.   In the first quarter of 1979 the average estate agent's fee ranged from a low in Scotland of 1.5 per cent of the selling price of the average house, increasing progressively on the journey to the south where it was 2 per cent, and reaching a high of 2.4 per cent in Greater London. This means, for example, that a vendor in Greater London selling a £23,000 house (the average house price in London at the time) would typically pay his estate agent approximately £565. The amount would have been lower if sole agency was used and higher for multiple agency. In the south more people use multiple agency than sole agency, although the charge for the latter can be nearly ½ per cent less.

36.   The first quarter of 1979 was a seller's market. In a buyer's market, when it is more difficult to sell houses and more money has to be spent on advertising, the amounts would increase. These increases will, however, tend to be lower in the south than in the north. Some agents are prepared in certain circumstances, particularly where local competition is strong, to negotiate fees below their normal level.

7.   Estate Agents in Other Countries
(amplified in Exhibit 2)

37.   Comparisons with estate agencies in other Western countries are difficult, since practices, charging methods, services provided and other costs associated with selling a house vary considerably from one country to another.

8.   Sole and Multiple Agency

38.   The kinds of service which are likely to be offered under sole agency and multiple agency are qualitatively different. A sole agent, relatively sure of obtaining a commission, is usually prepared to risk larger outlays on a broad service to the vendor; under multiple agency, expenditures are more cautiously incurred and the service is correspondingly more selective — speed of sale may become the most important consideration.

39.   We are unable to conclude that one form of agency is better value for money than another. Multiple agency is more costly to provide and consequently more expensive for the vendor, but it has certain advantages which may lead to a quick sale. The choice between the two, where it is available, may depend on local market conditions. However, the choice is not freely available in many parts of the country. The contrast between the south, where both methods are used, and the north, where agents practise sole agency almost exclusively, is as striking today as it was ten years ago. The reasons for this are neither simple nor easily explained, but we believe that, if there is a consumer demand for multiple agency, it should not be frustrated.

9.   Profitability

40.   We measured profitability in terms of net profit per principal (by 'principal' we mean directors as well as sole traders and partners). Return on capital employed has not been used as a measure of profitability since it is inappropriate for a service industry employing relatively little capital.

41.   Firms of estate agents were divided into three categories, namely: single office firms ('small'); other firms with an income in 1978 of up to £½ million ('medium'); and those whose income in 1978 exceeded £½ million ('large').

42.   The average income for the small firms was about £39,000 in 1978 of which 60 per cent was derived from fees earned on the sales of domestic properties. The average net profit per principal for the small firms was £8,600 in 1978 compared with around £6,000 in 1976 and £7,000 in 1977. In 1978, over two-thirds of these firms had a net profit per principal of less than £10,000.

43.   The medium-sized firms had an average of some 3.5 offices per firm and the average income per firm in 1978 was about £162,000; about 55 per cent of the income was derived from sales of domestic property. The average net profit per principal for the medium-sized firms was £12,200 in 1978 compared with around £9,000 in both 1976 and 1977. Nearly one-third of these firms had a net profit per principal in 1978 of over £15,000 and about one-quarter were between £10,000 and £15,000.

44.   The large firms had an average of nearly ten offices per firm in 1978, and an average income per firm of just over £1 million. A little under half the income came from fees on the sale of domestic properties. The average net profit per principal for the large firms was £23,300 in 1978, having been £21,500 in 1977 and £17,800 in 1976. In 1978, one-third of the firms achieved a net profit per principal between £20,000 and £30,000 and another one-third £30,000 or more.

Patrick sauntered back to his office, wondering as he went, whether the material Sally and he had gathered contained within it the seeds of a solution to Robert Rorty's problem.

Only when he sat down at his desk again did he realise that his most pressing problem was to dispose of a second cup of cold coffee without Sally knowing.

Exhibit 1
Consumer Attitudes
Extracts from the Price
Commission Report.
The Survey

To establish more clearly the attitudes of the public to estate agents, we commissioned the British Market Research Bureau Ltd (BMRB) to carry out a consumer survey in early 1979.

They interviewed 699 buyers and 499 sellers of domestic properties in England and Wales who had effected property transactions during the previous three years. It was established during prior group discussions and pilot interviews that respondents generally had an excellent recall of events and a high level of interest and cooperation was obtained. Below we summarise the main points. Some tables of percentages do not add up to a total of 100 per cent either because respondents were offered multiple choices, the results are rounded or we have only selected the most significant answers.

Sellers
Methods Employed

Four hundred and ninety-nine sellers were asked which methods they used and which were successful.

Per cent

	Total trying method	Proportion successful	Proportion unsuccessful
Estate agents	80	73	7
Personal contacts	20	14	6
Private newspaper advertisements	21	9	12
Private 'For Sale' boards or posters	17	2	15
Other methods	3	2	1

Source: BMRB report

It appears that people tend not to be enterprising when selling their homes, as over two-thirds (68 per cent) tried one method of selling only.

It is interesting to note that nearly one-half of those using private advertising were successful in selling their property. Nearly three-quarters of those using personal contacts were also successful, but no doubt personal contacts were used mainly when good opportunities occurred. Although private 'For Sale' boards and posters were little used, a one-eighth success rate was achieved with this method.

Selling without estate agents tended to be more prevalent where the property was cheaper, under £10,000.

Reasons for Using
Different Methods of
*Sale*Users of estate agents were asked their reasons for doing so. Replies were widely spread, including:

	Per cent
Convenience	27
Speed of transaction	19
Coverage/access to buyers	17
Is the normal/only way	13
They are well-equipped/know what to do	10

Source: BMRB report

When those who had not tried estate agents were asked why, the main answers were that 'they were not necessary/we sold quickly' (59 per cent) or economy/expense (30 per cent).

When the majority who did not advertise privately were asked for their reasons, most of the answers reflected inertia:

	Per cent
Left everything to the agent	27
Too much bother/inconvenience	22
Not necessary/sold quickly	22

Source: BMRB report

Of those who sold by private newspaper advertising, 52 per cent gave economy (avoiding having to pay agent's fees) as their reason. The rationale for other selling methods was not clear.

In order to cause respondents to think more deeply about their choice, a number of factors were listed which, from the results of group discussions, seemed to be important. All sellers were asked which of the factors were the more important. The answers were:

	Per cent	
	Those using estate agents	*Those selling privately*
Speed of finding a buyer	61	40
Getting a good selling price	43	35
Convenience of negotiation	28	14
Time taken up with negotiation	7	4
The cost incurred	3	21
The financial rates involved	2	1
Other factors	2	4

Source: BMRB report

Speed and a good selling price clearly emerged as the main considerations, although the cost factor was important to many of those selling privately.

What Do Estate Agents
*Do?*Those who had sold through estate agents were then asked what services have been provided. The responses were:

	Per cent		
	Provided	*Not provided*	*Not sure*
Drawing up property description	92	6	2
Suggested and agreed on price	87	12	1
Newspaper advertisements	77	18	5
Help with negotiations	74	22	4
Display of details in office	63	15	22
Provision of 'For Sale' board	62	36	2
Circulation of details via waiting list	60	16	24
Showing prospective buyers round property	30	64	6

Source: BMRB report

It is significant that agents tended to provide more services for the more expensive properties, including showing buyers around. This service was also more common in the South where, of course, house prices are also higher. 'For Sale' boards are used more frequently for cheaper properties.

How are Prices Fixed? The fixing of property prices and the agent's role in this important activity were then explored further. All sellers who sold through an estate agent were shown a card of alternative responses. This obtained the following results:

	Per cent
No estate agent involvement	13
Agents suggested price — vendor accepted	42
Vendor and agent agreed price together	28
Agents suggested price — we raised it	11
Agents suggested price — we lowered it	3
Agents involved in some other way	3

Source: BMRB report

Thus the agent has a very important influence on asking prices. Only 14 per cent of these sellers positively changed the agent's suggested price, although 28 per cent claimed the price was jointly agreed.

Further probing showed that 38 per cent of sellers said they compared their properties with others in deciding the price, 23 per cent said they decided what it was worth, and 9 per cent had a valuation carried out. Forty-two per cent said they just accepted the agent's advice.

Success in Obtaining the Desired Price Nearly two-thirds (62 per cent) of sellers through estate agents claimed they obtained the price they wanted, and 36 per cent did not. The remaining 2 per cent were not sure.

Expectations and Realisation of the Time Taken to Sell Among those selling through agents there was a very wide range of expectations as to the length of time it would take to obtain a satisfactory offer and to exchange contracts. Extreme optimists hoped for success in a week or so and pessimists expected a delay of over six months in each case.

	Per cent	
	Time expected to be taken	
	To acceptance of offer	*From acceptance of offer to exchange of contracts*
A month or less	31	19
One or two months	19	43
Three months	18	19
Four to six months	15	5
Over six months	3	1
Not sure	14	13

Source: BMRB report

In the event a significant proportion were disappointed, particularly in the time taken to secure exchange of contracts.

	Per cent	
	Time actually taken	
	To acceptance of offer	*From acceptance of offer to exchange of contracts*
More time than expected	33	45
Less time than expected	38	11
Same time as expected	15	32
Not sure	14	12

Source: BMRB report

Estate Agents' Charges   There appears to be some ignorance among the public about estate agents' charges. Most people (86 per cent) who sold through an agent had the terms of business explained to them by the agent, and of these only 11 per cent were offered a choice of terms. Eleven per cent said no explanation was given. Agents charges were said to be calculated as follows:

	Per cent
Simple *ad valorem* percentage of price obtained for property	63
Others	27
Don't know	10

Source: BMRB report

Three-quarters of those selling through estate agents were finally charged as quoted, most of the remainder receiving no quote.

Two-thirds of those who were charged on a simple *ad valorem* basis could remember how much they paid.

	Per cent
1% or less of selling price	11
1¼% or 1½% of selling price	22
1¾% or 2%	29
2¼% or 2½%	27
2¾% or 3%	3
Over 3%	7

Source: BMRB report

If no sale was effected by the agent, 58 per cent thought they would pay no fee and 27 per cent thought they would pay expenses, a registration fee or some unspecified charge. Fifteen per cent did not know. The no sale no fee concept (contingency charging) varied by regions.

Percentage Expecting 'No Sale No Fee'

Total	North	Midlands/Wales	South	London*
58	34	47	71	82

* Small sample
Source: BMRB report

It is interesting to compare the costs incurred by those who sold property privately; 41 per cent of these sellers spent money on advertising as follows:

	Per cent
Less than £10	48
£10 to £29	24
£30 to £39	7
£40 plus	7
Don't know	14

Source: BMRB report

Satisfaction with Estate Agents   Sellers through estate agents were then asked whether they were satisfied with the services offered. The responses were listed under five headings:

				Per cent
	Very or quite satisfied	*Mixed feelings*	*Not very or not at all satisfied*	*Did not reply/don't know*
Sales effort before offer	78	10	9	1
Advice on price	79	6	8	5
Effort after offer	70	6	16	6
Overall services	73	14	12	—
Value for money	45	21	32	—

Source: BMRB report

On most aspects the level of satisfaction was high — 70 per cent or more. Clients were less satisfied in terms of value for money, where less than half were very or quite satisfied. Two-thirds of those dissatisfied with value for money said the charges were not justified or that it was a lot of money for a little work. A minority of clients expressed dissatisfaction with the advice given on prices and success in obtaining them, while others said that little interest or effort was shown or that poor results were produced.

Probably the final test is the likelihood of sellers using estate agents again in the future. The answers below indicate that well over half the people asked, including those who did not use agents, will probably use estate agents' services next time, but a third are unlikely to do so.

The likelihood of using an estate agent for next sale	Per cent Sellers	
Very likely	34	} 60
Quite likely	26	
Not very likely	20	} 34
Not at all likely	14	
Not sure	6	

Source: BMRB report

Buying   The 699 people who had bought property during the previous three years were asked a different set of questions to establish their attitudes and practices.

How Property was Found and Bought

How Found	Per cent	How Bought	Per cent
Estate agents	60	Estate agents	74
Through personal contact	15		
Private newspaper advertisements	11	Direct from vendor	22
Calling at 'For Sale' boards	8	Others	4
Other/not stated	6		

Source: BMRB report

Estate agents are the main method used by buyers to find and buy a property. Their significance is particularly great in London and the South of England, and for those buying more expensive properties. However, some 40 per cent of properties were not found through estate agents and, indeed, 20 per cent of buyers did not use estate agents at all. The number of people not using estate agents was high in the North, the Midlands and Wales and where the value of the property was less than £10,000.

Reasons for Using Estate Agents   When those who found their houses through estate agents were asked why they did so the answers were as follows:

	Per cent
Better choice of properties	32
Convenience	16
Agent had particular property we wanted	14
Moving to new area	9
Knew agent before	7

Source: BMRB report

As with sellers, the same group of buyers were shown a list of reasons derived from group discussions, in order to probe further their reasons for using estate agents:

	Per cent
Speed in finding properties	46
Getting a good property for the money	34
Convenience of negotiation	34
Direct contact with the vendor	9
Financial risk involved	6
Costs incurred	4
Not stated	5

Source: BMRB report

It seems these buyers felt that estate agents can provide a range of houses quickly and efficiently and this is their main reason for using them.

Number of Agents Used The number of agents used varies greatly and the difference between regions is of particular interest:

Per cent

Number of agents supplying details	Total	Midlands and Wales	North	South	London
1	21	20	38	13	20
2	12	19	10	10	8
3—5	31	30	30	37	24
6—9	19	15	9	27	18
10+	15	10	10	16	26
Don't know	3	6	3	1	4

Source: BMRB report

Buyers who had found their house through an agent were asked what services he had provided for them.

Per cent

Details by post	48
General details of all properties	37
Details by telephone	25
General advice on prices	20
Accompanied visits to empty properties	20
Accompanied visits to occupied properties	15
Looking for property	15
Introduction to solicitor	13
Introduction to a mortgage	12
Introduction to a surveyor	10
Advertising specifically	3
None of these	15

Source: BMRB report

Clearly the main function of estate agents, as far as buyers are concerned, is to supply details of properties, and other functions were performed only by a minority, a fifth or less, in each case. The extent to which buyers are accompanied on visits to properties is low and the number of introductions made to other professional help, particularly in connection with mortgages, is less than might be expected, and indeed shows this is less important than the Commission were told by the professional bodies.

Estate Agents' Charges The majority (83 per cent) of buyers who found their houses through estate agents were not charged by agents for their services but, perhaps surprisingly, 12 per cent were charged a fee. Most (66 per cent) of those charged did not know what the charge was for, and the remainder mentioned specific searches, telephone expenses, advertising and valuations.

Once an offer to purchase had been accepted, over half (56 per cent) of these buyers paid the agent a deposit, but two-thirds of the deposits paid were less than £200. Interest was rarely, if ever, paid on the deposit by an estate agent.

Future Intentions Finally, all buyers were asked about their future intentions for using estate agents to buy their next home:

Per cent

Very likely	42	} 76
Quite likely	34	
Not very likely	10	} 17
Not at all likely	7	
Not sure	7	

Source: BMRB report

Buyers in the A/B social grade were more likely than average to use agents as were buyers of more expensive property and buyers living in London and the South. Conversely, the least likely were those in the lower social grades, those aged over 44 and those living in the North. However, nearly half (47 per cent) who bought without using an agent last time are likely to use one next time.

The main reasons given for deciding to use an agent in the future were:

	Per cent
The number/range of properties available	23
Speed of transactions	20
Agent helpful and informative	10
Have (always) used agent before	7

Source: BMRB report

Exhibit 2 *Estate Agents in Other Countries*

Levels of Charges   **Level of Charges in Other Countries**

Country	General level of charges %	Structure of ad valorem charge
USA	6—7	simple
Canada	5—7	simple
Germany (FR)	5—6	simple
France	4—8	tapered
Italy	6	tapered
Belgium	3—5	tapered
Switzerland	3—5	mix of simple and tapered
New Zealand	2.5—5	tapered
Sweden	3—5	simple
Denmark	1.5—4.5	tapered
Spain	2—3	simple
Irish Republic	3.5 Dublin 2.5 elsewhere	simple
UK	*1.5—2.5*	*mix of simple and tapered*
Netherlands	1—2	tapered
Norway	1—2	tapered

There appears to be a strong tendency for the rates in all countries to conform to 'norms', frequently under the influence of trade associations or because of legal control. In France and the Irish Republic, for example, the rates generally charged are legal maxima. The rates in New Zealand are set by a statutory licensing authority, whilst those for Belgium and the Netherlands are the scale fees of the national trade associations. Trade associations in the USA and Canada also have a long history of rate fixing and, although the practice is now illegal in both countries, the standard charges have generally been maintained through informal mechanisms.

A number of points should be noted when considering the table above:

(a) We have been led to believe that the high charges in the USA and Canada are related to the high quality of service given. (In the USA title insurance greatly reduces the cost of conveyancing.)

(b) In the Netherlands it is common practice for both the vendors and purchasers to be charged commission by the agent, although this practice is being examined by the Ministry of Economic Affairs. Payment of the agent's fee is frequently divided between vendor and purchaser in some of the German provinces and, indeed, in a seller's market, the whole commission is often paid by the purchaser. In France, also, fees are sometimes split between vendor and purchaser.

(c) Contingency charging (i.e. the 'no sale — no fee' practice) is common in other countries.

(d) In some countries, for example Denmark, Belgium and Norway, a minimum fee is charged.
(e) The cost of advertising is included in the fee in Germany (FR), France and Sweden, and sometimes in the Netherlands.
(f) Auctioneers sell the majority of domestic properties in the Irish Republic.

Operating Methods   The main function of an estate agent is to transfer information from sellers to buyers. The most interesting method of doing so revealed by our international comparisons is through the Multiple Listing Systems operating in the USA and Canada. Under a Multiple Listing System (MLS) a number of firms in a particular local market contribute details of the properties coming on to their books to a central pool. A list of all the properties in the pool is periodically drawn up and distributed to the participant agents. Where the agent who finds the buyer is not the agent who found the seller, the commission is split between the two.

In the USA and Canada, MLSs are generally administered by local associations, or real estate boards. Over the last 30 years these local boards have developed considerable power to inhibit competition by denying new entrants access to the central pool of listings. Anti-trust action has, on occasion, been taken to curb such behaviour in the USA and similar proceedings are in prospect in Canada.

The argument in favour of the MLS approach is that it raises the efficiency with which information is transmitted from vendors to prospective buyers by increasing:

(a) the exposure given to listed properties; and
(b) the scope for computerised data handling. Given the localised nature of real estate markets, economies of scale in data handling can only be exploited to the full where different agencies in the *same area* cooperate to pool their listings. This is the kind of cooperation found within a MLS. In the UK, on the other hand, the pooling of listings (and therefore the use of computerised techniques) has been limited mainly to single firms with a string of offices in *different* local markets. The potential gains from cooperation of this sort appear far more limited.

It is arguable that market efficiency would be increased still further if sellers and buyers had direct access (for a reasonable fee) to MLS listings. This is one of the proposals currently being considered by the US Federal Trade Commission. Its implementation would substantially reduce the role played by estate agents and an alternative method of administering the system would be needed.

Industrial Structure and Franchising   In each of the countries for which detailed information was obtained, estate agency has traditionally been a highly fragmented industry, dominated by sole traders and partnerships. In North America, however, the position has begun to change rapidly in recent years, with the growth of:

(a) national real estate brokerage chains; and
(b) franchising organisations.

The main force behind the emergence of national chains has been the existence of economies of scale in advertising and promotion. These economies have become increasingly important as families have become more mobile; local brokers have been less able to rely on referred and repeat business, and advertising has become a more vital source of trade.

The franchise movement represents a response by small brokers to increased competition from national and regional chains. Each franchisee must pay an initial franchising fee (ranging from $1,000 to $10,000 in the USA), plus annual charges calculated as a percentage of gross income. In return for the fee, the broker receives:

(a) the benefit of national advertising;
(b) training at the schools run by the franchising companies;
(c) access to particulars of the properties listed with other firms under the franchise umbrella.

Many US brokers believe that the structural changes taking place in the industry are such that, in another five years, 70—80 per cent of the sales of single family homes will be controlled by fewer than ten big companies.

This case was prepared by Hugh Murray of the London Business School, 1973.

CASE A5
Josiah Doncaster Ltd

On the 4th of March, the board of Josiah Doncaster met for the second time in three weeks. The main item on the agenda, as before, was what decision to take on the proposed New Product Strategy, which arose out of the Consultant's Report commissioned by the Marketing Director.

Established in 1740, the company had built up a world-wide reputation for fine household china. Its management was paternalistic, very conservative financially, and committed to preserving company traditions. Yet over the last 10 years the company had extended its product range into industrial porcelains for high-voltage insulation, and it had been very successful.

Bill Hawkins, the newly appointed Marketing Director, opened the meeting with an aggressive presentation. At 35, he was a good 20 years younger than anyone else on the board; and with a Harvard M.B.A., he was the only member of the board with formal management training.

"I hope that certain members of the board have reconsidered their positions since our last meeting. As far as I am concerned, my recommendations of three weeks ago still stand. Let's go through them once again, shall we? What are the main facts from the Consultant's report? Let's take them one by one, shall we?

(a) At a £4.50 selling price per filter unit, and a market size of 1 million units, the present market size is £4.5 million.

(b) One company, Western Ltd, has an estimated 85% market share.

(c) The market does not like working under a monopoly, and especially as Western Ltd do not give volume discounts.

(d) The number of buying points is estimated at 20,000, of which 220 in Birmingham, 150 in London, and 70 in Manchester, take 55% of the total.

(e) There are 35 manufacturers of equipment powered by compressed air, who dominate the market; and 15 major suppliers of air compressors.

(f) Western's don't make a thing themselves — they assemble bought-in parts. So could we. There is no technical barrier to our entry into this market.

(g) Their estimated fixed costs are thought to be £100,000; with variable costs estimated at £2.7 per unit. Total cost/unit on sales of 850,000 is thought to be £2.82.

(h) Our fixed costs are estimated at £180,000; but our variable costs are clearly lower than theirs. We estimate them at £2.12 per unit. On any kind of volume the total cost of our ceramic core is down to ½p each; their sintered bronze core costs them 60p to buy in.

(i) We have a patented technological edge over Western in the ceramic core. They can only filter down to 64 microns with the sintered bronze; whereas we can tailor ours down to any desired filtration level.

(j) Finally, we have a name which is known and respected. Everyone has heard of Doncaster. We have a 200 year reputation for quality.

. . . So I say let's make our move. Look here . . ." He went over to the new flip chart, which was mounted on an easel, by the Adam fireplace. Pointing, he said,

"Page 1.   Strategy: Exploit the anti-monopoly feeling of the market, our cost advantage, and our product superiority, by launching our Filter Unit against Western.

Page 2.   Tactics: Price 10% below Western. Give 25% bulk discount. Personal selling to the key buying points, and the equipment manufacturers. Sell to the rest by direct mail and trade journal advertising.

Page 3.   Targets:
10% of the market in Year 1.
15% of the market in Year 2.
25% of the market in Year 3.

Page 4.   Costs:

Sales in units	100,000	150,000	250,000
Fixed cost/unit	£1.80	£1.20	£0.72
Variable cost/unit	£2.12	£2.12	£2.12
Total cost	£3.92	£3.32	£2.84

Page 5.   Profit/Loss:
The average price per unit is £3.48; our estimated position is

        a £0.44 loss/unit year 1 i.e. £44,000 loss
        a £0.16 profit/unit year 2 i.e. £ 24,000 profit
        a £0.64 profit/unit year 3 i.e. £160,000 profit.

Page 6.   Conclusion: The downside risks are small. Breakeven is at 13% of the market. With all we have going for us, there should be no problem in reaching breakeven, and soon!

. . . If we are to do our duty to the shareholders of this company, our action is clearly indicated. Our duty is clear. No further hesitation. Let's approve the project. Let's go!"

"Bill, your last remarks are totally uncalled for. This Board does not need reminding of its duty to its shareholders," said Paul Doncaster, almost before Hawkins had sat down.

"Sorry Paul. I apologise. I guess my enthusiasm ran away with me."

"It's my job to see that it doesn't run away with all of us. Your proposition, as you have outlined it, is too one-sided, too easy. No real account has been taken of the risks involved. And risks there are. When you have had as much experience as I have, you will realise that taking on a market leader is no easy task — especially when they are as strongly entrenched in the market as Western is in this one. 85% market share — that's market domination with a vengeance!

Filtration is their business, and they do it well. There is no complaint anywhere in the report of their product performance, nor of their service, nor of their price. Only what amounts to a general comment that it would be nice if they were not quite so dominant! What good is that to go on? There are another 11 filter manufacturers in the market. And what have they done? Very little. They have tiny, specialised sections of the market. And their total market share adds up to what? 15% — amongst the 11 of them!

No account has been taken of Western's competitive reaction. React they will. Quickly. And hard. This isn't marginal to them as it is to us — it is their bread and butter! Market-share loss to us would hit their profits hard. The 25% market share targeted for the third year would reduce their gross profits by 25%. No company would take that quietly. We wouldn't. Why should we expect them to do so?

They have all the original equipment manufacturers sewn up; and as a result, automatically get all the replacement re-orders from the users in the factories. On average these filters last 6 years. Moreover, I doubt if any buyer regards them as a significant cost item. Take the 440 chief buyers . . . in total they spend per annum about £2,475 million, i.e. £5,600 each. Since the replacement parts are bought throughout the year, this amounts to about £470 per month. This is hardly major expenditure, for the buyer of a large company.

Finally, remember that these filters are safeguards to extremely expensive machinery, and they are often specified under the terms of the guarantee. The incentives to save pennies, at the potential risk to thousands of pounds' worth of machinery is small."

"What you say about the buyers may be right, Paul; but the Engineer is certainly aware of these filters." Bob McGregor, a dour Scot, in his mid-sixties, and Works Director, went on, "There is a point barely made in the Report. The life of these units averages 6 years. We find, like everyone else, that we have to clean the sintered bronze every three months. We use a caustic soda solution, then neutralise it with a weak acid. It is a costly operation, both in materials, labour, and sometimes in machine down-time. Why don't we say with our new filters, you throw away the core, and put in a new one?"

"If we did that, we'd really have to lower the price of the filter cores, and that would give the game away. The only difference between our Filter Unit and that of Western is the filter core. They even look alike, except for the difference in colour. And just because we have a price advantage, I don't see why we should charge a superior filter at a lower price in the market place. Incidentally, the Report says that the market likes the clear plastic bowl, because they can see the residue left by the filter. But I remember, and my staff have looked it up, that there was a court case in 1962, when one of these plastic bowls exploded, after an air pressure surge down the pipe line. There was a lot of publicity at the time. Very unfavourable. Don't let me lose sight of the fact that 80% of this company's profits, almost £1.74 million, come from the household china division. Anything that might put that at risk needs to be looked at very closely. If we go into this field at all, then we can't risk the use of a plastic bowl. We must use something stronger, a metal, or a metal alloy." John Davies, the longest serving member of the Board, and the Financial Director, finished speaking abruptly, when he saw that Hawkins had risen to his feet to make a reply.

"But to do that, John, would be to go against what the market demands. You must give the market what it wants."

"No Bill, we don't have to in this particular case," said Paul Doncaster. "I'm not altogether happy with the proposal as it stands, and I think that other members of the Board feel the same. Perhaps we would be well advised to commission a more general survey into potential new products, which don't involve a risk to our main product line, and don't involve taking on a dominant market leader.

I propose, notwithstanding your enthusiasm, Bill, that we take no further action on this Report, and commission a more general survey into the possibility of product diversification. I formally propose this to the Board. May I have your votes please?"

CASE A6
Scripto Pens Ltd

In September of 1959 Mr Paul J. Brown, Managing Dirctor of Scripto Pens Ltd of London, England, was evaluating his company's current competitive situation in the British ball-point pen industry. He was particularly concerned about a recent pricing move by the Biro Swan company, Scripto's largest competitor, and was wondering what, if anything, Scripto should do in response to the move.

Background

In 1956 the Scripto Pen Corporation of Atlanta, Ga., USA, purchased the Scroll Pen Company of London and renamed the new company Scripto Pens Ltd. Prior to its acquisition by Scripto, Scroll had traditionally concentrated on the manufacture and sale of ball-point pens in the 'medium' price range. Ball-point pens in this range usually sold at retail for a price somewhere between 50p and £1.30. These pens were designed so that the original ink cartridge, when empty, could be replaced by a refill cartridge, which Scroll also manufactured.

After the 1956 acquisition, Scripto Pens Ltd continued to manufacture a medium-priced line of ball-point pens and ink refill cartridges under the SCROLL brand name. At the same time, however, the company brought out a line of ball-point pens which it marketed under its own brand name of SCRIPTO. Most of the models in this line were also in the medium price range, although the line did include a few higher priced models. As time went on the company began to place major emphasis on the SCRIPTO brand and gradually to phase out the SCROLL brand. As of late 1959, the old line of SCROLL pens was still being manufactured, but only on a limited scale.

Scripto manufactured the ball-point pens which it supplied to the domestic British market in a plant adjacent to its offices in London. The manufacturing process was one of mass production utilizing much specialized machinery. In 1956 the plant had an annual production capacity of 12.5 million ball-point pens and ink refill cartridges and employed over 450 workers.

To sell its products Scripto maintained a force of 24 full-time salesmen. These salesmen sold about two-thirds of the company's total volume to 1,000 wholesalers. Wholesalers, in turn, sold SCRIPTO and SCROLL pens to many thousand retail dealers located throughout the British Isles. These retail dealers included stationers, department stores, drug stores, newsagents, tobacconists, and other miscellaneous outlets. The remaining one-third of the company's sales volume was generated by Scripto salesmen selling directly to 15,000 retailers and to five or six large chain organisations. Generally speaking, both the wholesalers and retailers through whom Scripto sold its pens also carried the pens of competing manufacturers.

Scripto allowed all wholesalers a 25% mark-up on the price at which they sold to retailers. Retailers, in turn, were granted an average mark-up of 30% to 35% (depending on the model), regardless of whether they purchased from wholesalers or from Scripto's direct salesmen. Neither wholesalers nor retailers were granted additional discounts for volume purchases.

Despite the fact that Scripto sold direct to a number of retail outlets, the company made an effort to protect its wholesalers as much as possible so as to ensure that these wholesalers would devote maximum effort to the sale of Scripto's products. Thus, Scripto made it a practice never to sell directly to retailers at a price below that being charged by the wholesalers. Moreover, direct salesmen tried not to visit retailers who were already being adequately serviced by wholesalers. In most cases wholesalers did not seem to mind the fact that Scripto salesmen were selling direct to some retailers. Mr Brown, Scripto's Managing Director, felt this was due to the fact that even when a Scripto salesman did visit a retailer directly, he did so only about once every six weeks; consequently his efforts very often resulted in repeat orders for pens or refills for the wholesalers who visited these retailers in the interim; on the whole, Mr Brown felt Scripto's wholesaler relationships were quite satisfactory.

The retailers whom Scripto salesmen visited, in turn, generally welcomed the opportunity to deal directly with the company, the main advantages being that company salesmen offered on-the-spot delivery, in-store display service, and immediate attention to retailer or customer complaints.

To back up the sales plan, Scripto annually budgeted an amount equal to approximately 15% of total factory sales for advertising and promotion. Of this amount, about 12½% was allocated to newspaper and television advertising; the remainder was set aside for promotion of Scripto's products to wholesalers and retailers. Prior to 1959 the company had never used up the total amount of its annual advertising and promotion budget. Approximate actual expenditures since 1957 were as follows:

1957:	£220,000
1958:	£260,000
1959:	£300,000 (estimated)

Trends in the Sales of Ball-point Pens

The English ball-point pen industry had been expanding at an extremely rapid rate for several years prior to 1959. From sales of approximately 11 million ball-point pens in 1952, the industry had grown to the point where, in 1959, sales were estimated at 86 million units, a seven year increase of almost 800%. Meanwhile, sales of fountain pens and mechanical pencils had remained fairly constant. Exhibit 1 presents the trends in unit sales of writing instruments in the British Isles.

In pounds sterling, industry-wide sales of ball-point pens and ink refill cartridges had risen from about £3.7 million in 1952 to an estimated £14.0 million in 1959, an increase of about 375%. Exhibit 2 shows the magnitude of sterling sales of writing instruments between 1952 and 1959.

During this same period, the average price of an individual ball-point pen dropped measurably. An indication of the magnitude of this drop is given in Exhibit 3.

Mr Brown had conducted some informal market research into the public's pen buying habits and had reached some tentative conclusions concerning the reasons why people bought pens. He felt that the primary reason for the tremendous increase in the popularity of ball-point pens was that people felt that they represented an ideal compromise between the permanence and attractiveness of an ink writing instrument and the convenience, cleanliness and inexpensiveness of a lead pencil. Generally speaking, Mr Brown felt that a ball-point pen was an impulse purchase. To most people a ball-point was neither a large enough nor an important enough purchase to demand much forethought. Finally, Mr Brown believed, on the basis of his experience, that the following factors, in order of importance, most influenced the sales of a particular brand of ball-point pens:

(a) Quality of pen
(b) Availability of brand in a large number of retail outlets
(c) Price
(d) Appearance and attractiveness of pens and retail display material
(e) Media advertising

Composition of the Industry

As of 1956, when Scripto bought out the Scroll Pen Company, there was one other major manufacturer of ball-point pens in the United Kingdom. This company, Biro Swan Limited, was the largest in the industry. Biro Swan had about 45% of the

Exhibit 1 *Trends in the Unit Sales of Pens in the UK*
Source: Board of Trade, London

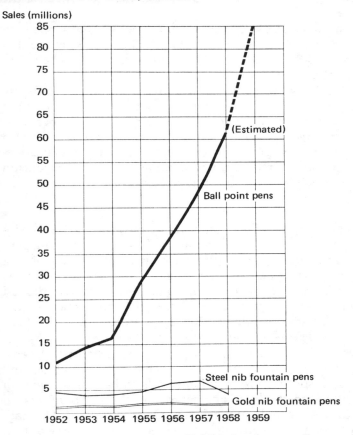

Exhibit 2 *Trends in the Sale of Ball-Point Pens in the UK*
Source: Board of Trade, London

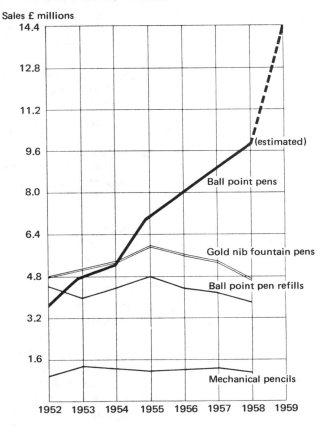

Exhibit 3 *Average Factory Price per Ball-Point Pen*
Source: Board of Trade, London

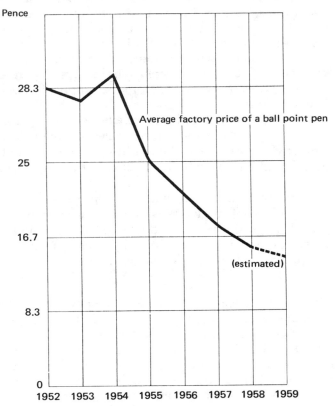

1 Refill cartridges manufactured by one company,
generally speaking, could not
be used in the ball-point pens
made by other manufacturers.

1956 sterling sales volume of ball-point pens and ink refill cartridges,[1] Scroll had about 22% and a number of other small manufacturers together accounted for the remaining 33% of the market.

At the time of Scroll's acquisition by Scripto, all of the above companies concentrated their major efforts on the manufacture of ball-point pens which sold at retail in the medium (50p to £1.30) or high (£1.30 and up) price ranges. They also, of course, manufactured refill cartridges for these pens.

In September of 1957 a controlling interest in Biro Swan Ltd was acquired by the BIC Pen Company of France.[2] Following this transaction it was rumoured within the trade that an overall internal management re-organisation occurred within the ranks of the Biro Swan Company. At the same time it was also rumoured that Biro Swan began a programme to expand significantly its production capacity for ball-point pens. This management re-organisation and expansion of production capacity supposedly continued for about a year.

2 BIC was the largest French manufacturer of ball-point pens and had almost 80% of France's annual 100,000,000 unit market.

Introduction of a Low-Priced Line of Ball-Point Pens by Biro Swan

3 'Non-refillable' meant that once the original ink cartridge went dry, it was not possible to replace it with a refill cartridge. Non-refillable ball-point pens were sometimes also known as 'throw-away' pens.

Following this year of preparation, Biro Swan made a move which marked the industry's first large scale departure from its traditional emphasis on marketing pens in the medium price range. Thus, in August of 1958, Biro Swan introduced the first low-priced line of ball-point pens to be seen in England. This new line of pens, which was initially launched in the Midlands and then quickly expanded to the rest of England, was sold under the 'BIC' brand name. Three pen models made up the line: the non-refillable[3] 'BIC Crystal' retailing at 20p; the non-refillable 'BIC Clic' retailing at 30p; and the refillable 'BIC Coronet' retailing at 40p.

To announce the introduction of its more low-priced line of ball-point pens, Biro Swan made heavy expenditures on consumer advertising. Throughout England extensive use was made of both spot television commercials and advertisements in local newspapers. In this widespread advertising campaign, the company placed major emphasis on trying to create heavy public demand for the 20p 'BIC Crystal'. To achieve this goal, the company's advertising strongly stressed the price appeal of the new pen.

Biro Swan had little difficulty getting retailers all over England to carry the new low-priced line. In attempting to achieve intensive distribution for the new line, Biro Swan followed its traditional policy of selling both through wholesalers and direct to the retail trade. For its selling activities the company employed a force of 'van salesmen' who operated more in the capacity of 'order takers' than as 'salesmen'. Thus, they visited wholesalers and retailers, took orders, and immediately filled these orders from the supply of merchandise which they carried in their vehicles.

One fundamental difference existed in the pricing policies of Biro Swan and Scripto. Whereas Scripto's direct salesmen made it a point never to undersell the company's wholesalers when visiting a retail account, Biro Swan salesmen would grant an additional 'wholesale' discount to any retailer who ordered in sufficient quantity.

Biro Swan's venture with the 20p, throw-away pen proved to be extremely successful. As of August 1959, one year after its introduction to the public, production of the 'BIC Crystal' had grown to the annual rate of 53 million units. This figure compared with the annual production rate for the 'BIRO' medium priced ball-point pen line of seven million units.

Scripto's Reaction to the Introduction of the 'BIC Crystal'

Biro Swan launched its 20p BIC pen shortly after Mr Brown arrived in England from the United States to take over as Managing Director of Scripto Pens Limited. By coincidence, Mr Brown happened to be travelling in the Midlands at the time that the 'BIC Crystal' was introduced to the public there in August 1958. Upon noticing the apparent initial success of this low-price competitive pen, Mr Brown hurried back to London to assess the overall situation and decide what, if anything, Scripto should do in response to Biro Swan's move.

As soon as it became evident that 20p ball-point pens were going to become tremendously popular in the eyes of the English buying public, Mr Brown decided that Scripto must also introduce a comparable low-price line in order to protect its overall interest in the ball-point pen industry. At the same time, however, Mr Brown felt that the introduction of a 20p Scripto pen should be viewed primarily as a defensive move. In other words, although he felt it essential that Scripto eventually market a pen in the low-priced field, he thought that the company should continue to place primary emphasis on its medium-priced line of pens. Mr Brown felt that there would continue to be a strong market for medium-priced ball-point pens; consequently he thought that the medium-priced line could continue to be the most profitable segment of Scripto's business. He therefore decided that Scripto's strategy should be to 'knock the pins out from under the BIC Crystal' by introducing a 20p Scripto pen, while at the same time attempting to keep sales of Scripto's regular line of medium-priced pens at a normal level.

Before Scripto could come out with a 20p ball-point pen, Mr Brown felt it would be necessary to increase the company's production capacity. If demand for a 20p Scripto were high, it might easily surpass the factory's 1958 capacity of 12.5 million pens annually. Therefore, in September, 1958, Mr Brown initiated steps to increase plant capacity by designing and installing a number of new high-speed, special purpose machines that automated various stages of the production process which were previously performed by hand. By early 1959 this programme of expansion through automation had enabled Scripto to cut its factory force from 450 to 400 employees while, at the same time, increasing production capacity from 12.5 million units to 40 million units.

Simultaneously with his programme to increase production capacity, Mr Brown made an effort to 'add more value' to Scripto's medium-priced pens. The quality of these pens was improved by increasing the ink supply in each cartridge 50%, installing a new metal tip on one end of the pens, and by introducing more stringent quality control. This programme of increased quality was in line with Mr Brown's desire to continue to place major emphasis on medium-priced pens. By making the above improvements, he felt that Scripto's competitive position in that field would be strengthened.

Finally, Mr Brown embarked on a project to design a new 20p pen. In undertaking this project Mr Brown felt that, if possible, Scripto should come out with a 20p pen which would be superior in quality to the 20p 'BIC Crystal' and yet which still could be sold at a satisfactory profit to Scripto. The quality of the first pen that was designed seemed to be equal, but not superior, to the 'BIC Crystal'. Like the BIC, it was non-refillable and did not have a retractable point. In spite of the fact that this pen had no substantial quality advantages, Mr Brown decided to introduce it to the trade as an interim competitive measure to help arrest the gains being made daily by the 'BIC Crystal'. Consequently, in April of 1959 Scripto's wholesalers and dealers were offered the opportunity to stock the new 20p pen and sell it as the 'SCROLL Longline'. Despite the fact that the introduction of the 'Longline' was not backed up by any consumer advertising, total sales of the new pen reached the 5 million mark by the beginning of September.

Meanwhile, Mr Brown succeeded in developing a second ball-point pen model which Scripto could profitably sell at retail for 20p and which had the added advantage of a retractable point. Because of this added feature, Mr Brown felt that the new model was just what was needed to compete successfully against the 'BIC Crystal'.

Accordingly, Mr Brown named the new model the 'SCRIPTO BOBBY' and made plans to introduce it to the public. During the beginning of August, Scripto salesmen made a concerted effort to sell advance supplies of the 'SCRIPTO BOBBY' to wholesalers and retailers all over England. In selling the new pen, the salesmen emphasised the fact that Scripto had plans to promote its introduction to the public by means of a widespread television and newspaper advertising campaign. Beginning the first of September, Scripto had lined up a five week schedule of frequent spot TV commercials devoted solely to the 'BOBBY'. Following this period of intensive TV advertising, Mr Brown planned to promote the new pen through a series of advertisements in local newspapers all over England during the remaining months of 1959.

In anticipation of this year-end advertising campaign to introduce the 'BOBBY', Mr Brown had conserved on advertising expenditures early in the year. Up until the beginning of September he had spent only about £68,000 of his £300,000 advertising budget. Consequently, he planned to spend about £240,000 on the introductory advertising campaign for the 'BOBBY'.

Mr Brown had designed the format of this campaign with the idea in mind of directing it almost as much toward wholesalers and retailers as toward the general public. This strategy was in line with Scripto's policy of maintaining strong wholesale and retail relationships. Thus, it was with the feeling that wholesalers and retailers would be favourably impressed by the prestige of TV, that Mr Brown had decided to make such heavy use of this medium.

As a result of the August selling efforts of Scripto's salesmen, about 1,750,000 'BOBBY' pens had been distributed to the trade by the beginning of September. Although Mr Brown did not, as yet, have any specific figures, he thought that these 'BOBBY' pens had already begun to move off the retailers shelves at a fairly brisk rate in spite of the fact that the consumer advertising programme had not yet commenced. Meanwhile sales of Scripto's medium-priced ball-point pen lines had continued at what Mr Brown considered to be a 'normal' level.

The Situation of August 1959

As of August 1959, Scripto was marketing a full line of ball-point pens with models in every price range. Sales of the 20p line, both in units and in pounds sterling, were still minimal when compared to sales of the company's medium-priced line. However, the company was poised to launch its £240,000 introductory advertising campaign for the 'BOBBY' in September.

A list of the company's most important ball-point pen models, along with the price schedule at which each pen was sold, is shown in Exhibit 4.

Exhibit 4   *Scripto Pens Ltd Price List as of 15 August 1959*

	Price to Wholesalers (Dozen)	Price to Retailers (Dozen)	Purchase Tax (Dozen)	Retailer's Margin (Dozen)	Retail Price (Each)
	£	£	£	£	£
SCRIPTO LINE					
Low-price pens					
'Bobby'	1.00	1.33	0.33	0.74	0.20
Medium-price pens					
'250'	2.50	3.33	0.83	1.84	0.50
'450'	4.72	6.30	1.57	3.29	0.93
'T200'	6.50	8.67	2.17	4.40	1.27
High-price pens					
'T650'	7.70	10.27	2.57	5.16	1.50
'Satellite'	17.50	23.33	5.83	11.62	3.40
Refills	1.75	2.33	0.58	1.29	0.35
SCROLL LINE					
Low-price pens					
'Longline'	1.00	1.33	0.33	0.74	0.20
Medium-price pens					
'320'	3.50	4.67	1.17	2.32	0.68
'420'	4.00	5.33	1.33	2.70	0.78
'520'	5.75	7.67	1.92	3.97	1.13
Refills	1.75	2.33	0.58	1.29	0.35

Exhibit 5   *Biro Swan Ltd Price List as of 15 August 1959*

	Price to Wholesalers (dozen)	Price to Retailers (dozen)	Purchase Tax (dozen)	Retailer's Margin (dozen)	Retail Price (each)
BIC LINE	£	£	£	£	£
LOW-PRICE PENS					
Crystal	1.00	1.33	0.33	0.74	0.20
Clic	1.50	2.00	0.50	1.10	0.30
Coronet	1.95	2.60	0.65	1.55	0.40
REFILLS					
(Clic & Coronet only)	0.75	1.00	0.25	0.55	0.15
BIRO LINE					
MEDIUM & HIGH-PRICE PENS					
Minor	2.92	3.90	0.98	2.32	0.60
Citizen	3.80	5.07	1.27	2.66	0.75
Retractable	4.42	5.90	1.47	3.43	0.90
Stylist	5.75	7.67	1.92	4.21	1.15
Deluxe	10.50	14.00	3.50	7.70	2.10
Squire (each)	1.45	1.92	0.48	1.10	3.50
Magnum (each)	1.58	2.12	0.53	1.15	3.80
REFILLS					
Recharge	1.50	2.00	0.50	1.10	0.30
Magnum	1.73	2.30	0.58	1.32	0.35
Insert	1.95	2.60	0.65	1.55	0.40

Biro Swan, meanwhile, was also marketing a full line of ball-point pens; its low-priced line being sold under the 'BIC' brand name and its medium and high-priced lines under the 'BIRO' brand name. Biro Swan was currently producing BIC's at the rate of 53 million units per year and BIRO's at the rate of about 7 million units per year. Biro Swan's August 1959 price list is shown in Exhibit 5.

Announcement of Biro Swan's Price Change

On August 26th the management of Biro Swan suddenly announced to the trade that, effective September 1st, big price cuts would be made on all pens and refill cartridges in the medium-priced BIRO line. Pen reductions were to range from 33⅓ % off on the BIRO MINOR (old retail price 60p, new price 40p) to 7½ % off on the BIRO MAGNUM (old retail price £3.80, new price £3.50). Retail prices of refill cartridges were to be cut in half. Prices of the low-priced BIC line were to remain unchanged. Exhibit 6 shows Biro Swan's new price list.

Dealer margins on each unit in the BIRO line were to remain the same from a percentage point of view, but would be reduced in absolute money terms. To compensate for the resulting devaluation of stocks presently in the hands of wholesalers and retailers, Biro Swan proposed a special 'bonus' offer (see Exhibit 6). A London Financial Times newspaper article announcing the price change also indicated that Biro Swan had plans to launch a £1 million advertising campaign to introduce the price cuts to the public.

Excerpts of the letter which Biro Swan's management sent to the trade to announce the forthcoming price cuts are reproduced in Exhibit 7.

Exhibit 6 *Biro Swan Ltd Price List as of 1 September 1959*

	Price to Wholesalers (dozen)	Price to Retailers (dozen)	Purchase Tax (dozen)	Retailer's Margin (dozen)	Retail Price (each)
BIC LINE	£	£	£	£	£
LOW-PRICE PENS					
Crystal	1.00	1.33	0.33	0.74	0.20
Clic	1.50	2.00	0.50	1.10	0.30
Coronet	1.95	2.60	0.65	1.55	0.40
REFILLS					
(Clic & Coronet only)	0.75	1.00	0.25	0.55	0.15
BIRO LINE					
MEDIUM & HIGH-PRICE PENS					
Minor	1.95	2.60	0.65	1.55	0.40
Citizen	2.77	3.68	0.92	2.00	0.55
Retractable	3.45	4.60	1.15	2.65	0.70
Stylist	4.73	6.30	1.53	3.57	0.95
Deluxe	7.50	10.00	2.50	5.50	1.50
Squire (each)	1.25	1.68	0.42	0.90	3.00
Magnum (each)	1.45	1.92	0.48	1.10	3.50
REFILLS					
Recharge	0.75	1.00	0.25	0.55	0.15
Magnum	1.00	1.33	0.33	0.74	0.20
Insert	1.00	1.33	0.33	0.74	0.20

Exhibit 7 *Excerpts of Letter from Biro Swan Management to Biro Swan Wholesalers and Retailers*

26th August, 1959

Dear Sirs:

On September 14th, we are announcing to the public the most-important-ever news concerning the genuine Biro range.

All Biro prices will be substantially reduced from 1st September; all pen prices will be down by at least 20p, most refill prices will be slashed by half.

... Advanced techniques backed by new, ultra-modern machinery have enabled us to make significant reductions in our production costs, at the same time as increasing the quality of them.

The new prices will give the Biro range a far wider appeal than ever before. Enormous demand is anticipated, and with it will come greatly increased turnover, and larger profits for you. Trade margins remain, as they always have been, the most generous in the ball-pen field. The terms on which you buy the Biro range coupled with our Super Discount scheme give you really worthwhile profits on fast-moving merchandise.

We fully appreciate that your existing stocks are devalued by this operation, and we are therefore giving you this advance notice, together with the opportunity to claim a free special bonus during the month of September. All orders received by us between September 1st and September 30th inclusive, for pens and refills in the genuine Biro price range will be invoiced at the new trade price. All orders must be for immediate delivery. The goods will be delivered to you, plus a free bonus of the same goods ordered by you equivalent to the difference between the old and the new retail value of your order. We feel that you will appreciate that this method of adjustment causes you the least effort, and is absolutely straightforward and fair to you and all our customers . . .

The National Advertising starts on September 14th and continues until Christmas. We know that it will create enormous demand for the genuine Biro ball-pen, and at the same time ensure repeat business in refills. You can save in this demand simply by stocking up, displaying, and selling the genuine Biro range.

Yours faithfully,

Sales Manager
Biro Swan Limited

*This case was prepared by
Kenneth Simmonds and Jules
Goddard of the London
Business School
© Kenneth Simmonds, 1980*

CASE A7
Henshall Confectionery

Among Peter Avery's duties at Henshall Confectionery was responsibility for the Vendomatic account. Since the Christmas break ten weeks previously when Peter took over the account, the account performance had been disappointing. Sales had slipped by nearly 20% on the previous year and the contribution of £6,000 for the ten weeks looked decidedly sick.

Vendomatic held the franchise from the Transport Authority for stocking the automatic chocolate vending machines on the Authority's premises. Special chocolate packs were supplied to Vendomatic by both Henshall and its major competitor Pastile at a standard price agreed annually with the Vendomatic and Transport Authority management. The price allowed a commission to Vendomatic on the volume sold and a royalty to the Transport Authority. From time to time, the vending machine price to the customer could be adjusted, but given the mechanical limitations of the machines, the bulk of the adjustment was made by the confectionery companies with changes in the quantity of chocolate in the packs.

The vending machines contained either three or five slots with two allocated to chocolate — one for a Henshall pack and one for a Pastile pack. Henshall's and Pastile's brands were advertised widely with high public brand awareness and both firms offered a milk chocolate, a plain chocolate and a nut and raisin chocolate. Vendomatic, however, was not prepared to stock the machines with more than one brand at a time from each competitor. Their staff servicing the machines would, they claimed, be involved in unnecessary costs if they had to carry more than two chocolate lines. Staff frequently had to carry supplies up and down escalators in use and for a considerable distance along corridors. Furthermore, they would need to spend more time packing in their vans if they had multiple brands from each supplier. The agreement reached was that each supplier would supply one of its brands each week and could change the brand for the Monday delivery.

Each Monday, Vendomatic provided both competitors with a return showing for each the brand used in refilling the machines during the preceding week and the quantities placed. These returns for the past ten weeks are shown in Exhibit 1. While nut chocolate represented the smallest placements for Henshall's, Peter Avery calculated that if he eliminated nut chocolate altogether in favour of plain chocolate, he could increase the £6,000 contribution for the ten weeks by a further £500. With the added requirements of its manufacture, nut chocolate remained the most expensive even after adjustment of the chocolate and nut content. Contributions for the ten weeks were:

	Packs (000s)	Contribution Per Pack	£
Plain	71.2	4.0p	2,848
Milk	49.6	3.6p	1,786
Nut	47.6	3.0p	1,428
	168.4		£6,062

Exhibit 1 *Henshall and Pastile Brand and Volume Returns*

Week	Henshall Brand	Packs (000s)	Pastile Brand	Packs (000s)	Total Packs (000s)
1	Plain	17.2	Milk	17.2	34.4
2	Nut	15.3	Plain	18.7	34.0
3	Plain	19.7	Nut	16.0	35.7
4	Milk	15.9	Nut	19.5	35.4
5	Plain	14.9	Milk	20.2	35.1
6	Milk	14.8	Plain	18.0	32.8
7	Nut	17.9	Plain	14.6	32.5
8	Milk	18.9	Nut	15.3	34.2
9	Nut	14.4	Milk	19.5	33.9
10	Plain	19.4	Milk	14.2	33.6
	TOTAL	168.4		173.2	341.6

This case was prepared by Kenneth Simmonds of the London Business School.
© *Kenneth Simmonds, 1980.*

CASE A8
Albright Ltd

Victor Lonergan seemed to be swimming around in figures. Ever since July when he joined Albright Limited as Personal Assistant to the new Managing Director, Graham Peake, Peake had kept him hard at work analysing historical pricing data. Victor had completed his Bachelor's in Marketing and was prepared for some figure analysis, but he was inclined to think that Peake as an electrical engineer had a bad case of 'compulsive calculosis'. Against his strenuous objection that pricing should be based on an assessment of customers' attitudes to product prices and not on historical cost and price measurements, Peake was now insisting that Victor prepare a written price policy for Albright for the ensuing year, justified in historical terms. "The trouble with business graduates and accountants", said Graham "is that they calculate everything in discrete terms. Somehow, the training doesn't allow for the feedback and system thinking which is the basis of most market processes."

Annual plans for 1981 were due to be submitted by Peake at the end of September to the board of the Beta Group. Albright was a wholly-owned subsidiary. The Chairman had asked Peake to come up with an increased contribution to consolidated profits and he was personally anxious to avoid any slip in the group's earnings per share. A slip might cause an adverse reaction on the stock market just at a time when some were looking for tangible results from his first four years in the chair. As he told Peake "There are only two things the stock analysts care about from a metal components group and those are profits and more profits. And Albright has had an abysmal record so far."

The Beta Group manufactured a wide range of metal and plastic parts, components, sub-assemblies and small products. Albright specialised in standard wall switches and sockets for lights and electrical appliances and was one of the few group subsidiaries with a standard product line. Nevertheless, there was no marketing organisation as such, and the standard group pattern of an engineering trained managing director and a strong financial director was evident. Apparently, Peake had had a disagreement with the Finance Director shortly before Victor's arrival when he complained about the incomprehensibility of the standard cost calculations for the long list of individual items in Albright's range. Peake told Victor he found it impossible to grasp price—volume—cost relationships for individual items from the cost figures because of the large range, fluctuating volumes and dominating percentage of common costs. "There's hardly any difference conceptually between single, double and treble switches, for example, yet we have a set of standards and variations for each — and not one of the costing staff has been able to interpret what it means when every month seven lean variations on standard are gobbled up by seven fat variations. About the only cost figures I can use out of the accounts are the general classification headings and a rough guess as to how they vary." He showed Victor the following breakdown he had developed:

Classification	Percentage of Total Cost	Short Term Variation with Volume	Long Term Variation with Volume
Direct Labour	19	100% Variable	90% Variable
Direct Materials	16	100% Variable	90% Variable
Indirect Expenses	12	100% Variable	90% Variable
Works Expenses	39	50% Variable	90% Variable
Distribution Expenses	3	50% Variable	90% Variable
Selling Expenses	5	Fixed	50% Variable
General and Administrative Expenses	6	Fixed	50% Variable
	100		

The first task Peake gave Victor was to calculate an index of price per average item for each period that followed an adjustment in Albright's price list over the past seven years. Currently Albright's price stood at £1.19 for an average item.

Next, Peake had Victor calculate similar figures for Maynard Switches Ltd, Albright's leading competitor. He asked Victor to calculate an average ratio of Maynard's item prices to Albright's and adjust the Albright average item price by this ratio to give an estimate of Maynard's average item price. This exercise proved to be more straightforward than Victor at first expected. Apparently, Maynard had consistently raised all item prices at the same time by more or less the same percentage. They had also led Albright and the seven or eight smaller competitors with price rises and since April, Maynard's average wholesale price had stood at 12½% above Albright's. Victor's estimates are tabulated in Exhibit 1.

Peake then asked Victor to analyse the published accounts and other estimates of sales revenue for Maynard and the smaller competitors. Maynard was an independent firm and its 1979 accounts are summarised in Exhibit 2. From the published accounts of the smaller competitors, none held over 10% of the market, and they confirmed the Albright sales staff estimates that these firms together

Exhibit 1 *Albright and Maynard: Average Item Prices, Volume and Market Share Estimates — The Historical Pattern*

	Competing Average Item Prices (From Price Lists)			Estimated Market Volume (Exhibit 3 Column 2 Adjusted) M. Items	Albright		Maynard	
Period Ruling	Months No.	Albright Average £	Maynard Average £		Sales (Actual) M. Items	Market Share %	Sales (Est. *) M. Items	Market Share %
May 74—Feb 75	10	.51	.51	35.2	6.9	(19.6)	14.5	(41.2)
Mar 75—Dec 75	10	.56	.56	32.5	6.1	(18.8)	14.2	(43.7)
Jan 76—Jun 76	6	.60	.60	19.5	3.5	(17.9)	9.0	(46.2)
Jul 76—Apr 77	10	.65	.69	27.2	6.1	(22.4)	8.9	(32.7)
May 77—Jun 77	2	.69	.69	6.3	1.4	(22.2)	2.1	(33.3)
Jul 77—Nov 77	5	.80	.80	15.8	3.3	(20.9)	5.9	(37.3)
Dec 77—May 78	6	.87	.87	19.9	4.0	(20.1)	7.9	(39.7)
Jun 78—Mar 79	10	.94	.99	34.1	7.9	(23.1)	10.4	(30.5)
Apr 79—Oct 79	7	1.04	1.05	25.1	5.8	(23.1)	7.7	(30.7)
Nov 79—Mar 80	5	1.19	1.19	18.1	4.0	(22.1)	6.1	(33.7)
Apr 80—Aug 80	5	1.19	1.34	18.3	4.4	(24.0)	5.1	(27.9)

*Maynard Estimate = Market — 3 (Albright Volume)

Exhibit 2   *Maynard Switches Ltd: Summary of Accounts*

	1979 £m	1978 £m
Turnover	14.6	13.1
Profit before Taxation	0.4	1.4
Taxation	0.2	0.7
Dividend	0.4	0.4
Current Assets		
Cash	0.4	0.4
Debtors and Pre-payments	2.2	1.8
Stocks	3.3	2.8
	5.9	5.0
Less Current Liabilities		
Bank Overdraft	3.5	2.4
Creditors	1.3	1.6
	4.8	4.0
Net Current Assets	1.1	1.0
Fixed Assets	3.2	3.4
Total	4.3	4.4
Financed by:		
Debentures and Loans	2.7	2.6
Shareholders' Funds	1.6	1.8
	4.3	4.4

accounted for under 50% of the market. Just as Albright had followed Maynard's price lead in the past, these smaller firms had waited for Albright before they too raised prices. There were a few imports as well, but British building and wiring codes gave some protection. The Sales Manager thought that unless UK suppliers pushed their prices well out of line with cost, no foreign firm would be able to gain enough volume to get costs below Maynard's.

From the estimate of total industry revenue, Peake now had Victor calculate industry volume. He first calculated 1979 average item price for Albright from its volume and sales totals, and dividing this into industry revenue gave an estimate of 43 million items for the industry as a whole. On the assumption that industry volume had moved more or less in step with the Index of Construction Output, Peake then extrapolated backwards to 1974 to get the industry volume estimates shown in Exhibit 3.

Exhibit 3   *Annual Indicators of Volume and Price*

Calendar Year	Index of Construction Output (1970 = 100)	Estimated Industry Volume (1979 = 43m.) (million items)	Wholesale Price Index All Manufactured Output (1980 = 100)
1974	94	43	35
1975	86	39	44
1976	85	39	51
1977	83	38	63
1978	88	40	72
1979	94	43	88
1980 (8 months est.)	95	29	100

Victor had begun by now to disbelieve all of his figures. There were too many estimates, assumptions and averages involved. But Peake was far from finished. He had Victor adjust the estimated market volume from a calendar basis to give volume estimates for the periods over which Albright and Maynard prices had held constant. Victor did obtain fairly reliable figures on the item quantities sold by Albright in each period but Peake had him make the heroic assumptions that any volume change for Albright was directly reflected in Maynard's sales and tripled by similar shifting between Maynard and the other competitors. The resulting market share figures, shown in Exhibit 1, left Victor doubting whether they meant much at all.

Finally, Peake thought it would be interesting to see how prices had varied in real terms. Using the wholesale price index for all manufacturing output as a deflator, he had Victor calculate real revenues per item from the Albright and Maynard financial figures as shown in Exhibits 4 and 5.

Now, a week after Peake's meeting with the Chairman, there had been a subtle change in Peake's attitude. All the figures seemed to have become Victor's. He was left with 'his' figures to prepare 'his' price policy.

Exhibit 4 *Albright Limited: Annual Sales, Item Revenue and Market Share*

Calendar Year	Sales (£m)	Profits Before Tax (losses) (£m)	Volume (million items)	Item Revenue Actual (£)	Item Revenue 1980 Prices (£)	Market Share (%)
1974	4.2	0.4	8.5	0.49	1.40	19.8
1975	4.0	(0.2)	7.3	0.55	1.25	18.7
1976	4.5	(0.3)	7.2	0.63	1.24	18.5
1977	5.8	(0.1)	7.8	0.74	1.17	20.5
1978	8.0	0.4	8.8	0.91	1.26	22.0
1979	10.2	0.2	9.8	1.04	1.18	22.8
1980 (8 mth est.)	8.1	0.3	6.8	1.19	1.19	23.4

Exhibit 5 *Maynard Switches Ltd: Annual Sales, Item Revenue and Market Share*

Calendar Year	Annual Report Sales (£m)	Annual Report Profits Before Tax (losses) (£m)	Volume (Sales Item Revenue) (million items)	Item Revenue Actual* (£)	Item Revenue 1980 Prices (£)	Market Share (%)
1974	9.1	1.9	18.5	0.49	1.40	43.0
1975	9.2	0.9	16.7	0.55	1.25	42.8
1976	8.9	0.3	14.1	0.63	1.23	36.2
1977	8.5	(0.1)	11.2	0.76	1.21	28.9
1978	13.1	1.4	14.1	0.93	1.29	35.2
1979	14.6	0.4	13.8	1.06	1.21	32.1
1980 (8 mth est.)	11.1	N.A.	8.7	1.28	1.28	29.7

*Exhibit 1 Adjusted to Calendar Year Basis

This case was prepared by Kenneth Simmonds of the London Business School. © Kenneth Simmonds, 1971.

CASE A9
British Electrical Supplies Ltd

Executives of British Electrical Supplies Ltd were divided over the price action to take on their Powerite insulating compound. Some wished to lower the price to £0.50 to counter a decreasing market share, others wished to leave the price at £0.60 because they considered the increased margin more than compensated for the lost volume. As the annual price list was due for circulation, an early decision was being called for by the Sales Office Manager.

Powerite was sold to a wide range of manufacturers for incorporation in electrical motors. BES was not certain of the exact market size, but as near as the Sales Department could estimate, about 5.2 million lbs would have been purchased during the year that was just ending. Of this volume BES sold the largest share, around 45%, and the remainder was produced by two competitors with more or less equal shares of the market. Powerite was stronger than the competing compounds, although they all fulfilled the same function — and many customers preferred it for this reason. Moreover, BES had a high-quality image in the electrical supplies field and some customers claimed that there were fewer imperfections in Powerite shipments and that Powerite would last longer in operation.

In August of each year BES circulated an annual price list to customers and the sales staff followed this up by making supply arrangements with the largest customers. Salesmen were paid on a fixed salary basis and represented BES's full line to their customers; Powerite normally took only a small part of their time.

Up to August, competitors had not announced their prices for the ensuing year and appeared to be waiting for BES before making any price moves. Until the previous year their prices for compounds competing with Powerite had always been the same as the BES price, but when BES had raised the price from £0.50 to £0.60 per lb a year ago neither competitor had followed suit. This had caused BES's market share to decline, as can be seen from the following figures:

	Powerite Price (per lb)	Powerite Sales (million lbs)	Estimated Total Market (million lbs)
Current year	£0.60	2.3	5.2
Last year	£0.50	2.7	4.9
2 years ago	£0.50	2.3	4.4
3 years ago	£0.50	1.7	3.8

Powerite and the competing lines had been introduced as an insulating compound only six years previously and demand had grown rapidly as other insulating materials were replaced. Sales executives felt that future growth would be more moderate and depend largely on the demand pattern for electric motors. There was little likelihood of any technological breakthrough to replace the compound in the next four or five years. In order to get more precise figures for Powerite, they listed the major accounts for the insulating compound and questioned the responsible sales representatives as to the likely growth from each and which buyers might switch volumes to different suppliers as prices changed. From this exercise they estimated that the total market for the ensuing year would be 5.4 million lbs if both BES and competition maintained their current prices, and possibly 5.5 million if BES reduced the Powerite price to meet the competition. The Powerite share they estimated would be 2.1 million lbs or 2.7 million lbs, respectively. If, on the other hand, the competition were to raise price to match Powerite the total sales would be likely to fall to 5.0 million lbs, although Powerite would still sell 2.7 million lbs.

Should Powerite remain above the competition indefinitely, the Sales Manager estimated that there might be a further fall of 15% off the estimate for next year, as the arguments of the competing sales representatives convinced more purchasers to switch. With the current price differentials, though, this would probably be the limit of the BES market share decline, given the premium image held by many customers. The Sales Manager pointed out that this meant only a 33.3% market share and would lose BES its leadership strength. In the light of such figures he felt BES had no real alternative but to reduce price.

The Factory Manager took the opposite view. Powerite was manufactured in a separate department with its own departmental foreman and its profit figures showed separately in the monthly return covered by the Factory Manager's report. While he naturally preferred to have volume production, the Factory Manager calculated that he would still show a higher profit with the 33.3% market share. Moreover, he was certain that competitors would shortly raise their prices because their current costs with lower volumes were higher than his own and they would currently be recording losses. His arguments were based primarily upon the tabulation of production cost per lb for varying volumes shown in Exhibit 1, prepared by the accounting section at his request.

Exhibit 1 *Powerite Estimated Cost per lb for Varying Volume*

	Volume in million lbs				
	1.8	2.1	2.4	2.7	3.0
	£	£	£	£	£
Direct labour	0.1180	0.1150	0.1120	0.1150	0.1180
Materials	0.0590	0.0590	0.0590	0.0590	0.0590
Scrappage	0.0057	0.0051	0.0047	0.0053	0.0054
Powerite department expense					
Class I[1]	0.0170	0.0170	0.0160	0.0150	0.0150
Class II[2]	0.1055	0.0905	0.0791	0.0704	0.0633
General works expense[3]	0.0393	0.0383	0.0373	0.0383	0.0393
Cost of Manufacture	0.3445	0.3249	0.3081	0.3030	0.3000
Selling & Administration expenses[4]	0.2067	0.1949	0.1849	0.1818	0.1800
Total	0.5512	0.5198	0.4930	0.4848	0.4800

1 Indirect wages, packing, maintenance, supplies etc.
2 Supervision, depreciation, etc.
3 Allocated on direct labour (33.3%)
4 Allocated on works cost (60%)

This case was written by José R. de la Torre, Institute of International Business, Georgia State University, and is not intended to demonstrate either effective or ineffective handling of administrative matters.

CASE A10
White Electric Inc

Mr Jack Heinen, Vice-President of WEI's international division, walked into Charlie Gessel's office on a late Friday afternoon in November 1971. He was returning from a staff meeting called by Mr Robert Griffith, White's Executive Vice-President for Operations, regarding the launching of WEI's new microwave oven. The company was gearing up to meeting supply commitments for its pre-Christmas introduction of the product. In this connection, Mr Heinen had been asked to attend the meeting to represent any interest White International might have in the matter.

After sitting down and lighting an excellent Havana that he had picked up on his last trip back from London, Mr Heinen told Charlie that International had been asked to prepare a quick but reliable estimate on the microwave oven's potential in overseas markets. The urgency of the matter was such that a preliminary report had to be ready for next Wednesday's staff meeting, at which production and marketing budgets for 1972 were going to be revised. Jack Heinen left the room leaving behind a thin trail of smoke. Charlie reached for the phone, called his wife, and asked her to cancel any engagements for the following week. It looked like a dandy!

Company Background

White Electric Inc was a medium-sized manufacturer of household appliances, aerospace components, power systems, and other related electric machinery. The company had had 1970 sales of $350 million, of which $105 million were overseas (excluding Canada). Total profits were $21.5 million.

The domestic appliance market accounted for almost 40% of WEI's US sales, or $95 million. This figure represented less than 2% of the total home appliance market in the US, which had exceeded, at retail prices, the $14 billion mark in 1970. Each of the industry giants — Sunbeam, General Electric, General Motors, Singer, Westinghouse, American Motors, Arvin Industries, Ford and others — had annual sales of household appliances of $200 to $500 million in the US market. In addition to these, there were approximately 80 manufacturers in the industry which were considered medium to large in size.

White Electric had three other divisions which did various amounts of business. The Aerospace Products Division did mostly subcontract work in government-related business and had declined in pace with the recent general slowdown in that sector. Sales of aerospace products dropped to less than $40 million in 1970. Of this amount slightly more than 5 per cent were export sales. All foreign sales were handled by the division's staff in accordance with foreign supply provisions written into their various contractual obligations with defence and commercial establishments abroad. The high degree of technical sophistication involved, as well as strict national security restrictions, precluded any other division from handling these sales.

The Machinery Division had been acquired in the late 1930's and incorporated into White's growing business during that period. A strong competitor both nationally and internationally, the division had reached a plateau in sales since the mid-1960's. Increased competition at home and abroad were principally responsible for this state of affairs. Sales in 1970 were approximately $60 million in the US. In addition, White International handled the Machinery Division's export sales on a commission basis through their foreign affiliates and distributors. These exports amounted to over $10 million in 1970.

The fourth division, Power Systems, manufactured generators, motors, and similar equipment for a wide array of customers. However, 80% of the division's business was done with large utilities throughout the US and abroad. Total 1970 sales were $57 million, of which nearly $5 million were export sales generated and handled by the division's own staff.

The international division, White International, in addition to acting as an export agent for the Machinery Division, controlled manufacturing, assembly, and sales operations of household appliances throughout the world. It had consolidated sales (exclusive of machinery) in excess of $88 million and profits of $4.5 million in 1970.

WEI had been founded in the early 1920's by Bill White, an aggressive ex-GI who loved to tinker with electricity. He began by manufacturing electric fans and toasters, and was soon into vacuum cleaners, refrigerators and electric ranges. In 1938, Mr White acquired the nearly bankrupt Coleman Electric Works and transformed it into the electric machinery division of White Electric Inc. His brother-in-law, Mr Robert Wassle, took charge of the new division. Fuelled by war-time orders, both the division and the company grew dramatically through 1945.

The company took good advantage of the postwar surge in consumer demand, adding new lines to its household division. Among these, washing machines and home freezers were particularly successful. During the same period, the company diversified further into the aerospace and power fields. This diversification stemmed from the experience gained as a war contractor.

Following Mr White's death in 1953 and a brief period of reorganisation, Mr Wassle assumed the chairmanship of the Board. A public offering in 1955 greatly diluted the controlling interests of the White and Wassle families, but provided much needed capital for expansion.

Mr Wassle's young and dynamic son, Bill, had played a key role in the firm's development throughout this period. As Vice-President of the household products division, he had moved the firm into the fields of convenience household items, such as air conditioners and dishwashers, items that soon experienced rising demand as income levels grew in the 1960's. Simultaneously, he had launched WEI into the international arena. The first foreign investment was made in 1955 in Canada. This was soon followed by moves into the United Kingdom, Mexico, Germany and Italy. By 1961 a new international division, White International, was formed to coordinate all foreign operations.* Mr Robert Griffith, a marketing professor at a leading US business school, was hired for the job.

In 1966 Mr Wassle assumed the presidency of WEI and Mr Griffith became Executive Vice-President for Operations. Jack Heinen, former manager of White International's UK subsidiary and later European regional director, was named to head the international division. Two years later Charlie Gessel joined the division. At 32, he had four years of experience in consumer durables and had acquired recently an MBA with major concentrations in marketing and international business.

Exhibitis 1 & 2 provide financial information on WEI and its various divisions. Exhibits 3 & 4 detail the organisation of the firm and of its international activities.

*The export activities of the power and aerospace divisions were not assimilated in the new division due to very special technical and sensitive problems.

The International Division

The international division was formed in 1961 to deal with the specific problems that derived from operating in various countries. When Bob Griffith took over the management of the division, WEI had five subsidiaries with combined sales of less than $6 million. Profits from foreign operations were less than $200,000 in that year.

The formation of the EEC provided the stimulus to a European recovery similar to the post-war consumer boom in the United States. Both Griffith and Wassle agreed that this was the market to pursue and they launched a major expansion drive in the Continent. Major capital expenditures soon were made in the UK and Germany. In 1963 the smaller Italian subsidiary merged with a domestic

Exhibit 1   *Summary of Consolidated Financial Statements[1] for White Electric Inc. (millions of dollars)*

	1970	1969	1968	1967
Net sales	349.7	321.7	305.6	261.4
Cost of goods sold	257.8	231.2	221.7	187.0
Operating profit	91.9	90.5	83.9	74.4
Sales and Administrative expenses	29.2	26.8	24.2	21.4
R&D Expenses	15.3	15.7	12.5	11.3
Other expenses	1.7	1.6	1.8	1.8
Before-tax profit	45.7	46.4	45.4	39.9
Income tax	24.2	24.5	23.9	21.1
Net profit	21.5	21.9	21.5	18.8
Cash and securities	16.7	13.2	11.8	10.2
Other current assets	99.4	92.7	87.0	72.9
Net fixed assets	38.4	35.1	33.7	25.8
Total assets	154.5	141.0	132.5	108.9
Current liabilities	32.1	30.1	30.3	25.2
Long Term debt	10.3	8.3	14.5	10.5
Equity	112.1	102.6	87.7	73.2
Total	154.5	141.0	132.5	108.9

1. Includes all subsidiaries, foreign and domestic, owned 50% or more, and a proportionate amount of the accounts of minority-owned subsidiaries.

manufacturer to expand in that highly competitive market. This last move proved very successful as the Italian appliance industry established its dominance over the rest of the EEC in the years ahead.

That same year, a regional office was opened in Geneva to coordinate all selling and manufacturing activities in Europe. Jack Heinen assumed the post of European Director from his previous job of heading the UK subsidiary. In the next two years sales activities expanded to every country in Western Europe. Manufacturing facilities were also added in Spain and Sweden to cover two important markets outside the EEC. Total European sales, including imports of household appliances from the US division but excluding other corporate exports to Europe, reached $25 million in 1965.

Activity in other areas of the world was fairly quiet during this period. The Canadian operations were totally integrated with the US division. In addition to Mexico, two more ventures were started during this period: a wholly-owned subsidiary in Brazil and a minority (35%) investment in Australia. When Jack Heinen assumed the direction of international in 1966, however, he initiated a change of policies which included increased emphasis on developing countries.

During the following five years, subsidiaries were added in El Salvador, Peru, Venezuela, South Africa, Philippines, Thailand and India; licensing agreements were also concluded with firms in Japan, Israel, Chile and Colombia; and two new regional directors were named to coordinate activities in Latin America and in Africa-Asia-Australia (AAA).

A rather complex organisational structure had developed at White International in order to cope with the widely dispersed system of affiliates. The basic corporate philosophy of decentralised units applied in principle, but with many

Exhibit 2   *Divisional Performance of White Electric Inc 1967—1970* (millions of dollars)*

	1970		1969		1968		1967	
	$m	%	$m	%	$m	%	$m	%
Corporate Sales	349.7	100.0	321.7	100.0	305.6	100.0	261.4	100.0
(consolidated)								
Aerospace Division	39.2	11.2	41.1	12.8	45.3	14.8	38.3	14.7
Power Systems Division	57.4	16.4	52.4	16.3	47.2	15.4	39.6	15.1
Machinery Division	70.2	20.1	67.3	20.9	67.7	22.2	64.5	24.7
Household Appliance								
Division	94.8	27.1	87.2	27.1	81.8	26.8	70.3	26.9
International Division	88.1	25.2	73.7	22.9	63.6	20.8	48.7	18.6
Corporate Profits	21.5	100.0	21.9	100.0	21.5	100.0	18.6	100.0
(consolidated)								
Aerospace Division	(1.1)	(5.1)	1.6	7.3	4.3	20.0	3.5	18.8
Power Systems Division	6.0	27.9	5.6	25.6	5.0	23.3	4.5	24.2
Machinery Division	6.7	31.2	6.6	30.1	6.6	30.7	6.0	32.3
Household Appliance								
Division	4.3	20.0	4.0	18.3	3.7	17.2	3.0	16.1
International Division	5.6	26.0	4.1	18.7	1.9	8.8	1.6	8.6
Corporate Profitability (% of sales)								
WEI		6.1		6.8		7.0		7.1
Aerospace Division		(2.8)		3.9		9.5		9.1
Power Systems Division		10.5		10.7		10.6		11.4
Machinery Division		9.5		9.8		9.7		9.3
Household Appliance								
Division		4.5		4.6		4.5		4.3
International Division		6.3		5.6		3.0		3.3

*Sales and profit figures for the Aerospace, Power Systems, and Machinery divisions include both foreign and domestic activities. Figures for the Household Appliance Division include only the United States and Canada. The International Division accounts for the remaining corporate activity outside North America.

Exhibit 3   *Organisational Structure of White Electric Inc*

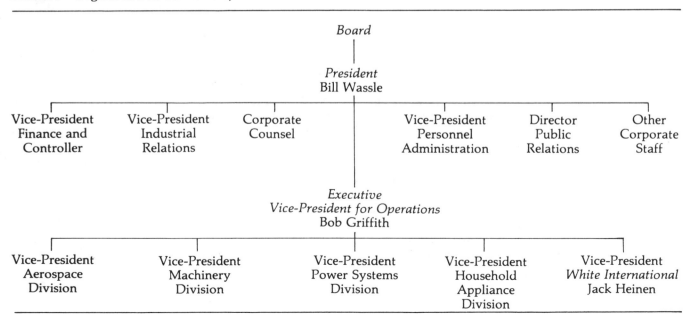

Exhibit 4 *Organisational Structure of White International*

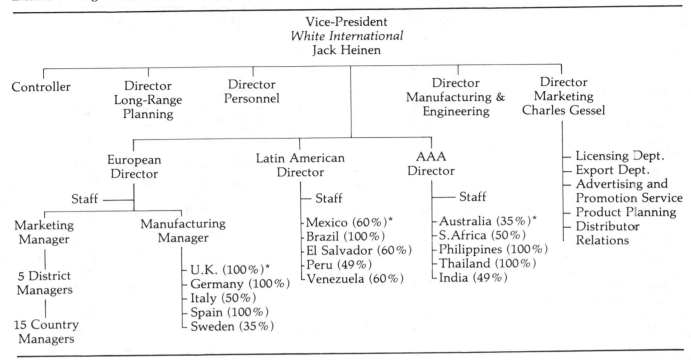

*Figures denote percentage ownership held by WEI in the subsidiary

exceptions and modifications. The basic structural unit was the division management and its three regional profit centres. Each regional director had lone responsibility over the various sales and manufacturing subsidiaries in his region and was accountable for overall performance and profitability. But the patterns differed at this level. The European office, for example, had separate management for the marketing and manufacturing functions. This region was characterised by extensive integration of operations and close centralised control at the regional level. A fairly large staff in Geneva assisted the director in carrying out his duties in this connection. The AAA region was the opposite. Its director resided at corporate headquarters and travelled extensively. He had only two assistants on his staff and each country manager was responsible for all operations in his country. The third region, Latin America, consisted of a mixed pattern with some centralised control and functions, but with a large degree of independence at the country level.

The divisional staff provided a series of services to all regions and subsidiaries. The most active group was the marketing group under Charlie Gessel. In addition to coordinating all export and licensing activities, Charlie's staff provided technical assistance and served as a means of communication in matters pertaining to three major areas: advertising and promotion, product planning and R&D, and distributor relations. Three groups provided these services. The first group was responsible to answer any request for assistance as well as to keep all marketing personnel at the regional and subsidiary level informed on what the US and each other were doing to promote their products. The second group's principal function was to serve as liaison between the R&D department of the US household division and the various subsidiaries. New product development information, requests for design changes, and product line planning were some of the typical concerns at this level. The distributor relations group kept distributors happy throughout the globe with conventions, technical assistance, management seminars, contests, prizes and the like.

In performing their various functions, members of the division's staff could

.and did, in fact, rely to a large extent on their counterparts in the domestic division. The greatest dependency was in the product area. While some subsidiaries did some product development work, most of it was performed by the domestic division.

The Microwave Oven The R&D department of the household appliance division had been working on a design for a home-use microwave oven since 1965. A first model was test marketed in mid-1969, but was judged to be unsatisfactory. Very high costs (over $500 at retail level) and other technical problems resulted in its demise.

By 1971 the company had reached what they considered an extraordinary commercial design for a microwave oven. Production costs were such that, given traditional channel mark-ups, the retail price would fall in the vicinity of $350, or 20% below the cheapest competitor then in the market. The management of the domestic division agreed to launch the product in time for the seasonal peak at Thanksgiving and Christmas. The following strategy was agreed upon.

Product The design would be conventional and portable. It would feature a side opening door with black glass, and two dials, the top indicating time in seconds up to 5 minutes and the bottom calibrated in minutes up to 30. It was compact (20" x 14" x 15") and could be built into a wall or cabinet, or set on a counter top.

Microwave cooking operates through high-frequency radio energy which sets the food molecules vibrating. This generates heat which 'cooks' the food from within. Any non-food and non-metallic material is not affected, e.g. dinnerware, glass, plastic and paper. The method is very fast as evidenced in the following cooking times: hamburger in 1 minute, a 12 lb turkey in 90 minutes, frozen lobster tails in 5½ minutes, a 4 lb rolled rib roast in 23 minutes, defrost a 12 oz steak in 90 seconds, and bake a cake in 5 minutes.

The company was planning to add a microwave oven to one of its standard ranges in 1972. Also under consideration had been the addition of a browning unit that would allow meats to be browned either before or after cooking. This had been dropped for the moment given the need to go into production and the desire for lower costs.

Price Variable production costs had been estimated at approximately $150 per unit. A margin of $100 per unit would allow a 40% mark-up for the trade and still keep the retail price below $350. Most competing units sold for around $400—$450, with some going as high as $1000.

Distribution WEI was planning to hold distribution to certain channels such as company distributors, department stores and selected appliance dealers. After much debate it was agreed that discounters would not be given the line in 1971. Once the results of the coming season were clear, that decision would be reviewed.

Promotion A budget of $250,000 had been set for the six-month period July—December 1971. Heavy emphasis was placed on magazines, principally of the type of *Better Homes and Gardens* and *Good Housekeeping*, supplemented with some coverage in *Time, Life* and other popular women's magazines. A second category of expenditure was point-of-purchase and promotional literature. These had been distributed to all agents and dealers. Finally, some newspaper advertising was carried out selectively in a few communities.

The approach was high-brow, although the price factor was prominently displayed. The copy emphasised time-saving and modernity. Advertisements focused on the good looks of the cabinets, occasionally accompanied by an elegantly dressed woman. The words 'speed', 'reliable', 'modern', and 'safe' were highlighted. Sample cooking times were provided for a range of foods.

*   *   *

Exhibit 5   *White Electric, Inc.*

Microwave ovens heat up again

Microwave ovens, those fast-cooking wonders whose glowing sales were doused a few years ago by a flood of safety criticism, are hot once again. In 1968, when the ovens were first catching on, sales of home units leaped from a scant 3,000 to nearly 20,000. But growth soon sagged after a spate of adverse safety reports. Now, boosted by heavy pre-Christmas promotion, sales may top 100,000 — a 75% jump over 1970's total.

"This is the year," beams Robert I. Bruder, president of the Atherton Div. of Litton Industries, Inc., which claims 10% of the market. "We're selling a product whose time has come." Bruder says that one of the chief reasons for the strong performance is that all safety problems have been resolved. "Safety was a great concern to consumers a year and a half ago," he recalls, "but we and other responsible manufacturers have met the new federal safety requirements." Still, safety crusaders find the sudden resurgence disquieting, since many of the ovens rushed to stores for Christmas did not bear the new federal certification seal.

While microwave ovens now coming off the production line must indeed meet more stringent standards, the fact remains that the units currently available for purchase fall into two categories: safe and less safe. Under the Radiation Control for Health & Safety Act, ovens manufactured after Oct. 6, 1971, cannot leak microwave emissions in excess of 1 milliwatt per square centimeter of oven surface at the time they are sold. The units must also be designed so that leakage will not exceed five times that level at any time during their 'useful' life. The Bureau of Radiological Health is charged with policing these standards. But before the mandatory federal ruling, the voluntary industry standard was 10 milliwatt/cm^2 — and a lot of ovens made prior to the Oct. 6 cut-off date are still sitting on the shelves.

No guarantee. "The risk is small from ovens that meet the voluntary industry standard," assures Herbert Klein, assistant to the director of the Bureau's Div. of Electronic Products. "But we cannot say absolutely that no public health hazard exists." However, the radiation expert adds: "I personally would feel confident to purchase one of them."

Manufacturers face other hurdles before they can meet the 75% jump in sales predicted for next year. Consumers remain shy of the hefty prices, generally around $400 but sometimes as high as $1,300. And despite the cleanliness and speed (16 minutes for a 5-lb. roast), home owners question how useful a microwave oven is.

For one thing, microwaves cannot brown, so everything from chicken to chops turns out an unappetizing gray. (Commercial food operations, which are expected to buy 25,000 units this year, usually brown microwaved meat in regular ovens before serving.) Size is also a problem. "You can't cook a big turkey in many of them," admits Anthony A. Celio, sales vice-president at Norris Industries' Thermador Div. The industry hopes to sidestep such shortcomings by pushing the units as auxiliary cookers or building them into conventional ovens. Litton estimates that by 1975, one of every four ranges sold will include a microwave unit.

Price cut. As for price, the higher volume has already begun to shrink costs. Despite the additional expenses of special sealing devices, safety interlocks, and safer viewing screens, "prices dropped 20% in the last 12 months," says Litton's Bruder. "We're looking for another 10% in the first half of 1972, and possibly 10% more in the last half."

Retailers agree with the manufacturers that sales will continue to climb sharply. Noting the crowds flocking in for demonstrations over the holiday season, Herman Platt, merchandising manager for the May Co. in Los Angeles declared confidently: "The public used to diddle around. But now the market is really starting to jell."

Source: *Business Week*, November 1971

Back at his desk on Monday morning, Charlie Gessel was getting ready to tackle his assignment. He had gathered all the information he needed on the US campaign (summarised above). He also learned that sales of WEI's oven had reached 1000 units during the first month in the market, from October 15 through November 15. Management was hoping for a total of 3000 units by the end of the year. Also, that week's *Business Week* carried a brief note on the new product and the tone seemed optimistic (Exhibit 5).

A trip to the division's library yielded some comparative information on various countries (Exhibits 6 and 7). Given the need for a quick first reaction Charlie realised that there would be no time to contact the various subsidiaries and regional offices for additional information. This, of course, would have to be done at a later time.

Other information obtained on short notice included shipping costs and likely tariff schedules. The oven weighed approximately 30 lbs and occupied a volume of nearly 3 cubic feet. On this basis it was estimated that shipping costs would range between $5 and $20 per unit depending on distance and mode of transportation. Tariff duties varied widely, with the EEC countries averaging 10% of CIF value and some Latin American countries going as high as 100% CIF value.

Having reviewed this information, Charlie prepared to write a three-part report that would deal with:

a) A preliminary assessment of the world-wide potential for WEI's new microwave oven. This would include estimates on the market potential of various countries based on a general knowledge of the business and those areas. It

Exhibit 6   *Selected Demographic Data*

Country	Population (millions) 1968	GNP/Capita ($) 1968	Electric Consumption (KWH/capita) 1964	People per auto 1969	Phones 1968	T.V. 1969	Radios 1969
					(per thousand population)		
US	201.1	3980	5200	1.9	519	392*	1431
Canada	20.8	2460	6290	2.7	419	294	679
Argentina	23.6	820	529	11	65.4	381	106
Brazil	88.2	250	302	28	16.7		
Chile	9.4	480	631	33	32.4		
Columbia	20.0	310	268	79	26.1	111*	19*
Mexico	47.6	530	333	30	22.1	255	45
Peru	12.8	380	274	39	11.9		23
Venezuela	9.7	950	797	15	37.7	174*	72*
Belgium	9.6	1810	1643	4.2			
Denmark	4.9	2070	1517	3.8		197*	107*
France	49.9	2130	1823	3.7	122*	131*	182*
Germany (W)	60.2	1970	2441	4.1	149*	192*	302*
Italy	52.8	1230	1308	5.4	116*	117*	88*
Netherlands	12.7	1620	1677	5.1	188*	163*	250*
Spain	32.6	730	713	12.0	71*	23*	85*
Sweden	7.9	2620	5141	3.4	456*	270*	378*
UK	55.3	1790	2895	4.0	102*	246*	487*
Australia	12.0	2070	2414	2.7			
India	523.9	100	59	545.0			
Israel	2.7	1360	1251	16.0			
Japan	101.1	1190	1631	6.8			
S Africa	19.8	650	1575	11.0			
Thailand	33.7	150	30	126.0			

* = 1966 Data

Exhibit 7   *Saturation Rates for Selected Appliances in Selected Markets (percentage of households owning the product)*

Product	1961	US 1966	1970	EEC 1963	UK 1963	Japan 1963	Japan 1968	France 1968	Germany 1968	Italy 1968
Television	90.2	94.6[a]	95.0	34	82	85	96.4[b]	64	80[c]	66
Radio	96.6	97.4	99	79	76	83	72	n.a.	69	n.a.
Record player	50.1	58.8	n.a.	28	39	n.a.	24	n.a.	69	n.a.
Refrigerator	98.4	99.3	99.8	40	30	40	78	73	79	68
Vacuum cleaner	73.5	76.4	n.a.	42	72	—	54	51	80	19
Electric mixer	67.0	69.5	n.a.	21	5	n.a.	n.a.	n.a.	55	n.a.
Dishwasher	5.1	10.8	23.7	—	—	n.a.	n.a.	n.a.	2	3
Electric iron	96.8	97.4	99	81	91	95	n.a.	n.a.	n.a.	n.a.
Washing machine	74.8	72.9	91.9	n.a.	n.a.	65	85	50	61	40
Range	98.8	98.1[d]	99	n.a.	n.a.	n.a.	n.a.	3[e]	53[e]	n.a.
Clothes dryer	19	31.1	40.3	n.a.	n.a.	n.a.	n.a.	n.a.	n.a.	n.a.
Freezer	19.4	26.4	29.6	n.a.	n.a.	n.a.	n.a.	n.a.	11	n.a.
Air conditioner	10.5	20.0	36.7	n.a.	n.a.	n.a.	4	n.a.	n.a.	n.a.

a. Colour: 14.7% B & W 79.9%
b. Colour: 5.4% B & W 91.0%
c. Colour: 3.0% B & W 77.0%
d. Electric: 40% Gas: 58.1%
e. Electric range only, gas not available.

would include also a detailed description of the principal factors considered in reaching conclusions about each market's potential.

b) A preliminary assessment of the applicability of the US marketing strategy to those markets of the world considered as having some potential for the product. Included here would be some tentative suggestions about whatever appropriate modifications would be necessary in these various markets. Also included would be a proposal as to how to supply these markets over the next twelve months.

c) An indication of the type of information required from the various areas under consideration. This section of the report would consist primarily of a plan and budget proposal to conduct necessary marketing research activities in the following weeks in order to verify the tentative conclusion above. The results of this research would allow WEI to make a firm recommendation for action to the company's management and take the necessary steps to meet production and marketing requirements for selected foreign markets. It would be highly desirable to have this information on hand and processed by the end of the year.

*This case was prepared by
Shiv Mathur, of the London
Business School. It was written
with the cooperation of
Dexion management. Facts
and figures have been disguised
to preserve confidentiality.
Financial support was provided
by The British Overseas Trade
Board.
© London Business School,
1976. Revised 1981.*

CASE A11
Dexion Overseas Ltd

In November 1975, Mr John Foster, recently appointed Managing Director, and Mr Keith Galpin, Marketing Manager, of Dexion Overseas Limited (DOS), were attempting to give new direction to Dexion's overseas activities. Dexion had, over the years, grown substantially but somewhat haphazardly in its export markets and it seemed to the two managers that it was time for a full review of the company's present position and future overseas activities. They were particularly concerned with DOS's operations in Africa and the Middle East as these regions characterised the changing political and economic conditions in most of Dexion's overseas markets.

**Dexion-Comino
International Ltd**

Dexion-Comino International Ltd, was founded before the Second World War to manufacture slotted angles invented by Demetrius Comino as a solution to the recurring need for easily erectable and demountable industrial structures. What was initially jokingly referred to as 'industrial meccano' soon acquired wide acceptance. Mr Comino's initial investment of £14,000 in a 4,000-square foot factory in North London had by 1968 grown into a 200,000 square-foot site at Hemel Hempstead producing well over 50 million feet of slotted angles. By 1973 Dexion was well established as a worldwide name with wholly owned subsidiaries in North America, Europe and Australia, with exports accounting for over 60 per cent of the UK factory's total turnover.

Product Range

As the group's turnover and geographic coverage had increased, so had the company's range of products. What had started as ordinary slotted angles (known as DCP — Dexion Catalogue Products) that could be erected by almost anybody, had gradually grown in sophistication. By 1975 Dexion was a world leader in manufacturing and installing complete materials handling systems.

In the developed countries the continuing search for more efficient techniques of storage and materials handling resulted in a rapid growth of the 'unit load concept' (various small parts being containerised for efficient storage) — and in particular the use of pallets. Dexion systems like 'Speedlock' adjustable pallet racking were developed to meet this need. The Speedlock range permitted vertical storage to a height limited only by the height of the building itself. When fitted with wheels the racks, then known as 'Poweracks', could be mounted on steel rails permitting the closing down of an aisle and opening up of a new one at the touch of a switch.

By 1975 Dexion manufactured a whole family of products that served particular applications. 'Apton' square tube framing had been designed for the smarter display of goods; 'Clearspan' and 'Impex' shelving for better storage of hand-loaded goods; and 'Maxi' for storing small items. The basic DCP range was also modified and extended to meet entirely new applications. For example, DCP products that were usually used for storage had been modified to facilitate the construction of prefabricated housing units in developing countries. The growth of new products in many instances had also produced growth for DCP products as they constituted basic ingredients of the more advanced designs.

Overseas Activities

Until 1970 overseas growth of Dexion's activities had been largely organic. As

Exhibit 1   *Licensed Product Sales, Royalty Income and Products Licensed*

Country (year of agreement)	Licensee 1974 Sales (£s)	Royalty Rates*	Products Licensed
Spain (1957)	650,000	£13,000 per annum (fixed sum)	DCP, pallet racking
Portugal (1957)	620,000	2%	DCP, Apton, Speedlock
New Zealand (1959)	210,000	2%	DCP
India (1960)	420,000	Profit participation agreement	DCP, Apton
El Salvador (1961)	50,000	4%	DCP
Canada (1964)	1,950,000	£25,000 per annum (fixed sum)	DCP and accessories
Mexico (1964)	1,170,000	2%	DCP, Apton, Speedlock
Brazil (1966)	490,000	4%	DCP, Apton, Speedlock
Argentina (1966)	160,000	4%	DCP, Speedlock
Peru (1967)	230,000	£4,000 per annum (fixed sum)	DCP
Jamaica (1968)	87,000	4%	DCP
Nigeria (1970)	490,000	4%	DCP and accessories
S. Africa (1971)	325,000	4%	DCP, Apton, Speedlock
Hungary (1971)	650,000	£65,000 (lump sum royalty)	DCP

*Expressed as percentage of turnover unless otherwise indicated.

Dexion products had gained popularity, the company had set up subsidiaries in North America, Europe and Australia. In other countries of the world Dexion had appointed distributors to stock and retail the products. Where local demand was fairly substantial but import restrictions prevented direct export and circumstances did not justify a subsidiary, local manufacturers had been licensed to produce and sell some products in the Dexion range. By the early 1970s Dexion had licensing arrangements with manufacturers in various parts of the world (Exhibit 1), although few were in Africa and the Middle East.

The actual agreement varied from licensee to licensee and reflected the company's attitude at the time the agreement was actually signed. Agreements usually specified a royalty income based on a percentage of turnover, often with a minimum annual payment. Dexion had little control over the pricing and marketing policies of its licensees, though sometimes restrictions were placed on their export activities. As the majority of licensees were mainly concerned with building up strong positions in their home markets, pressure to export to third countries in competition with Dexion's own direct export activities was not a major factor. The problems as seen at Dexion headquarters were not so much of licensee exports to third country markets, but of ensuring that they developed their home markets and that licensee income due was in fact repatriated. Since many of the licensee markets had recurring balance of payment problems the actual collection of royalties was of continuing concern.

Competition with Dexion products both in the UK and overseas had multiplied. Dexion, however, had maintained its market leadership in the UK. Overseas, in adddition to budding indigenous manufacturers, Dexion was facing growing competition from Italian and Continental exporters and lately the Japanese and Indians. But Dexion products were well established and the company prided itself on having a much more comprehensive product range and better design and other back-up services than the non-European competition. Cheaper

British steel gave Dexion exports a very real advantage, but it seemed that the position was gradually changing. Mr Foster was getting increasingly concerned about Japanese and subsidised Indian competition in the Middle East and the gradual erosion of the cost advantage of using steel made in Britain.

Dexion Overseas Limited In 1970 Dexion-Comino International Ltd had set up Dexion Overseas Limited (DOS) as a separate company within the organisation to look after and coordinate its entire overseas export and licensing activities. Markets where Dexion had established subsidiaries or associates were excluded. In order to supervise distribution closely, DOS had divided the overseas market into five regions and appointed regional sales managers (RSMs) located in London to oversee Dexion's interests in each of these areas. The five regions were: (1) the Middle East and North Africa, (2) Europe, (3) the Rest of Africa, (4) the Far East and Southeast Asia, (5) the Caribbean and South America. Exhibit 2 gives DOS results for 1973 to 1975 and Exhibit 3 gives a breakdown of 1975 results by region.

Exhibit 2   *DOS Operating Results (£000s)*

	1973	1974	1975
Invoiced sales	5,672	6,444	6,914
Gross profits*	1,076	1,770	2,088
Variable distribution costs	156	221	290
Gross profit (after distribution costs)	920	1,549	1,798
Home office and regional expenditure	565	560	703
Operating profit	355	989	1,095
Miscellaneous income (including royalties)	94	122	136
Interest	(13)	(75)	(75)
Profit before tax	436	1,036	1,156

*After deducting transfer prices payable to Dexion-Comino International Ltd.

Exhibit 3   *Allocation of 1975 DOS Results by Region (£000s)*

	Invoiced Sales		Gross Profit	Regional Expenses
Middle East and North Africa	3,016		1,006	96
Europe	1,829		378	33
Africa	1,090		408	42
Far East	257		61	26
Caribbean, and South America	426		142	49
Miscellaneous	296		93	13
Total	6,914		2,088	259
Variable distribution expenses			290	
Gross profit (after distribution)			1,798	
Less:				
Regional expenses		259		
Central expenses		133		
Marketing and promotion		104		
Administration and rent		130		
Technical		77		
Total			703	
Operating profit			1,095	

Direct exports and involvement in the Far East and Central and South Europe were comparatively small. Dexion's operations in Europe were mature in nature and the increasing similarity between the UK and continental Europe in terms of competition, products and customers had gradually resulted in most of Western Europe being treated as an extension of the home market, at least so far as the existing product range was concerned. With UK entry into the EEC in 1973, this similarity between the home market and continental Europe was becoming even more obvious, although differences in channels of distribution remained.

Keith Galpin had carried out a detailed analysis of the various international markets that could provide it with substantial business in the future. This analysis had incorporated not only informed views within the company but also interpreted demographic and economic data. The attempt was to highlight not only those markets which would continue to grow, but also select those which could become major profit generators in future. This exercise had brought to light some Southeast Asian and Middle Eastern countries which could be the target for more concentrated attacks.

DOS was of the opinion that during the next five years the company's business in the oil-rich countries of the Middle East and North Africa would expand much more rapidly than elsewhere. This called for a strategy that took into account the prominent position of the region. But the company felt that such a strategy would be applicable in principle to most overseas activities of the company, and Africa generally might follow the developments in the north.

DOS's International Policy
Markets and Organisation

Galpin divided the Dexion market in Africa and the Middle East roughly into three kinds of buyers. *Bazaar buyers* were customers who bought mostly DCP-type products to erect small and fairly crude storage and other structural units. Though DOS had no hard data on the buying behaviour of these customers, it was generally believed that they designed their requirements themselves or with some help from local Dexion dealers. Their main criteria for buying Dexion products in preference to those of other suppliers were price and availability. The demand was more for the less sophisticated Dexion products and an important characteristic of the buyer was his lack of awareness and perhaps need for more sophisticated storage and material handling systems.

The second group were *installation buyers*. Installations could vary from small simple racking units (similar to those put up by the bazaar buyer himself) to complete warehouse units made up of products such as Speedlock pallet racking and Impex hand-loaded shelving. This type of business was invariably handled by local distributors, sometimes with the help of Dexion staff, and often required detailed designs and site construction. This design and construction service was increasingly being provided by the local distributor, although Dexion's UK-based units assisted with jobs which were outside the resources and capability of a particular distributor.

There was occasional demand for relatively large and sophisticated systems requiring special resources such as system analysis, structural design, subcontracting, contract negotiation, financing, project management, etc., outside the scope of any distributor. DOS referred to this third type of business as *project business* and it invariably involved sales and implementation resources not available locally from a distributor even when supported by a local Dexion salesman. Support of the local distributor for this type of work was by the payment of a negotiated commission.

In order to serve the growth in both installation and project business, DOS had established in London a technical services cell (see Exhibit 4 for organisation chart). The regional sales managers could refer their design problems to this unit and the cell itself undertook some marketing activities. It stayed in touch with UK-based architects, specifiers and designers to influence them to use Dexion equipment in projects they were associated with. The cell had developed over the years the expertise to quote for and supervise a wide variety of overseas projects. Its links with the regional sales managers were close.

Exhibit 4 *DOS Organisation Chart*

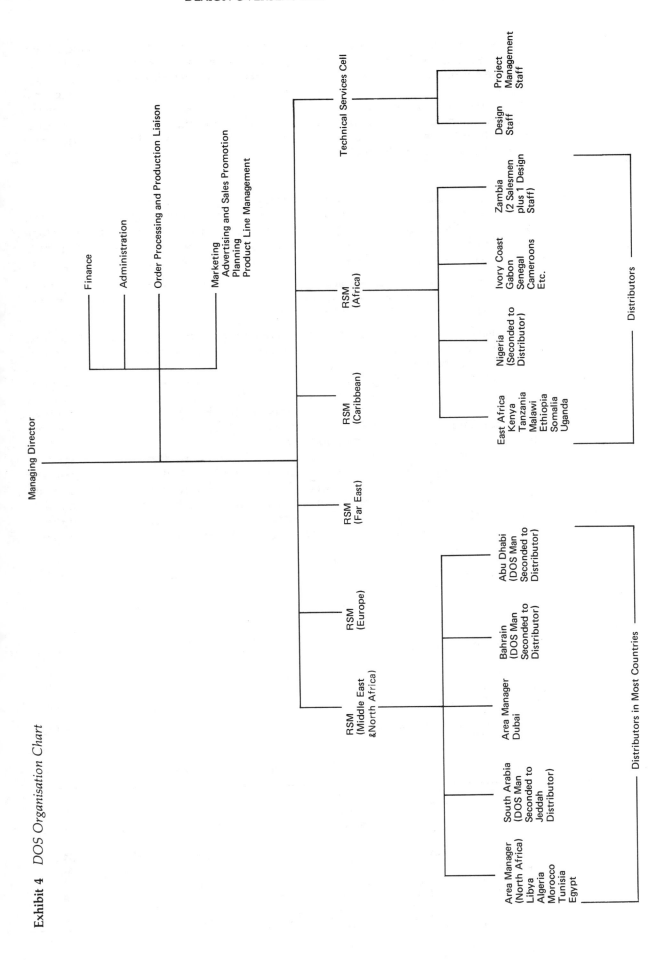

NB: Full-time distributor staff looking after DOS sales and design in Kuwait, Oman and Lebanon.

As part of its central marketing function the DOS staff at headquarters attempted to coordinate the advertising and sales promotion campaign for Dexion products in national markets. Films, pamphlets and information material in various languages had been prepared. The marketing department together with regional staff undertook to arrange seminars in various overseas capitals aimed at specific audiences. The marketing department also looked after the promotion of individual products and retained staff product managers who coordinated the activities for a particular product in the regions.

Pricing DOS was supplied by the plant at Hemel Hempstead at a transfer price that reflected the direct costs of production and an allocation of works and general overheads. DOS, in turn, set prices for its distributors by adding a percentage markup to cover the cost of its own operations and provide a satisfactory profit.

In Mr Foster's view, the essence of DOS's policy on distributor pricing was:

> A question of competitive activity — we should evaluate what price competitive products are selling at and adjust our margins to account for the comparative advantages and disadvantages of Dexion goods.

Distributors in national markets were quoted different prices to take into account expected local distributor mark-up, the prices of competitive products, and the local customers' ability to pay. For example, during 1974, when transfer prices charged to DOS rose by 15 percent (Exhibit 5 (a)), there was no corresponding across-the-board increase in prices charged to customers. European customers were charged only an extra 5 percent, while Middle East prices went up the full 15 percent in sterling prices. When the devaluation of sterling had been accounted for, however, the local prices ended up lower.

As a result of the policy of value pricing, the markups distributors charged on various Dexion products differed considerably. Exhibit 5 (b)) gives an indication of gross margins by product category. Though DOS informally indicated to its distributors in various national markets the price at which they should retail their products, it did not, and in management's view could not, lay down firm directives. This policy had both its advantages and disadvantages. The company did not

Exhibit 5 (a) *Increase in Transfer Price to DOS, 1974*

	Cost Increase		Percentage Costs	Increase
Steel	− 5%	on	40%	− 2.0%
Auxiliary material	20	on	35	7.0
Accessories	10	on	10	1.0
Other costs	0	on	15	0
Volume down 30% on budget				9.0
Total increase in transfer price				15.0%

Exhibit 5 (b) *DOS Product Margins (excluding project sales) (£000s)*

	1973			1974		
	Sales	Gross Profits	Percent	Sales	Gross Profits	Percent
DCP	2,079	610	29.3	2,530	874	34.5
Apton	305	120	39.3	481	164	34.1
Speedlock	1,120	238	21.3	1,347	393	29.2
Others	590	108	18.3	570	107	18.8
Total	4,094	1,076	26.3	4,928	1,538	31.2

retain any firm control on its prices and occasionally found distributors in well-protected or prosperous markets charging exorbitant markups. But with its flexible pricing policy, DOS had built for itself an extensive distributor network. Distributors, it was hoped would in turn set retail prices to maximise their own and consequently DOS's profits. That this did not always happen was seen as a largely unavoidable consequence of using independent companies as part of the distributor system.

Africa The Regional Sales Manager (Africa) had for administrative convenience divided the countries south of the area of Arab influence into four areas: East Africa, Zambia, Nigeria, and the erstwhile French West Africa. The four areas were roughly equal in terms of market potential and four area managers were based in convenient local capitals. Though Dexion had a distributor in virtually every African capital, choice had been limited and determined more by the distributor's general business standing and connections with the local government than by previous experience of selling products related to storage and materials handling.

Apart from South Africa and Nigeria, the region was comprised largely of developing countries with foreign exchange problems and complicated systems of tariff and exchange controls. Often there was no dearth of demand for Dexion products but a noticeable lack of buying power for foreign products. This was in the regional sales manager's view the single most important impediment in exporting to the African market. There were few areas where concentrated marketing effort could be justified. Not only was the entire region plagued by controls but it was also in a state of constant economic and political flux.

Many suppliers besides those in the developed countries had found it possible to meet the less sophisticated level of African demand. Continental, Japanese, and Indian exports abounded, but Dexion with its wide and well-established network of distribution had a firm grip and in some countries like Tanzania had almost wiped out the use of competitive products. In virtually all markets, small local manufacturers making a restricted range of generally low quality products were a continuing threat. In the regional sales manager's opinion, what Dexion had and

Exhibit 6 *Africa: Orders Received (£000s)*

	1973			1974			1975		
	DCP	Other	Total	DCP	Other	Total	DCP	Other	Total
Ethiopia	32	—	32	25	2	27	16	—	16
Ivory Coast	12	—	12	5	3	8	38	7	45
Kenya	26	—	26	18	5	23	55	8	63
Nigeria	44	61	105	60	79	139	103	109	212
South Africa	3	8	11	11	9	20	16	56	72
Sudan	44*	—	44	—	—	—	—	—	—
Tanzania	—	—	—	5	—	5	18	—	18
Zambia	74*	35*	109	61*	71*	132	140*	279*	419
Zaire	5	13	18	1	2	3	—	—	—
Others									
Cameroons									
Gabon									
Ghana									
Gibraltar	85	26	111	72	29	101	49	8	57
Senegal									
Niger									
Etc.									
Total	325	143	468	258	200	458	435	467	902

* Project activity.

the competition did not, were the local contacts and a name for quality and service that was well established.

It was not the overseas exporters who provided the major threat in African markets but the growing desire in most developing countries to set up their own production units. As the outlay for such a project would be about £500,000 it was well within the reach of most governments, if not individual entrepreneurs. It was possible that the small African markets would not support economic production units. But there was always the possibility of some countries getting together to come to tariff arrangements to form a quasi common market or to look actively for regional exports. Some countries in East Africa and French West Africa had shown just this sort of inclination and this was seen as the thin end of the wedge at DOS headquarters.

The richer countries of Africa — Nigeria, Zambia, and South Africa — were different in their purchasing behaviour. Areas of industrial concentration had resulted in a demand for a host of Dexion products and services. To South Africa and specially Nigeria, in spite of the presence of local licensees, Dexion directly exported the more modern systems, which were not manufactured locally. In Zambia, the company had obtained a large contract to design, supply, and erect a complete materials handling and storage system. The Zambian case characterised an obvious trend in buying behaviour. Developing country governments keen to put up large industrial complexes, often with the help of overseas funds, increasingly contracted for the complete supply, design, and erection of turnkey projects.

Middle East and North Africa

The regional sales manager (Middle East) described his region:

> In spite of popular beliefs it's not all gold. For us there are three to four countries that contribute most of the sales. And it would be fair to say that in most countries the results are directly proportional to the effort we put in. When I say "we", I mean "we" — the local distributors have far too much on their plates and are often so badly organised that they need all the assistance we can give. The real selling force is frequent visits and resident expatriate staff — people who are willing to live in Arab countries and promote the Dexion name. And they are harder to find than you would imagine.

In spite of the massive oil revenues there was a growing inclination in some Arab countries to ban foreigners from setting up purely trading companies. The United Arab Emirates, Iraq, Iran, and Algeria had formulated, or were in the process of formulating, controls for limiting the activities of foreigners. Others like Libya, who were at that moment big customers of DCP products, had already outlined their intention to set up their own slotted angle plants to reduce the economy's dependence on imports.

Everywhere there was an explosive industrialisation underway. All over the Middle East new plants were being constructed and the host countries, while embarrassingly rich financially, lacked human skills and infrastructure to cope with the growth. Even Iraq and Algeria, while attempting to lower their reliance on foreign companies, recognised the necessity to permit foreigners to bid for and undertake large projects. In fact, almost all Dexion's business in Iraq, Algeria, Iran, and a substantial portion of that in Saudi Arabia had been obtained by negotiating large contracts. (See Exhibit 7)

Though the growth in project activity was generally welcomed by Dexion management, it had, created some organisational problems. Contract negotiation took a comparatively long time and resulted more often than not in 'next year's sales and this year's expenses'. The regional sales managers, were always under considerable pressure to maintain expenditure within agreed budgets and treated project activity with mixed emotions. However, when the organisational problems, both within DOS and with the local distributors had been overcome, the profits were very welcome. Gross profits on successful tenders in the Middle East were broadly similar to those obtained on the sale of hardware alone.

Exhibit 7 *Middle East and North Africa — Orders Received (£000s)*

	1973			1974			1975		
	DCP	Other	Total	DCP	Other	Total	DCP	Other	Total
Abu Dhabi	73	7	80	155	25	180	285	33	318
Dubai	32	11	43	78	3	81	85	27	112
Iraq	147*	—	147	478*	2	480	209*	4*	213
Libya	377*	21*	398	356*	17*	373	252*	60*	312
Oman	18	15	33	58	80	138	130	104*	234
Saudi Arabia	65	48	113	134	247	381	257	369†	626
Bahrain	18	9	27	35	34	69	25	21	46
Qatar	9	—	9	17	3	20	25	—	25
Algeria	—	1,235†	1,235		47*	47	—	—	—
Others Cyprus Egypt Iran Jordan Kuwait Lebanon Malta Pakistan Syria Tunisia Yemen	94	14	108	294	29	323	91	9	100
Total	833	1,360	2,193	1,605	487	2,092	1,359	627	1,986

*Project activity.
†Projects not broken up by product groups.

Competition in the Middle East was strongest from the Japanese, Italians, and Indians in the supply of DCP-type hardware and from Japan and Germany in the project market. The Japanese and Germans often had a slight edge on Dexion as they had been able to quote for complete turnkey projects. In Libya, DOS's distributor had established very good links with the local government and Dexion products had reached a large market share, but only by pricing below DOS's normal markup to offset the price advantage of Italian products. In Saudi Arabia and the U.A.E., which still constituted the bulk of the hardware business, DOS's response to competition had been first to pare margins and second to promote slightly more advanced systems like Speedlock. In spite of overseas and local manufacturers crowding these markets, there was still ample opportunity for all. Saudi Arabia and the U.A.E had five-year plans that budgeted a threefold increase in public expenditure — justification enough for the most forceful of selling efforts.

Alternative Possibilities With its target of achieving a 15 percent annual increase in sales and profits, DOS management was aware that a series of long-term strategic decisions had to be made. These decisions would have to encompass almost all the activities of the company and would have to bear in mind that 100 percent owned subsidiaries would be difficult to establish overseas. They included:

1. Should the company continue to license overseas manufacturers to produce the DCP range in areas of high tariffs and foreign exchange problems, or should the licensing policy be extended to cover more products and markets? In particular, should DOS agree to permit the manufacture of the Speedlock and Apton range in Nigeria?

2. If licensing was not a viable option, in view of local government hostility to royalties, should DOS look to joint ventures?

3.   Another possibility could be to discontinue all overseas manufacture and cancel where possible the existing licensing arrangements and manufacture and export from the U.K., or another suitable European base.

4.   Which markets should be focused on and with what products?

5.   Should the existing policy be changed?

6.   Was there any need to restructure the distribution strategy?

The list of issues which needed to be questioned and sorted out seemed endless. DOS management was also aware of the fact that it would be impossible to put hard figures on many of these options but Mr. John Foster felt that the data he had were reliable, in the sense that they were indicative of the situation. He was particularly aware that the issues were interrelated (e.g. the company could not have a production policy that required licensing arrangements and a marketing strategy that required distributors) and the direction that DOS's total strategy took should at least be compatible within itself.

*This case was prepared by Kenneth Simmonds of the London Business School. © Kenneth Simmonds, 1972.

CASE A12
Dorcas International Corporation

Dorcas International manufactured a line of electric razors and over the years had built a significant market position in most of the developed countries. There had been recent signs, however, that the electric razor market had matured to a point where competition on price, and therefore cost, would be the outstanding characteristic of the industry over the next half dozen years. Recognising the changed situation, Jorg Moroney, the Dorcas President, had established a central

Exhibit 1 *Summary of Cost and Revenue Data for Dorcas International System*

			Country					
	Unit	General	A	B	C	D	E	F
1. Annual sales volume in 4 years' time for alternative average prices to wholesale	'000 units							
$9.00			50	150	250	80	250	50
8.50			55	160	320	120	300	60
8.00			60	180	340	160	350	70
7.50			65	210	370	190	500	80
7.00			75	250	400	200	600	100
2. Variable cost of local marketing, selling, and distribution per average unit	$		.50	.60	.40	.40	.20	.50
3. Corporation tax rate	%		30	50	40	20	50	40
4. Customs tariff on imports based on transfer price	%		40	60	25	25	10	20
5. Transport costs per unit of transfers								
Among A, B, C, F	$	.10						
Between D and others	$	.20						
Between E and others	$	.20						
Existing production capacity								
6. Volume limit	'000 units			400	300		400	
7. Fixed production cost per annum (including interest and depreciation)	$'000			800	1,100		1,200	
8. Variable production cost per average unit	$			3.00	2.00		2.00	
Additional production capacity								
9. Fixed production cost for plant with annual volume								
200,000 units	$'000	800						
300,000 units	$'000	1100						
400,000 units	$'000	1350						
500,000 units	$'000	1500						
10. Variable production cost per average unit from new plant	$		1.50	2.00	1.80	1.80	1.50	1.80

management services group to look into the question of concentrating further expansion of production into a smaller number of sites, in order to gain greater scale economies.

In setting up this group, however, Moroney indicated that he did not intend to dispense with a policy of holding operating units to profit achievement. While profit achievement had always been applied quite loosely, each manufacturing unit had been free to set its own price for its local markets and for supply to other marketing units.

The task of proposing a plan for future plant expansion fell to Stephen Morse as head of the new management services group. He decided that the first essential in preparing his recommendations was to collect basic cost and revenue data for the Dorcas International system. This he did, and as he considered the current situation irrelevant to the problem, he projected market growth, alternative price-sales figures and cost estimates for four years ahead in current dollars. These are summarised in Exhibit 1. All this involved many simplifications, but Morse felt they would not materially affect a decision. For example:

1.   Export duties and rebates were ignored as immaterial.

2.   Any new capacity would take about two years to build and cost variations among alternative sites were unpredictable.

3.   About 30 percent of fixed production cost was represented by depreciation in the first year (15 percent of plant cost). As depreciation reduced, it would be more or less offset by increased repair cost. The three existing plants could continue production at the indicated figures indefinitely. Plants would have little scrap value.

4.   Tax rates applied to non-remitted funds only, but as Dorcas had large borrowings in each country no profit remittances were envisaged in the foreseeable future.

The next task seemed to be to calculate some sort of approximation to an optimum and then to mould this into reasonable management recommendations.

CASE A13
Alfa-Laval Thermal

In November 1975 senior members of Alfa-Laval's Thermal subdivision based in Lund, Sweden, had come together to review the subdivision's strategy. The subdivision was a major international force in the manufacturing and marketing of thermal products. It still held — as it had done over the last two decades — the position of dominant market leader in its chosen product area; but small cracks appearing in its structure and strategy were causing some managerial concern.

Alfa-Laval's International Organisation

Alfa-Laval was in 1975 one of the largest Swedish companies. The original establishment had been founded in 1883 and over the years the company had diversified into a wide range of businesses. A fundamental Alfa-Laval philosophy, however, was its intention to remain in the manufacture and marketing of industrial products.

The company's activities could be divided into three broad categories:

Industrial Equipment — centrifuges, pumps, thermal equipment and installations for the food industry, power production, mechanical engineering industries, shipbuilding, the chemical, pulp and paper industries, as well as for environmental control.
Dairy Processing Equipment — special processes and complete plants for dairies and certain beverage industries.
Farm Equipment — equipment and systems for milking, feeding, manure removal, hygiene and cooling.

In 1975 there were four major company divisions: Farm, Separation, Thermal and Dairy, and Rosenblads. Activities which could not be easily incorporated into one of the four divisions were referred to as 'Other Companies and Units'. The divisions were profit centres each responsible for a defined range of products and applications, producing for sale to the Group's worldwide marketing network and monitoring and influencing worldwide performance within the scope of their business mission.

Alfa-Laval market companies, as listed in Exhibit 1, provided outlets for the Group's products in many countries of the world. In countries with less demand, Alfa-Laval had distributors and commission agents. Senior management felt the coverage more than adequate for the Group's current needs.

Over the years, many market companies had drifted away from their original role as outlets for Alfa-Laval products. Some had set up manufacturing operations, enabling them to cut down freight costs and reap the advantage of a better local presence. It was, however, neither technologically nor economically justified to move all stages of production to local sites and the more highly capital intensive production tasks remained in Sweden for almost all products. As a consequence, the overseas manufacturing establishment needed for any one product was not large and the local market companies had generally combined local manufacturing for various products and divisions under one roof. These manufacturing activities had often expanded to such an extent that the term 'market company' had become a misnomer.

In a few instances the manufacturing activities of market companies had expanded to include production for export to other Group companies. For items that were manufactured by market companies for export within the Group, 'Product Centres' at Divisional Headquarters in Sweden attempted to coordinate

Exhibit 1 *Geographical Distribution of Market Companies*

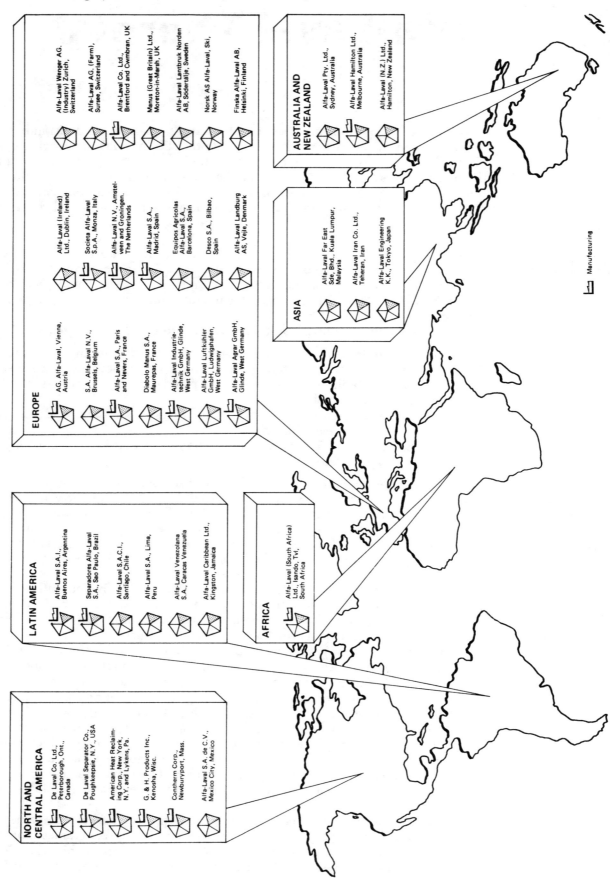

Exhibit 2 *Geographical Distribution of Manufacturing Units*

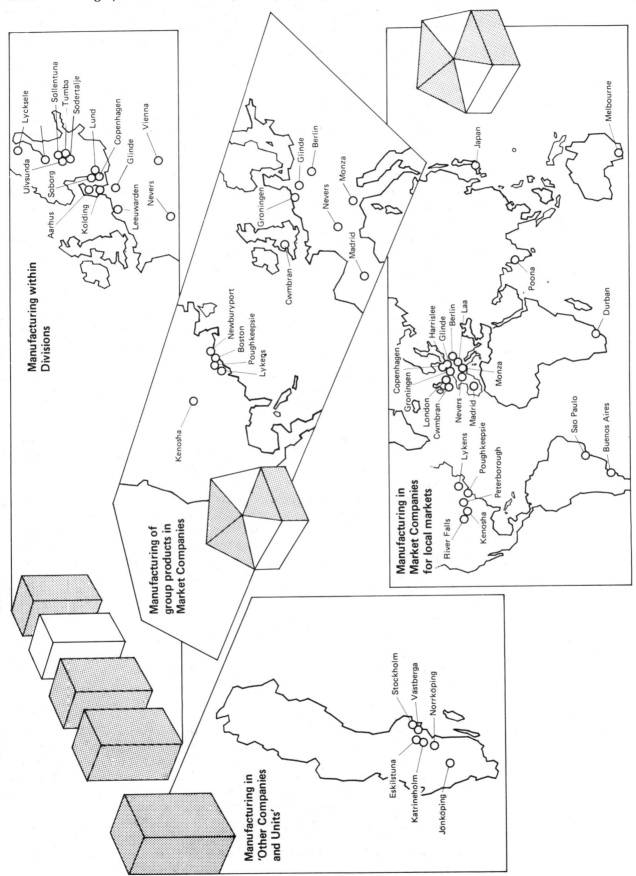

Manufacturing within Divisions

Manufacturing of group products in Market Companies

Manufacturing in Market Companies for local markets

Manufacturing in 'Other Companies and Units'

the manufacturing activities of the various units. Production for local markets, however, was considered the sole responsibility of the domestic market company. Exhibit 2 shows the breakdown of manufacturing activities for the Group.

Though some market companies manufactured both for the local market and the Group, there was a significant difference between the manufacturing activities of market companies and divisions. Production within divisions was in higher volumes, involved larger capital investments and greater R & D, and produced a much more comprehensive range of products. For example, the basic plates for heat exchangers were pressed only in Lund, Sweden, while frames and other components were made in Germany, Spain, the USA and some other countries.

Liaison Between Customer, Market Company and Divisions

The primary contact for either a Scandinavian or overseas customer was the local market company. In some instances, the customer could have a choice of two or more market companies, but such instances were rare and Alfa-Laval attempted to ensure that in any one market there was only one representative for a particular product or service. In many instances the local market company was competent to deal with all aspects of customers' requirements. In others, especially in cases of small market companies and complicated enquiries, there was a need to refer the enquiry to the division concerned.

Just as 'Product Centres' within divisions coordinated manufacturing, so 'Application Centres' coordinated and assisted market companies with marketing. A market company requiring assistance would get in touch with the appropriate 'Application Centre' and the Application Centre would answer the query or arrange for further assistance.

For the less sophisticated products, the local market company was usually competent to deal with customers. For products like Farm and Dairy Equipment, where a complete system had often to be designed and tendered for, the liaison between the market companies and the division concerned had been developed through frequent contact. Over the last few years the company had consciously promoted the sale of complete systems and often tendered bids on a turnkey basis, even to the extent of taking on the civil engineering work.

Application Centres were expected to keep abreast of both market and product development and provide advice to the market companies and the division's senior staff. An Application Centre was headed by a person designated 'Sales/Marketing Manager' but did not concern itself with the day-to-day sales activities of the market companies. However, it provided the only formal link between market companies on specific business possibilities. With the growth of system sales, large bids and more and more international customers, coordination was becoming increasingly important. The Application Centres attempted to keep track of major projects in their chosen industrial sector and provide an information service about them to the market companies. Within the Thermal and Dairy Division, however, it was felt that the flow of information was becoming far too one-sided. The Application Centres were providing services and information but receiving little information from the market companies about their general activities and their interest in particular projects.

The Thermal Sub-division

The Thermal and Dairy Division of Alfa-Laval had a total 1974 sales figure of Swedish Kronor 312 million*, representing a tenth of the Group's total turnover. The division was in turn divided into four subdivisions. The Thermal Subdivision was responsible for the world-wide sale of thermal products and prided itself on being able to sell anything in its product area, from small individual components to complete processes required for large and complex operations.

The key product in the thermal engineering field was the 'heat exchanger'. Heat exchangers were used whenever it was necessary to heat or cool any fluid. The conventional tubular heat exchanger, still used most frequently, consisted of a tube pack inside an outer casing with one fluid flowing through the tubes and the other

*Note: In December 1975 1 Swedish Krona = £0.12 or US $0.22.

fluid flowing around them at a different temperature and thus exchanging heat. The Alfa-Laval product strategy had been to concentrate on specially compact heat exchangers, based on more sophisticated engineering designs. There were four basic types of heat exchangers in the Alfa-Laval range of which the plate heat exchanger (PHE) was the most versatile and represented the bulk of the sales. The others were: spiral, lamella and closed-tube heat exchangers.

The principle of the plate heat exchanger is fairly simple. As shown in Exhibit 3, it consists essentially of a pile of metallic plates clamped together. Each adjacent pair of plates forms a 'flow channel' with the two fluids at different temperatures flowing in alternate channels. Gaskets separate each plate from the others, thus preventing the mixing of the two fluids. Though the basic concept is comparatively straightforward, it is essential that the material used for the plates, the corrugations on them, and the material for the gaskets, be chosen to fit the particular task in hand. Thus a corrosive fluid of high viscosity at a high temperature and pressure necessitates an entirely different solution from another under different operating conditions.

Exhibit 3 *Plate Heat Exchangers*

Plate heat exchanger (PHE)

Alfa-Laval plate heat exchangers are assembled on the construction kit principle from individual standard channel plates that can be arranged according to the needs of the specific duty.

The plates are assembled in packs and clamped in a frame, each adjacent pair of plates forming a flow channel with the two media flowing in alternate channels. Different channel groupings can be chosen to give the desired pressure-drop characteristics and flow pattern. Two or more independent sections, separated by special connection plates, can be housed in the same frame. The gaskets separating the plates — which may be made of different materials according to the nature of the medium — prevent any mixing of the two media in the unit.

Flexible construction system

The construction system used for Alfa-Laval plate heat exchangers makes it possible to tailor them exactly to the requirements of varying working conditions throughout their wide range of applications. A plate unit is easily opened for inspection and cleaning of the plates and gaskets, but it can also be cleaned in place by detergent circulation, in which case it need not be dismantled at all.

The special corrugations of the channel plates generate an intensely turbulent thin-layer flow. They also stiffen the plates so that extremely thin-gauge material can be used. This improves the heat transfer coefficient and at the same time makes it economically feasible to use such expensive materials as titanium.

Typical applications

Plate heat exchangers are maids of all work. Their handiness, high thermal efficiency and flexibility make them far and away the most economical choice in a host of applications, subject only to the pressure and temperature limits of the type.

This is true above all in the food industry with special reference to pasteurisation and sterilisation of cheap food and beverage products, where heating costs must be kept to a minimum and regular cleaning of the equipment is an essential feature of the high standard of hygiene demanded today.

Other suitable fields are general heating and cooling duties. Dissipating the heat from engine and machinery coolants — for example on shipboard and in stationary power plants — is a field in which plate heat exchangers have proved their worth many times over. Another natural application for the plate type of unit is heat recovery in cases where a small difference in temperature between the media means that only a really efficient heat exchanger can do the job economically.

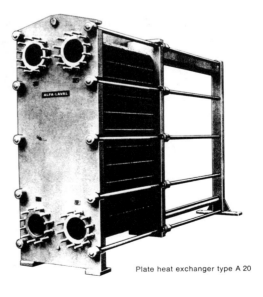

Plate heat exchanger type A 20

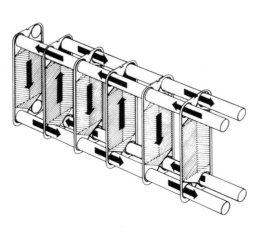

Flow pattern in a plate heat exchanger

Alfa-Laval prided itself on its lead in the design of the most efficient engineering solutions for various operating conditions. The choices of plates, material, size, corrugations and gaskets were carefully examined to provide a tailor-made match for a customer's thermal requirements. Often it would be necessary to include other types of heat exchangers and ancillary equipment, such as cooling towers and air coolers, to meet the complete requirements of a client. The Thermal Subdivision had gradually expanded and diversified its activities in these fields to meet the market. In fact, this emphasis on technical competence and coverage had been explicitly recognised by the Subdivision in 1968 in its 'Business Mission and Policy' statements:

> We are in the 'heat transfer' market and should act and become known as 'thermal engineering specialists'. Our goal is to develop, produce and market on a worldwide level, thermal engineering equipment and processes of a high technical standard and to get a growing share of the world market.

> It is our aim to obtain a reputation among engineering customers as the most reliable supplier in our range and also to maintain our reputation as the biggest and most advanced supplier of heat exchangers, including software services.

With the growing software needs, the Application Centre at Lund expanded to take on a number of qualified thermal engineers capable of designing complicated systems and of consultation on a wide variety of design problems. There was also a gradual shift in the development section at Lund towards the development of large PHE's and those made of special materials for difficult operating conditions. Emphasis on the manufacture of large units and complete systems gave Alfa-Laval a competitive edge in the more advanced uses. The quality of Alfa-Laval products had always been good, but with steady attention to quality, it had become difficult by 1975 for company officials and customers to recall an example of outright failure of an Alfa-Laval component. After-sale service was mainly limited to replacing plates and gaskets which had succumbed to wear and tear.

By 1975 the Thermal Subdivision had five Application Centres in its Marketing Department at Lund (Exhibit 4). Market companies requiring assistance on an enquiry were free to get in touch with the relevant Application Centre, but were under no compulsion to do so. Market companies were given direct access to the comprehensive computer programmes that had been written to calculate

Exhibit 4   *Thermal Subdivision — Organisation 1975*

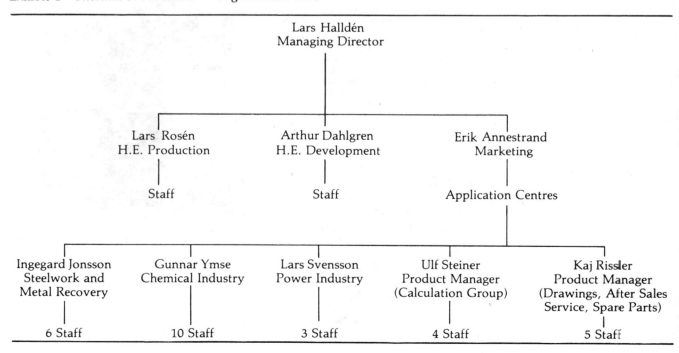

specific heat exchanger requirements, and a back-up service assisted with technical drawings and after-sale service. The Marketing Department also offered training for marketing personnel in the technical aspects of the heat exchanger business. For all these services there was little or no direct charge, as Lund believed that these services more than paid for themselves through increased sales and better customer liaison; and gave the company the very advantage that it was eager to retain in a market that was becoming increasingly competitive.

Thermal know-how was particularly important in the chemical, steel, power and mining industries. These market segments were distinguished by large orders and large HE units, often involving international contracting. Thermal management saw a great opportunity here for expansion in sales. While few products from other Alfa-Laval divisions were sold along with HE's to these industries, Thermal could draw on its strength of a complete thermal line and use its extensive application know-how to effect. In 1975 the Subdivision's 'Business Mission' was amended to read:

> We shall also promote marketing of complete functions for the large and fast-growing central cooling market. That can be done by selling complete installations for seawater or cooling towers or by selling installation software with our heat exchangers.

> We shall have the largest resources, the best know-how with superior products and a reliable delivery capacity.

On large bids, or on business that might involve international contracting or be of continuing importance to the Group, market companies could if they wished approach the Application Centre for an advantageous transfer price on centrally produced components to enable them to make a more competitive quote. Frequently, a market company would ask for assistance to get Alfa-Laval products specified at the design stage for a major contract; but in keeping with the company's policy of autonomy for its market units, the rule was quite clear — assistance was given by invitation, rather than any Head Office imposition.

Competitive Position The greater part of Alfa-Laval's heat exchanger orders (about 75%) were accounted for by plate heat exchangers, which competed with conventional tubular heat exchangers and PHE's of other makes. The tubular HE was by far the most widely used HE for industrial application and had a surprisingly strong hold on the American market. Acceptance of the PHE as a suitable replacement, however, was growing. For application in the marine, dairy and other fields, where compactness and hygienic or environmental effects of heat exchangers were major considerations, the competition was all between different makes of PHE's. In marine and dairy industries, moreover, Alfa-Laval's other subdivisions had strong process know-how. Exhibit 5 shows a breakdown of Thermal PHE sales by industry of application.

Through conscious choice Alfa-Laval had not involved itself in the market for conventional tubular HE's which were fabricated in a large number of countries by many small, highly competitive but technically less advanced companies. In the view of Alfa-Laval management this market, though many times larger than that for PHE's, was generally more suited to small local manufacture and was not one where a company like Alfa-Laval could compete effectively.

The mix of small, medium and large PHE's sold from Lund had altered over the years as shown in Exhibit 6. Exhibit 7 also indicates the increase in size of orders serviced from Lund. Thermal Subdivision sales were shifting towards larger units and larger customers. This shift was not altogether an unwelcome change. The percentage of profit contribution from small PHE's for 1974 was not very significant and the segment was coming under increasing fire from small national competitors. They had cut prices in order to break into a stronghold where Alfa-Laval had earlier had great market and technical superiority.

In 1975 there were about twenty PHE manufacturers in the world. Of these,

Exhibit 5   *Thermal Division Plate Heat Exchanger Sales by Industry of Application*

	1970 %	1972 %	1974 %
Power	2	3	2
Factory	5	4	4
Mining	1	1	1
Steel	12	15	18
Chemical, Organic	14	13	12
Chemical, Inorganic	18	15	15
Marine	18	20	21
Brewing, Fermentation	7	7	7
Dairy Plant	12	12	10
Other	11	10	10
	100	100	100
Index of Invoice Value Adjusted to 1974 Prices	83	78	100

Exhibit 6   *Thermal Division Plate Heat Exchanger Sales and Profitability by Size*

	% of Total Thermal Subdivision Sales		% of Total Thermal Profit Contribution
	1974	(1975) (Est.)	1974
Small PHE	13	(10)	4
Medium PHE	51	(48)	40
Large PHE	12	(19)	35

Exhibit 7   *Thermal Division Plate Heat Exchanger Sales by Size of Order and Model*

Size of Order in Swedish Krona	% of Total Number of Orders	
	1972	1975
Below 50,000	92	80
50 — 500,000	7	18
Above 500,000	1	2
	100	100

	% of Total Unit Sales	
	1972	1975
Small	48	34
Medium	52	56
Large	—	10
	100	100

about seven were of any significance. The more important competitors were:

1. APV — UK   4. Vicarb — France
2. Schmidt — West Germany   5. Ahlborn — West Germany
3. Hisaka — Japan   6. DDMM — Denmark

There were very significant variations in the market share of these main competitors. Alfa-Laval now held perhaps 50% of the world market for PHE's, as against 60% in 1970. APV was the leading contender, with Schmidt and Hisaka following to take much of the remaining volume. Even more noticeable, however, was the different level of technical services provided. Competition was largely confined to small and medium PHE segments. The bigger specialised products and systems that Lund was putting on the market faced little or no competition. Alfa-Laval's advanced designs, protected by patents, had given the company substantial cost advantages which the smaller companies found difficult to match. For applications in which the competition for plant construction was international, then, Alfa-Laval held a very high percentage of the market share.

The international distribution outlets for the leading competitors as estimated by Alfa-Laval staff are listed in Exhibit 8. Not all could be thought of as competitors in the international PHE market. Some could more adequately be described as national companies with export activities.

Of the really international competitors, APV of the UK was the closest, with a broad range of activities in thermal engineering and a wide distribution and marketing system. APV had fifteen affiliated companies in the principal industrialised countries and numerous agents across the globe. In a manner similar to Alfa-Laval, APV had developed a wide variety of technical information and computer programmes to promote its products. APV was particularly strong in the chemical, food and dairy industries.

Competition from the remaining companies had been largely confined to domestic markets and even then often in specialised segments of the market. But the competition, when faced, could be very real indeed and there were increasing instances of prices and quotations undercutting Alfa-Laval by as much as 15% or 20%, and these companies seemed to be gradually looking further afield for business.

In spite of its great strength and momentum, Alfa-Laval was receiving small bits of information from various market companies that were causing concern. The Japanese company, Hisaka, for instance, had captured about 85% of the Japanese

Exhibit 8   *Alfa-Laval and Competitors' Distribution Systems*

	Affiliated or Associated Companies	Licensees	Agents
APV	15 in principal industrialised countries	—	Numerous globally
Schmidt	Austria	—	10—15
Hisaka	—	1 in UK 1 in USA	Australia, India, Korea, Taiwan, Netherlands
Vicarb	—	—	10
Ahlborn	—	—	10—15 Several agents in same country
DDMM	—	—	5—10

Exhibit 9 *Penetration of Market Segments*

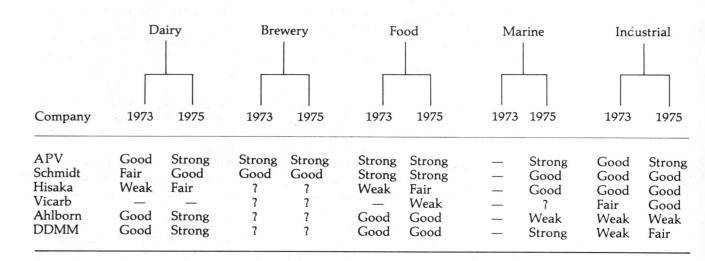

INDUSTRIAL SECTOR

Company	Dairy 1973	Dairy 1975	Brewery 1973	Brewery 1975	Food 1973	Food 1975	Marine 1973	Marine 1975	Industrial 1973	Industrial 1975
APV	Good	Strong	Strong	Strong	Strong	Strong	—	Strong	Good	Strong
Schmidt	Fair	Good	Good	Good	Strong	Strong	—	Good	Good	Good
Hisaka	Weak	Fair	?	?	Weak	Fair	—	Good	Good	Good
Vicarb	—	—	?	?	—	Weak	—	?	Fair	Good
Ahlborn	Good	Strong	?	?	Good	Good	—	Weak	Weak	Weak
DDMM	Good	Strong	?	?	Good	Good	—	Strong	Weak	Fair

Exhibit 10 *New PHE Models Introduced 1965—1975*

Company	Number of PHE's Introduced 1965—73	Number of PHE's Introduced 1973—75	Expected Introduction
Alfa-Laval	8	1	
APV	3		1
Schmidt	12		1
Hisaka		3	1
Vicarb	4		1
Ahlborn	3 (2 withdrawn)	1	
DDMM		4	

market and was looking enviously at the European and North American markets. There were rumours that Hisaka, DDMM and the French company, Vicarb, were about to expand plate pressing capacity and might extend the size-range of PHE's they manufactured. DDMM and the French had been having some success in getting into the coveted marine market. Exhibits 9 and 10 summarise Alfa-Laval's information about competition in various industrial sectors and indicate the changes taking place.

Product Development Philosophy

Product Development in the Alfa-Laval group of companies continued to build on the very impressive technological lead that the company had established. There had been a steady expansion of the range of thermal equipment offered and the company had most recently ventured into central cooling systems. Instead of providing individual HE's for the many local requirements in various parts of a factory, these developments made it possible to provide a single central cooling system. Such systems meant a substantial change not only in the hardware sold by the company, but also in the software service provided. Some Thermal managers believed that the emphasis should be to educate the market on the economic and technical benefits of single large PHE's and associated complete systems, and to explain that these benefits far outweighed the disadvantages. Smaller but parallel systems could provide a built-in back-up facility in the event of technical failure of single large units. Alfa-Laval management pointed to the absence of technical failure to emphasise the very low probability of such an event.

The philosophy of the development department at Lund, as shown in the following extract, was to retain Alfa-Laval leadership through creative new products:

A brief historical sketch of the 1950's and 60's shows clearly that the key concepts for successful companies have been production and marketing. The company that realised the importance of building up an efficient, rational, production apparatus in the 50's and learnt to do so, was able to compete most successfully. In the 60's, which can be characterised as the decade of marketing, it was the companies who concentrated on developing their marketing capability that laid the best foundation for favourable development.

In the future, production engineering and marketing are unlikely to have the same decisive importance as in the past. They are, of course, still two important components of a company's operations, but their importance from the point of view of competition is declining. Most companies know how to run their production and marketing operations, so standards in these respects have now become more uniform.

It is research and development that will be the big thing in the future. Although product development has always played an important part in corporate strategic planning, the constantly changing external demands on both our company and our products means that in the future it will not be enough to concentrate only on the traditional engineering aspects. We shall have to broaden the base of product development in future and integrate it into the corporate strategic planning process in a more concrete manner.

An ambition to lead the market demands products of a very high standard and, by the same token, product development of a very high standard. It is not enough for our products to satisfy the demands of the market; they must also be technically superior to those of our competitors.

The Thermal marketing group, however, believed that the development of new products and systems should follow an increase in the application know-how within the company, including:

1. The search, within known and established processes, for areas of application:
    where heat exchangers have not previously been used;
    where compact heat exchangers have not previously been used, but where other types such as tubular heat exchangers are already used;
    where it is possible to deliver a high degree of process know-how.
2. The search for applications of the company's product mix in new processes.

Only a small part of the company's application resources had been directed in the past towards these objectives. The division's Application Centres had been more occupied in providing technical and commercial support to the field organisation within established markets. This past orientation was partly an outcome of the technical superiority of Alfa-Laval's products which had created their own markets in areas where the competition was not troublesome. There had been, however, a gradual change in the attitude of Lund's marketing personnel, who now felt that with the increase in competitive activity and pressure on Alfa-Laval's profits and margins, the Application Centres should adopt a more aggressive stance. Marketing personnel felt that they should be informed as a matter of course of all important activity, especially large projects in their respective industrial sectors, and not have to sit and hope that the marketing companies would have the goodness to get in touch with them. To face the growing competition, the Marketing Department saw the remedy in aggressive central marketing activity.

There was another school of thought, however, that argued for decentralisation of product development rather than centralisation of marketing. Frequent discussions had taken place as to whether it would be preferable to retain the relatively large development group working internationally with the national market companies or build small engineering groups in each of the major national companies. Until now the primary responsibility for product development had rested with the division, but it had been found practical to keep some development activities close to production and sales in market companies. Thus most of the development work for cooling towers had been done in Spain, where the relevant production unit was located.

Pricing Policy   The Thermal Subdivision administered a complicated pricing policy. Despite a general acceptance that this policy was unsatisfactory, it had not been changed because the various alternative suggestions were either too cumbersome to implement or did not accomplish what the Subdivision considered to be the central purpose of its pricing strategy — that is, to maintain divisional autonomy and, at the same time, provide the required incentive to maximise total company performance. Management's attitude had been to accept the 'devil you know'. A company catalogue laid down the internal sales prices for products calculated as shown in Table 1; note that these are disguised percentages but should be taken as actual for the purpose of this case.

Table 1   Calculation of Internal Sales Prices

Standard Variable Production Costs, Stock Holding Charges etc.	*Production Cost*
Work's Overheads, Specially Installed Equipment	*Manufacturing Price* (MP)
Product Division's Charge for Development and Coordination	*Approx. 30% on MP*
Product Division's Profit Charge	*Approx. 20% on MP*
	Internal Sales Price (Catalogue)
Market Company Cost Charge	*Average 40% on MP*
Market Company Profit	*Average 10% on MP* *Customer Sales Price* (CSP)

Interdivision sales took place at the manufacturing price, and in about 80% of the cases the market companies paid the catalogue price less a discount varying according to the country of destination. The size of the discount was determined through negotiation between the management of the Thermal Subdivision and the respective market company, though occasionally Group management was involved. The discount for a particular market company, however, remained constant unless there were very special reasons. The aim of this market discount was to allow for the different competition, and hence price levels, that had grown up in the different country markets. In Germany, for example, Alfa-Laval held a leading market share; but Germany was a large, price-conscious market and under continual competitive pressure.

Where it was felt that a particular order was of such importance to the Group that a particularly low price should be quoted, it was possible to request a special discount. This happened for under 10% of the business, but the assessment of whether an order justified a specially preferential price had become one of the major concerns of the Application Centres at Lund.

A number of dysfunctions of the pricing system had been recognised. These statements are taken from internal subdivision papers:

> It appears that the subsidiary is treated as an external customer. Since the easiest way for a subsidiary to improve its profitability is to obtain extra discounts from the product division, attention is drawn to the wrong quarter. But, on the other hand, the price system does not guarantee that the subsidiary gets enough freedom of action, e.g. in external pricing. The information transferred to the subsidiaries via the price system does not correspond to the actual position for the current decision.

> A subsidiary company can show good profits at the expense of a product division in Sweden.

> Each fixed internal pricing system has effects on resource allocation. To use a price system with a resource allocating purpose without either informing the units involved or drawing out the consequences must be condemned. The relation between different product divisions (e.g. competition for the favours of the subsidiary) or between different subsidiaries (e.g. competition for the same international buyer) can be serious.

> The structure of the internal pricing system provides the subsidiary with little incentive to increase its volume. There is a tendency to 'skim' the market.

> The Internal Sales Price is determined by a pre-calculated standard catalogue price. A preliminary calculation such as this is always based on a number of assumptions about volume, distribution of joint costs, depreciation and interest on fixed assets. Each estimation of these costs is more or less arbitrary and, in turn, is based on a number of more or less unspoken assumptions. With the present system for internal sales price calculation, it is hard to relate the cost calculation to the actual decisions.

As the Thermal Subdivision found itself dealing more and more with large international customers, problems were becoming evident on large bids with regard to division of profits, differences of price levels, and differences in technical solutions suggested by various Market Companies. For the Thermal Conference of 1975, a partially fictitious case had been written to open the discussion as to how the marketing approach, particularly pricing, should be amended:

The Case of a Major Opportunity

Alfa-Laval has market companies (MkA, MkB, etc.) in 6 countries: A, B, C, D, E and F. There are 3 contractors competing to obtain the main contract:

> Contractor 1B has its head office in country B and subsidiaries in countries C and D.
> Contractor 2E has its head office in E.
> Contractor 3F has its head office in F and a subsidiary in B.

The ultimate customer, an end-user, is located in country A and local regulations require 20% of the equipment to be manufactured in A. Alfa-Laval's MkA in A has local assembly facilities for some types in the product range, but not the types specified in the quotations.

Step 1   MkA informs Thermal about the project, stating which contractors are bidding.

Step 2   Thermal forwards information to MkB, MkE and MkF where the 3 contractors have their head offices. Since the project is at a very early state, none can obtain material for a quotation but must wait.

Step 3   Contractors start work in project design and MkC, which has previously collaborated with Contractor 1B's subsidiary in C on other projects, receives an enquiry without knowing which project it refers to.

Step 4   MkB, MkD, MkE and MkF now also receive enquiries from Contractor 3F's subsidiary in B. All enquiries except the one to MkF are forwarded to Thermal for coordination. MkA receives an enquiry direct from the end-user.

Step 5   MkC, which has its own manufacturing facilities for some products, makes its own technical solution and its own price quote to Contractor 1B's subsidiary in C, still unaware of which project is involved.

Step 6   Thermal makes its calculations and prepares quotations with a recommended technical solution and bid price, which are then forwarded to our MkA, MkB, MkD, MkE and MkF.

Step 7   The reaction to Thermal's proposal from the various Mk's are:
A: Our MkA accepts and quotes the price proposed by Thermal direct to the end-user and persuades him to specify plate heat exchangers.
B: Relations with Contractor 1B have previously been good and MkB has virtually a fixed price level for this customer. Contractor 1B is committed to a particular technical solution for this kind of application and MkB will, therefore, not accept the Thermal proposal.
C: MkD has generally been able to maintain a very high price level and, therefore, does not approve the level recommended by Thermal. The technical solution is acceptable.
D: The quotation is accepted and passed on to Contractor 2E.
E: It is discovered that MkF has already submitted its own quotation to Contractor 3F, with almost the same technical solution but at a higher price than the one recommended by Thermal.

Step 8   Thermal advises that its technical solution and price level should be used regardless.

Step 9   Contractor 1B gets the order.

Step 10   What happens now to relations between Alfa-Laval and the Contractors? *Contractor 1B* is irritated because Alfa-Laval has also quoted direct to the end-user and takes the line that Alfa-Laval is competing with its own customer. Discovers that Alfa-Laval has different price levels in different countries and will in future ask for quotations from several Alfa-Laval offices. Is annoyed that we argue for different technical solutions for the same application, depending on the country in which the discussion takes place. We can, however, counter this by pointing to a different operational experience in different countries.
Contractor 2E has no problem.
Contractor 3F has also discovered that Alfa-Laval has different price levels in different countries, and having previously done business with MkF on other projects now suspects that he has been overcharged on previous occasions. Will not give Alfa-Laval another chance.

Step 11   Contractor 1B places the order with MkB.

Step 12   What efforts have the Alfa-Laval market companies made and what permanent changes have resulted?
A: Has persuaded the end-user to specify PHE's. Has passed on Thermal's quotation. Gets the after-sales service.
B: Has passed on Thermal's quotation. Has carried on technical and economic discussions with the customer to explain away the differences in price and technical solution. Has secured the order. Has lost some of its goodwill in its relations with Contractor 1B. Has lost a customer — Contractor 3F's subsidiary in B.
C: Has worked out its own technical solution. Has written its own quotations.
D: Has passed on Thermal's quotation. Has had its price level cut.
E: Has passed on Thermal's quotation.

Subjects for Discussion   How should we modify our organisation and methods to ensure:

closer contacts and coordination with main contractors;
involvement at an earlier stage;
a correct price policy;
optimum technical solutions?

How can we keep the question of division of profits out of the quotation work and ensure that a fair division is made *after* the order has been secured?
Who should be responsible for:

the technical solution;
the price level;
making the quotation?

The Way Ahead   Though 'The Case of a Major Opportunity' was fictitious, it was sufficiently accurate to characterise the sort of problems that the Thermal Subdivision was facing in the international marketplace. The discussion brought home to all participants that fairly fundamental changes were called for, both in terms of distribution strategy and cross-country sales. Management was keen to decide what a future Thermal Subdivision should be like, what it should do, how it should control, and how such an organisation should be reached given the constraints of a hundred years of organisational tradition. Some managers felt that the well-established organisational culture was going to be a major stumbling block, that changes should be moderate and gradual. Others disagreed.

This case was prepared by Kenneth Simmonds of the London Business School. © Kenneth Simmonds, 1980.

CASE A14
Metropolitan National Bank Ltd

As Chief Properties Manager for the Metropolitan, Brent Elliott held overall responsibility for negotiating purchase of new sites, construction of new premises and disposal of properties no longer required by the bank. Metropolitan operated over one thousand branches in the United Kingdom; consequently Brent was concerned with numerous building and renovation projects at any one time.

Brent was annoyed. His professional competence had been indirectly criticised during a recent regional management meeting when the Properties Division was blamed for failing to provide adequate teller windows and floor area for waiting customers in a branch opened only six months previously. Design and construction of this particular branch had extended over four years and there had been more new office building in the immediate vicinity than expected when the designs were drawn up. Moreover, no competitor banks had moved in to take up the additional growth. Anyway, Brent was sure the design would have been adequate, had it not been for the rapid growth in the number of outside customers who cashed cheques at the branch but who did not hold accounts there.

By presenting their cheque card with their cheque, customers could withdraw cash from any branch of a British bank. This arrangement had encouraged customers changing their home or office address to leave their account with their original branch and to switch to the nearest convenient bank for cashing their cheques. The frequency of cash withdrawals had also increased with inflation since banks had retained the £50 limit for a cheque card withdrawal, partly to avoid an increase in the costs of cashing stolen cheques supported by stolen cheque cards.

It seemed to Brent that heavy traffic through the new branch was an indication of success in choosing a good site, not a cause for criticism. Still, he planned to avoid criticism in future by asking a consulting firm to develop a standard procedure for forecasting customer traffic for any potential branch location. Before he did so, however, Brent thought he should make a preliminary list of the considerations that the consultants should allow for in their procedure.

CASE A15
Premier Publishing Group (A)

Book Publishing The publishing of books is significantly different from the provision of many other products in terms of the crucial role of the editorial staff. Book publishing has the usual functional areas of production, sales and, in certain cases, accounting and marketing; but to a lesser or greater extent these are dominated by the editorial function. This is partly a reflection of tradition, but also relates to the rather special character of the publishing industry.

Any book publisher will generally handle a relatively large number of books every year and, in many ways, each book is an individual entity. Obviously, most books are produced in similar ways and indeed almost all are sold as part of a list rather than individually, but otherwise each book is clearly different. It is to cover the management of these differences that the editorial function exists. The relevant editor is concerned particularly with negotiations with the author, the content of the book, and its presentation. However, there are some crucial decision points on a specific book which must involve other opinions besides that of the editor and these can be categorised as the contract stage where a contract is signed with a specific author, the typescript approval stage where a manuscript is accepted for publication, and the print run and pricing decision where both the detailed presentation of the book is agreed as well as its recommended retail price and the actual print run.

Book Markets Obviously the book market is not homogeneous and can be considered in various segments. Within the book trade it is common to distinguish between:

(i) *General Trade:* books which are generally sold through several trade bookshops and mainly to individual customers.

(ii) *Library Supplies:* there are a number of specialist wholesalers who supply to local authority libraries. Some books are produced specifically for the library market.

(iii) *Educational:* whilst many educational books are actually sold via bookshops they are generally, in the primary or secondary sector, ordered in large volume by schools and local education authorities. In the tertiary sector books are bought by individuals, but on the basis of recommendation particularly by course lecturers and professors.

Market Size The most extensive figures for publishers are issued by the Department of Industry — they are estimated to cover about four-fifths of total sales and receipts of general printers and publishers (Table 1).

During 1973/75 the book trade suffered very severe inflation particularly in terms of paper costs. The general response was not to match this completely with price rises, but rely on low percentage margins and higher volume to cover overheads (Tables 2 & 3).

Table 1   Sales of UK General Printers and Publishers (£'000s)

Books	1973	1974	1975
Hard Back			
Bibles	4,484	5,143	7,185
School Texts	19,709	22,704	26,026
Technical & Scientific	37,591	44,822	53,032
Fiction, Literature & Classics	28,029	29,908	39,057
Children's	17,636	23,209	26,892
Other	45,369	60,382	72,631
Paper Back			
School Texts	17,167	22,767	27,738
Technical & Scientific	7,503	8,898	11,911
Fiction, Literature & Classics	23,100	30,070	41,036
Children's	7,019	8,870	10,346
Other (incl. Bibles)	13,953	15,607	17,925
TOTAL	221,559	272,382	333,780

Table 2   Price Indices (1970 = 100)

	1973	1974	1975
Paper Prices (Printing & Writings)	122.3	173.8	221.3 (4q. 228.5)
Wholesale Price Index (Books)	126.3	149.2	186.1 (4q. 197.5)
Retail Price Index (Not Food)	124.4	143.4	177.5 (4q. 190.3)

Table 3   Number of Titles Issued

1950	17,072
1955	19,962
1960	23,783
1965	26,358
1966	28,883
1967	29,619
1968	31,420
1969	32,393
1970	33,489
1971	32,538
1972	33,140
1973	35,254
1974	
1975	

Source: The Bookseller

Who Buys?   The Book Promotion Feasibility Study (BPFS) did a considerable amount of research on book-buying habits. The BPFS found that regular book-readers (who read at least one book a week) tend to be educated over the age of 16, non-manual working class, women, and aged between 45 and 64. It also found that there was a close correlation between interest in books and education level, as Table 4 shows.

Table 4   Interest in reading books

Adults educated up to the age of:	Not interested in reading books (per cent)
up to 16 years	43
16—18 years	23
over 18 years	16

Source: BPFS

The BPFS research only covered the period December 1973 to March 1974; the following figures must therefore be treated with caution, since this period may not be representative of the year as a whole. The BPFS estimated that 164 million books were read for 'light reading' and 128 million books for 'serious reading', by adults in the period covered. A breakdown of these figures is shown in Tables 5, 6 and 7.

Table 5   Breakdown of the 164 m 'light' books read

Category	Percentage	Number of books (m)
Crime/Thrillers	38	62
Romance	20	33
Western/War	14	23
Humour	5	8
Other light reading	23	38

Source: BPFS

Table 6   Breakdown of the 128 m 'serious' books read

Category	Percentage	Number of books (m)
History/Religion	25	32
Biography/Autobiography	16	20
Academic/Technical	16	20
Hobbies/Instructional	14	18
Classics	11	14
Travel/Guides	9	12
Other serious reading	9	12

Source: BPFS

Of these 292 million books read, nearly 60 percent were borrowed from a source outside the reader's household; a breakdown is given in Table 7.

Table 7   Breakdown of the 292 m books read

Source	Percentage	Number of books (m)
Borrowed from library	48	137
Owned by reader or other member of household	41	120
Owned by non-member of household	11	35

Source: BPFS

However, the proportions are very different, depending on whether the books are 'serious' or 'light'. Nearly 50 percent of 'serious' books read had been bought; but bought books accounted for only just over 25 percent of 'light' books read.

Tables 8, 9 and 10 show some of the principal distinctions in buying habits between hardbacks and paperbacks.

Table 8   Hardbacks and paperbacks: volume and value (%)

	Volume	Value
Paperbacks	48	28
Hardbacks	52	75
Total	100	100

Source: BPFS

Table 8 shows that, of the books covered in the survey, hardback books cost about three times as much as paperbacks.

Table 9   Hardbacks and paperbacks: light and serious (%)

	Paperbacks	Hardbacks
Light	59	25
Serious	41	75
Total	100	100

Source: BPFS

Table 9 shows that paperbacks accounted for 70 percent of light books bought, whereas hardbacks accounted for nearly 65 percent of serious books bought.

Table 10   Hardbacks and paperbacks: gifts and other readers (%)

Reason bought	Paperbacks	Hardbacks
For self	67	25
Gift for:		
other adult	11	12
child	22	63

Source: BPFS

Table 10 shows that, whereas the majority of paperbacks were bought for reading by the buyer, most hardbacks were bought as a gift for a child. Gifts for other adults, on the other hand, were drawn almost equally from paperbacks and hardbacks.

Table 11   Frequency of visiting a bookshop

Frequency	*Percentage of adults*
Once a week or more	14
Once a fortnight	6
Once a month	16
Once every 3 months	17
Less often	28
Never	20

Source: BPFS

The frequency of visiting a bookshop is obviously important, and Table 11 shows that there is a significant minority of fairly frequent visitors.

Prices: The Net Book Agreement

The publishing industry is one of the few industries where resale price maintenance is allowed. The arrangement by which this is organised is called the Net Book

Agreement, an agreement signed in 1957 by all members of the Publishers' Association. This agreement set out the conditions of resale price maintenance, which are as follows:

A publisher, in publishing a book (this also covers pamphlets, maps and other similar printed matter) decides for himself whether to make it a 'net' book, or a 'non-net' book. If he decides to publish the book at a net price, then he gives notice to the retailer of standard conditions of sale, which require the book to be sold at the full 'net' price (fixed from time to time by the publisher), and this main condition of sale is relaxed only in the following circumstances:

(i)   If the book has been held in stock by the bookseller for more than 12 months since his latest purchase of that particular book, and if it has been offered to the publisher at cost price or at the proposed reduced price whichever is the lower, and the offer has been refused by the publisher.

(ii)   If the book is second-hand, and it is more than 6 months after the date of publication.

(iii)   If the purchaser is a library or institution, authorised by the Council of the Publishers' Association.

In practice, nearly all books (except most school textbooks and a large proportion of Bibles which are customarily purchased in bulk) are published at 'net' prices.

The Net Book Agreement was upheld by the Restrictive Practices Court in its judgement in October 1962, because it recognised that properly maintained book prices were necessary to ensure that the public continued to have access to the 38,000 different books published each year, and the quarter of a million books in print at any one time. The Court also held that the Net Book Agreement helped to keep the prices of books in general down, and considered that price-cutting, if permitted, could reduce the number of titles issued — works of probable literary or scholastic value being amongst those books no longer published.

The bookseller usually gets a 33 to 35 percent discount off the published price of a net book bought on subscription, i.e. pre-publication or for stock. While this discount applies to some other net books too, many of the academic technical and higher educational titles still earn only 25 percent — as do single copies. There is also a small order surcharge, charged by some publishers, of up to 5 percent. Postage and packing is rarely charged, since it is liable to VAT, whereas books themselves are zero-rated. In fact, Britain is the only EEC country to have books zero-rated — because the Government was persuaded that there should be no tax on knowledge — and the industry is pressing for books to be zero-rated throughout the EEC.

Premier Publishing Group

Premier Publishing Group Limited is a medium sized, London based, publishing company with an annual turnover of £4 million and over 100 employees. It is a wholly-owned subsidiary of Premier Limited, which is a private company. They print around 400 titles annually and an analysis of the titles by imprint is given in Table 12.

Only Bullseye is an exclusively paperback imprint. Many of the titles published are actually reprints: the approximate breakdown is shown in Table 13.

Major decisions on any book are taken at the 'Friday Meeting'. This meeting is chaired by Herbert Wilson, the Managing Director, with Harold Heath, deputy Managing Director, Frances O'Connor, Editorial Director, Anthony Jenkins, Sales Director and Chris Canashan, Marketing Director. Relevant members of the editorial and production staff are also present. The organisation structure is shown in Exhibit 1. The agenda for a typical Friday Meeting is attached as Exhibit 2.

Table 12

Imprint	General Classification	Number of Titles (1974)	% Sales
Premier			
Premier	General Fiction and Non-Fiction	82	34
Books for Leisure	Leisure and Vocational Training	31	9
Thrills	Popular 'Library' Crime	19	2
Dogs for All	Dog Series	1	2
Bleeding Hearts	Popular 'Library' Romance	46	4
The Eye	Occult, Witchcraft	4	4
Premier Library Service		35	4
Juvenile	Childrens' Books	—	3
Education			
School Texts		17	5
Scientific and Technical		11	4
Premier University Library		6	4
Bullseye			
Bullseye	Popular Fiction & Non-Fiction	69	26

Table 13

	Reprints	New
Premier	30%	70%
Education	70%	30%
Bullseye	45%	55%

Typically, any individual book is subject to three major decision points (see Exhibit 3).

1. *The Contract*   All books are produced on a contract basis, although the stage at which the contract is signed can vary from an idea to a virtually completed typescript.

2. *Typescript Approval*   The full typescript is, of course, available at this stage. Various members of the meeting will have had the opportunity to read it and the planned blurb (see Exhibit 4).

3. *Print Number and Pricing*   At this stage the final price and print-run must be agreed. It is generally true that it is most economic for the initial print run to cover about 2 years' duration.* The relevant print run may vary from a few hundred to 100,000 in the case of a hardback, or somewhat more in the case of a paperback. At this stage a costing analysis is available (Exhibit 5). Although there are certain differences between imprints, the actual costings can be compared with an 'ideal' or target breakdown to achieve 10% net profit on turnover:

*In fact, it is standard accounting practice to write-off book stocks at the end of the year, two years after publication. Up until this time book stock is valued at cost (around 35% of revenue).

Table 14 'Ideal' Breakdown of Costs and Revenues

	Retail sales price (%)	Manufacturers sales price (%)
Sales at retail sales price	100	
Sales at manufacturer's sales price	60	100
Production Costs	21	35
Royalty	9	15
Overheads**	24	40
NET PROFIT	6	10

Note: Royalties are paid on a rate directly linked to book sales. However, on certain books advance royalties may be given which are not covered by those actually 'earned'.
**For a breakdown of overheads see Exhibit 8.

However, all costings are done on the basis of 100% sales. In fact it is often the case that some books are written off and remaindered (i.e. sold substantially below cost) — this write-off can reduce the title profitability considerably. The average write-off cost per imprint for 1975 was:

Table 15 Write-off Costs as % of Turnover

Premier	3.8
Thrills	1.4
Dogs for All	2.4
Juvenile	7.5
Bleeding Hearts	1.7
Leisure	3.4
The Eye	11.2
Premier Library Service	10.9
School Texts	9.2
Scientific & Technical	11.5
Premier University Library	21.6
Bullseye	2.6

The previous decisions of Friday Meetings are monitored to ensure that the sum of the decision on each imprint is close to the net profit percentage targets (on the basis of full sales) by means of the estimate appraisal form prepared on a fortnightly basis (see Exhibit 6).

General Information Information on individual title performance is produced as a result of the computer invoice analysis on a weekly basis. This information indicates sales by title and imprint on a weekly net basis. Terms of sale are complex and variable in the publishing business, but facilities do exist for many forms of sale or return — the invoicing system therefore only registers sales net of returns. Inevitably the weekly computer reports circulated to the sales director and the editorial staff are voluminous and the sales director has a card index on title performance maintained by his staff from the computer records — a typical blank card is shown in Exhibit 7.

The twin pressures of a difficult market place and cost inflation forcing cash-flow problems in terms of funding stock were generating greater and greater pressures for better decision making on both books and also the print-run level and pricing, to ensure a higher level of real profitability.

Exhibit 1 *Premier Organisational Structure*

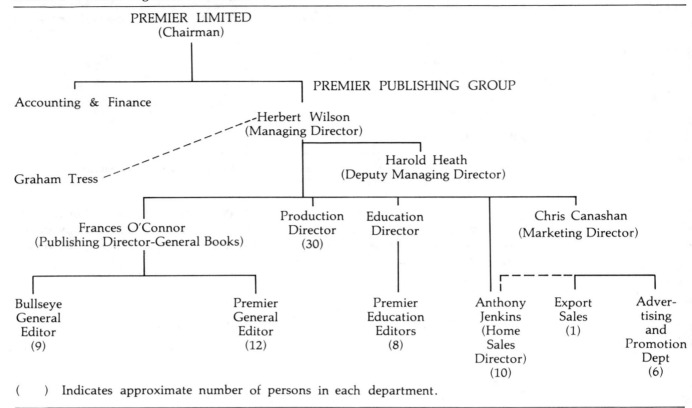

( ) Indicates approximate number of persons in each department.

Exhibit 2 *Agenda*

Typescript Approval Contract, Print Numbers and Prices Meeting to be held on Friday, April 11, at 10.00 at 3 Rochester Square

CONFIRMATION OF FINAL PUBLICATION DATES: May 12, 19 and 27

PREMIER BOOKS

1. *Typescript Approval*

DISTRACTIONS	Herbert Krans	ZH
MAE WEST	Albert Henchley	ZH
MORNING AT LAST!	Andrew Black	AH

2. *Contract*

THE QUESTION	Vincent Tewson	AH

3. *Print Numbers & Prices*

COREN IN THE COUNTRY	Alan Coren	ZH
NEEDLE	Francis Queen	ZH
AUTUMN TEARS	Charles Smith	ZH
FULL MOON AND GRASS	Bill Fainlight	WT
FOURTH MAN UNDER	Wilson Abert	WT
A CORRIDOR OF SILENCE	Bill Hill	WT
CHRISTMAS STORY	John Vincent	WT
LONDONERS AT WORK	Walter Henry	ZH
NEW CENTURY ENCYCLOPAEDIA (rp)		MH

DOGS FOR ALL

3. *Print Numbers & Prices*

REARING OF DOGS (rp)	Smythe Allen	AG

Exhibit 2 (Continued)

PREMIER/BULLSEYE

1. *Typescript Approval*

Industrial Studies Series:

ACTION AT WORK	Stone	BF
STUDYING FIGURES	Wellpton	BF
RIGHTS AT LEISURE	Higgins	BF
WORK FOR PAY	Boyson	BF

BULLSEYE

2. *Contract*

REEVE'S TALE	Emmanuel Hargrave	HP

BLEEDING HEARTS

1. *Typescript Approval*

LUCIFER'S SON	Jane Desiree	SP
I LIKE COUSCOUS	Patricia Wallace	SP

2. *Contract*

DISTANT WINTERS	Sarah Boyd	SP

3. *Printer Numbers & Prices*

CASTLE OF FEAR	Naomi Jenkins	SP
THE RUTHLESS BUS DRIVER	Naomi Jenkins	SP

BOOKS FOR LEISURE

For Discussion

THE COMPLETE GOLFER	Bill Saunders	BB

3. *Print Numbers & Prices*

MODEL SOLDIERS	Michael Jones	BB
FOOTBALL FITNESS	Tony Watson	BB
BETTER TENNIS	Bill Mottram	BB

SCHOOL BOOKS

3. *Print Numbers & Prices*

WHO AM I?	Paul Ballard	CM

Exhibit 3 *PPG Publishing Sequence*

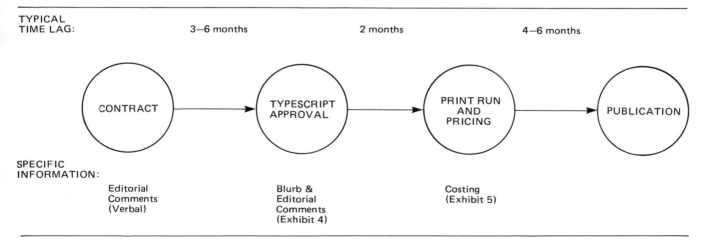

TYPICAL
TIME LAG: 3–6 months   2 months   4–6 months

CONTRACT → TYPESCRIPT APPROVAL → PRINT RUN AND PRICING → PUBLICATION

SPECIFIC
INFORMATION:

Editorial Comments (Verbal)

Blurb & Editorial Comments (Exhibit 4)

Costing (Exhibit 5)

Exhibit 4 *Advance Title Information*

TITLE:	Morning At Last!	PRICE:	£3.50
AUTHOR:	Black	PUB. DATE:	September '75
IMPRINT:	Premier	SIZE:	Demy 8vo
CATEGORY:	Fiction	ILLUS:	—

AUTHOR: Andrew Black, The Pines, Rickmansworth, Hertfordshire.

BLURB: Morning At Last!

In the tense months that followed the murder of the Israeli athletes at the Munich Olympics, the Arab—Israeli quarrel reached a new pitch of hatred and violence.

Set against the continuing underground war of assassination and parcel bomb, *Morning At Last!* tells the story of a group of people who strive to bring about a settlement. Their leader is Anis Kubayin — codename Saladin — a man who seeks to win the world's attention with a major act of sabotage in Israel.

For this he requires a professional, and he finds one in Stephen Roscoe, an ex-army officer who retains all the lethal skills he has learned in the SAS, an English gentleman farmer and a man of honour.

Flying into the Middle East, Roscoe leaves behind him a fractured affair; but before long finds amidst the mounting dangers of his mission a girl who brings him fully alive as only flirtations with death have done before.

No less ruthless than Roscoe, no less complex, is Yaacov, the brilliant young Israeli officer who hunts him all the way to their final confrontation.

In *Morning At Last!* Andrew Black has welded fact and fiction in a wholly new and successful manner, producing a real depth of characterisation, continual suspense and a crescendo of excitement which is all the more startling for being drawn from events which daily make the world catch its breath.

Morning At Last! is a major breakthrough for Andrew Black who is already well known to the public.

SELLING POINTS:

1 . We have a three-book contract with this author who is going to build up a series based on Roscoe. Foreign reactions to *Morning At Last!* have been excellent.

2 . *Morning At Last!* is extremely publicisable as is the author who was the founding proprietor of *Public News.*

Exhibit 5

					Title	Unmarried Father
			3.25	20.8.76	Date	
				2500	Print: number	Author D. Barber
			£3.00	£2.75	Price	Imprint Premier
				60p	Unit cost	ISBN 0 09 122130 7
				425	Composing/Reimposing	
				66	93 **Book** Reproduce and proof	Format Demy 8VO
				43	Corrections 10 % of composition	Extent 192 OF
				15	Fees Copyright Translation / Illustration Offset / Design Editorial	Illus. —
					Artwork	Printer A/P
					Blocks	Binding canvas WB
					Make ready	Jacket 3 Cl
				148	Machining text from type	Pub. date 3.2.75
				271	Machining: plates / ends Paper: text V or 18AW / illus: 90gm / ends:	Advance £750

						Royalty 10% to 2500 / 129 to 5000
£	£	£	£968	Sheet cost		
			423	FC & E/FC & S / Binding @ £ 141		
			5	Brasses		
			31	Jacket: Artwork		
			35			
			— 3	Blocks/Plates		
			60	Machining		
			66	Paper		
			25			
			39	Lamination/Varnish/Overgloss		

PROVISIONAL		FINAL	
Print number		Print number	
Bind number		Bind number	
Price		Price	
Date		Date	
Initial		Initial	

£	£	£1645	£1645	Production bound cost	
		165	165	+ 10%	
		108	99	Allocation for 2%	
		1918	1909	Total	
				Royalty 80/20	
		684	627	Home 2280 (6840) 10% (6270) 10%	
		95	90	Export 570 (1567) ass 5%	
				Cheaps (8710) 6%	
			33	Unearned advance	
				Editorial royalties	
£	£	£2697	£2650	Total cost	

BINDING DETAILS

Folding	7.92
Gathering after	18.36
Forwarding	44.37
Cases	16.56
Coverdale	15.10
2025	13.15
Sundry	13.60
Thread	.54
Setting up	13.86
	140.96

				Revenue	
		4425	4056	Sales home 35.31	
		968	888	Sales export 43.37	
				Sales cheap	
				Subsidiary rights	
£	£	£5393	£4944	Total	
		2697	2650	Less total cost	
£	£	£2696	£2294	Gross profit/loss	
		2157	1978	Less 40 % overhead	
£	£	£ 539	£ 316	Net profit/loss	
£	£	£9.99 %	£	Net profit/loss on two-third sales	

Free copies 150　　　　Est. No. 411

Prepared AP	Checked tm.

Exhibit 6 *Estimate Appraisal*

HARDCASE IMPRINTS		PRICE MEETING			CUMULATIVE FROM MAY 22		
		New	Reprint	Total	New	Reprint	Total
PREMIER	No. of Titles						
	Profit Ratio %						
	Unit A.S.Y.						
	Unit Prodn. Cost						
	Average Print Qty.						
THRILLS	No. of Titles						
	Profit Ratio %						
	Unit A.S.Y.						
	Unit Prodn. Cost						
	Average Print Qty.						
DOGS FOR ALL	No. of Titles						
	Profit Ratio %						
	Unit A.S.Y.						
	Unit Prodn. Cost						
	Average Print Qty.						
JUVENILE	No. of Titles						
	Profit Ratio %						
	Unit A.S.Y.						
	Unit Prodn. Cost						
	Average Print Qty.						
BLEEDING HEARTS	No. of Titles						
	Profit Ratio %						
	Unit A.S.Y.						
	Unit Prodn. Cost						
	Average Print Qty.						
LEISURE	No. of Titles						
	Profit Ratio %						
	Unit A.S.Y.						
	Unit Prodn. Cost						
	Average Print Qty.						
THE EYE	No. of Titles						
	Profit Ratio %						
	Unit A.S.Y.						
	Unit Prodn. Cost						
	Average Print Qty.						
P.L.S.	No. of Titles						
	Profit Ratio %						
	Unit A.S.Y.						
	Unit Prodn. Cost						
	Average Print Qty.						
HARDCASE TOTAL	No of Titles						
	Profit Ratio %						
	Unit A.S.Y.						
	Unit Prodn. Cost						
	Average Print Qty.						

EDUCATIONAL IMPRINTS		PRICE MEETING			CUMULATIVE FROM MAY 22		
		New	Reprint	Total	New	Reprint	Total
SCHOOL TEXTS (19)	No. of Titles						
	Profit Ratio %						
	Unit A.S.Y.						
	Unit Prodn. Cost						
	Average Print Qty.						
S. & T. (21)	No. of Titles						
	Profit Ratio %						
	Unit A.S.Y.						
	Unit Prodn. Cost						
	Average Print Qty.						

		PRICE MEETING			CUMULATIVE FROM MAY 22		
		New	Reprint	Total	New	Reprint	Total
P.U.L.	No. of Titles						
	Profit Ratio %						
	Unit A.S.Y.						
	Unit Prodn. Cost						
	Average Print Qty.						
EDUCATIONAL TOTAL							
	No. of Titles						
	Profit Ratio %						
	Unit A.S.Y.						
	Unit Prodn. Cost						
	Average Print Qty.						
PREMIER INTERNATIONAL	No. of Titles						
	Profit Ratio %						
	Unit Prodn. Cost						
	Average Print Qty.						
BULLS EYE	No. of Titles						
	Profit Ratio %						
	Unit A.S.Y.						
	Unit Prodn. Cost						
	Average Print Qty.						
TOTAL ALL IMPRINTS							
	No. of Titles						
	Profit Ratio %						
	Unit A.S.Y.						
	Unit Prodn. Cost						
	Average Print Qty.						

Exhibit 7

AB/WN   SALES CONTROL CARD

DATE	PERIOD SALE	TOTAL	DATE	PERIOD SALE	TOTAL	DATE	PERIOD SALE	TOTAL	DATE	PERIOD SALE	TOTAL	MIN. STOCK	PRINTED
												1: GRATIS	B/EVEN
												2: SPECIAL SALES:	BOUND DATE
												DM.	
												3: ON SALE	PRINTED
												MONTH STOCK OUT	
													B/EVEN
													BOUND DATE
													PRINTED
													B/EVEN
													BOUND DATE

MONTHLY	SERIES (IF ANY)		AUTHOR:	PRICE	PUBLICATION DATE
WEEKLY	TITLE				

Exhibit 8   *Breakdown of Overheads (%)*

Salaries	27
Occupancy	5
Distribution	25
Advertising and Sales Promotion	10
Management	8
General	25

This case was prepared by Kate Gillespie under the supervision of Ulrich Wiechmann, as the basis for class discussion rather than to illustrate either effective or ineffective handling of an administrative situation. © President and Fellows of Harvard College; The Darden Graduate Business School, University of Virginia; and l'Institut pour l'Etude des Méthodes de Direction de l'Entreprise (IMEDE), 1977.

CASE A16
Carnation Foods Company Ltd

In late 1974 Tony Merry, Managing Director of Carnation Foods Company Ltd, UK, was considering raising the price on the company's non-dairy coffee creamer, Coffee-mate. The product's main ingredient, vegetable fats, had recently tripled in cost, dramatically reducing the company's margins on the product. Also, due to a shortage of glass in the UK, Carnation UK had recently been forced to buy more expensive German glass for packaging Coffee-mate. Coffee-mate's percentage gross margins, previously in the high 40's, were currently in the high 30's, and Carnation UK's parent company, Carnation Foods, USA, was urging Merry to improve them.

Merry was also considering what effect the present situation might have on the rest of Carnation's product line. Prior to his appointment as Managing Director in early 1974, Merry had been Marketing Director of Carnation UK for five years. During that time the company had launched nationally four new products or product lines (including Coffee-mate) and was currently planning the national launch of a fifth product in February 1975. Meanwhile, Carnation's traditional product, evaporated milk, was experiencing declining sales and margins.

Carnation UK had applied to the British Price Commission for permission to raise the retail per-ounce price of Coffee-mate by 30%, based on the higher ingredient costs. The Commission had not denied the request within 30 days, so Carnation remained free to raise the price anywhere up to 30%. The company had to take the chosen increase in a single step, however; i.e. Carnation could not take 10% one month and 20% the next without applying again to the Price Commission.

According to Price Commission regulations, Merry had 28 days to decide his new pricing.

Carnation Foods Company

The US parent firm was founded as a partnership between Tom Xerxa and E.A. Stuart in 1899. The new company began manufacturing condensed milk in an old converted hotel building near Seattle, Washington, N.W. America. After the first two years, which were difficult for the company, Stuart bought his partner's share and became sole owner. Stuart had faith in his new product and installed can-making machinery and a French homogenizer (which prevented cream from rising to the top in the can). He also began to increase public awareness of Carnation Milk by advertising in newspapers and on shop signs.

Soon, Stuart began to breed his own cows to ensure a plentiful supply of high-quality milk. After extensive research and specialised breeding, his cows held world records for milk production. Stuart adopted as a slogan for his product: 'Carnation Milk from Contented Cows.'

After World War I, Carnation began to expand its sales of milk internationally and to diversify into other product lines. The first product diversification was into the fresh-milk and ice-cream business. In 1929 Carnation entered the pet-food market, first in animal feed and later in dog food.

Carnation opened its World Headquarters in Los Angeles in 1949, and Carnation's sales expanded rapidly thereafter. Carnation had since introduced instant powdered milk, a chocolate flavoured drink, mashed potatoes, instant breakfast food, Coffee-mate, canned meats, sandwich spreads, canned dog food, cat foods, canned potatoes, and an all-beef canned dog food. In 1973 worldwide sales had increased to one and a half billion dollars, making Carnation the sixth largest food corporation in the world.

Carnation Foods Company Ltd, United Kingdom

Carnation Milk became known in Europe during the first World War, when it was supplied to soldiers serving overseas. After the war Europeans continued to buy the product. In 1921 Carnation entered a 60—40 joint venture with Pet Milk Company. The new company, American Milk Products (AMP), began to acquire overseas companies for the production and marketing of condensed milk. During the twenties AMP acquired 14 such companies, 8 in Europe.

Originally, Carnation had envisioned AMP as a vehicle to introduce new products world-wide. Pet Milk, however, had a directly competing product line. Furthermore, neither parent wished to introduce new products to AMP for fear that the other would profit from their technology. AMP, therefore, became a holding company, with each parent receiving dividends from the subsidiaries. The UK subsidiary had been AMP's last acquisition. It had previously been a family-owned company of declining sales and profits.

The turn-around at Carnation UK after 1930 was attributable to the efforts of one man, Harry Bond. Bond joined the UK subsidiary as Managing Director in September 1929, just after AMP acquired Carnation UK. Trained as an accountant, Bond had extensive managerial experience in the finance and accounting functions.

By 1932 Bond had succeeded in reversing the downward trend in profits. Later generations of Carnation management attributed Bond's success to the tight control he established over the company's operations. All Carnation UK managers were held strictly accountable to Bond for the performance of their departments, and no major decisions were taken without his personal approval.

During the 1930s Bond replaced many of the managers remaining from the previous management with men of his own choosing. Most management staff hired by Bond came from accounting backgrounds similar to his own. These personnel were structured into the very centralised organisation Bond believed was needed to control the company's operations.

The company's basic policies which evolved under Bond centred on the premise that Carnation UK would do one thing and do it well. The company's business was defined as the manufacture and sale of evaporated milk. Because the company by now had a branded product with an excellent consumer franchise, little emphasis was placed on the marketing functions. The marketing which was done was handled by the sales department. In Bond's view the market for Carnation Evaporated Milk was mature and could not be greatly expanded. He therefore concentrated on controlling costs and increasing efficiency as the means to higher profits.

In 1961, two years before he was to become Managing Director, Barrenger was appointed as Carnation's first Marketing Director. Barrenger joined the company in 1935, and like Bond he was an accountant by training. Barrenger had served Bond in a variety of posts over the years starting first as a junior accountant. In 1943 he became chief accountant; in 1948 head of the production department; and in 1953 he was moved to the job of Financial Director. The assignment as Marketing Director was prompted by Bond's desire to expose Barrenger to the marketing side of the business before he assumed the job of managing director.

Bond retired in 1963, leaving to his successor a profitable and financially sound one-product company. When Barrenger assumed the position of Managing Director, he did little to change the organisation or the basic policies established by Bond. Barrenger believed strongly, as had Bond, in tight centralised control and customarily spent a large portion of his time reviewing the financial accounts prepared for him by the accounting department. Managers who worked in the company under both men concluded that their managerial outlook was very similar.

In 1966 Pet Milk sold its 40% interest in AMP for just over $43 million. Shortly after the sale, AMP was merged into Carnation, becoming the Carnation International Division. With the change in ownership, the relationship between subsidiary and parent company also changed. The UK company became part of a large, rapidly growing US corporation, which was assuming a more active role in the management of its overseas subsidiaries. The only regular communication between AMP and its subsidiaries in the past had been in the area of financial reporting.

In early 1967 the new president of the recently created Carnation International Division, H.L. Lucas, requested all subsidiary general managers to begin proposals for product line expansion. Lucas was ambitious for his new division and anxious to see it develop into one of Carnation's major operations. The new request met with some resistance in the UK. Barrenger believed that Carnation UK was a milk company. They were earning a respectable return on sales, and Barrenger saw little reason to enter new product lines.

In the summer of 1968 all the European subsidiaries, including the UK, were visited by members of the corporate staff of Carnation. The purpose of these visits was to review each subsidiary's market situation and to begin to formalise plans for new product introduction. Barrenger had serious reservations about the introduction of new products. He believed that Carnation UK was an excellent milk company and should not try to be anything else. Barrenger agreed, however, to move ahead with the test marketing of Coffee-mate, a non-dairy coffee creamer that Carnation had been selling successfully in the US since 1962. A young product manager was transferred to the UK from Carnation's headquarters in Los Angeles to assist with the test market.

In 1968 Barrenger also received a visit from Lucas himself. During his visit Lucas stated his belief that the International Division had tremendous growth potential and expressed hope that the UK subsidiary would play a major role in developing the European market. Before leaving to visit other Carnation subsidiaries, Mr Lucas asked Barrenger for a commitment to introduce five new products in the next five years. Lucas believed that with the introduction of new products, Carnation UK would be able to attain 15—20% growth in annual sales and profits in the coming years. Despite its interest in product expansion overseas, Carnation expected the national subsidiaries to remain financially independent as they had in the past.

Approximately six months after Lucas's visit, Mr Barrenger received a letter from Lucas asking him to consider the matter of choosing his successor. Barrenger, who was 61 at the time, was told that it was Carnation corporate policy that its employees be allowed to retire at the age of 65. Mr Lucas explained that he wanted Barrenger's successor to have several years' experience working in the company before he assumed the role of Managing Director. Therefore it was necessary that Barrenger begin the search for his replacement immediately. Lucas suggested that the person chosen to become the next Managing Director have a background in marketing consumer products.

In 1968 Tony Merry was hired as Marketing Director and Assistant Managing Director of Carnation UK, with the understanding that he would become manager of the company after a couple of years. Merry had previously been the manager of the consumer products division of a large British multinational company and had also held positions in sales management and advertising. Merry had been attracted to Carnation because of its commitment to product-line expansion and growth. During his years as Assistant Managing Director, Merry was put in charge of new-product introduction, while the Managing Director handled the milk business. When Merry joined the company, the marketing department consisted of himself and the product manager for Coffee-mate. During the next five years, he expanded his marketing team to a total of five — himself, three product managers, and a market analyst. Merry was anxious that Carnation UK move from a company controlled from the top to a company which encouraged initiative from its younger managers. Barrenger, however, considered the product managers to be 'brash young men' and Merry often found himself acting as a buffer between Barrenger and the product managers.

Within the company, Barrenger remained the sole point of contact with the parent company. Barrenger stated that after forty years with Carnation, he had

Exhibit 1 *Carnation Foods Company Ltd   Balance Sheet for the Year Ended 30 September 1974*

	£		£		
Bank Balances and Cash	225,153	Bank Overdrafts	3,493,348		
Accounts Receivable	2,920,912	Short Term Bank Loan	500,000		
Payments in Advance	81,892	Accounts Payable	1,440,855		
Inventories	5,956,630	Accrued Expenses	141,590		
		Taxation			
Total Current Assets	9,184,587	Payable 1 October 1974			290,000
		Current			56,000
Property, Plant and Equipment	2,596,110		346,000		
		Amounts due to holding company and fellow subsidiaries			279,333
		Less: Amounts due from holding company and fellow subsidiaries			136,815
			142,518		
		Total Current Liabilities	6,064,311		
		Deferred Tax Provision	672,862		
		Capital and Retained Earnings			
		Capital authorised, issued and fully paid			
		2,520,000 shares of £1 each			2,520,000
		Retained earnings			2,523,524
			5,043,524		
	£11,780,697		£11,780,697		

Source: Company records

Profit and Loss Account for the Year Ended 30 September 1974

	£
Profit for the year before taxation	694,078
Taxation	465,060
Profit for the year after taxation	229,018
Balance brought forward from the previous year	2,294,506
Balance carried forward	£2,523,524

gained the trust of headquarters in Los Angeles. He believed, however, that there was sometimes a tendency for headquarters to get too much involved with the details of the subsidiaries. Headquarters' approval was necessary for any capital expenditure over $600. Barrenger recalled one time when he had wanted to build a factory for powdered skim milk, but the idea had been turned down. Although he had not spoken much with the heads of the other European operations, Barrenger believed that Carnation UK was one of the more autonomous subsidiaries.

Each summer Barrenger met with the Chairman of Carnation to review the operating results and the budget for the next year. In the summer of 1973 Barrenger was able to point to a £1.2 million bottom line, and the Chairman had complimented him on 'running a tight ship' (see Exhibit 1 for financial data on Carnation UK).

In early 1974 Barrenger retired and Merry became Managing Director of Carnation UK.

Coffee-mate in the UK

Coffee-mate was first formulated and introduced in the United States in 1962. Powdered creamer sales had grown at a high rate in the US, and Coffee-mate had an 18% penetration of the coffee-whitening market. In order to achieve such a high penetration, Carnation USA had invested heavily in advertising and promotion. Several competitors, including private brands, had later entered the market, but Coffee-mate had retained brand leadership with nearly half the market.

Coffee-mate had been formulated for use in American-type ground, percolated coffee. Coffee-mate was a totally non-dairy product, basically a blend of corn syrup and vegetable fats premixed in liquid form and sprayed against an updraft of hot air to remove the moisture. The finished product, a white powder, was packaged in an amber jar designed for especially long shelf life. Prior to the introduction of Coffee-mate, all coffee creamers were powdered cream and tended to go rancid after a time.

Carnation believed that Coffee-mate possessed several characteristics which were of interest to a consumer. Coffee-mate was highly soluble and produced a creamier cup of coffee than coffee made with milk. It possessed only eleven calories per level teaspoon, or half the calories of milk needed to whiten coffee. On an average-serving basis, Coffee-mate cost less than milk, and, unlike milk, it did not chill coffee. Furthermore, Coffee-mate offered conveniences in use and storage. Even an open jar would stay fresh for a long time.

1   Coffee-mate was not suitable for whitening tea. In 1974 only 4% of Coffee-mate purchasers in the UK used it to whiten tea.

The average Briton was not a heavy coffee drinker. Unlike the US, the UK consumed more tea than coffee.[1] The British coffee drinker defined a really good cup of coffee as being ground coffee made with cream. This kind of coffee, however, was drunk mainly at restaurants. Instant coffee, on the other hand, was purchased by 95% of households in the UK. Although cream was recognised as the best whitener, only 2% of coffee in the UK was whitened with cream. Milk was used in 83% of the coffee, evaporated milk in 3%, and 12% of the coffee was drunk black.

In many cases instant coffee was simply added to hot milk to produce coffee-flavoured milk. Fresh milk was readily available in most UK homes, 70% of which received home deliveries, and milk prices were heavily subsidised by the British government.

Test Market: 1965—69

In late 1965, Carnation UK put Coffee-mate (three and six ounce sizes) into test market. The product was imported from the US and marketed in the same package used in the American market. The Midlands, with approximately 15% of the UK population, was chosen as the test area. The Midlands was considered demographically representative of the UK, i.e. it was not the conservative north nor the progressive south. On the surface, the Midlands looked like the average area for coffee consumption.

Although the sales force achieved a 70% distribution of Coffee-mate in the Midlands area, the test market floundered. Carnation UK attributed the poor test results to several factors (see Exhibit 2 for a sales history of Coffee-mate). One was the unquantifiable differences in coffee-drinking habits in the Midlands. The Midlands was the home of sterilised milk, and the people there showed a preference for strong chicory-flavoured coffee. Therefore, Midlander tastes in coffee and milk (whitener) were not truly representative of the UK.

With hindsight, Coffee-mate's price at the time of introduction was seen as being too high. It was introduced to the test market at 22.5p for the 6-ounce size and 12.5p for the 3-ounce size. Carnation UK concluded that the high price gave

Exhibit 2   *Five-Year Sales History of Non-Dairy Coffee Creamers (Cases)*

	1968	1969	1970	1971	Fiscal years 1972	1973	1974
12/3 oz							
Carnation	20,400	47,000	119,348	107,414	158,340	150,000	140,000
Compliment						28,000	76,000
12/6oz							
Carnation	19,300	58,000	220,526	271,934	406,640	430,000	520,000
Compliment					5,790	33,200	124,000
12/11oz							
Carnation	—	—	21,384	74,746	158,406	216,000	290,000
6/2lb							
Carnation	—	—	—	29,686	79,587	100,000	125,000
1000/3 g & 24/ 1 lb							
Carnation	—	5,205	9,463	7,380	2,760	8,000	18,000

Source: Company records

Coffee-mate a premium, luxury-product image. The price was subsequently dropped to 21.5p (6-ounce) and 12.0p (3-ounce) in 1967.

Table 1   Test Market Gross Sales for Coffee-mate

	1965	1966	1967	1968	1969
Sales by weight ('000s kilos)	22	57	49	60	166
Sales by value (£)	23,800	63,400	52,700	56,200	151,300

Also, at the same time that Coffee-mate went into test market, Cadbury's, a large UK foods firm, launched nationally a non-fat instant dry milk 'Marvel'. As a secondary point in its advertising, Marvel presented itself as a coffee whitener. Instant milk was actually a poor product for whitening. It dissolved slowly and merely whitened without adding flavour. Carnation, however, believed that there was a certain amount of confusion in the mind of the consumer between the two products. Marvel, selling at half the price of Coffee-mate, could tend to attract the purchaser who wanted a powdered whitener for convenience alone. Carnation UK believed, however, that some consumers were beginning to trade up from Marvel to Coffee-mate.

National Launch: 1969   In late 1969 Carnation UK decided to launch Coffee-mate nationally. Sales had been climbing since the price readjustment in 1967, and Carnation had begun to detect a shift towards purchases of the larger-size jar (see Exhibits 2 and 3 for sales and price history of Coffee-mate). At the beginning of the test market, 70% of Coffee-mate sales were in the three-ounce size. By 1967, only 50% of sales were in this size. Carnation UK believed that a trend toward volume usage had definitely emerged. The company had also begun to receive sporadic requests for Coffee-mate outside the test-market area. In late 1968 Coffee-mate was placed in selected areas outside the Midlands. Despite a lack of any sales support in the outside areas, sales did occur. Furthermore, during the test market Carnation UK had been importing Coffee-mate from the US. Margins had been low due to transport costs

2. In the years 1970—73 Coffee-mate's advertising budget remained at a relatively constant £250,000, despite increasing prices for advertising time and space. Preference was given to television advertising.

and import duties. Margins on Coffee-mate would increase dramatically when Carnation's own plant came on stream in 1971.

Carnation UK supported its national launch of Coffee-mate with television advertising in the spring (£125,000) and a magazine follow-up (£75,000).[2] Coffee-mate's primary advertising claim was its superiority over milk in taste and texture: 'Coffee-mate makes every cup of coffee taste like coffee made with cream.' As a secondary point, the advertisements stressed Coffee-mate's convenience.

At the time of national launch, Carnation UK projected Coffee-mate sales at 350,000 equivalent three-ounce cases for the first year. At this volume Coffee-mate would break even during the year. The first year resulted in nearly twice the projected sales, 660,000 cases, and a profit of £42,000.

Development years: 1970—74

During 1970 sales of Coffee-mate continued to grow and an 11-ounce jar was introduced late in the year. Also, Carnation UK introduced a two-pound catering pack and soon captured half of the commercial market. The commercial market was much more price intensive than the grocery market, and until 1972 Coffee-mate's competition in this area was from powdered milk.

In December 1971 Carnation UK's new Coffee-mate factory at Dumfries came on line. The factory, which cost £1,500,000, had a three-shift capacity of 19 million pounds a year. The percentage gross margins on Coffee-mate rose dramatically from 38% to 48%.

In 1972 Cadbury's put their own non-dairy coffee creamer into test market in the London area. Cadbury's was one of the largest British foods companies. Cadbury's produced a wide product line including tea, chocolate, cakes, etc. and had a sales force six times that of Carnation (600 salesmen versus 100 at Carnation). Unlike Carnation UK, Cadbury's made direct deliveries to the larger stores.

Cadbury's new coffee creamer, 'Compliment', was packaged and advertised similarly to Coffee-mate, with the exception that the Cadbury name was more prominent on the Compliment jar than Carnation's was on the Coffee-mate jar. Compliment was produced by an agglomerated process which formed the product into large granules and caused the product density to be lower than powdered form. Because of the lower product density, two teaspoons of Compliment were needed to achieve the same whitening effect as one teaspoon of Coffee-mate. A three-

Exhibit 3 *Development of Consumer Prices for Coffee-mate and Competing Products, 1968—74*

	Size	1968	1969	1970	1971	1972	1973	1974
Consumer Price for Coffee-mate (local currency)	3oz	12p	12p	11.4p	11.4p	11.5p	11.4p	12p
	6oz	21½p	21½p	18.7p	18.7p	19.2p	19.1p	21.5p
	11oz	—	—	—	30p	31.2p	31.3p	35.0p
Consumer Price for Cadbury's Compliment	3oz					12.0p	11.7p	11.5p
	6oz					21.0p	20.2p	20.5p
Consumer Price for Tesco 'Coffee White' (private label)							16.5p	18.0p
Price Changes and Dates for Coffee-mate	3oz	Reduced 0.8	—	—	Decimal- isation			Price Rise
	6oz	Reduced 2.8 1/1/68	—	—	2/15/71			3/1/74

Source: Company records

ounce jar of Compliment, however, looked bigger than a three-ounce jar of Coffee-mate.

Compliment was introduced into the London test market in three and six ounce jars at a price higher than Coffee-mate. The local television advertising support given the product was estimated at a national equivalent of £350,000. Cadbury's stated objective was to double the market for non-dairy coffee creamers and to achieve for themselves a 50% share of the market. Carnation UK increased television expenditure in the London area during the time of Compliment's test market and put samples of Coffee-mate into two national magazines.[3]

After ten months of test market, Compliment had only gained 10.5% of the London market. Compliment was then launched nationally at a price parity with Carnation.[4]

During 1973 Carnation UK held four group discussions with London-area housewives to determine their attitudes toward non-dairy coffee creamers. Two groups were users of non-dairy creamers and two were non-users

Of the non-users, the majority claimed to drink more tea than coffee. In fact, many did not consider themselves to be 'proper' coffee drinkers. Non-users considered instant coffee as a convenient hot drink, one you would drink when you did not want to dirty the teapot. Instant coffee was purchased by price, not quality. Non-users considered creamers like Coffee-mate and Compliment to be expensive, although there seemed to be no real awareness of the product's price. Milk, on the other hand, was not expensive, because 'you always had it in the house anyway.' This group made very little distinction between powdered creamers and powdered skim milk and perceived Coffee-mate as being a high-quality skim-milk product. A few who had tried powdered creamers had found them greasy, not creamy, and complained of a grease slick floating on top of the coffee.

The users, on the other hand, claimed to drink more coffee than tea and were much more concerned with the quality of their coffee. Users' main reason for buying a creamer was the product's taste and flavour, and they made a firm distinction between creamers and powdered milk. Users saw other product benefits as being convenience, saving milk, and not cooling coffee. Creamers were generally seen as not being expensive, the relative cost of cream often being quoted. Most users, however, used two teaspoons of Coffee-mate (the label said one), claiming that this produced a better colour. Coffee-mate was preferred over Compliment, which was perceived as being more expensive. Although Carnation UK discovered a certain amount of brand loyalty to Coffee-mate, few people could tell the difference between Coffee-mate and Compliment in a blind test.

Carnation UK estimated that in 1974 Coffee-mate was bought by 7% of UK households and accounted for 3% of whitened coffee in the UK. Compliment was estimated as having only about 2% penetration of households.

At the moment, Coffee-mate offered the grocer certain advantages over Compliment. It was the brand leader by a large margin, and it required a smaller space investment than did Compliment.[5] Cadbury's was anxious to improve the distribution of its product, however, and might be expected in increase promotional efforts. Cadbury's was also introducing a nine-ounce jar of Compliment, which looked bigger than the eleven-ounce Coffee-mate. Cadbury's had asked the British Price Commission to allow a 43p price on the new size.

Carnation UK was currently considering production of a one-pound bag or box of Coffee-mate to sell through retail outlets. The company was already producing a one-pound bag for sale to commercial users, but believed that a box would be more attractive to retailers and guarantee less breakage and waste. The cost of putting Coffee-mate into a box was little more than putting it into a bag. The company's production facilities, however, could not be adapted for box-making until eight months to a year. Carnation was tentatively thinking of retailing the box at 65p — assuming that the prices on the other jars would be raised in accordance with increased costs. At a price of 65p, percentage gross margin on the box would be around 53%.[6] Carnation UK could employ an outside agent to begin producing one-pound boxes immediately. Percentage gross margin, however, would be reduced to 50%.

Other Product Lines
Carnation Evaporated Milk

During the years of Coffee-mate's development the market for Carnation UK's traditional product, evaporated milk, had begun to decline at three to four percent a year. In 1974 the market declined 7.3%, although the Carnation brand declined only 3.1% (see Exhibit 4 for a profitability history of the Carnation UK product line). The margins were also decreasing on the domestic sales as table 2 shows:

Table 2   Net Margins of Domestic Evaporated Milk, Fiscal Year 1968—74

Year	F68	F69	F70	F71	F72	F73	F74
Net Margins	27.9%	28.7%	26.3%	26.5%	25.4%	23%	18.6%

One of the reasons for the decline in margins was the price control on milk which the UK had retained since the last World War. The decline in sales, however, was chiefly attributed to changes in consumer tastes. The steady users of evaporated milk had been introduced to it during the war, and this group had begun to die off. Despite the decline of the total market, Carnation retained a 38% share of market by volume, the highest in the industry.

Evaporated milk in the UK was chiefly used as topping on tinned fruit. In the latter half of the sixties, Carnation UK began a campaign to encourage the use of evaporated milk in cooking. (This idea had been successful in the US.) During the late sixties and early seventies Carnation UK spent £300,000 per year promoting different recipes. Although the commercials were rated as being very memorable, the recipes themselves, such as 'crêpes suzette', were considered by many consumers to be 'too high class.' Carnation UK believed the campaign was successful, however, since a recent survey placed recipe usage of Carnation Milk at 30% of total usage.

During the 1970s, however, the ratio of advertising to promotion of Carnation Milk had fallen. In 1970 Carnation spent £370,000 on advertising and £48,000 on promotion; and £203,000 on advertising and £186,000 on promotion in 1974. Carnation was planning to further cut advertising by 50% in the fiscal year 1975 in order to free funds for promotion.

The evaporated milk industry in the UK was in a state of over-capacity, and Carnation was currently exporting 40% of its own production in order to keep the brand profitable. Carnation UK's major export market was the West Indies, where evaporated milk was primarily used for feeding babies. Carnation International

Exhibit 4   *Sales and Profits by Products, Fiscal Years 1969/70 — 1973/74*

	1969/70		1970/71		1971/72		1972/73		1973/74	
Total Net Sales ($)	17,203,000		19,125,000		26,010,000*		27,980,000*		39,625,000*	
Total Net Profits After Taxes	1,123,000		985,000		1,565,000		1,518,000		1,708,000	
Major Product Lines	% total net sales	% total operating profit	% total net sales	% total operating profit	% total net sales	% total operating profit	% total net sales	% total operating profit	% total net sales	% total operating profit
Evaporated Milk	88.4	92.6	80.5	122.8	74.6	85.7	72.6	80.9	58.4	87.7
Coffee-Mate	8.0	3.6	10.8	7.3	13.5	19.7	14.1	27.2	13.1	47.9
Go-Cat	0.8	(0.6)	4.5	(39.3)	7.1	(11.3)	7.9	(6.0)	14.2	(24.2)
Other	2.8	4.4	4.2	9.2	4.8	5.9	4.0	5.9	6.9	20.0
Dog Food	—	—	—	—	—	—	1.4	(8.0)	7.4	(31.4)

* Estimated exchange average £1 = $2.53 fiscal 1971/72
£1 = $2.40 fiscal 1972/73
£1 = $2.45 fiscal 1973/74

Source: Company records

decided which areas of the world subsidiaries would receive as export markets. The decisions were made on the basis of location, manufacturing capacity, and the subsidiaries' past history of handling the product.

Go-Cat   In October 1970 Carnation launched nationally its third major product, Go-Cat. Merry had reservations about introducing the product. Carnation International, however, had decided to push a world-wide product line of pet foods, and Go-Cat was currently performing well in other European markets. Go-Cat , a dry cat food, came in three flavours and provided a cat with complete nutrition. It had the further benefit of staying fresh in a bowl, allowing a cat to eat whenever it liked. As in the case of Coffee-mate, Carnation UK had arranged to import the product from the US during its early stages.

In the UK 18% of the households owned cats, whereas 25% owned dogs. The pet food market was £80 million (1970 retail prices). Of this, £25 million was in cat-food sales. Since 1968 unit sales had been growing at 10% a year. About 50% of all cat-food sales was divided among three major all-meat brands, while the other sales were in brands which included cereal additives. At the time Carnation UK introduced Go-Cat, there was one other dry cat food on the market.

Before putting Go-Cat into the test market , Carnation UK had tried it in a home placement test similar to ones that had been done by other European subsidiaries. The UK test achieved scores higher than any others in Europe. (Go-Cat was already selling successfully in Denmark where home-placement scores were lower.) In 1968 Go-Cat entered test market and during the first year sold 55,000 cases — 10% above target. After one year in test market, a Carnation survey showed that 70% of potential consumers were aware of Go-Cat, 30% had purchased it at least once, and 18% were currently using it.

Although Go-Cat's share of the dry cat food market was only 8% in 1971, it increased substantially thereafter. (See table 3.)

Table 3   Sales of Dry Cat Food in the UK

	1972		1973		1974	
	(£'000)	(%)	(£'000)	(%)	(£'000)	(%)
Go-Cat	1155	35	2200	49	3700	53
Felix	924	25	1100	24	1700	24
Munchies	627	19	500	11	900	13
Purina	594	18	700	16	700	10
TOTAL	3300	100	4500	100	7000	100

There remained, however, a certain amount of consumer rejection of the idea of dry cat food, and, at best, dry cat food had only reached 11% of the total cat food market — as opposed to 20% in the US. Despite hefty trade deals in 1973, Go-Cat had only acquired a 40—50% distribution.

In late 1973 Carnation UK was informed that they would soon be unable to continue to import Go-Cat from the United States. The US plant had reached capacity and was only able to supply its own domestic market. Although Carnation UK was building its own cat-food factory (at a cost of £3 million), this factory would not come on stream until late 1975. The Go-Cat factory in France, however, would be able to add another packing line to handle the UK demand.[7] This packing line could be in operation within six months.

Carnation UK agreed to pay the French subsidiary for the new cooker which cost £300,000. French law, however, would not allow Carnation UK to make a direct capital investment in France. The payment therefore had to be made through transfer pricing. Due to tax on business profits, this, in effect, raised the price of the cooker to £600,000. The French subsidiary, furthermore, requested that the payment be completed over a single year.

At the same time, sales of Go-Cat in the UK had flattened and began to decline

7. The French plant was currently supplying the French and German markets.

due to several competitive changes. During fiscal 1975 two new competitors in dry cat food had entered the market, each spending twice as much on advertising their product as Carnation on Go-Cat. One competitor which was showing particularly strong growth was a product of Pedigree Pet Foods, the largest pet-food company in Europe and holder of 65% of the pet-food market in the UK. Also in 1974 three major companies launched semi-moist cat food products, supporting them with heavy promotion. In March 1974 Carnation UK had increased the price of Go-Cat, putting it at a slight premium compared with its competitors. The competition took this as an opportunity and began heavy trade promotion. Carnation UK believed, however, that its competitors would soon follow their example and raise their prices.

Go-Dog   In August 1974 Carnation UK began the national launch of Go-Dog, the second dry dog food on the UK market. Purina was already selling a similar product to retailers and direct to kennels and breeders.

Go-Dog had been in test market for the past eight months and had encountered more resistance than had Go-Cat. The test market covered the London, Anglia and Southern TV districts — an estimated 30% of the potential UK food market. Carnation UK believed that the results of the test revealed that the consumer was indifferent to the product. While customers cited convenience as an advantage of dry food, 32% of trial users surveyed by Carnation UK replied that their dogs liked the product, while 35% replied their dogs disliked it.

The national launch itself fell short of sales expectations. Carnation UK was not able to achieve high distribution for the new product and concluded that dry food lacked credibility with the trade.

Pedigree had recently followed Carnation UK in introducing a dry dog food called 'Loyal'. It appeared likely that two other brands might enter the market as well.

Carnation believed that dog owners were not yet convinced that dry dog food should be fed regularly to their dogs. Although Go-Dog by itself provided a fully balanced meal, there appeared to be confusion in the mind of the consumers between Go-Dog and 'mixers', cereal biscuits which were added to tinned food. The mixers provided roughage without providing any nutrition. Although Go-Dog was cheaper than tinned food, consumers often compared it with mixers, noting that it was much more expensive.

A recent survey revealed that only 20% of potential consumers of Go-Dog had ever tried it, and of those, 45% had bought only one pack.

Pet Accessories   A new line of pet accessories was also launched nationally in 1974. Carnation International had acquired two pet accessory plants in Denmark and Italy during 1972—73. The plants, two of the largest in Europe, had been bought at a relatively high price and, consequently, Carnation UK was buying the accessories at what Merry considered a high transfer price. The other European subsidiaries were already selling pet accessories and Carnation International wished to expand sales to England, where the market was expanding at about 20% a year. Merry agreed, but restricted distribution to 200 grocery stores, an estimated 10% of the possible grocery outlets for these products.[8] He was attempting to capture only 1% of the almost £30 million market in fiscal year 1975.

One reason why Merry resisted entering quickly into the pet accessory market was the strong competition Carnation would face. A subsidiary of Pedigree Pet Foods, Thomas' Limited, dominated the pet accessory market in the UK with over 75% share of the market, and only very small operations competed against it. A subsidiary of Shell Petroleum Company had entered the market and was rumoured to be pulling out. On the other hand, Hartz, the largest pet accessory company in the United States, had announced that they would soon enter the UK.

8. Approximately 25% of total pet accessory sales (by value) were made in grocery outlets. The other 75% were made in pet shops or related outlets.

Slender Carnation UK was currently planning a national launch of 'Slender' for February 1975. Slender was a powdered diet food which when mixed with milk, produced a low-calorie, nutritious, light meal. Slender had already become a successful product in the United States. Slender was also a high-margin product — over 40% gross margin despite import duties — and Carnation UK believed that it would not be a drain on company resources.

The total UK market for slimming aids and calorie-controlled foods was expanding at a per annum real growth rate of 10%. The current market at retail sales was £52 million. Carnation UK believed that the potential for the market was much greater, noting that 50% of British women were overweight, but only 9.1% had ever used a slimming product. The main channel for slimming products was the chemist. (Chemists accounted for 75% of the meal-replacement market.) The media support for slimming products was relatively high, about 13% of sales.

Slimming products which were intended as meal replacements accounted for £8 million in retail sales. According to a Nielsen audit, the meal replacement sector was the fastest growing sector of the market, about 11% per year by volume and 17% by value. Adverse advertising from consumer groups, however, had caused the market to decline in 1974.

The meal replacement market could be divided into three product groups: 75% of sales were biscuits, 10% were chocolate bars, and 15% were powdered mixes (mainly soups). Two-thirds of the total meal-replacement market was held by one company, Pfizer, which was the first to introduce slimming biscuits in 1961.

Since 80% of the purchasers of slimming products were women and 62% of these were between the ages of 15 and 44, Carnation UK tested Slender in a three-week home placement test involving 199 housewives who had attempted to slim or control their weight within the last year. The housewives were, on the whole, favourably impressed by Slender, especially as a meal substitute once a day. There also appeared to be little resistance to price. Some participants, however, considered drinking a meal to be 'not normal'.

Carnation UK planned to sell Slender through chemists. They already had a six-man medical salesforce which had sold evaporated milk and pet foods to the larger chains.[9] Since Slender was expected to be a seasonal product, selling more in the traditional slimming months of the summer, Carnation UK was anxious to establish distribution early. They had allotted £215,000 for advertising during the February launch. Two-thirds of this amount was budgeted for television, the other third for magazines.

9. One large chain in the UK accounted for 50% of retail sales. Five other cooperatives accounted for another 40%.

The Pricing Decision As Merry pondered the question of raising Coffee-mate's price, several issues came to mind. First, he had to decide how high to raise the price. He did not have to take the full 30% allowed by the Price Commission. Although costs per ounce for manufacturing Coffee-mate had risen dramatically, Merry wondered how long costs would remain at their current 'high'. Commodity prices in the past had traditionally peaked, then fallen. In the past few years, however, commodity prices had steadily increased and in some cases dramatically increased. It had become harder

Table 4 Average Gross Margin: Coffee-mate (1974)

	Per kilo[1]	%
Net Sales[2]	£0.84	
Cost of Sales	£0.44[3]	
Gross Margin[4]	£0.40	47.6

1. Kilos sold had increased 34% in 1974 over 1973; 22% in 1973 over 1972; 75% in 1972 over 1971; and 58% in 1971 over 1970.
2. Sales to trade. Trade mark-up was approximately 24%.
3. Current cost of sales had increased to £0.52.
4. Margin before marketing costs.

to predict what an average price over a few years would be. If Merry did not take the full 30% increase immediately and the price for vegetable fats fell, the Price Commission would not allow him to take the same increase later. Merry was also aware that he had not taken the full price increases allowed by earlier decisions. (See table 4 for gross margin calculation.)

Cadbury's had filed for a similar price increase on its current sizes of Compliment and for a price of 43p on its new 9-ounce size. Cadbury's was applying for increases on its complete milk line as well, and Merry suspected that the Price Commission would take a close look at Cadbury's request.

Merry could also spread the 30% increase in various proportions over the three sizes of Coffee-mate. The purpose of the 30% increase was to allow Carnation to maintain its pence-per-ounce margin on the product. Carnation was simply required not to exceed a 30% price increase on an equivalent ounce basis based on its present sales distribution over the three retail sizes. Merry believed, however, that the only size with enough volume to matter was the 11-ounce size.[10]

Although Coffee-mate had built up a certain brand loyalty among consumers, Merry wondered about its price sensitivity. Law required that Carnation wait 28 days after establishing new prices before offering 'pence-off' promotions. Coffee-mate's 11-ounce size and Compliment's 6-ounce size were often promoted in such a way. Prolonged promotions were expensive, since they required the company to guarantee the retailer's margin at the list price.

Merry believed, on the other hand, that Carnation UK could not sustain the decreased margins on Coffee-mate while continuing to support its other newly-launched products. Also, Carnation International was very anxious about the decreased margin, which was now well below the margins for Coffee-mate in the US. Merry's predecessors had always presented a favourable 'bottom-line' at the annual review, and Merry suspected that Carnation International had come to expect increased profits each year.

10. Carnation UK could also produce a 12-ounce size to sell at the same price as the 11-ounce size for a reduction in gross margin of 1%.

This case was prepared by Robert Mills and Michael Thorpe under the direction of Kenneth Simmonds. © London Business School, 1977.

CASE A17
Waterpics

On January 3rd 1977 Ken Barkworth returned to his office, well pleased with prospects following recent developments in his business. He was in a very good frame of mind as he welcomed the two consultants he had employed to advise him how to develop his company and market the new product, Waterpics.

"Morning, Jim. Morning, Peter," said Ken. "Well, I've some more news for you. After the big order from Japan, we've just received another order for 20,000 Waterpics from our new Taiwan agent, and I've managed to get the Greene Group to offer £22,500 for 65% of Barprint's equity. This means that my brothers wouldn't be breathing down my neck any more to get their money back; Greene's would buy out both of them for cash (see Exhibit 1). Such a deal can take a lot of worry off my shoulders, as it would remove my obligation to my family. Of course, I'm grateful for their help in the early seventies, when they each dipped in £6000 for shares. It's just a pity that they were unable to provide more at the time when I needed money to get Waterpics off the ground. Still, everything seems to be working out fine. Sales prospects now look good, and this year I'm aiming for a quarter million at least. I still remain as Managing Director of Barprint and have 30% of the equity, but there'll be no cash flow worries to divert me from the development of the Waterpic product. The Greene Group, which is a publicly quoted printing company (see Exhibit 2), see me as strengthening their product range, developing the group's marketing organisation and rapidly expanding turnover through Waterpics. Eventually I have the chance of becoming their Group Marketing Director, but I have a free hand here and our relationship has not changed. I can't miss this opportunity, even though I have other options, including gearing up to buy out my brothers."

Jim and Peter looked at each other, but said nothing. They wondered if Ken really was doing the right thing, given an optimistic plan that Drummers Limited had recently drawn up for marketing Waterpics in a big way.

Barprint Limited

Barprint Ltd was the firm Mr Barkworth had bought with his two brothers for £3000 in 1967. He planned to undertake contract printing for firms in the Oxfordshire

Exhibit 1 *Barprint Ltd 1977 Family Tree*

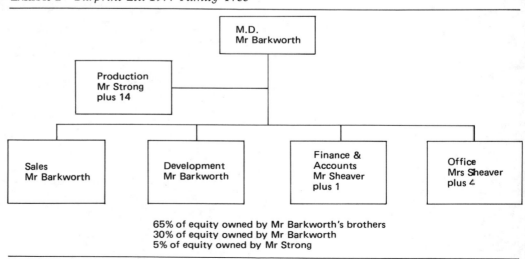

65% of equity owned by Mr Barkworth's brothers
30% of equity owned by Mr Barkworth
5% of equity owned by Mr Strong

Exhibit 2 *Greene Group Data*

Financial Data			1975 (£'000s)	1976 (£'000s)
Share Capital (1,300,000 at 20p)			266	266
Share Premium			10	10
Reserves			45	37
Minority Interests			47	47
Deferred Tax & Tax Equalisation			85	92
			453	452
	Stock	97		89
	Debtors	460		460
	Cash	14		3
	Overdraft	(165)		(144)
	Creditors	(372)		(382)
	Dividends	(16)		(16)
Net Current Assets			18	10
Property			83	78
Plant			291	290
Goodwill			61	74
			453	452

Stock Data	1975 (£000s)	1976 (£000s)
Turnover	1,753	1,955
Net trading profit before tax	66	38
Dividends	16	16
EPS (including extraordinary items)	1.6p	2.2p
Share Price high	29p	16p
low	13p	10p

area, using his own local sales experience and industry knowledge, which had been gained over twenty years spent with Stevenson's, a leading printing firm. He also planned to switch the company from Letterpress printing over to the more modern Litho techniques. And everything did work out as he hoped. In 1968 he persuaded Alan Strong, an old colleague from Stevenson's and a man he knew he could rely on, to join him and support the production side of the business. They did well together and by 1970 turnover exceeded £70,000, yielding a £10,000 profit.

This rapid growth introduced new problems. Barprint soon needed larger premises, but the only sites on the market required a large increase in sales to support the extra overhead. In 1970 two salesmen from Stevenson's, Bill Rickey and Stuart Bridges, approached Mr Barkworth, saying that they could obtain £150,000 print contracts on an annual basis. As this amount of new business could make a move possible, Mr Barkworth jumped at the chance and an additional company, Barprint Sales Ltd, was formed. Rickey and Bridges became directors, taking a 12% commission on all sales they generated for this company. As Exhibits 3 and 4 show, turnover improved dramatically during that year.

The 1972 sales target was over £200,000 now that Rickey and Bridges had joined. Mr Barkworth therefore invested in more production equipment, signing a hire purchase contract for £20,000 on two Heidelberg presses. In addition, he set up an in-house photographic processing department as part of a plan to develop the creative side of the business.

By July 1972 Ken Barkworth realised that something was drastically wrong. Sales were lower than in 1971. As Ken said, "My suspicions were further aroused when Lucy, a secretary, burst into tears in the office. She bawled, 'I've just been fired!' Apparently, Bridges had been involved with Lucy during a difficult period in his marriage, but was now removing her from the scene. Clearly this was an action

Exhibit 3 *Barprint Limited: Sales, Profit and Growth History*

Year	Sales £'000s	Post Tax Profit/(Loss) £'000s	Production Staff	Admin. Staff
1967	10.4	0	n/a	n/a
1968	21.3	(4.3)	n/a	n/a
1969	36.0	0	n/a	n/a
1970	71.1	9.2	n/a	n/a
1971	128.2	14.4	32	15
1972	110.1	(21.4)	21	11
1973	145.4	3.8	22	11
1974	199.8	18.6	20	11
1975	200.1	(7.1)	17	12
1976	223.5	4.9	18	11

Exhibit 4 *Barprint Ltd. : Financial Data (£'000s)*

	1971	1972	1973	1974	1975	1976
Share Capital	1.2	1.2	18.0	18.0	18.0	18.0
Revenue Reserves	4.7	(15.0)	(10.9)	3.2	(3.7)	1.1
Shareholders' Funds	5.9	(13.8)	7.1	21.2	14.3	19.1
Stock and WIP	10.0	4.7	18.6	23.6	20.3	42.9
Debtors	29.9	16.8	32.3	41.9	50.6	39.8
Cash	0.6	0.1	—	0.1	0.1	0.2
Current Assets	40.5	21.6	50.9	65.6	71.0	82.9
less						
Creditors & HP accounts	28.7	27.4	58.0	61.0	76.4	65.2
Overdraft (secured)	8.6	14.4	28.3	28.5	33.5	30.0
Directors' Loan	7.6	10.4	—	0.5	0.5	1.1
Net Current Assets	(4.4)	(30.6)	(35.4)	(24.4)	(39.4)	(13.4)
Deferred Taxation	—	—	—	(5.7)	(.9)	(4.9)
Development Costs	—	—	—	—	5.6	5.9
Fixed Assets	10.3	16.8	42.5	51.3	49.0	31.5
Net Assets	5.9	(13.8)	7.1	21.2	14.3	19.1
Sales	128.2	110.1	145.4	199.8	200.2	223.5
Purchases	38.1	37.6	55.2	63.6	81.7	87.4
Wages	27.1	33.6	31.2	40.8	39.4	39.1
Sundry	3.0	6.2	5.4	6.9	6.4	5.6
Gross Trading Profit	60.0	32.7	53.6	88.5	72.7	91.4
Overhead	45.6	54.2	49.5	68.0	78.8	87.5
Development Cost	—	—	—	0.6	5.6	5.9
Net Trading Result	14.4	(21.5)	4.1	19.9	(11.7)	(2.0)

that could not be endorsed on these grounds. Further investigation showed that this was not the only area where Bridges, and Rickey too, were displaying a lack of discretion.

"Sales were down but their expense claims had doubled and I could not see how reduced commission earnings were paying for their new 3-litre BMW's. I soon learned, through an old friend, that my two Sales Directors were placing orders elsewhere for 14% commission. Naturally, this resulted in a parting of the ways and was for me a salutary lesson in judgement. You mustn't get too dependent on people you don't really know; otherwise one stroke of bad luck can finish you."

With the dismissal of Rickey and Bridges, Barprint Ltd was in serious difficulty because this happened only 6 months after moving into the new factory and taking on all its extra fixed costs. With no prospect of meeting the sales target, drastic cost reductions were necessary. Thirty percent of the production and administration staff were laid off, the in-house photographic facility abandoned, and Strong and Barkworth themselves acted as both operators by night and administrators during the day. Although the 1972 loss was over £20,000, post-July costs were contained, and sheer hard work produced a break-even over the last 3 months that gave Mr Barkworth the confidence to continue, against the advice of his accountants. His two brothers helped; each bought 5850 £1 shares (at par) to improve the capital position.

Over the next two years performance gradually improved, but the 1975 economic recession hit the printing trade severely. Despite maintained turnover, cost inflation removed Barprint's profit and the squeeze on margins as local firms competed for the available business made for poor long-term prospects. As Ken observed, "You're damn lucky nowadays if you make even one third Gross Profit in the contract print business."

Development of Waterpics

Ken Barkworth had always worried about the vulnerability of printing to economic fluctuations. As a service trade, it was particularly susceptible to firms cutting back on overheads during hard times. Moreover, as Ken said, "I wanted a product of my own that I could sell to industry rather than be at the beck and call of local firms — I didn't want my company to remain bespoke printers."

As is usual in such situations, getting the product idea proved the most difficult problem. Mr Barkworth wanted to move out of contract printing, but could not see how — until he met an old Swiss friend, Bernard Schropp.

The chance stemmed from a breakthrough in the mid-sixties, when Bernard Schropp invented a multi-colour printing machine. In the old days, multi-colour jobs required a different print run and press for each colour. Schropp's new machine had the advantage that up to twenty-eight colours could be deposited in a single run and in hitherto unattainable thicknesses.

This new machine had not been exploited across the world. A consortium of German printing firms had recognised the threat to their own enormous investment in the old technology and so had purchased Schropp's patents. This defensive cartel successfully restricted the diffusion of the new process by preventing the sale or lease of the machines. However, through his friendship with Bernard Schropp, Mr Barkworth was aware of the technique, and by the early seventies he had formed the seeds of an idea to exploit its potential in a way which did not threaten the German companies.

Using the inventor as a go-between, he persuaded the consortium to lease him two machines over ten years for only £1500 per annum each. This was arranged on the understanding that they were not used for colour printing of business materials or any field which competed directly with the Germans. Although Mr Barkworth did not get exclusivity in the United Kingdom, there were only three machines permitted there, of which Barprint had two. Indeed, worldwide, there were only eight; and Mr Barkworth was the only man who had displayed the initiative and innovation to adapt the machines to a special purpose.

Ken Barkworth's idea was to print watercolours in a pallet form on card, and to deposit these colours to a thickness considerably greater than that possible by other printing processes. The product could then be used by children as an alternative to normal watercolour paintboxes, whereby the children were presented with a complete kit of brush, outline drawings and palletised paints at a cheap price in a convenient form. It took a year to perfect, but the idea proved technically feasible and Ken was able to announce a Waterpic range in mid-1975.

The idea of pressure-feeding watercolours through a special press was unfortunately not wholly patentable. Nevertheless, Mr Barkworth was reasonably happy about a technology lead, for other printers were too blinkered to look beyond their original markets and toy manufacturers did not have the printing expertise or flair to even consider such a product. Even so, he wanted to get the new product off the ground as soon as possible, just in case anyone was working on a similar principle.

Waterpics were basically complete painting kits in themselves. All the user provided was water, so there was no stain or mess. Each kit contained a brush (or two), up to ten paints and/or glitter and glue, plus outline drawings to colour in. These drawings ranged from simple pictures of animals, birds, fairy stories, to more complex badges, cut-out models, Christmas cards, jig-saws. In all, there were now seventeen different kits in the complete Waterpic range, although in mid-1975 he only had three, Painta Pic and two Paint'n Glitta packs (see Exhibit 5).

Since then Mr Barkworth had naturally devoted much of his time to developing the Waterpic range, as Exhibit 5 shows. He had also been thinking of other possible applications, but as yet had taken little action so that he could direct his attention to the successful launch of this new paint product. Nevertheless, he had two other applications which he was ready to exploit later.

Exhibit 5 *Waterpics Range*

Painta Pic	: 7 ranges: Kits of Birds, Animals, Footballers, etc . . .
Paint'n Glitta	: 2 ranges: Xmas cards and Greetings cards
Painta Cutout	: 5 ranges: To make Animals, Dolls, Ships, Monsters, etc . . .
Painta Play	: 5 ranges: Cutouts of Ali Baba, Snow White, etc . . .
Painta Game	: 3 ranges: Jigsaw, Horse Trial, Snakes and Ladders
Painta Palette	: 3 ranges: Palette and outline drawings
Paint'n Glitter Pics	: 3 ranges
Painta Mobile	: 3 ranges
Painta Badge	: 3 ranges
Painta Puppet	: 3 ranges
Painta Silver Jubilee	: 3 ranges
Painta House	: 3 ranges
Paint by Numbers	: 3 ranges
Painta Stencil	: 3 ranges
Paint'n Collage	: 3 ranges
Painta Gallery	: 3 ranges
Paint & Learn Books	: 3 ranges

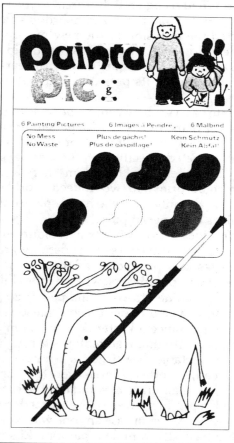
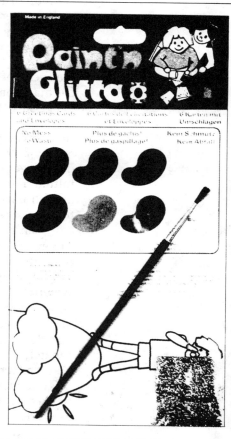

Exhibit 6 *TV Regions Marketing Information*

	Midlands	Tyne-Tees	UK
Population ('000s)	9350	2850	55,500
% 0—14 yrs.	23.5	25.5	24.0
% CDE socio-economic group	30.4	35.0	31.2
No. households ('000s)	2730	875	16,400
Persons per household	3.42	3.25	3.38
No. newspapers	23	9	130
Poster sites	10,800	4050	75,000
Cinemas	356	186	1970
No. retail establishments	97,000	28,000	690,000
of which self-service/ supermarket	3400	1150	24,000
Av. weekly household income (£)	45.54	40.54	46.16

Marketing Strategy

Ken Barkworth, who was a Fellow of the Institute of Marketing, explained the development as being primarily aimed at removing Barprint's vulnerability in bespoke printing. "Initially I was thinking of using basic Waterpic kits for the premium gift market for sales promotions. Naturally the price for products used as give-aways is low and the quality unimportant. But by the end of the development stage, I found I could offer a high-quality product, higher than required by this market, and one which could perhaps command greater profits in other areas. So my thinking changed a bit."

The Managing Director of one merchandising company approached by Mr Barkworth showed a great deal of enthusiasm for the new product. His company was Lupus Toy Kits, the children's play and pleasure subsidiary of a national confectionery manufacturer. He had his marketing services staff design a pack and ordered 10,000 simple Painta Pic Kits for a test market in the Tyne Tees TV Region. Exhibit 6 gives the details of this test area. Within two weeks, Lupus had sold out and repeat orders were soon supplied. On the basis of this success, Ken Barkworth accepted the package and price dictated by Lupus' expertise and experience as suitable for the market. He therefore implemented a basically similar product/market concept for his own launch as Waterpics in 1976.

Although he was most encouraged by the Lupus test market, Mr Barkworth also conducted some local experiments to test the consumer acceptance of Waterpics. As an active member of the local Round Table, he often became involved in voluntary work for local orphans and deprived children. Mr Barkworth offered Waterpics as gifts and the children, especially the 4—10 years age groups, were thrilled. They had never seen anything like it before. Moreover, Mrs Barkworth's friends were unanimous in their delight. As she said, "They thought it was such a cheap and original way of keeping the kids quiet on a rainy day." Ken's own doubts that the children might damage relatively fragile outline drawings were quickly dispelled when he saw them use a Waterpic kit. They soon became engrossed in the discipline of colouring within the boundaries and indeed respected the fragility of the product by treating everything most delicately.

With his own experience and the grounds for optimism from Lupus, Ken Barkworth felt he was on to a winner.

Waterpics Launch

The standard retail price was set at 25p, based on the Lupus experience. Mr Barkworth decided to produce to order and therefore set about visiting contacts in the toy trade. Barprint took stands at five major European toy fairs in early 1976 (including the Brighton Toy and Hobby Fair).

Much interest was aroused by the new product, but Mr Barkworth was surprised that the major toy wholesalers and retailers did not seem to be the major potential outlets. He recalled, "I was amazed at the interest from large retail chains like Boots and Woolworths and from the foreign import agents. Toyshops seemed less interested; I was talking mainly to chain store buyers about direct supply. Furthermore, about 80% of the enquiries came from buying houses abroad. It was then I decided that the product had a lot of international potential. So, I decided to change the packaging, look for foreign customers and at home aim at the multiple retail chains who were diversifying into the play market. It's funny, you know, I still can't see why the traditional toy trade isn't as keen as these other outlets, and it's exactly the same abroad."

Consequently, Mr Barkworth added French and German translations of the English instructions on each package. By the year end, he was pleased with the progress of orders (as shown by month in Exhibit 7). He found the German and Far East breakthrough most encouraging, although orders remained sporadic. Even so, he had no difficulty in meeting the call-off rate, as capacity was well in excess of demand.

Exhibit 7   *Waterpic Orders Billed*

Year		£	Units	Destination
1975		14000	100000	UK (Lupus)
		15000	n/a	UK premium market
1976	January			
	February	5500	50000	UK (Lupus)
	March	3000	25000	West Germany
		3000	25000	Sweden
	April	5500	50000	UK (Lupus)
	May			
	June	1000	8500	Eire
	July	5500	50000	UK (Lupus)
	August	3000	25000	Netherlands
		3000	25000	West Germany
	September	3000	25000	Belgium
		2000	17000	Hong Kong
	October	6000	50000	Australia
	November	16500	150000	UK (Lupus)
	December			

As mentioned earlier, Barprint had leased two of Schropp's multi-colour printing machines and had adapted them for watercolour work. The normal printing process was used to prepare the tri-lingual card packs and the paint deposition was the technologically critical middle stage of the production process. Watercolours were pressure fed into the Schropp press, which simultaneously injected anything up to 10 colours and glue on to the card. Three cards could be stamped xt each pressing and in one hour up to 400 pressings could be completed. An hour's drying time was necessary and then the packs went on for final processing. This involved folding, adding the paintbrush, and finally covering in cellophane. The only fixed limit on output was the maximum 1200 cards per hour realistically obtainable from each machine. Although the machines were believed to be reliable, they were the only specially adapted two in the country and standby plant was thus not available. Nevertheless, Ken Barkworth was thoroughly familiar with their technology. The capacity of the card printing section was flexible and could be varied easily to suit the needs of the Schropp machines without affecting the costings (see Exhibit 8). Final processing was more critical on capacity. Mr Barkworth felt that his 1977 staff of 14 could 'just about cope with nearly 2 million packs per annum', but that thereafter, for every 50,000 extra packs per month, an extra hand would be required in production processing. Apart from this, there were no constraints other than machinery. He could get another, but would have to purchase outright this time for nearly £20,000 (or £60,000 with an automatic feed which would save two men and halve drying time).

Exhibit 8 *1976 Waterpic Production Costs*

Basis:	Batches of 10,000 units Labour @ £2 per hour Materials @ current prices		
Series 1	Painta Pac Painta Puppet Painta Stencil Paint'n Glitter Pictures Paint'n Collage	}	*i.e.* simple paint kits. Average nett direct cost = £0.054.
Series 2	Painta Game Painta Gallery Painta Mobile Painta Badge Paint by Numbers	}	*i.e.* all advanced kits. Average nett direct cost = £0.06.
Series 3	Painta Play Paint & Cut Outs Painta Letter Paint'n Glitter Cards Painta House	}	*i.e.* all complex kits, cutouts and sets. Average nett direct cost = £0.075.

It is anticipated 1977 costs will be 11% higher.

In 1976 Ken Barkworth spent most of his time, after production and development, worrying about the cash flow and how much it would constrain him from developing Waterpics' potential. Already he had spent a lot of money on the new product development, and now he had to worry about new trade capital commitments. As he said, "I didn't know how much credit the toy trade demanded, particularly abroad. Moreover, with about 65% of product cost in labour, the Waterpic value added was good. Now I felt I would have to hold some finished goods stock and all these factors led to the need for more working capital, and that's not even including extra staff to permit expansion. The trouble was that I did not know how much we might require." Nevertheless, he still wanted to expand the range and visit more toy fairs to find new agents for exclusive contracts overseas, for Ken wanted to expand the sales vigorously and quickly.

At the beginning of the year, the Waterpics range was just Painta Pic, Paint'n Glitta, Painta Palette, Painta Game and Painta Play. Ken proudly reminded Jim and Peter of the range expansion to that shown in Exhibit 5 by December 1976. All the new product ideas came from Mr Barkworth, who received his inspiration at the Toy Fairs, from his family, or even from new agents. These sources brought eleven new ideas between January and November.

At the same time, Ken was visiting many European countries. Following the Toy Fair tour at the beginning of the year, he went to France, Germany, Italy, Scandinavia, Spain, Yugoslavia and Switzerland. He also continued to take stands at all major Toy Fairs and buyers Ken met at these Fairs were appointed as agents in eight countries: France, Germany, Finland, Sweden, Luxembourg, South Africa, Hong Kong and Australia.

Each agent was given an exclusive contract lasting one year. Mr Barkworth was particularly pleased with the Finnish agent — and was proud that he had broken into one of the highest income per capita countries in the world. However, he was also expecting great things from the Dutch agent. Although few orders had been received from the Netherlands, Mr Barkworth was often comparing him with the largest foreign orderer in Germany: "That chap Van Venken is superb, unlike Neumann at Konfields, who always keeps me in the dark. I know all about the most appropriate range and product concepts for Holland. Van Venken experiments with pricing and is particularly aggressive in his approaches to new distribution channels. I'll soon be getting a big order out of him and we'll establish ourselves there because I'm told what's going on in the market so I can respond very quickly."

A geographical breakdown of Waterpics orders is given in Exhibit 7. So far, the greatest sales in Europe had come from Germany. This was also the country with the fastest growth in disposable income.

Life in Barprint was getting very exciting. But the sales development in the UK was sporadic and the bulk of the turnover still came from Lupus. Mr Barkworth felt it was time to take more positive action in the home market by summer 1976, as he was growing impatient with Lupus, whose headquarters staff were still test marketing and had not yet gone national with Waterpics into its core 3000 outlets. Moreover, he was running down the fixed assets on the normal printing side of the business to cope with an annual turnover of about £100,000. He therefore needed to replace the lost print sales in 1977.

United Kingdom Market   Mr Barkworth felt that financial constraints prevented him from developing his own sales organisation. He nevertheless wanted to expand sales considerably, to his short-term target of two million packs in a year. Unfortunately, he was anxious regarding his ability to obtain such orders on his own and he wanted to avoid another Rickey and Bridges situation. Therefore, he set about appointing a UK national distributor.

Ken Barkworth congratulated himself on uncovering, at his first attempt, a highly desirable agent. He recalled, "One Sunday, whilst digesting the Business News, I came across an intriguing box number which was offering to market new business ideas. I wrote off, but restricted my enquiry to the Waterpics development, not my other ideas, and very quickly Mr Peter Piers, the Managing Director of Drummers Limited, sent an enthusiastic reply. We met and I was most impressed

---

Exhibit 9

---

17 November 1976

FROM: Mr Peter Piers
TO: Mr Kenneth Barkworth

RE: *Outline UK Marketing Plan for Waterpics with exclusive UK distribution by Drummers Limited*

Product Concept

Painting toys providing a changing range of pursuits for children's pleasure. Product rotation will be constant within the overall broad range limits of pictures, cutouts and plays.

Good quality and value are very important. The sale must be at a reasonable price to fit the child's and the mother's budget. The product will then have year round purchase probability; it will not be directed exclusively at the special gift market segment, as impulse buying will be important.

Packages and Price

We propose 3 Waterpic series:

Series 1:	Painta Pac
(basic units to	Painta Puppet
retail at 39p/pack)	Paint'n Stencil
	Paint'n Glitta Pictures
	Paint'n Collage
Series 2:	Painta Game
(basic units to	Painta Gallery
retail at 39p/pack)	Painta Mobile
	Painta Badge
	Paint by Numbers
Series 3:	Painta Play
(complex kits, with	Paint and Cut-Outs
2 brushes, to retail	Painta Letter
at 49p)	Paint'n Glitter Cards
	Painta House

Drummers Limited will sell nationally and place emphasis on Series 3. We will have exclusive rights in the UK and will grant normal trade terms to toy customers. Such terms are considered appropriate as they broadly match the trade margins available on similar types of product that compete for shelf space, such as children's crayon sets. Moreover, they more than match Lupus, which is the only direct competitor.

Display and Promotion

Drummers will use its national salesforce to promote Waterpics, but will initially concentrate efforts in the Midlands area. In April we have booked 20 thirty-second slots (prime time) in the Midlands TV area. The adverts will be consumer orientated, as our field force will, during March, concentrate on selling in to the trade.

For sale through retail outlets we will utilise standard metal display units from which the packs will hang. Each stand is capable of taking 300 packs and its cost of £20 will be amortised over 3 display stock orders for Series 1 & 2 packs.

Drummers Limited will prepare its own brochure covering the Waterpic range.

Distribution

Our national salesforce of ten men already covers 5000 outlets in the toy trade. We will actively canvass these. Once we have established a regular turnover pattern with these outlets (within, say, two years), we would hope to broaden our distributional coverage to other types of outlet.

Where we encounter Lupus distribution, we will not hold back from pushing Waterpics. The Drummer Waterpics have a much broader range (Lupus takes only 3 products) and we have the advantage that our higher price offers the dealer greater profit despite identical discount levels (to the toy trade).

Target Sales 1977: 1.25 million packs.

---

by Drummers' list of successes which included, in the toy market, Rolf Harris's Singing Yo-Yo. This product had been the most notable new toy launch in the 1970's, so I asked Mr Piers to develop a UK Sales Plan for Waterpics." The details of this plan are contained in Exhibit 9. Mr Barkworth continued to Jim and Peter, "I was very pleased with his plan and appointed Drummers on December 10th as sole representative for the UK for one year. It was understood that I would continue supplying Lupus' 350,000 packs over the period, at the end of which a review of the situation would take place. It was tacitly agreed that if Drummer achieved sales of 1.2 million packs by their efforts in the UK, then a longer-term contract would be forthcoming. This, of course, leaves me free to do what I really like — that is developing the Waterpic range and establishing the kits overseas. I hope you two

Exhibit 10   *1977 Export Orders*

Country	Agent	Orders (units)
Japan	Konfields	400,000
Germany	Elbfridt	400,000
Malta		7,500
S. Africa	Feldman	75,000
Benelux	Mandema	40,000
Finland	U. Marketing	40,000
Iceland	Hollkenson	1,000
Australia	Woolworths	55,000
France	Letraset	Negotiating for 100,000
Taiwan	Wellchosen Corp.	20,000
Canada		5,000
Kenya		
Nigeria		
Israel		146,500
Greece		
USA		
TOTAL		1,250,000

Exhibit 11 *Waterpics Discounts 1977*

Average discounts in the toy trade are 27.5% to wholesaler and 33.3% to retailer, with 5% normally granted for cash settlement.

Manufacturer's Selling Price (MSP) is calculated:

a) Lupus :

Retail Price	25p
less VAT @ 8%	23p
less Retailer 33.3%	15.4p
less Lupus 33.3%	10.3p*

b) Drummers (Series 1 & 2) :

Retail Price	39p
less VAT @ 8%	35.9p
less retailer's 33.3%	23.9p
less wholesaler's 27.5%	17.3p
less 5% cash	16.5p
less Drummers 33.3%	11.0p

Calculation for Drummers Series 3 is identical, though MSP is, of course, different.

c) Exports: Series 1 & 2 Manufacturer's Selling Price:

> Orders of 2500 : 16p
> Orders of 5000 : 15p
> Orders of 10000 + : 14p

> Series 3 MSP:

> Orders of 2500 : 18p
> Orders of 5000 : 17p
> Orders of 10000 + : 16p

> (1976 MSP for exports averaged 12p)

*Lupus, when agreeing 'deals' with large multiples, have been known to reduce their margin to as little as 18%. This has never affected the Barprint selling price, however.

Exhibit 12 *Selected Export Market Data*

	UK	France	Germany	USA	Japan	Netherlands	Sweden
Population ('000s)	55668	51250	61284	207049	104606	13190	8110
% 0—14	24.0	24.5	22.2	27.9	23.6	27.0	20.8
No. households ('000s)	16397	16671	21990	63374	23085	3932	2778
Persons per household	3.4	3.1	2.8	3.3	4.5	3.4	2.9
No. households with 3 or more people ('000s)	8667	8604	10504	34225	17932	2276	1386
Passenger cars per 1000 pop'n.	222	256	253	448	99	212	291
TV sets per 1000 pop'n.	293	214	272	409	219	233	310
GDP per capita (1975) £	1667	2532	2712	2856	1811	2405	3403

can help me quickly implement Drummers' ideas in the international market, although I must say I think I've done pretty well myself at the Toy Fairs so far. Look at the 1977 overseas orders!" Ken Barkworth then handed over Exhibit 10 to the consultants. Exhibits 11 and 12 show the ruling selling prices and terms for Waterpics and selected statistics in the different markets.

PART B
Market Assessment and Measurement

Assessments of the number of potential customers and their motivations and decision-making patterns are the foundations on which every marketing plan is built. Skill in seeking out information about the market, interpreting it, and piecing it together for decision making in the firm is a fundamental requirement of the marketer.

This case was prepared by Jules Goddard and Kenneth Simmonds of the London Business School.
© *Kenneth Simmonds, 1981.*

CASE B1
Hirondelle

First launched as a brand of wine in 1969, Hirondelle was an outstanding success. Sales grew from 23,000 cases in 1969 to 750,000 in 1974. A *Sunday Times* quality survey in December 1973, titled 'The Good, The Bad and the Undrinkable', placed two of the three Hirondelle styles top and the third style second, after tests on 350 cheap wines. Using a base wine from Austria, liberally laced with Rumanian and Bulgarian wines, Hedges and Butler, the wine merchant subsidiary of Bass Charrington Ltd, seemed to have hit on a perfect taste for the British palate.

Basic wine sources had to be changed from time to time for supply reasons. Indeed, the very success of Hirondelle had meant that only a short while after the *Sunday Times* verdict, Hedges and Butler were switching to Italian sources merely to keep pace with the demand. Nevertheless, with strict attention to the quality and 'finish' of the wine, a consistent Hirondelle taste had been maintained. Hedges and Butler had, in fact, shaped a new category of wine for Britain, a standard of quality brand; not *chateau* perhaps, but certainly not plonk either.

The Advertising Brief

The success of Hirondelle had been attained without any media advertising at all. But in 1976, in a reaction to a flattening sales curve, the account was placed with J Walter Thompson Company Ltd. The brief that Hedges and Butler gave JWT included the data given in Exhibits 1 to 6 and the following rationale for putting advertising muscle into the brand.

Early Success

At least four reasons can be given for Hirondelle becoming joint brand leader (with Corrida) of the table wine market without advertising support:

a) The introduction of Hirondelle coincided with the advent of grocery off-licenses and with the formation of a grocery sales force at Hedges and Butler.

b) In its early years, before it had its imitators, Hirondelle offered unique value for money.

c) The rapid growth in popularity of table wine has coincided with a rapid growth in grocery/supermarket distribution, for which Hirondelle was explicitly designed.

d) The 1973 *Sunday Times* survey provided excellent free publicity for the brand.

Why Advertise?

In common with nearly all other alcoholic drinks, the table wine market reached a peak in early 1974, since which it has declined. This recession has been a problem

Exhibit 1　*Historical Performance in a Market Perspective*

	Hirondelle Sales[1]	UK Clearances of Still Table Wines[2]		Table Wine Penetration,[3] All Adults
	Cases ('000s)	Cases ('000,000s)	Increase (%)	(%)
1968	0	7.4	22	
1969	23	7.3	−1	
1970	88	7.1	−3	
1971	164	9.4	32	33
1972	510	11.5	22	33
1973	696	16.0	40	35
1974	757	16.3	2	43
1975	678	16.0	−2	46

Source: 1. Hedges & Butler
2. Customs & Excise
3. T.G.I.

Exhibit 2　*Hirondelle User Profile*

	Hirondelle (%)	All Table Wine (%)	Heavy Users of Table Wine (3+ bottles per month) (%)	Total Population (%)
SEX				
Men	50.6	48.8	71.9	48
Women	49.4	51.2	28.1	52
SOCIAL CLASS				
AB	41.2	22.2	40.3	11
C1	32.0	30.0	33.7	23
C2	18.5	29.1	15.4	33
D	6.2	14.3	8.7	22
E	2.0	4.4	1.9	11
AGE				
15—24	24.1	19.1	21.0	19
25—34	28.4	21.6	27.9	17
35—44	17.9	16.2	17.1	15
45—54	13.8	17.9	17.3	16
55—64	10.5	14.0	10.8	15
65+	5.2	11.3	5.9	18

Exhibit 3　*Hirondelle Competitive Position*

Table-Wine Brand	Sales[1]		Awareness Levels, All Adults[2]	
	Bottles (%)	£ (%)	Spontaneous (%)	Prompted (%)
Hirondelle	4.2	4.1	5	20
Corrida	4.4	4.0	4	24
Don Cortez	3.7	2.9	3	28
Mateus Rosé	2.7	2.8	12	35
Nicolas	1.9	2.0	1	7
Charbonnier	0.9	1.2		
Baton	0.6	0.5		
All Other	81.6	82.6		

Source: 1. Nielsen Dec. 75/Jan. 76
2. N.O.P. 1976

Exhibit 4 *Table Wine Advertising Expenditure, 1975 (£)*

	TV	Press	Total
Blue Nun	—	89,300	89,300
*Corrida	101,900	300	102,200
†*Langenbach	108,600	—	108,600
Mateus	—	186,000	186,000
Goldener Oktober	—	86,700	86,700
Others	175,500	686,700	863,300
Total for Group	386,000	1,049,000	1,435,600

*London and Southern only
†Final quarter only

Source: MEAL

Exhibit 5 *Hirondelle Distribution: Percentage of Outlets Serviced*

	Total Outlets	All Off Licence	Pubs	Restaurants/ Residential	Clubs
Dec. '72	9	24	5	9	2
Dec. '73	10	25	7	9	2
Dec. '74	13	30	9	14	3
Dec. '75	12	32	7	10	3

Exhibit 6 *Off Licence Distribution and Sales*

	Total Off Licence Outlets	Grocery Total	Grocery Multiples Only	Specialist
Number	31,500	18,500	3,900	11,300
Per cent selling:[1]				
Any wine	92	90	100	98
Hirondelle	32	34	21	31
Corrida	20	21	42	21
Don Cortez	23	27	38	19
Mateus Rosé	54	43	75	74
Nicolas	15	13	38	20
Per cent of total wine sales:[2]				
All wines		30	20	
Hirondelle		64	58	

Source: 1. Stats MR Dec. '75
2. Nielsen Dec. '75/Jan. '76

for Hirondelle, but other factors also argue for advertising weight to be put behind the brand:

a) The number and quality of Hirondelle's competitors, particularly Corrida, Don Cortez and Nicolas, have improved, thus narrowing its lead as the best value-for-money table wine.

b) The major retail chains, such as Sainsbury and Marks and Spencer, are developing their own lines of table wine.

c) If, as some evidence suggests, Hirondelle's brand leadership is due more to its distribution share than to its rate of sale per outlet, then growth in the future can only come from becoming more competitive on the shelf, since its retail penetration would appear to be at a maximum.

d)   The consumer is becoming more sophisticated and requires some justification for Hirondelle's premium price over other branded wines.

e)   Corrida, its major competitor, has just begun to advertise.

Summary   Faced with this dilemma — a static market and increasing competition, especially on price — how can Hirondelle increase its share? In the past share growth has come from increased penetration which is now levelling off; thus we must go for higher sales per outlet through an improved consumer franchise.

Low awareness of Hirondelle and lack of reassurance about its quality are fundamental barriers to increased trial and loyalty. Currently Hirondelle, in common with other non-advertised brands, is not a well-recalled name.

We believe that awareness and reassurance can be improved by advertising. Furthermore, advertising can begin to differentiate Hirondelle from other cheaper products in a way that is less easily imitated than product quality or price.

The Advertising Plan   In response to this brief, JWT produced four advertisements, two of which are shown in Exhibits 7 and 8. Their rationale was as follows:

Objectives of the Advertising   In line with the client's diagnosis of Hirondelle's current problems, the aims of any advertising for the brand must be:

a)   To stimulate trial by increasing awareness of the brand name.

b)   To reinforce repeat buying of current users by reassuring them of the quality and pedigree of the brand.

c)   To differentiate the brand from other cheaper products, thereby justifying the price premium.

Advertising Target Group   ABC$_1$ wine drinkers and under 45's account for around 60% of Hirondelle usage, and potential heavy users of Hirondelle are thought to come from the same group, though generally younger.

The target group for the advertising is therefore: ABC$_1$, aged 20—45.

Advertising Approaches   In ten group discussions of twelve advertising ideas, those which have met with the most favourable reactions are those that:

a)   Clearly position the brand as a mid-market 'everyday' wine — not a plonk, nor (in any way) a fine wine; a table wine.

b)   Communicate that it is consistent and reliable, so you can be sure of what you are buying every time.

c)   Endorse the fact that it tastes good — for instance, the *Sunday Times* survey of cheap wines in 1973 voted it top.

d)   Talk in a sensible, down-to-earth way about a sensible, down-to-earth brand (avoiding references to wine lore and preciousness).

e)   Indicate that it is available as a range.

Target Responses   This leads to the following responses being sought:

a)   I will never be disappointed with Hirondelle: it is consistent *and* good (evidenced by the *Sunday Times* saying so).

b)   Hirondelle is a no-nonsense, straight-talking branded wine (not plonk, not a fine wine).

c)   It is a wine which has the tradition and history of real wine without the pretension or pomposity.

d)   It comes in red, white (dry and sweet) and rosé.

Exhibit 7

IT'S ABOUT AS LIKELY AS A DUFF BOTTLE OF HIRONDELLE.

In 1973, in a comprehensive survey of the less expensive wines, *The Sunday Times* found that Hirondelle was "excellent value for money."

In fact, of more than 350 wines tasted, Hirondelle came top in two of its three categories (medium-dry white and rosé wines) and a close second in the third (vin ordinaire).

In 1975, the *Daily Express* also described Hirondelle as "excellent," and, in a survey conducted last year, placed it first in the 1½ litre category of red table wines.

These surveys only serve to reflect the public's view of Hirondelle over the years: a wine that's not only good, but one that's consistently so.

Hirondelle is selected and shipped by Hedges & Butler, wine merchants since 1667. It is available in red, sweet white, medium-dry white and rosé.

Hirondelle.
Every bottle is guaranteed.

Exhibit 8

IT'S ABOUT AS LIKELY AS A DUFF BOTTLE OF HIRONDELLE.

In 1973, in a comprehensive survey of the less expensive wines, *The Sunday Times* found that Hirondelle was "excellent value for money."

In fact, of more than 350 wines tasted, Hirondelle came top in two of its three categories (medium-dry white and rosé wines) and a close second in the third (vin ordinaire).

In 1975, the *Daily Express* also described Hirondelle as "excellent", and, in a survey conducted last year, placed it first in the 1½ litre category of red table wines.

These surveys only serve to reflect the public's view of Hirondelle over the years: a wine that's not only good, but one that's consistently so.

Hirondelle is selected and shipped by Hedges & Butler, wine merchants since 1667. It is available in red, sweet white, medium-dry white and rosé.

Hirondelle
Every bottle is guaranteed.

Media Selection Press has been chosen as the medium to be used, since it is considered vital that the copy, which tells people in more detail about Hirondelle, should be read. This would not be possible on posters, and television is too costly.

Publications have been selected to avoid making Hirondelle look like a grocery brand, although it is intended that it should be bought primarily in supermarkets. To this end, therefore, publications which are adult/general interest orientated have been selected, and not those that are housewife/food orientated. (JWT's proposed media schedule is given in Exhibit 9, and Exhibit 10 shows the comparative cost analysis of press alternatives that were considered.)

Creative Interpretation Given the need to communicate directly the consistent and reliable nature of Hirondelle, the 'Unlikely Situations' campaign is proposed, with the headline, 'It's about as likely as a duff bottle of Hirondelle'.

Development of the Campaign One of the strengths of the 'Unlikely Situations' idea is that it lends itself to unending variations on the same theme. Consumers will be curious to see the 'latest joke' in the series, much as they do with Guinness advertising. But since there is a host of 'unlikely' subjects which, however original in conception — and humorous to some — might offend more readers than they're worth, the following creative guidelines have been put forward to control the development of the campaign:

a) Each subject should be designed to involve, amuse, delight and startle, rather than unpleasantly shock and upset for the mere sake of it.

b) Nothing in the emotional values of an individual advertisement should run the risk of alienating consumers by association with that which is clinical, cold, off-putting or down-market.

c) Whilst it is important that the ideas become more involving and subtle as the campaign moves on, each subject should be fairly quickly comprehensible.

d) The subjects should be highly original.

e) Because the nature of the material, and its quality, is so much at the mercy of subjective opinion, it might, when opinion is divided within, be worth relying on the *vox populi* without.

g) And, to end at the beginning, each subject must be not only highly unlikely, but as unlike the preceding one as we're ever likely to get.

The Advertising Decision It fell to Vern Johnson, the senior brand manager of Hirondelle, to prepare a response to JWT's advertising proposal. As it happened, he had just received the latest Target Group Index (TGI) Survey published annually by the British Market Research Bureau (BMRB). One of the statisticians in the company had extracted Hirondelle usage figures from the 1976 survey and compared them with figures for 1972 and 1974. These are given in Exhibit 11, with definitions of the terms used by TGI given in Exhibit 12. (Fieldwork for the TGI survey is conducted in the spring and early summer of the year in which it is published.) Vern wondered, as he cast his eye over the TGI data, whether JWT's creative solution and media strategy were consistent with these latest findings and whether, more generally, the right message was being communicated to the right people at the right time.

Exhibit 9

(JWT) Media Department London

CLIENT HEDGES AND BUTLER LIMITED   PRODUCT   HIRONDELLE   PERIOD   1976/77   AREA   NATIONAL

1976-77

Week commencing Monday	July 28 5 12 19 26	August 2 9 16 23 30	September 6 13 20 27	October 4 11 18 25	November 1 8 15 22 29	December 6 13 20 27	January 3 10 17 24 31	February 7 14 21 28	March 7 14 21 28	April 4 11 18 25	May 2 9 16 23 30	June 6 13 20 27	SUMMARY
Sunday Times Mag		O	O X	O	X X	O			O	O	X	O	£51050
Observer Mag.		O O	O X	O	X O X	X			O³	O X	X		£29867
Daily Telegraph			A	A A	A A	A		A	A A	A A	A A A	A	£23017
Readers Digest				O	O O					O O	O O		£12800
Evening Standard			A	A	A A	A A		A A		A A	A A	A	£10120
Punch		O	O	X	X O	O			A O	O X	O X	X	£9196
Cosmopolitan			O		O	O				O	O	O	£8855
Country Life		O	X	O	X	O			O	O O	X O		£6730
Illustrated London News			O	O	O O	O		O		O	O O	O	£5760
Mayfair			O	O	O O			O		O	O O		£5700
Geographical Mag.			O	O	O O	O		O		O	O	O	£4088

Production   £167,183
Reserve for   7,000
rate increases   5,817
                   ─────────
                   £180,000

NOTES   O = Page 4 colour bleed   X = Page B/W bleed   A = 33 cm + 5 col

	Coverage	Average OTS
Heavy Wine Users	87%	16.0
Hirondelle Users	88%	17.0

Exhibit 10   *Comparative Cost Analysis of Alternative Press Media*

Publication	Cost per Page 4-colour bleed[1] (£)	Heavy Users of Wine Coverage[2] (%)	Cost per '000 (£)	All Hirondelle Users Coverage[2] (%)	Cost per '000 (£)
Mayfair	950	17.1	3.23	13.6	2.61
Penthouse	980	16.2	3.53	13.2	2.76
Geographical Mag.	511	8.0	3.72	8.9	2.14
Men Only	1100	16.7	3.83	13.1	3.13
Illustrated London News	720	8.2	5.07	5.8	4.64
Good Housekeeping	1584	12.7	7.25	15.4	3.83
Punch	968	7.5	7.50	8.9	4.08
Harpers and Queen	667	4.9	7.94	5.8	4.30
Homes and Gardens	1375	10.0	7.99	11.7	4.36
Readers Digest	3200	23.3	8.00	31.0	4.86
She	1485	10.6	8.15	14.8	3.74
Observer Magazine	3097 (2047)[5]	21.9	8.23 (5.44)	25.0	4.62 (3.05)
Observer	— (1980)	19.0	— (6.07)	26.2	— (3.48)
Country Life	745	5.2	8.27	5.0	5.60
Cosmopolitan	1771	12.2	8.43	14.3	4.62
House and Garden	1339	8.7	8.98	8.5	5.87
Field	385	2.4	9.16	1.4	10.13
New Scientist	759	4.6	9.60	3.5	8.07
Daily Telegraph Magazine	4194 (2829)[5]	25.3	9.66 (6.51)	26.1	6.00 (4.05)
Daily Telegraph	— (2557)	23.6	— (6.31)	25.0	— (3.82)
Ideal Home	1595	9.4	9.90	10.0	5.95
Evening Standard	2250[4] (920)	13.2	9.95 (4.07)	9.7	8.68 (3.55)
Sunday Times Magazine	5470 (3190)[5]	31.6	10.09 (5.88)	33.0	6.18 (3.60)
Sunday Times	— (3052)	35.2	— (5.05)	34.7	— (3.28)
Vogue	1552	8.6	10.48	12.4	4.67
Tatler	550	2.9	11.00	2.7	7.63
Radio Times	7900 (4200)[5]	36.7	12.53 (6.66)	38.6	7.64 (4.06)
TV Times	6743	30.9	12.69	27.6	9.12
Tit Bits	1450	6.4	13.18	4.2	12.83
Economist	1050	4.3	14.18	3.2	12.20
Weekend	3080	10.0	18.01	8.5	13.44
Guardian	3300[4] (1402)	10.7	18.03 (7.66)	9.6	12.79 (5.43)
Daily Mail	5250[4] (1750)	16.2	18.88 (6.29)	17.2	11.36 (3.78)
Financial Times	4250[4]	12.9	19.23	6.5	24.56
Woman's Journal	935	2.7	19.89	6.9	5.08
Times	4202[4] (1732)	10.7	22.83 (9.41)	7.3	21.32 (8.79)
Woman and Home	2662	5.9	26.35	15.1	6.57
Brides	1224	1.4	48.96	2.5	18.26

Notes: 1 Bracketed prices = black and white for 33 cm + 5 c or equivalent in tabloid.
2 TGI 1975
4 ½ page 4-colour/equivalent.
5 Full page.

Exhibit 11 *Users and Non-Users of Hirondelle Wine*

	All Users				Solus Users				Major Users				Minor Users				Non-Users
	'000	% down	% across	index	'000	% down	% across	index	'000	% down	% across	index	'000	% down	% across	index	'000
1972:																	
ALL ADULTS	1219	100	3.0	100	146	100	0.4	100	463	100	1.1	100	611	100	1.5	100	13538
MEN	661	54	3.4	114	88	61	0.5	127	242	52	1.2	110	331	54	1.7	113	6469
WOMEN	558	46	2.6	88	57	39	0.3	75	221	48	1.0	91	280	46	1.3	88	7069
15—24	306	25	3.9	131	34	24	0.4	123	125	27	1.6	141	147	24	1.9	126	2648
25—34	346	28	5.1	172	30	20	0.4	123	146	32	2.2	191	170	28	2.5	168	2730
35—44	215	18	3.4	114	23	16	0.4	101	72	16	1.1	101	120	20	1.9	127	2373
45—54	189	16	2.8	96	18	13	0.3	78	73	16	1.1	97	98	16	1.5	99	2467
55—64	115	9	1.8	61	30	20	0.5	130	32	7	0.5	44	54	9	0.8	57	1974
65 OR OVER	48	4	0.7	23	11	8	0.2	44	15	3	0.2	18	23	4	0.3	22	1346
AB	543	45	10.6	355	63	43	1.2	345	231	50	4.5	397	249	41	4.9	326	3087
C1	417	34	5.2	175	38	26	0.5	132	149	32	1.9	165	229	38	2.9	192	3853
C2	187	15	1.2	42	32	22	0.2	59	62	13	0.4	36	94	15	0.6	41	4435
D	67	5	0.7	25	12	8	0.1	35	19	4	0.2	18	37	6	0.4	27	1789
E	5	0.4	0.1	5	1	1	*	12	3	0.6	0.1	7	1	0.2	*	2	375
1974:																	
ALL ADULTS	2678	100	6.5	100	309	100	0.7	100	1126	100	2.7	100	1243	100	3.0	100	16646
MEN	1355	51	6.9	106	147	48	0.7	99	556	49	2.8	104	652	52	3.3	110	8066
WOMEN	1322	49	6.1	94	162	52	0.7	100	570	51	2.6	97	590	48	2.7	91	8580
15—24	645	24	8.5	131	71	23	0.9	124	280	25	3.7	135	293	24	3.8	128	3037
25—34	761	28	10.6	163	83	27	1.2	155	338	30	4.7	172	340	27	4.7	157	3405
35—44	480	18	7.7	119	51	16	0.8	109	172	15	2.8	101	257	21	4.1	137	2654
45—54	370	14	5.5	85	43	14	0.6	84	161	14	2.4	87	167	13	2.5	82	3094
55—64	282	11	4.6	71	39	13	0.6	85	108	10	1.8	65	135	11	2.2	74	2415
65 OR OVER	140	5	1.9	29	22	7	0.3	41	67	6	0.9	33	51	4	0.7	23	2041
AB	1103	41	20.4	316	90	29	1.7	223	448	40	8.3	305	565	45	10.5	349	3189
C1	857	32	9.3	144	102	33	1.1	148	361	32	3.9	144	395	32	4.3	143	4946
C2	496	19	3.6	56	77	25	0.6	75	234	21	1.7	62	185	15	1.3	45	5127
D	167	6	1.8	28	31	10	0.3	45	61	5	0.7	24	75	6	0.8	27	2589
E	54	2	1.4	22	8	3	0.2	30	22	2	0.6	22	23	2	0.6	21	795
1976:																	
ALL ADULTS	2794	100	6.7	100	260	100	0.6	100	1099	100	2.6	100	1435	100	3.5	100	16092
MEN	1339	48	6.7	100	115	44	0.6	93	495	45	2.5	94	728	51	3.7	106	7714
WOMEN	1455	52	6.7	100	144	56	0.7	106	604	55	2.8	105	707	49	3.3	94	8378
15—24	606	22	7.9	118	79	30	1.0	165	233	21	3.0	115	294	20	3.8	111	2794
25—34	1025	37	13.9	207	45	17	0.6	98	442	40	6.0	227	539	38	7.3	212	3355
35—44	433	15	6.9	103	39	15	0.6	99	135	12	2.2	82	259	18	4.2	121	2811
45—54	369	13	5.5	81	39	15	0.6	92	146	13	2.2	82	185	13	2.7	79	2975
55—64	221	8	3.7	55	31	12	0.5	83	84	8	1.4	53	106	7	1.8	51	2181
65 OR OVER	140	5	1.8	28	27	10	0.4	58	59	5	0.8	30	53	4	0.7	20	1976
AB	860	31	17.4	259	53	21	1.1	174	347	32	7.0	266	460	32	9.3	270	3035
C1	1099	39	11.2	166	103	40	1.1	168	428	39	4.4	165	568	40	5.8	167	5032
C2	591	21	4.4	65	70	27	0.5	83	232	21	1.7	65	289	20	2.1	62	4879
D	199	7	2.2	33	24	9	0.3	42	71	6	0.8	29	105	7	1.2	33	2274
E	45	2	1.1	16	9	4	0.2	36	21	2	0.5	19	14	1	0.3	10	873

Exhibit 12   *Terminology Employed in Target Group Index Surveys*

User Classifications

All Users:	Have drunk in the past 6 months.
Solus Users:	Drink only the one brand (of all brands of table wine).
Major Users:	Drink the brand most often but also drink other brands.
Minor Users:	Have drunk in the past 6 months but drink another brand most often.
Non-Users:	Drink the product but have not drunk the brand in the past 6 months.
Adult Users:	Aged 15 or over.
Social Grade:	Social grade is normally based on the occupation of the head of his or her household. It is assessed by the interviewer when attempting to place the questionnaire and is therefore based on information given personally and verbally by the respondent. Interviewers are supplied with a list of occupations within industry to guide them in their assessments.

Social grade	Social status	Head of household's occupation
A	Upper middle class	Higher managerial, administrative or professional
B	Middle class	Intermediate managerial, administrative or professional
C1	Lower middle class	Supervisory or clerical, and junior managerial, administrative or professional
C2	Skilled working class	Skilled manual workers
D	Working class	Semi and unskilled manual workers
E	Those at lowest levels of subsistence	State pensioners or widows (no other earner), casual or lower-grade workers

This case was prepared by Patrick Barwise and Kenneth Simmonds of the London Business School.
© Kenneth Simmonds, 1973.

CASE B2
Chubb and Son Lock and Safe Company Ltd

Introduction*

In May 1971 the advertising agency of Maisey Mukerjee Russell was in the process of formulating its recommendations for a major client, Chubb and Son Lock and Safe Company Ltd. MMR had been awarded the Chubb account in mid-1970. It had immediately done a brief initial study of the market and Chubb had agreed to a preliminary campaign to answer some of the problems which came to light in this study and also agreed that the agency complete their market research programme. MMR was now in a position to propose a broad, long-term strategy, using the full research results. Also during the last year, Chubb had streamlined the operation of its Wolverhampton factory; sales could now be increased by 25 per cent before capacity constraints became binding. Both Chubb and MMR were in agreement that the agency's recommendations need not be limited only to advertising, but could cover other elements of the marketing mix.

*Certain dates and figures have been disguised.

Chubb and Son Lock and Safe Company Ltd

The foundations of Chubb went back to 1818 when the family company was established at Wolverhampton, the traditional home of the locksmith's cottage craft. In 1835 the company started to manufacture safes in London, transferring this operation also to Wolverhampton in 1907. Chubb became a limited company in 1882, but did not go public until 1948. Since that time it had expanded into a worldwide group with a diverse and sophisticated range of activities, all falling broadly into the area of security (see Exhibit 1).

Exhibit 1 *Chubb Company Structure*

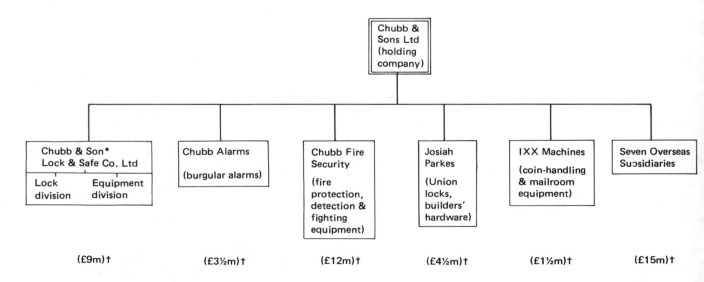

* The client in this case
† Estimated 1971 turnover

Exhibit 2 *Group Performance 1967 to 1971 (Worldwide*)*

31 March	1967 (£m)	1968 (£m)	1969 (£m)	1970 (£m)	1971 (£m)
Turnover	21.7	30.0	38.4	41.5	47.2
Trading profit	2.5	3.1	4.0	4.2	4.5
Net interest	(0.1)	(0.3)	(0.4)	(0.4)	(0.7)
Profit before tax	2.4	2.8	3.6	3.8	3.8
Taxation	(1.0)	(1.3)	(1.7)	(1.8)	(1.6)
Profit after tax	1.4	1.5	1.9	2.0	2.2
Minorities and pref. dividend	(0.1)	(0.1)	(0.1)	(0.1)	(0.1)
Attributable earnings	1.3	1.4	1.7	1.9	2.0
% earned on ordinary capital†	25.0%	21.9%	24.3%	27.4%	29.8%

* Figures do not add up due to rounding
† After tax, adjusted

MMR's client was the Chubb and Son Lock and Safe Company Limited which manufactured locks, safes and fire-resisting and banking equipment. Other Group companies produced and sold burglar alarms and other detection devices, and fire detectors and extinguishers. The Group as a whole was the biggest of its kind outside the USA; Exhibit 2 summarises its performance for the period 1967—71.

Sales growth had been strong for the previous decade; the Chairman, Lord Hayter — who represented the Chubb family on the board — summarised the reasons in his 1970 annual review to shareholders:

> Some years ago when our turnover began to show signs of rising to today's formidable total, I used to tell my friends that I lay awake at night wondering who on earth was going to buy it all again next year, but of course I need not have worried. At a time when prisons in this country have never been so full it is not surprising that our turnover of security products should be at record levels. The increase in crime is not peculiar to this country — the more civilized a country becomes, the more there is of petty theft, larceny, shopbreaking, shoplifting and safebreaking.

The Lock and Safe Company (hereafter referred to as 'Chubb') consisted of a Lock Division and an Equipment Division. Lock sales for 1970 were still only about half as much as equipment sales, but were growing at a faster rate. Lock sales showed a 64 per cent increase on 1967 against only 19 per cent for equipment.

Chubb's Distribution and Selling Organisation

In general, the final consumer for locks was a private individual — a householder — who did not purchase direct from Chubb, although a small number of large orders came from organisations. To reach the final consumer Chubb dealt through 1,200 registered lock stockists. In 1970 turnover went to the different classes of stockist in the following proportions: wholesalers (including branches) 43 per cent, ironmongers 23 per cent, builders' merchants 20 per cent, locksmiths 7 per cent, and others 7 per cent. Through these outlets there were a range of possible ways by which locks might reach the general public. The most important of these are shown in Exhibit 3.

The equipment market was in contrast predominantly industrial, with Chubb largely selling direct (although about 20 per cent of sales came through a network of six agents). Since security products were not repeat-bought by the same customer, there was no list of equipment accounts. Safes were marketed under the name of Chatwood Milner as well as Chubb.

The Chubb salesforce was divided into five areas, with an average of three lock salesmen and five equipment salesmen in each area, reporting to an area manager. The area managers in turn reported to the two divisional managers. A

Exhibit 3 *Distribution of Locks*

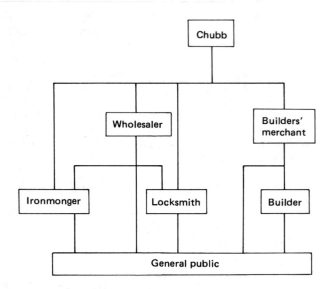

marketing director was in overall charge, assisted by a marketing services manager.

Most of the Chubb salesmen had not spent their whole careers in selling, nor were they 'drummers'. The company felt that American-style pressurised selling would be inconsistent with its quality image. Its basic marketing stance was that the best way of selling was to provide products that really solved the customer's security problems. Any risk of jeopardising its excellent reputation must be avoided. In line with this policy, lock salesmen were paid straight salaries plus a small share of a commission on the total sales of the division. There was another argument behind this decision: it was felt that the individual salesman could not really influence sales, which depended on people with whom he had no contact (the general public), rather than on those to whom he was selling (the trade). In contrast, equipment salesmen — who sold direct — were paid salaries and individual commissions.

Chubb's sales effort was supported by advertising. Until 1970, when the account was moved from Everetts Ltd to MMR, Chubb's advertising had aimed principally to maintain the 'quality' image, announce new products when appropriate, and in a gentle way keep the name of Chubb before the public.

Chubb's Market Position

There was no inexpensive way of accurately assessing market shares in Chubb's various markets. The government had no appropriate industry data, while the major individual firms only published turnover figures in aggregate — not broken down by product market. Nevertheless, Chubb clearly dominated the fast-growing security lock market, with a share of at least 75 per cent. Its strongest competitors here were probably Ingersolls, Yale and Bramah. Chubb's reputation for excellence in security locks was nowhere better attested than in a letter received by the company in 1959:

> Dear Sir,
> I am 55 years of age and I have spent 35 years of my life as a burglar. I have opened many kinds of locks in my career as a criminal, yet I have never known any burglar who has successfully opened a Chubb mortice deadlock, myself included. You can take it from me that your lock is definitely invulnerable to light fingered gentlemen of my profession, (. . .)
> Herbert H. Smith   Yorkshire's ex 'Burglar Bill'

Exhibit 4   *Advertising Expenditures: Chubb & Competition*

	1968 (£'000)	1969 (£'000)	1970 (first half) (£'000)
CHUBB			
Lock division	12.6	3.6	6.9
Equipment division			
Chubb safes	3.8	2.6	6.5
Chatwood Milner safes	4.6	5.0	2.3
Record cabinets	5.3	3.8	0
Cash dispensers	0	1.7	0
	13.7	13.1	8.8
OTHER GROUP COMPANIES			
Josiah Parkes ('Union')	0	0	0
Chubb Alarms	2.9	6.4	2.0
Chubb Fire Security	0	0	4.2
COMPETITION			
Yale Locks	6.1	4.2	1.9
Yale & Towne	0.5	3.0	0.6
Ingersoll Household Locks	3.1	5.9	0
Legge Locks	0	5.4	2.1
John Tann	0	0	0

Source: Media Expenditure Analysis Limited (MEAL)

Chubb's presence in the larger (but slower-growing) general lock market was far less significant; the group as a whole was represented by Josiah Parkes Ltd's 'Union' brand, however. The market leader was probably Yale, closely followed by Union.

The equipment division had well over half of the UK safe market, the major competitor being John Tann. Chubb was also a force to be reckoned with in the markets for fireproof cabinets and for cash dispensers.

Exhibit 4 gives advertising expenditures for various Chubb and competitive accounts for the period 1968 to 1970.

Demand Influences

The demand for security products — especially in the industrial sector — was strongly influenced by the insurance companies. Many sales were made to customers with buildings that were either new, or that had recently been burgled. In both these cases an insurance company was likely to specify minimum security standards. Moreover, these standards were becoming more stringent. Exhibit 5 gives the amounts paid out by members of the British Insurance Association for various crime losses for the year 1967 to 1971.

Exhibit 5   *Insurance Company Crime Losses 1967 to 1971*

(Excluding uninsured losses or losses covered outside the BIA membership or under marine or motor policies)

Type of policy	1971 (£m)	1970 (£m)	1969 (£m)	1968 (£m)	1967 (£m)
Money	2.5	2.0	2.1	1.8	2.4
Goods in transit	2.3	2.1	2.1	1.9	1.8
Commercial and industrial premises	5.2	5.8	6.0	4.8	5.0
Household	7.7	7.0	6.2	4.8	4.0
All risks	3.6	3.7	3.4	3.0	2.7
Total losses	21.3	20.6	19.8	16.3	15.9

Another influence was the police, who ran an advisory service for the public with the aid of local crime prevention officers. A private householder might well consult his local CPO in the early stages of thinking about installing a peripheral security system for his home. The CPO was not allowed to recommend a single brand; he would have to mention either no brands or several.

Again, people having a new house (or factory) built might leave the security side to the architect or builder. Or they might consult a locksmith or ironmonger. There were many 'experts' in the field.

The Preliminary Study

When MMR was first given the Chubb account, one of its first actions was an informal telephone survey of 80-odd 'city influencers'. These were executives with professional knowledge of the London stock market — men in banking, insurance, stockbroking and so on. They were simply asked what they thought about the Chubb group, and in particular, how big they thought it was.

Most respondents seemed unaware of the size of the group: it was regarded as basically a 'conservative' manufacturer of safes, 'very much concerned with reputation and product quality'. Estimates of turnover were mostly around £5 million per annum. This perception of the group as being so much smaller than the reality doubtless accounted for its rather low level of trading on the market. The premium rating which Chubb had previously enjoyed on the stock market (i.e. an earnings multiple several points higher than the FT-500 Index) had recently been largely eroded. Chubb's growth during the 1960s had presumably not been fully perceived by the market.

Before beginning any pilot creative work, MMR also felt it essential to obtain basic attitude research data on Chubb and its position within its several target markets. It therefore carried out three small-scale surveys, as follows:

a) 50 direct interviews of members of the public
b) 25 direct in-store interviews of ironmongers
c) 75 direct or telephone interviews of senior managers, mostly company secretaries, and companies in manufacturing, distribution and service sectors.

Asked to name three brands of lock, the general public recorded the following measures of 'simple, unprompted awareness': Yale 85 per cent, Chubb 60 per cent, Union 47 per cent, 'Mortice' 39 per cent and Ingersoll, 38 per cent.

There was clearly confusion about exactly what a mortice lock was — many people believing that it was a brand. On prompted awareness the only brand to obtain 100 per cent was Yale, apparently viewed as a generic product. Unprompted recall of advertising was zero, while only 20 per cent of respondents 'thought' they had seen a recent Chubb advertisement that was used for prompting. The survey also showed that the image for Chubb was 'bland and unexciting'. The locks produced by Chubb were regarded as 'more expensive but of rather better quality than the competition'. Overall the public seemed apathetic towards the product field — a lock was a lock unless somebody particularly recommended a certain brand.

Among retailers, unprompted awareness of Chubb, Yale and Union brands was 100 per cent, but unprompted awareness of advertising was extremely low. Most retailers were aware that Chubb advertised, although they could not remember any advertising they had seen. When shown two recent advertisements, however, most claimed they had seen them. Chubb locks were considered harder to sell by retailers, as they were generally more expensive. Some retailers complained of the absence of promotional material either in-store or above the line. The comparison was made with pharmacists, where the customer comes to buy only at the order of his doctor — in this case the insurance man.

The company executive survey concentrated on fire protection equipment and safes. Except in the area of fire protection equipment for computer files, advertising recall was minimal. On a test of simple, unprompted awareness of brands of fire protection equipment, substantial scores were only obtained by two brands:

Chubb 44 per cent and Remington Rand 41 per cent. Only 20 per cent of respondents claimed to have fire protection equipment in some form or another. Many different reasons were given by the other 80 per cent. A common delusion was that the standard anti-burglar safe was fireproof.

When respondents were asked to name safes, only three brands were forthcoming: Chubb, Chatwood Milner and John Tann, in that order. Very few executives knew the brand of their safe. Only half of the sample claimed to have a safe at all (and half of these admitted to safes more than 10 years old). Typical reasons for non-ownership were: 'If we were going to be burgled, a safe wouldn't keep them out'; 'Only means more expenses'; 'Must get one — one day'.

The Preliminary Proposals

On completion of the preliminary study MMR reported to Chubb that there was a clear need for a massive education effort. The markets for Chubb's products were characterised by the indifference and ignorance of the buying public — both as private individuals and as companies — and the same was true of the financial community. All UK citizens were potential Chubb customers — some in more than one market sector — and a campaign in the general national media would therefore be effective. Chubb's market position across its product lines, moreover, would make it the main beneficiary of changed attitudes towards the principle of security.

MMR recommended that the campaign aim for a massive emotional jolt in order to overcome the consumer apathy and resistance. An analogy was drawn with the anti-smoking campaign. The prime message would be the need for home security. The copy used, though, should also sell Chubb as a maker of locks as a complement to its image as a maker of safes.

MMR also recommended that the bulk of the budget be spent on a series of full-page advertisements in the Sunday press and major national weeklies, allocated to reach the A, B and C1 social classes. In MMR's words, 'the message should reach them right where they are most vulnerable, in their own homes, where they least expect it, and when they have most time to digest the full implications'.

MMR was charging a flat annual fee for its services, as opposed to the usual practice of receiving remuneration in the form of a 15 per cent discount from media owners. MMR passed such discounts on to the client.

While discussions were continuing on these proposals and the copy being prepared, Chubb authorised MMR to continue with a second phase of market research. MMR's full research programme consisted of a large and detailed survey of the lock trade, plus smaller studies of potential purchasers of locks and equipment.

Consumer Attitudes

The consumer research was carried out by means of a series of in-depth discussions among groups of eight or ten consumers guided by a psychologist. Questions were not asked, but the group gently led into the areas to be explored. The recorded discussions were later analysed and salient points identified. Street interviews were then used in an attempt to quantify the importance of these points. Typical comments from these discussions were as follows:

1 'A lock is immaterial in a house — if they want to get in, they'll get in.'
2 'What's the point of having a very expensive front door lock if in fact they can just break the panel of glass beside it and still come in?'
3 'The man gets over it very quickly, but it's very disturbing to the woman to know that some unknown person has been through all her personal stuff.'
4 'If you have a Yale lock you'll get in much easier without breaking the door.'
5 'I shouldn't think Chubb would be easy to open — not for the price you pay for them . . . and a Chubb is morticed into the door.'
6 'Chubb doesn't sound like locks somehow — sort of too cosy . . . chubby . . . has to sound emaciated like Yale.'

7   'The name Chubb always brings to mind a picture of a safe, but elderly people associated with it . . . wing-collars and spectacles . . .'

MMR staff felt that the principle of 'cognitive dissonance' clearly applied to the whole question of home security. In a report to the client they explained it this way:

Sometimes known as the 'it won't happen to me' syndrome. If a person is presented with a set of fully authenticated facts which that person finds thoroughly distasteful, the following processes occur in his or her mind:

1   The facts (and the conclusions drawn from them) are disliked.
2   This dislike sets up an anxiety state in the subconscious.
3   The anxiety leads to the transfer of the dislike from the facts to their source.
4   Dislike of the source reduces the credibility of that source.
5   The truth of the facts themselves therefore becomes dubious — and in the mind of the person involved they are no longer facts and can therefore be ignored.

This process is fairly rapid, particularly in cases where physical proof of the facts is lacking, and/or where the facts consist only of incontrovertible statistical probabilities. Consequently, it is essential that, after presenting the facts, action towards the recipient is taken at the earliest possible stage of this 'decaying of belief' period.

General conclusions from the study were:

1   The best-known name in locks was Yale, with Ingersoll coming a poor second and Chubb third.
2   Knowledge even of the existence of locking window catches was very low.
3   Locks were usually purchased when pressure (i.e. a burglary or the insistence of an insurance company) was brought to bear on the householder.
4   Although the man of the house was invariably the purchaser, the wife was usually the prime mover.

As it seemed to MMR that there was scope for increasing Chubb's sales of locks, the bulk of the research focused on this side of the business. But it was also suggested that there might be under-exploited market sectors on the equipment side, namely among professionals (e.g. accountants and solicitors). A brief study was therefore made into the incidence of fireproof cabinets in six different professions: results — and employment within each profession — are shown in Exhibit 6. There was some uncertainty as to the implications of these data in terms of marketing (e.g. is high incidence good or bad?).

Exhibit 6   *Ownership of Fireproof Cabinets among the Professions*

Professionals in London area (interviewed by telephone)	Number interviewed	Fireproof safe (%)	Fireproof cabinet (%)	Membership of institution(s): England and Wales (thousands)
Banker	8	100	75	64.8
Solicitor	8	88	50	23.6
Computer centre	8	75	38	—
Barrister	8	75	25	2.6
Accountant	8	38	38	43.0
Architect	8	12	25	21.3
Average:		65	42	—

The Trade Survey   The trade survey covered those 'experts' responsible for recommending security standards to the public, using personal structured interviews. Six samples were taken, comprising 182 'lock-stocking ironmongers' (one-third from Chubb's own stockists) and 20 each of locksmiths, architects, builders, insurance companies and crime prevention officers. About half of the respondents thought that the lock-buying public usually did not know which brand it wanted (see Exhibit 7). Except for the builders, who simply chose the brand themselves, the respondents in general did not recommend a single brand.

It seemed that Chubb's sterling qualities were appreciated by the architects, but that other factors militated against Chubb among ironmongers, locksmiths and builders. Ironmongers stated in a ratio of 3 to 1 that they preferred Chubb to Yale, but themselves used about the same quantities of each and sold twice as many Yale as Chubb locks. The apparent discrepancy between preference and sales may, however, have been due to the question asked about locks in general — Yale sales included also the cheaper, easier-to-fit rim latches. The reasons given for selling twice as many Yale as Chubb locks were:

1   Yale sells at a more favourable price (40 to 9 per cent).
2   Yale are easier to fit (18 to 4 per cent)
3   Yale packaging is better (9 to 4 per cent).
4   Yale name is slightly better known (69 to 64 per cent).

Of the ironmongers who were not Chubb's official stockists about half stocked Chubb locks, as shown in Exhibit 8.

Exhibit 7   *Recommendation of Lock Brands by Trade Channels*

Trade classification: (number in sample)	Ironmongers (182)	Locksmiths (20)	Architects (20)	Builders (20)	CPOs (20)
	(%)	(%)	(%)	(%)	(%)
'Public generally has no particular brand in mind'	51	65	100	55	35
of which: 'Recommends no brand or several'	32	30	45	—	35
'Recommends one brand'	19	35	55	55	—*
of which:					
Chubb	9	20	35	15	—
Yale	7	—	—	25	—
Union	2	—	—	10	—
Other	1	15	20	5	—

*CPOs and insurance companies did not recommend or approve single brands on their own. They held a far higher opinion of Chubb protection equipment than any other brand, however.

Exhibit 8   *Lock Brands Stocked by Ironmongers*

	All respondents (182)			Not Chubb stockists (121)
BRAND:	Chubb	Yale	Union	Chubb
	(%)	(%)	(%)	(%)
External door locks	63	86	40	45
Security door locks	70	60	18	56
Other (average of five items)*	44	17	3	16

*Includes window locks and bolts, and door viewers, chains and bolts

One puzzling finding from the ironmonger survey was that 42 per cent of enquiries at Chubb stockists were for Ingersoll, and 50 per cent of enquiries at non-Chubb stockists were for Ingersoll. MMR concluded that either public brand awareness of Ingersoll was greater than they had previously identified or that dealers had been so well indoctrinated by the Ingersoll salesforce that they inflated, perhaps involuntarily, the number of enquiries.

About half the ironmongers interviewed thought transparent packs would satisfy their customers, but only a quarter preferred transparent packs from their own point of view. Nearly two thirds of the sample said that when ordinary 'cardboard box' packs are opened, small items such as screws etc. are often dropped and lost. Yale were regarded, moreover, as having packs slightly more efficient than Chubb and considerably more attractive. Only 7 out of the 20 locksmiths thought that instructions in lock packages were good enough to enable a householder to fit the lock himself.

Only 6 per cent of ironmongers thought it would be helpful and improve business if they had a lockfitter on the staff; 48 per cent direct the customer to the locksmith; 21 per cent to a builder or carpenter, and 34 per cent claim that they give the customer explicit instructions on how to fit. Thus practically everyone who bought a lock from an ironmonger must either fit it himself or take it to someone else to fit. Interestingly enough, only 24 per cent of locksmiths said their customers came via an ironmonger, and only 30 per cent said the client purchases and the locksmith just fits.

'The public is becoming more security-minded', said 68 per cent of ironmongers, 70 per cent of locksmiths, 45 per cent of builders, 75 per cent of insurance surveyors and 94 per cent of CPOs. But the trade thought only 10 per cent of the customers wanted more secure equipment than standard locks and bolts. The traders' views of requirements were much different. Locksmiths said that windows were by far the greatest security hazard; 90 per cent of them said every household should have window locks and door chains; 60 per cent of architects said every household should have window locks or bolts; 55 per cent of CPOs said windows were a major security hazard, and 90 per cent said every household should have window locks or bolts.

Outlets reported the following devices other than locks as 'selling particularly well': door chains 73 per cent, padlocks and bars 70 per cent, bolts 64 per cent, window locks 28 per cent. The average order value for security devices in ironmongers' outlets was well above the average for other items they sold and a total security system could easily cost several hundred pounds. Most other items stocked, moreover, were comparatively simple to handle when compared with the questions that arose about the operation and fitting of security devices. Average earnings of counter-hands in ironmonger and locksmith outlets were £20 to £25 per week against a national average of £30, and there was a very high staff turnover rate. Purchasers of locks and other security devices earned well above the national average.

Major Strategy Questions

MMR now called an internal staff meeting to discuss the various findings available and to determine in outline what strategy they should propose to Chubb. It was felt that the strategy should aim to overcome problems in three broad areas, not necessarily of equal importance:

1 Company image, in particular the stock market's perception of Chubb's size.

2 Demand for the product-field. This presumably depended on whoever made the decision to purchase, and why. A factor here seemed to be the cognitive dissonance effect. In some cases, the same person might be the decision maker in more than one market sector.

3 Brand choice. This seemed to be somewhat affected by the views of the purchaser, or the advice given by an 'expert' not present during the purchase. But packaging, display, point-of-sale material and the actual counter-hand

could be important factors. These in turn might be influenced by the Chubb salesman.

Whatever decisions MMR came to about other elements of the marketing mix, there was no doubt that advertising strategy should be thought out from first principles. The wealth of information now available made a change of posture seem likely. The following questions needed to be answered:

1 Who should the target audience be?
2 What should the message be? Should ads be high or low in information content?
3 How fast a response was wanted?
4 Given answers to the above, roughly what medium or media should be used?

The final question on the meeting agenda — perhaps rather less pressing for the time being — related to testing. What recommendations should MMR make to test the effectiveness of a given ad, a given campaign, or a given overall marketing strategy? How could Chubb know what would work until it already had — if then?

*This case was prepared by
Kenneth Simmonds of the
London Business School
© Kenneth Simmonds, 1981.*

CASE B3
Piper Books Ltd

Shortly after the beginning of the firm's financial year on 1st February, Vernon Martin was promoted from a financial accounting post in Piper Books Ltd to the position of publisher for children's books. Early in March he was asked by the editor responsible for children's annuals to approve a proposal to produce a boy's annual on Great Sporting Achievements in time for the Christmas market. The mock-up of the annual appealed to Mr Martin, but the specification of the market for the annual was rather hazy and he found that no formal market research backed up the proposal and in fact no research had ever been carried out in the children's book group. Mr Martin decided to call in outside research consultants, but before he did so he was considering the questions that he would need answered most urgently.

Piper Limited was one of Britain's two largest publishers of trade books and had maintained a high rate of growth for ten years. While the past two years had been no exception, profits had shown no increase over this period. The lag had been attributed primarily to excessive stocks of titles printed in greater quantities than needed within their peak demand period, and top management had begun to place increasing emphasis on stock reduction. Mr Martin's appointment from accounting and his predecessor's departure were concrete evidence of their intentions. For the children's book group in particular, the end of year stock figure had been £400,000 against an annual turnover of just over £800,000, with the year's net profit before taxes showing no increase at £60,000.

Mr Martin was determined to improve his stock position and when the proposal for the sporting annual was presented, he was concerned that it might produce the opposite effect just in time for next year's balance date. The editor, John Attwood-Reilly, explained that he had already had several long sessions with the sales manager and his assistant discussing the mock-up of the annual and the probable sales level. They were now both satisfied with the proposal and were agreed on a budgeted sales figure of 11,000 copies. While sales could vary from this figure, the minimum would be 7,000 barring a major recession. This would allow for minimum orders from the buyers in the major chains and only scattered orders from smaller outlets. On the other hand, if the publication was received very well, then a higher volume of initial orders and repeat requests could bring the figure to 15,000, or even more if stocks were immediately available.

As the cost of printing extra copies was marginal, requiring little more than the paper cost at under £0.05 a copy, Mr Reilly recommended a print run of 15,000. Only 10,000 copies would be assembled and bound in the first instance and if the volume of first-round orders was high, a further batch could then be bound.

The price was set at £1.50 with a 33.3% discount to retailers and a further 15% to wholesalers. Mr Reilly and the sales executives felt that any attempt to change from the usual price for this sort of annual would be self-defeating. While the market might not be particularly sensitive to price changes of 15% in either direction, any increase in price might lead the trade buyers to classify the annual as too expensive and to switch the emphasis of their orders to other titles.

The number of major outlets in the United Kingdom for this sort of publication was about 7,500, and of these some 3,000 belonged to three chains: W.H. Smith, John Menzies and Boots. Each of these worked through a central purchasing office and probably 50% of the orders for the sporting annual would come from here — at wholesale prices. The Piper sales representatives were in frequent contact with the buyers and could expect them to make their selections for their Christmas line by late August with delivery in October—November. In addition to orders for their own chain, W.H. Smith also bought as wholesalers to other newsagent chains. Before Christmas particularly, there would be numbers of the country's 50,000 newsagents who added a few books to their line. The remainder of the outlets were comprised of some 800 department stores and 3,000 independent bookstores. Even though half the department stores belonged to chains, each store invariably purchased separately. Orders from this second grouping would be placed with the Piper field sales staff, or be sent in direct after their calls or as a result of direct mailings sent regularly to all outlets.

Unless Mr Martin made an exception and authorised sale-or-return offers, all sales for annuals of this sort would be firm. Sale-or-return, however, would induce buyers to increase their orders by as much as 30% when they were uncertain as to the saleability of a title.

Mr Martin could see that sales of 11,000 copies would produce a good profit, given the figures presented to him by Mr Reilly. These are set out in Exhibit 1. General overheads were running at about 10% of revenues and payment for the costs of the project would be made on the average only three months before receiving payment from customers. Beyond this, the only drain on his group's capital would be stocks of any unsold copies. A few might possibly be sold during the following year, but any quantity would have to be disposed of as remainders at little more than the material cost — say £0.15.

What gave Mr Martin real cause for hesitation was the total lack of any concrete market facts when he questioned Mr Reilly. Nothing seemed to be known about what sort of customers bought the type of annual that was proposed — whether it was the younger readers themselves, mothers, fathers or other relatives — the social class distribution of customers, or where they regularly purchased and how frequently. Nor was there any basis for calculating whether the proposal might not simply switch customers from other titles. In these circumstances, Mr Martin could feel little confidence in the sales estimates and he determined that he should make a first step towards more scientific management decision by commissioning some research into the market.

The best starting point seemed to Mr Martin to be the basic motivation of purchasers of annuals. After that, with the mock-up already available, he felt that competent market researchers should be able to pin-point the likely sales more accurately than the estimates put forward which allowed a 30% fluctuation in either direction. Further questioning within the children's book group had revealed a complete absence of any research results concerning consumer motivation, and Mr Martin felt that once the immediate problem had been covered it would be well worthwhile to start collecting a bank of basic motivation research in the children's trade book field.

Exhibit 1 *Great Sporting Achievements Annual*

	£
Estimated Revenue	
11,000 copies @ £0.90	9,900
Estimated Costs	
Text, copyrighted graphics & editorial overheads	2,700
Typesetting and proofing	1,000
Paper and printing (15,000 print run)	2,500
Assembling, binding, packing & delivery (11,000 @ £0.2)	2,200
General Group Overheads (10% of revenue)	990
	9,390
Profit	510

This case was prepared by Kenneth Simmonds of the London Business School. © Kenneth Simmonds, 1979.

CASE B4

Dornbusch Corporation

On completion of his B.A. in marketing through the sandwich course at Midland Polytechnic, Graham Stoddard was particularly pleased when he was recruited as UK product manager (electric razors) for the Dornbusch Corporation. Dornbusch had a world-wide name in the consumer electrical products field and its brands had been aggressively promoted for many years. The firm had a reputation as a leader in marketing practice and as an excellent training ground for senior marketing posts later in an executive's career.

To Graham's growing astonishment when he started his new job, he could find from internal Dornbusch records no hard data about what was happening in the user market for electric razors and very little on the outlet market. Large retail chains had been demanding and obtaining special deals and it was not clear where, and even at what price, Dornbusch razors were being sold. Promotion costs were running at 20% of revenue, but there appeared to be a very low correlation between promotion and sales patterns over the years.

Dornbusch's current sales were around 210,000 razors per annum — all aimed at the male market. Estimates from the IPC Marketing Manual put the UK market two years previously at 1.6 million units, of which around 10% were probably women's shavers. Dornbusch's estimated 15% of the men's segment placed them well behind Philips with an estimated 800,000 units and Braun with possibly 400,000.

Stoddard knew he could obtain more precise estimates of current sales from A.C. Nielsen surveys of outlets, but he decided that it was more important to find out where the future potential really lay. There had been years of expanding demand and much switching and upgrading by users. Was the future potential in first purchase, replacement or second use? Or was there little potential left at all? Of 20 million male shavers it had been estimated that 70% were still wet shavers. After a little questioning around, Graham was fairly certain that he would get immediate clearance for a research commitment of up to £10,000. On such a budget he estimated he could finance a survey of 2,000 adult males, provided he arranged for the analysis of the results internally and kept the data requested fairly short. He accordingly drew up the following five open-ended questions to be asked of 2,000 randomly selected males aged between 20 and 55:

> What type of razor do you now own?
> How long have you had it?
> What type of razor did you have before this one?
> Have you ever owned any other kind?
> When did you switch and why?

Graham hoped that armed with this information he could pull more through from internal sales records and fairly firmly establish the need for an ongoing feedback system.

Audit Answers Ltd had been recommended to Graham as young, keen and hungry. His approach to them confirmed that they were what he was looking for. They were well prepared to carry through the national survey for £10,000 and turn over the interview sheets to Dornbusch for analysis.

This case was prepared by Kenneth Simmonds of the London Business School.
© *Kenneth Simmonds, 1980.*

CASE B5
Chez Nouveau Furnishings

William Elliot, store manager for Chez Nouveau, was considering whether to submit a proposal to the Board for a major reallocation of floor space to customer services. Chez Nouveau was located in one of London's main shopping streets and its four floors were primarily devoted to household furnishing departments.

Six months previously, a two-week comparison of the daily traffic through the store and the daily number of purchases suggested that at least 77% of those entering the store made no purchases at all. In an effort to raise the percentage who bought in the store, Elliot had increased the frequency of manufacturers' demonstrations and special offers. These efforts had produced results. Electronic counters installed at both store entrances showed that over the past two months daily average store traffic had increased 3% to 2,330 and average daily purchases to 618.

The aim of the new proposals was to go one step further and increase both the percentage of customers acually buying and the average amount spent, through lengthening the time spent in the store. The entire top floor would be rearranged to provide a customer restaurant for light snacks and luncheons and an art gallery. There would be a reduction of 6% in the floor space devoted to Chez Nouveau merchandise, but Elliot estimated that he would be able to recoup two-thirds of the normal net revenue from the franchisees of the services.

Elliot's proposals stemmed from a second consultant study that had stationed researchers at both store entrances for two days to query a random sample of entrants about their purchase intentions. Those interviewed were invited to check back on leaving the store for a free canvas shopping bag. At that point, they were asked further questions about what they had bought in the store. Nearly 90% returned for the second set of questions, and the following summary of research was tabulated:

Intention to Buy No. of Items	No. of Replies	Actual Purchases					
		0	1	2	3	4	5
0	153	120	19	6	4	2	2
1	263	210	32	7	7	4	3
2	164	109	26	15	7	5	2
3	62	39	8	6	6	2	1
4	20	8	5	2	3	2	—
5	5	2	2	—	1	—	—
	667	488	92	36	28	15	8

Time Spent in Store	0	1	2	3	4	5
Under 20 mins	174	30	5	6	1	—
20 — 39	163	35	13	10	3	2
40 — 59	74	12	11	6	4	3
60 — 79	39	5	4	5	3	2
80 — 99	31	8	1	1	2	1
100 & Over	7	2	2	—	2	—
	488	92	36	28	15	8

This case was prepared by Kenneth Simmonds of the London Business School. © Kenneth Simmonds, 1980.

CASE B6
Stylo Custom Products

Peter Henley had finally received the results of the market test which he had asked the market research department to organise. A new rotating counter stand for Stylo watchstraps, for which Peter was brand manager, had been tested for four weeks in selected department and jewellery stores. The market research department's tabulations of the results are set out in Exhibits 1 to 3. Peter now had to frame his recommendations to management.

Stylo watchstraps were made for both women's and men's watches in a range

Exhibit 1 *Stylo Watchstraps Rotating Counter Stand Test: Measured Store Sales for Eight Weeks (£) (Underlined Figures Indicate Sales With Rotating Stand)*

Week:	1	2	3	4	5	6	7	8
Department Stores:								
1	38.5	42.0	36.5	39.2	45.7	43.8	44.9	44.5
2	31.0	33.5	30.1	31.7	32.2	28.9	28.8	30.5
3	19.7	21.3	18.6	20.0	21.8	16.3	19.2	19.3
4	34.7	37.4	33.8	35.6	42.0	39.2	42.6	42.8
Jewellery Stores:								
5	20.9	22.7	17.3	20.4	20.2	20.5	19.4	20.3
6	24.6	26.5	22.8	25.1	29.6	27.9	26.8	28.0
7	27.4	30.1	25.6	28.0	29.2	23.4	25.0	26.6
8	23.4	25.6	20.5	23.5	28.1	26.5	29.9	28.3

Exhibit 2 *Stylo Watchstraps Rotating Counter Stand Test: Pre-Test and Test Period Sales Averages*

	Pre-Test Average Sales (£)	Test Period Average Sales (£)	Average Increase (Decrease) (£)	Per Cent Increase (Decrease) (%)
Department Stores:				
Test Store 1	39.05	44.73	5.68	14.54
Test Store 4	35.37	41.65	6.28	17.75
Average	37.21	43.19	5.98	16.07
Control Store 2	31.50	30.10	(1.40)	(4.45)
Control Store 3	19.90	19.15	(0.75)	(3.77)
Average	25.70	24.62	(1.08)	(4.21)
Jewellery Stores:				
Test Store 6	24.75	28.07	3.32	13.41
Test Store 8	23.25	28.20	4.95	21.29
Average	24.00	28.14	4.14	17.25
Control Store 5	20.32	20.10	(0.22)	(1.09)
Control Store 7	27.77	26.05	(1.72)	(6.20)
Average	24.05	23.07	(0.98)	(4.08)

Exhibit 3   *Stylo Watchstraps Rotating Counter Stand Test: Analysis of Results*

Test Period:	Degrees of Freedom (Pooled Variance)			Student t Value	1-tail Probability
Test versus Control Groups:					
Department Stores	14			8.13	.000
Jewellery Stores	14			3.79	.002
Pre-Test Period Variance:	Degrees of Freedom	Sum of Squares	Mean Square	F. Ratio	Significance of F
Department Stores					
Between Test and					
Control Groups	1	526.702	526.702	14.010	0.006
Among Weeks	3	30.215	10.072	0.268	0.847
Group/Week Interaction	3	1.193	0.398	0.011	0.998
Error	8	300.760	37.595		
Total	15	858.869	57.258		
Jewellery Stores					
Between Test and					
Control Groups	1	0.010	0.010	0.001	0.980
Among Weeks	3	44.075	14.692	1.006	0.439
Group/Week Interaction	3	0.185	0.065	0.004	1.000
Error	8	116.880	14.610		
Total	15	161.150	10.743		
Test Period Variance:	Degrees of Freedom	Sum of Squares	Mean Square	F Ratio	Significance of F
Department Stores					
Between Test and					
Control Groups	1	1378.265	1378.265	41.801	0.000
Among Weeks	3	23.557	7.852	0.238	0.867
Group/Week Interaction	3	4.492	1.497	0.045	0.986
Error	8	263.775	32.927		
Total	15	1670.089	111.339		
Jewellery Stores					
Between Test and					
Control Groups	1	102.515	102.515	9.407	0.015
Among Weeks	3	10.307	3.436	0.315	0.814
Group/Week Interaction	3	2.182	0.727	0.067	0.976
Error	8	87.185	10.898		
Total	15	202.189	13.479		

of materials and designs. They were distributed nationally by the company's own sales force and supplied either on cards or in boxed quantities to be used to refill a fixed counter-top display unit. This unit contained three sloping trays, was made of clear plastic, and was initially supplied free of charge by Stylo. Peter considered that the new rotating stand would be a definite improvement. Not only was it cheaper, less bulky and requiring less counter space, but it could also carry and display almost three times the quantity of straps — about £300 in wholesale value when full.

Peter Henley's concern for the test was not just to find whether his current sales figure of £1.5 million would increase with the new stand, but also to gain data for use in persuading top management to spend up to £20,000 in replacing existing display stands. Advertising had not proved effective for watchstrap promotion and sales were highly dependent on point-of-purchase displays. Of some 11,000 outlets stocking Stylo watchstraps in the United Kingdom, 4,000 were estimated to use the current display stand — and more might be persuaded to adopt the new rotating display. For an order in excess of 2,000 units, the new stands would cost Stylo around £5 each from the manufacturer.

As the basis for the test, the market research department had located eight stores in which the old displays were in current use. Four of these were jewellery stores and four were department stores. The eight were carefully chosen from stores in the Greater London area so that they represented annual sales of Stylo watchstraps within the top 30% for stores of their type and showed little seasonality. Futhermore, stores were matched by similarity of store location and, for department stores, by the size and location of the watch department. Any store identified as showing any marked individual characteristic was eliminated and, of course, only stores in which management would permit a test were finally included.

At the beginning of the test, each store's old display stand was filled on the Thursday afternoon by a Stylo salesman, who left adequate stocks for the store staff to refill the displays as they normally would. For the next four weeks, the salesmen called on Thursday afternoons and recorded the weekly sales at the retail sales price. On the fourth Thursday, Stylo market research selected randomly two jewellery and two department stores and the salesmen replaced the old display stands in these stores with the new rotating model. Measurement of all eight stores then continued for a further four weeks.

CASE B7
The Shepherd

In March 1975 staff at Hutchinson Publishing Group, a London based private publishing group employing about 100 people with a turnover of £4m, faced a more than usually difficult decision on print-run for a new book. (In most publishing situations it is only economic to produce before release a number of copies to cover the first 12—18 months' sales — this varies from 1,000 to 60,000 hardbacks, depending on the book.)

The new book concerned was *The Shepherd* by Frederick Forsyth. It could be described very broadly as a short ghost story from a writer who had made an enormous reputation for himself as a writer of fiction thrillers. These two facts really summarised the sales forecasting problems. Frederick Forsyth was a dramatically successful author; short stories, however, do not generally sell in substantial quantities.

Within H.P.G. print-run and pricing decisions are usually taken at the 'Tuesday Meeting' held normally once a week with Charles Clark, the Managing Director, in the Chair. Each meeting has to consider both contract proposals and specific print-run and pricing decisions for 20 to 30 books across the various H.P.G. imprints, including Hutchinson, Arrow (paperbacks), Educational, Stanley Paul (Hobbies and Leisure).

The Tuesday Meeting also consisted of Harold Harris, deputy Managing Director, Francis Bennett, Editorial Director, David Roy, Sales Director and Brian Perman, Marketing Director, as well as relevant members of the editorial and production staff.

Although the question of *The Shepherd* had not been discussed formally at the Tuesday meeting, it seemed that the general view was that it was such a risky venture that a very restricted print-run should be produced for the Christmas trade of about 35,000 copies. Brian Perman, however, felt that further research might well be conducted to try and establish a further market estimate. His summary of the dilemma was:

Exhibit 1 *Yearly Sales of Frederick Forsyth's Earlier Books*

Day of the Jackal	1971	56050
	1972	42150
Published: June 1971	1973	4200
	1974	3000
	1975*	600
Odessa File	1972	84300
	1973	22040
Published: September 1972	1974	3090
	1975*	500
Dogs of War	1974	150000
	1975*	7000
Published: September 1974		

*Inclusive of March 1975.

	FOR		*AGAINST*
1.	Vast potential market of those who have enjoyed F's novels (Exhibit 1).	1.	*The Shepherd* is, unlike F's previous fiction thrillers, a ghost story.
2.	The story is set on Christmas Eve 1957. So it's Christmassy.	2.	The stock, should there be any in the shops after Christmas, will effectively 'die' for 9 months.
3.	*The Shepherd* is a flying story and Forsyth was a pilot — so good detail.	3.	Do people who like flying stories relish a supernatural twist in their entertainment?
4.	If the price can be kept under £1 or even thereabouts, Paul Gallico's *Snow Goose* is a good example of how well such a gift book can do. Length is immaterial.	4.	Forsyth — Gallico? *Snow Goose* a woman's book. All the evidence suggests a low female readership for Forsyth.
5.	It is important to achieve a low cover price. We must therefore print at least 30—40,000 copies.	5.	Add on promotion costs, etc. and in publishing terms, the price of failure is escalating alarmingly.

H.P.G. decided to experiment with a forecasting technique which has been well used in other fields but not in short-term sales forecasting, particularly in publishing — the 'Delphi' method. This method was originally developed by the Rand Corporation in the USA and has been widely used for predicting very uncertain events such as long-term futures.

The Delphi Method is essentially a formalised procedure whereby a panel of experts are asked to forecast a specific event or events and then provided with an opportunity to revise their estimate in the light of the average forecasts of the other panel members. In many ways the Delphi procedure does not differ from the 'committee meeting' type of forecasting, like the 'Tuesday meeting' already mentioned at H.P.G. The differences lie in the opportunity to select a wider spread of 'experts' than those who can be sensibly involved in a face-to-face meeting; and also the opportunity to provide feedback on other persons' views in an unbiased and clear manner.

The following criteria had been developed for effective use of Delphi in forecasting particular events:

1. The future events concerned occur due to the complex interaction of many forces.

2. Many elements in the projection of future developments related to these events are not easily quantifiable.

3. In a non-exact discipline, expert opinion . . . must, of necessity, substitute for the exact laws of causality found in the physical sciences.

Against these criteria, the *Shepherd* problem looked particularly appropriate.

The selection of a suitable panel is obviously critical and the final panel consisted of:

3   Booksellers: 1 large, 1 small, 1 wholesaler
2   Critics
3   Readers (non-specialists in publishing)
2   Publishing executives
2   Sales representatives   all in H.P.G
1   Overseas executive

With this panel a standard Delphi procedure was instituted. The only major problem was the design of the questionnaire, since obviously sales figures would mean little to some members of the panel. Hence a sales success scale of 1 to 99 was developed and various books by Frederick Forsyth and also other authors indicated on it (Exhibit 2). In fact, the sales success scale multiplied by a factor of 1600 yielded a reasonable approximation to the hardback copies actually sold. Participants were also asked to rank both themselves and the other type of participants in terms of the confidence they would attach to their forecasts, on a 9-point scale (Exhibit 3).

The panel participated in an initial evaluation based on copies of the manuscript and the cover design and the information that the book was to be published in the third week in October and sold at a cover price of £1.50 for an estimated 64 pages. The panel also participated in two repeat runs in which they were allowed to modify their estimates with information on panel average ratings and weighted averages, for the previous round. The weighted averages were derived from their confidence rankings for each type of participant. The results of the ratings given for the three rounds are shown in Exhibit 4.

Before Round 3 it became known that ATV had bought the film rights to *The Shepherd* and intended to show the film on peak TV time for Christmas Eve 1975. Panel members were informed of this fact before they produced their Round 3 estimates.

Both the sales and editorial areas expressed considerable doubts about the more optimistic views expressed in the Delphi estimates:

Exhibit 2

		Forsyth's other novels	Other Authors	Other Short Stories
	99	*Dogs of War*		
	75	*Odessa File* *Day of the Jackal*		
Sales Success Scale	50		Alistair Maclean*	
				Gallico†: *Snow Goose*
	25		Le Carré* Desmond Bagley*	
			Len Deighton*	St. Exupery†: *The Little Prince*
	1			

*Based on: Alistair Maclean: *The Road to Dusty Death*
              Le Carré: *Tinker, Tailor, Soldier, Spy*
              Desmond Bagley: *The Snow Tiger*
              Len Deighton: *Spy Story*

†Estimated first year sales only

Exhibit 3

	Own Rating	Panel
Booksellers	6.5	5.9
Critics	6.0	4.2
Readers	5.8	5.3
Publishing Executives	8.0	6.6
Sales Reps	7.0	5.6
Overseas Executive	5.0	4.8

Exhibit 4 *Delphi Panel Summary*

ROUND 1

Individual Assessments	Min	Most Likely	Max	
	25	60	85	Booksellers
	35	50	75	Booksellers
	50	60	70	Booksellers
	5	12	37	Critics
	30	55	85	Critics
	40	55	80	Readers
	10	25	55	Readers
	15	45	60	Readers
	19	22	31	Publishing Executives
	20	30	45	Publishing Executives
	16	22	31	Sales Reps
	20	35	50	Sales Reps
	20	35	55	Overseas Executive
Panel Average	23	39	58	
Self-Weighted Average	23	38	57	
Panel Average Weighting	24	39	58	

ROUND 2

Individual Assessments	Min	Most Likely	Max	
	25	70	80	Booksellers
	35	50	75	Booksellers
	40	50	60	Booksellers
	9	22	47	Critics
	25	50	70	Critics
	35	45	70	Readers
	22	35	60	Readers
	20	44	60	Readers
	22	28	34	Publishing Executives
	22	34	44	Publishing Executives
	12	25	31	Sales Reps
	20	35	50	Sales Reps
	20	35	55	Overseas Executive
Panel Average	24	40	57	
Self-Weighted Average	23	39	56	
Panel Average Weighting	24	40	56	

ROUND 3		Individual Assessments		
	Min	Most Likely	Max	
	25	75	80 ⎫	
	35	50	75 ⎬ Booksellers	
	50	70	75 ⎭	
	9	41	47 ⎫ Critics	
	25	50	75 ⎭	
	25	35	60 ⎫	
	20	35	60 ⎬ Readers	
	22	45	60 ⎭	
	22	28	34 ⎫ Publishing Executives	
	22	34	44 ⎭	
	28	37	62 ⎫ Sales Reps	
	25	45	50 ⎭	
	30	50	60 Overseas Executive	
Panel Average	26	46	60	
Self-Weighted Average	25	45	59	
Panel Average Weighting	26	46	60	

Both the sales and editorial areas expressed considerable doubts about the more optimistic views expressed in the Delphi estimates:

The figures are, after all, only a reflection of the view of 13 individuals, some with no experience at all of predicting book sales. We must recognise four important points:

i) Editorial and sales staff within H.P.G. have a proven record of, at least, considerable success in predicting book sales. Recent figures have indicated that for the 600 titles we publish every year, almost all of them sell at least 80% of their print-run within 2 years.

ii) There is a very significant difference between the views of H.P.G. personnel in the panel, particularly UK staff, and the rest of the panel: I calculate that these four only produce an average estimate in the last Round of 36, compared with the overall average of 46.

iii) I think the last round results were substantially affected by the ATV story: it is far from definite that it will happen this year and I think it should be discounted from the forecast. On this basis, the H.P.G. estimate for Round 2 was about 30.

iv) This is a very risky book — even by our standards. Given the fact that any copies we fail to sell by Christmas will have very low sales potential, we could really only value them at a remainder price of around 5p a copy. Even though, on the optimistic side, I realise that if we went out of print a rush reprint would still take 6—8 weeks, and hence would mean considerable lost sales, there seems to be a clear indication that we should underprint. As such, I feel a print run of 35,000 to 40,000 would be correct. After all, in Round 2 eight of the panel were at or below 35,000 copies in their minimum estimate.

At this stage Charles Clark convened a special meeting to make the print-run decision for *The Shepherd*. (See Exhibit 5 for estimated costs and revenues.)

Exhibit 5   *The Shepherd: Estimated Costs and Revenues*

35,000 copies @ £1.50

			£
Production Costs: Fixed			1160
Variable			8550
Royalty (Variable)			4180
Overheads			
Distribution		3200	
Advertising & sales promotion		1700	
Salaries		3200	
General		3200	
Group charges		1200	
			12500
TOTAL COSTS			26390
Estimated Revenue at Average Discounts			29400
NET PROFIT			3010

CASE B8
Distral

The Distral company has been selling a range of ready-cooked canned food in France for some ten years.

Following a market survey, it has become apparent to the management of Distral that a large proportion of French housewives never use such canned food. Distral has taken the decision to aim at this unexploited segment of the market. In order to do so, the Production Department has been requested to develop a new high-quality product which will be sold with an initially minimal margin. The strategy is thus to offer present non-consumers a product with an attractive price/ quality ratio to attract a first purchase and to create a favourable post-purchase impression.

The Production Department of Distral has developed five differently conceived prototypes which have been classed *a priori* according to four criteria:

PROTOTYPES: CRITERIA:	A	B	C	D	E
Natural appearance (no obvious additives)	3	5	1	4	2
Digestibility	5	2	4	1	3
Speed with which it can be prepared by the housewife	5	1	3	4	2
Meat/filling ratio	2	3	5	1	4

(The figures in the table relate to ranks; thus C is ranked first according to the criterion of appearance.)

The five products could be made at comparable costs.

Distral's Commercial Department considers this table to contain mere indications, and thinks it is essential to obtain additional market information before deciding which of the five prototypes to put on the market.

A firm of Marketing Consultants is brought in and proposes to supply Distral with the following information:

Code	Nature of Information	Price
I.1	Position of the five products according to the criterion 'Attractiveness of the packaging' on a scale obtained after a test carried out among a group of non-consumers.	F 2000
I.2	Position of the five products according to the criterion 'Natural appearance when the tin is opened'.	F 2000
I.3	Position of the five products according to the criterion 'Speed with which it can be prepared by the housewife'.	F 2000
I.4	Position of the five products according to the criterion 'Appetising appearance of the product once prepared'.	F 2000
I.5	Position of the five products according to the criterion 'Taste'.	F 2000

I.6	Position of the five products according to the criterion 'Meat/filling ratio'.	F 2000
I.7	Position of the five products according to the criterion 'Digestibility'.	F 2000
II	Ranking of the four principal reasons for non-consumption spontaneously stated by non-users of canned food, and percentage of housewives having stated each reason.	F 14000
III.1—5	Most common remarks made by non-user housewives after a home test of products A, B, C, D and E.	F 4000 (each)
IV	Percentage of non-consumer housewives who agree with the following statements:	
IV.1	'A woman ought to take a great deal of time over her cooking.'	F 4000
IV.2	'When you serve a dish, it has to look attractive on the table.'	F 4000
IV.3	'A main course has to contain a fair amount of meat.'	F 4000
IV.4	'Some ready-cooked food is in doubtful looking packaging.'	F 4000

N.B.　All the information (I, II, III, IV) can be regarded as reliable in view of the size and composition of the samples questioned.

The Management of Distral grants the Commercial Department a budget of F 36,000 for the purchase of surveys to assist in choosing one of the five prototypes.

You are in charge of the Commercial Department. Which of the pieces of information proposed by the Marketing Consultants would you first purchase? Then, after studying this piece of information (which the leader will give you), which would you then buy? Carry on like this until you have used up as much of your F 36,000 budget as you wish.

You then have to choose one of the five products, to justify your choice and your order of choosing pieces of information, and to set out the main lines of the advertising and promotion campaign for the chosen product.

Marketing Mix Decisions

The marketing mix is the pattern of controllable variables which the firm adjusts to change its marketing presentation. Each variable should be carefully adjusted to fit the needs of the market situation, making sure that in total the mix produces a coherent and consistent offering in which the variables are working in unison and not against each other.

This case was prepared by Kenneth Simmonds of the London Business School.
© *Kenneth Simmonds, 1981.*

CASE C1
Graham's Groceries Ltd

The supermarket chain invasion was beginning to bite in the late 1950's when George Graham took over the family grocery store in one of those exclusive little towns just past the Greater London green belt. George had nevertheless done remarkably well in the face of this cut-price, fish-finger invasion. As tenants' leases fell due, he had been able to expand to take the entire floor space of Graham's High Street building. This had given 500 square metres of store space and George was able to move early into self-service, while retaining counter service for fresh meat and fresh fruit and vegetables and even a little flower shop and coffee shop. Wherever possible, he included some high-priced and exclusive brand items in Graham's range. These items had a slower turnover, but the higher margins compensated somewhat and kept Graham's image above that of the standard supermarket.

By 1973 frozen foods were becoming increasingly popular and George decided to expand his range to include numerous gourmet items. He knew that many of his customers still did not own freezers, so to develop their custom he launched a 'Gourmet Club'. He set up a display in the centre of the store with a 16 cubic feet deep freezer as the centre-piece. Customers who signed up as Gourmet Club members could purchase the freezer at a price below the best discount house prices and pay the purchase price at £20.00 per month. To join the Club, customers signed an agreement to purchase a minimum of £20.00 per month of frozen foods from the Gourmet Club list at prices 5% below Graham's normal retail price. Purchases were recorded against a Club charge number and the customer billed the previous month's outstanding balance. The Club idea caught on rapidly and within six months had 100 members.

Many times Mr Graham was asked by potential Club members whether he would extend the scheme to refrigerators and freezer-refrigerators. This gave George the idea of adding a line of appliances and electrical goods to Graham's range. He could use one of the front corners of the store facing the High Street and extend the display right into the window. For appliances, wholesale prices were 50% below suggested retail prices. This would give a chance for special promotions, while still leaving substantially higher gross margins than Graham's store average of 19% on sales.

CASE C2
Financial Times Business Newsletters

In July 1976 Keith Foley, Marketing Manager for the *Financial Times* Syndication Department, was reviewing the marketing strategy for *Financial Times* Business Newsletters. The London *Financial Times* (*FT*) was a leading daily newspaper aimed at top business and financial executives; it had a strong readership and reputation in the UK and overseas, especially in continental Europe. Apart from the newspaper itself, the *FT* group published books and magazines, organised conferences, provided various information and research services, and supplied syndicated articles to other journals on a world-wide basis; newsletters were the responsibility of the Syndication Department.

In Foley's words, 'A newsletter is a periodical which seeks to supply current information on a topic in a very concise form, rather than a hotch-potch of features, advertising, etc, like a magazine . . . There's no advertising at all'. Most newspapers came out weekly, fortnightly or monthly. The fixed production and editorial cost of a newsletter could be as low as £5,000 or up to £10,000 per annum. Since a year's subscription could be in excess of £100, and the incremental copying and postage costs per subscriber were low (around 25p per issue), newsletters were potentially very profitable, depending on how many subscriptions could be generated and with what marketing expenditure. Here are some extracts from Keith Foley's description of how the *FT* marketed its ten Business Newsletters (see Exhibit 1).

At the beginning of 1976 we had nine established newsletters — we'd just dropped one at the end of 1975, and we hadn't yet launched *World Accounting Report*. I've got a budget of £36,000 for promotion of these established newsletters, £4,000 each. As you'll see, there are some which need more promotional attention and some which need less, but I'm under some pressure to stick to that rule. Still, if I spend, say, £6,000 on a particular newsletter, that's fine as long as I'm adequately covered by revenue . . .

The only way we can maintain profitability is to drop the dead ones and introduce new ones. It would be nice just to bring out new ones of course, but with the department as it is, we couldn't really cope with many more than ten — I guess twelve would be an absolute maximum. Anyway the product life cycle is fairly short: on an annual basis we might weed out two and bring in two, keeping the total constant . . . This gives an average life cycle of five years, but with great variability about the average (see Exhibit 2). Of course, one of the problems is knowing why such-and-such a newsletter has come down from its peak: it may be a cyclical effect of the big recession which began in 1973, or it may be that a lot of people were prepared to try it out originally because of the FT's reputation, and that gave it an artificial boost. Finally, the whole field is much more competitive than five years ago. Most of the competition comes from the States, where they've even got a newsletter on newsletters . . .

We've just done an analysis of our subscribers (see Exhibit 3 for the figures for *Euromarket Letter*). Our own sales split about 50—50 into UK and overseas, with most of the overseas being continental Europe . . .

Another thing is that if we drop a newsletter, we seem to be able to pick up most of the subscribers on other newsletters. I find this rather surprising, as there isn't an enormous degree of overlap. There is some in the case of *European Community Information* and *Business Letter from Europe*, which gives me a problem with priorities: if

Exhibit 1 *FT Business Newsletters* *(As at July 1976: £1.00 = $1.88)*

EUROPEAN COMMUNITY INFORMATION

(Monthly. £25.00/$65.00 p.a.)

Summarises all the main decisions and new initiatives of the European Commission, the Council of Ministers, the Court of Justice, the European Parliament and the Investment Bank. There are regular sections on: economics and finance, competition, labour matters, regional policies, legal affairs, external relations, associated states, agriculture, and statistics together with background information on the different institutions.

BUSINESS LETTER FROM EUROPE

(Weekly. £70.00/$175.00 p.a.)

The monitoring of key business developments on the continent is the prime aim of this letter. Concise weekly reports cover such key topics as developments and decisions in the Community institutions, duties and tariffs, finance and taxation measures, imports and exports, key business developments within individual European countries, industrial output, labour relations and agriculture; special emphasis is devoted to the key industrial and commercial sectors, with reports on the activities of all major European companies.

TAX NEWSLETTER

(Monthly. £55.00/$140.00 p.a.)

It is international in scope, because the widespread operations of modern business have to take both domestic and foreign tax laws into account. The news which is presented is guided by the principle of concentrating on worldwide developments likely to have a practical impact on business decisions. The newsletter is essential reading for those whose work requires them to keep up-to-date with international tax affairs.

PETRO·MONEY REPORT

(Fortnightly. £120.00/$300.00 p.a.)

Helps fill the growing need for detailed information from the Middle East and the world's financial markets on vital matters arising from the changing direction of oil money flows. The newsletter is primarily about finance and investment, though it does relate the deployment of oil revenues to economic and political developments both in the Middle East and elsewhere.

WORLD COMMODITY REPORT

(Weekly. £70.00/$175.00 p.a.)

Commodities are at the heart of the new relationship that is developing between the primary producers of the Third World and the industrialised economies. This newsletter, therefore, is a broadly international source of information about the weekly trends of the major minerals and foodstuffs. It reports on the production news, consumption trends, crop forecasts, new discoveries and their development, and the politics of commodities. All this is preceded by a regular in-depth look at a topical commodity or a geographical region.

EUROPEAN LAW NEWSLETTER

(Monthly. £55.00/$140.00 p.a.)

Provides vital information on the legal aspects of doing business in Europe. The emphasis of the information is to cast light on the practical consequences of each legal development. Among the decisions analysed are those which affect cross-border investments, marketing arrangements, and co-operation with foreign firms.

EURO-MARKET LETTER

(Weekly. £155.00/$390.00 p.a.)

A confidential report on international and domestic capital and money markets. The letter opens with a news summary of events occurring within the world markets. It usually concentrates on two or three significant items followed by a resumé of the rest of the news. This is normally followed by a section devoted to medium term financing. Under the heading 'Euro-bonds', details of rates and banking transactions are described, and a list of prices of recent dollar bond issues are also quoted. Detailed reports are given of domestic money markets in the major financial centres. Finally, there is a synopsis of the state of Euro-currencies followed by a short listing of selected Euro-dollar rates.

WORLD INSURANCE REPORT

(Fortnightly. £100.00/$250.00 p.a.)

In both the private and public sectors, those who must take high-level decisions on the insurance of major risks need to be kept well briefed on this unpredictable industry. Regular coverage of: Non life insurance, Reinsurance, Social and employee insurance, Legislation, Management, Company developments. Many other aspects are included. With insurance becoming one of the major financial liabilities these days, this newsletter becomes essential to those with more than a local interest in the subject.

NORTH SEA LETTER

(Weekly. £100.00/$250.00 p.a.)

From both the offshore and onshore developments of the North West Continental Shelf a vast new industry has emerged. The economic impact of North Sea oil will continue to pave the way for further opportunities. The North Sea Letter monitors the progress and the possibilities continually being opened up in this vigorously competitive area. It regularly covers: Exploration, Onshore activities, Offshore supplies, Production, People, Finance, and Politics.

WORLD ACCOUNTING REPORT

(Monthly. £55.00/$140.00 p.a.)

The emergence of the standard-setting bodies in the UK and US, and the trend towards harmonisation in Europe, started the ball-rolling. The rapid growth of the international accounting firms, the creation of the International Accounting Standards Committee, and the proposed formation of the International Federation of Accountants in New York, has further stimulated the need for a comprehensive publication about international accounting. Each month, within a geographical framework, World Accounting Report looks closely at how international accounting procedures have taken on fresh significance.

From these, the largest single collection of business newsletters published in the UK, there may be one or more which will be of particular interest to you. If there is, and you would like to see a specimen, please complete and return the coupon overleaf.

Prices quoted are UK only. Overseas rates are available on request.

Exhibit 2 *Subscription Levels at 1 January each Year*

Newsletter	1970	1971	1972	1973	1974	1975	1976
BLE	(1)	300	280	260	220	200	196
EML	(1)	130	210	250	240	240	250
A	(1)	80	100	70 (3)			
ELN		(1)	320	470	410	370	380
B		(1)	140	190	100 (3)		
TN		(1)	400	550	520	490	480
ECI			(2)	1290	1030	880	820
C			(1)	240	190	110 (3)	
D			(1)	180	120 (3)		
WCR				(1)	120	150	150
E				(1)	70 (3)		
PMR					(1)	180	200
F					(1)	110 (3)	
NSL						(1)	260
WIR						(1)	190
WAR							(1)

(1) Launched.
(2) Purchased from European Commission with 950 subscribers.
(3) Withdrawn.

I'm given access to a new European mailing list (as happened three months ago) which one do I promote? I can't promote both! . . .

Each editor is in complete control of what goes into his newsletter. Obviously, I take an interest in the editorial content, but I have no control over it at all — after all, I'm not the expert. I respect the editors as journalists, and they respect that my responsibility is the marketing . . . One thing about the production is that subscribers, although they're paying £100 or whatever, want to see something in a fairly cheap form. Because they see it as a kind of confidential service, they think if it's typewritten it's specially for them. So it's first class mail, typed and copied on cartridge paper, never on gloss . . .

The other side of the coin is what we do to increase subscription of current newsletters. Direct mail is by far the most effective way of improving sales, and the cost is still only about £200 per thousand even at today's postage rates. Display advertising doesn't really work, except insofar as we advertise in the *FT* — and we're able to get in — we get the space very cheap. Let's take *North Sea Letter* as an example of the kind of things we do.

Exhibit 3 *Euromarket Letter: Analysis of Subscribers as at 1 July 1976*

	UK	Europe	North America	Middle East	Far East	ROW	Total
Banks	65	77	14	7	11	9	183
Finance Institutions	12	2	2	2	1	1	20
Government	2	1	2	2	1	2	10
Mfg. Industry	6	6	2			2	16
Insurance Companies	1	1	1				3
Investment Companies	2	2	1	1			6
Private	1	4	1		1		7
Miscellaneous	4	2				1	7
Unknown	3	6	1		1		11
TOTAL	96	101	24	12	15	15	263

Exhibit 4 *Subscriptions to North Sea Letter: January to June 1976*

MONTH	JAN	FEB	MAR	APR	MAY	JUN
OPENING SUBSCRIPTIONS	258	248	248	250	255	268
Terminations	(55)	(37)	(20)	(12)	(16)	(11)
Renewals	44	29	18	11	12	8
NET TERMINATIONS	(11)	(8)	(2)	(1)	(4)	(3)
New subs: direct mail	0	5	3	2	11	20
New subs: advertising	0	2	1	2	2	0
New subs: misc	1	1	0	2	4	5
NEW SUBSCRIPTIONS	1	8	4	6	17	25
NET GAIN/(LOSS)	(10)	0	2	5	13	22
CLOSING SUBSCRIPTIONS	248	248	250	255	268	290

As at the 1st of January this year, we had 258 annual subscribers. For historical reasons, a lot of these — 55 altogether — terminated in January. Of these 44 renewed, exactly 80%, which is good — the average over all products is about 65%. We have an automatic system whereby each subscriber gets a renewal reminder two months before termination, with two follow-ups.

In February there was a big government announcement about the landing of the first North Sea oil. Based on that, I did a small mailing to about 1800 people — oil interests out of a directory. I normally do a mailing with three insertions: a letter, an A4 fly leaflet and an order card, all with similar graphics. This is part of the corporate identity we introduced back in November 1975. The leaflet includes a money-back offer for people who originally paid cash, and then decide after six issues that the newsletter does not meet their requirements: apart from the fact that this helps us to sell subscriptions, it improves our cash flow, and in practice hardly anyone decides to drop out.

On that particular mailing I got ten definitely attributable subscriptions — this may not be all, because despite the order card, and a note in the letter, some people insist on ordering with their own order forms or by letter, and we can't tie that subscription in with any particular promotion. This 'miscellaneous' category for *North Sea Letter* is 13 so far this year, as you can see from the monthly subscriptions record (Exhibit 4).

In May we changed *North Sea Letter* from fortnightly to weekly, and I did a mailing to over 10,000 people: three different lists, each coded separately. We also did a special offer, a map of the North Sea, showing all the blocks, fields and so on, which you get with your first issue if you take up a subscription — and which we're also offering to previous subscribers if they renew. The map cost just £80 for a run of 500, and it doesn't increase the postal cost of the first issue if someone takes up or renews a subscription. And it gives us something to talk about.

I've also spent a total of £550 this year advertising *North Sea Letter*. The ads are more light-hearted than the mailings, in order to get attention . . . I've done one in the *Petroleum Economist*, one in the *Oil and Gas Journal*, and two in the *FT*. All my ads are couponed, but again, it's hard to relate promotion to sales: as in April, I advertised in the *FT* and received 62 enquiries — but out of that 62 I can only show one definite conversion who used the coded order form. That ad cost me £90 on production, plus £84 for space — that's for a quarter-page. I get the space at 90% discount in the *FT* — when I can get it. Obviously, at that discount I get bottom priority, and I can never guarantee when I'm going to get in: this year, they're being so successful selling space that I'm always getting booted out . . .

There's another thing about advertising which worries me. I suspect that seeing adverts may have a bad effect on existing subscribers — it reduces the feeling of a confidential personalised service . . . In fact I'm seriously thinking of dropping it altogether — it costs a lot to get together, and there's such a hassle getting it into the paper, I'm beginning to think it's not worth the time and trouble. The only time that it is, is when we launch. For example, with *World Accounting Report* we got 450 replies to the first ad in the *FT* . . . But again, the main launch effort for *World Accounting* was direct mail. We did a large mailing in April, to people on seven different lists, that's 30,000 people altogether. And we're hitting another 6,000 in the States this month . . . That makes just over £7,000 I'll have spent on launch mailings, plus £700 on advertising and £200 on a press reception. The response has been very good — over 300 subscriptions to-date and still rising fast . . .

I think *World Accounting* is well-positioned and well-priced . . . What would normally happen is that I would get together with Dick Hall, who runs the Syndication Department, and we'd decide it's about time we introduced something new for profit reasons, and between us we'd put our heads together and think of a field where we think we would have a market. And then I would go into it in more research detail. I would have a number of subject areas to look at. It's a very informal process, which mostly takes place in corridors! Journalists hate meetings, of course, whereas I need them in order to know what other people think . . .

World Accounting was unusual, in that it was dreamt up by the guy who's editor. I did do some informal field research by telephone, using oblique rather than direct questions to check that there was need for such a publication. The object was not to modify the product concept, just to make sure it was viable . . . I did the pricing — talking with the editor, estimating the size of the market and what it would bear, given the competition etc; I also had the likely overheads and promotion costs, and of course our experience with all the other newsletters . . .

What else do we do? Well I don't really do any direct selling, because I'm not qualified to talk about international taxes or European law or whatever . . . I'd always review the content of a brochure, an ad or a letter with the relevant editor. He wouldn't have much direct marketing involvement, but if he was going on a visit he might ask me for some sample copies to give to the people he's interviewing, and then ask me on his return to write to so-and-so and try and sell him a subscription . . .

I've also got a huge stand which either goes as a window display downstairs, or which I set up at conferences. For overseas conferences I just send sample copies to go inside delegates' folders, or alternatively a small stand which goes out with the conference department staff, who of course I know. And obviously, we tend to mention *FT* conferences in our editorial, so we help each other . . .

One other thing we're playing with now is letting subscribers have extra copies of a newsletter at an extra charge of 10% of the initial subscription, for each extra copy . . .

This case was prepared by Jules Goddard and Kenneth Simmonds of the London Business School. © Kenneth Simmonds, 1980.

CASE C3
Grand Empereur

Something was wrong with Grand Empereur's performance. As the advertising agency executive working on the Grand Empereur account, Mary Travis was perplexed. Consumers had been very positive in their reactions to Grand Empereur in research, but sales were not measuring up to expectations.

Grand Empereur had been launched by Hedges and Butler, the wine and spirits division of Bass Charrington, in February 1975, to compete in the fast-growing grape brandy market. Brandy is a general term for spirit distilled from fermented fruit juice, usually grape, but also apple, peach, cherry and so on. The name 'Cognac', however, is legally reserved for brandy distilled from grapes in the region around Cognac in the West of France, although sometimes it is colloquially taken to mean any French or any good brandy.

In late 1977 brandies came in three price brands:

£8—£9.50   Napoleon and VSOP cognacs (Very Special Old Pale)
£6—£6.90   3-star cognacs
£4—£4.90   Grape (non-cognac) brandies.

Three Barrells, with a ten-year head start on Grand Empereur, was the only other heavily advertised grape brandy. Hedges and Butler's initial objective had been to win market leadership from Three Barrells within a few years, but it was now nearly three years after the launch and Grand Empereur had only 7% of this sector of the market against Three Barrells' 35%. And there was little sign of change.

In a nutshell, Hedges and Butler's strategy had been to design a brand that looked like a cognac but that sold at a grape brandy price. A great deal of effort and skill had gone into imbuing the bottle, the label, the name, the advertising, and indeed the entire presentation of the brand, with the kinds of values and symbols traditionally reserved for genuine 3-star cognacs. On price, however, it would be placed at the low end of the brandy range, competing head on with Three Barrells.

The idea was that Grand Empereur would steal share both from the famous cognacs and from the grape brandies. The Martell drinker, for example, would be that much more tempted to trade down to a grape brandy. Indeed, much of the growth of the cheap sector since 1972 had been at the expense of the cognacs, aided and abetted by the economic recession. Hedges and Butler had recognised this and had designed Grand Empereur both to encourage this trend and also to capitalise on it. The intended message was: 'Trade down on price but not on quality, or at least, on the appearance of quality'.

Simultaneously, the sheer style of Grand Empereur's presentation was felt by Hedges and Butler to offer something extra to the Three Barrells drinker: 'A brandy just as good, but in a bottle twice as prestigious'. In fact, Grand Empereur did manage to convey a quality image. Its squat, green, opaque bottle — reminiscent of the Grand Marnier bottle — looked, as many said, as good as a £7.50 cognac. In consumer tests Grand Empereur would invariably be placed alongside Martell and even Remy Martin as a very fine and costly brandy. On taste tests, too, Grand Empereur did sufficiently well for Mary Travis to rule out product quality as a problem.

On the advertising side, quality was not so certain. Two campaigns had been run since its launch, both of them accompanied by considerable below-the-line support (mainly trade discounts to get distribution in off-licenses) and point-of-sale promotions (including a national consumer competition shortly after its introduction to the market). In the pre-Christmas period of 1975, its first year in the market, £40,000 had been spent on a national press campaign, with the following objectives:

> a) To familiarise all brandy drinking adults with the new brand as rapidly as possible by:
>> i) creating awareness of the brand, its name and appearance, and generating familiarity and confidence in it.
>> ii) exploiting the intrinsic appeal of the name and packaging as a 'Cognac' with traditional Napoleonic connotations.
> b) To establish a clear brand identity to distinguish it from other grape brandies in terms of quality.

The theme of the campaign, typified by the advertisement shown in Exhibit 1, was episodes from the life of Napoleon, drawn in the style of a Rowlandson cartoon from the nineteenth century. Napoleon is, of course, recognised as the traditional symbol of quality in a brandy. This was the agency's way of bringing this symbol to life and making it proprietory to Grand Empereur.

Then, in Spring 1977, advertising had been resumed with a rather different campaign, but still with the object of establishing Grand Empereur as a well-known brandy. In particular, the task set for the campaign had been put like this:

> Due to widespread confusion over the meaning of 'Cognac' the role of the advertising is to present Grand Empereur simply as a fine French brandy. The advertising for 1977/78 is intended to cut through the confusion, the bogus historicism and traditionalism — the brandy myths — perpetuated by the major cognac brands in their advertising and philosophy.
>
> It is to project an image of quality for Grand Empereur, but without the pretentiousness displayed by the main 3-star cognacs.

The advertisements in Exhibits 2 and 3, both spoofs on contemporary competitive advertising, show two examples of how the agency intepreted this brief.

So far, £23,000 had been spent on this latest campaign, but with little evidence of any market response. With the vital pre-Christmas selling-in period already upon them, with the sales budget of 60,000 cases for the financial year ending 31st March 1978, seeming to be 50% too optimistic, and with the client calling for 'more substantial funds in order to "buy" greater distribution', Mary wondered whether the voluminous data at her disposal offered any clues as to what she should recommend to the client. Exhibits 4 to 11 summarise the general market data available to her and Exhibits 12 and 13 present the current Nielsen store audit data for the grape brandy market.

Exhibit 1   Punch, September 17 1975

*Napoleon Bonaparte, 1803.

Exhibit 2

from France.

What's more, the people who make it have been making fine brandies for years.

What's also nice to know is that a bottle doesn't cost you the earth.

Grand Empereur is smooth, warming and mellow.

Slip down a glass sometime.

And, as you do so, by all means strike a posture.

Slip your right hand under your jacket, and over the left side of your chest.

Let your heart beat proudly.

EVER GET THE FEELING ALL BRANDIES ARE THE SAME?

You may have noticed a tendency among brandy manufacturers to whack Napoleon on the bottle at the drop of a bicorn hat.

The trouble is, the gap between one brandy and the next, whether it's thought of as a 'Napoleon' brandy or not, can be as wide as the gap between Moscow and Paris.

Something the great man knew all about.

You can rest assured with Grand Empereur.

It has every right to be so named.

To start with, it comes

Because you'll be toasting the Great Emperor in a style he would have labelled authentic.

GRAND EMPEREUR
Fine French Brandy

Exhibit 3

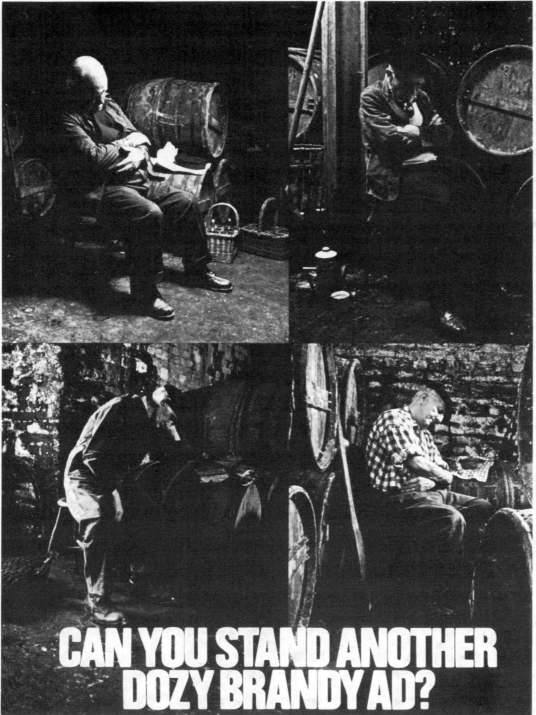

CAN YOU STAND ANOTHER DOZY BRANDY AD?

Second, making a fine brandy does take a bit of time. And it does help if the brandy makers have some experience to draw on.

Third, there's Grand Empereur.

In every respect, Grand Empereur qualifies as a fine brandy.

It's French.

The people who make it have been making fine brandies for years.

But – and this might really wake you up – a bottle doesn't cost you the earth.

Try a glass sometime.

You'll be surprised how smooth, warming and mellow Grand Empereur really is.

Napoleon, never a man to be caught napping, would have settled for nothing less.

Now, if you don't mind, I think we'll let our cellarmen get on with the job.

They've got those barrels to look after.

Just like everybody else.

A great many brandy advertisements over the years have taken place in the dark.

And that's probably where they've left most readers.

They've either been sent to sleep.

Or, if they have woken up from time to time, it's usually to be reminded, one way or another, that brandy comes in barrels. The barrels are in cellars. Cellarmen inhabit the cellars.

And both the barrels and the cellarmen have been maturing in the cellars for a very long, long time.

You may well ask, faced with the same information from everybody, how do you then tell the difference between one brandy and the next?

Or, indeed, what difference does it make?

Before you nod off again, allow us to light a few candles.

In the first place, it does help if the brandy's French.

GRAND EMPEREUR
Fine French Brandy

Exhibit 4 *Grape Brandy Sales*

	Grape Brandy ('000 cases)	Total Brandy ('000 cases)	(%)
1971	—	1450	0
1972	313	1740	18
1973	535	2229	24
1974	596	2056	29
1975	605	1834	33
1976	730	2029	36
1977 (to August)	723	1929	37.5

Source: Customs & Excise

Exhibit 5 *Spirit Sales by Outlet Type, 1976*

	On Licence	Off Licence
Number of Outlets ('000s)	120[1]	36
Sales:		
All Spirits	45%	55%
All Brandy	41%	59%
Cognac	60%	40%
Grape Brandy	15%[2]	85%

1 74,000 Public Houses, 16,000 Restaurants, 30,000 Clubs
2 Very small because of lack of acceptance by the major brewers of non-cognac as the optic brandy.

Source: STATS (MR)
NOP '76

Exhibit 6 *Ownership of Off Licences by Sector*, 1977 versus 1972*

	1972	1977	%
Specialist			
Brewery Owned	6,421	4,919	−23
Multiples	3,380	3,313	−2
Independents	3,387	3,368	−1
	13,188	11,600	−12
Grocer			
Brewery Owned	2,722	1,030	−62
Multiples	3,577	4,808	+35
Co-Ops	1,093	2,671	+144
Independents	8,771	13,726	+57
	16,163	22,235	+38
TOTALS	29,351	33,835	+15
Plus Pubs with Shops	6,528	3,382	−41
Percentage of Outlets Self-Service	9%	31%	

*Terms are defined in Exhibit 12.

Source: STATS (MR)

Exhibit 7 *Case Sales of Grand Empereur**

4-Week Period	1975	1976	1977	1978
1	—	1134	1604	2000**
2	906	561	2535	3000**
3	1319	966	892	2000**
4	2775	1845	1682	4000**
5	2200	2737	640	
6	1410	1389	1208	
7	1255	780	1209	
8	3800	1196	1248	
9	1764	1388	2516	
10	1169	1496	3022	
11	3658	6105	4276	
12	5985	7078	8000**	
13	6252	6695	7000**	
TOTAL	32493	33370	35832	

*One case = 12 bottles
**Sales   Forecast

Exhibit 8 *Grape Brandy Trade Price Structure: Price per Case, October 1977**

	Grand Empereur	Three Barrels	White Swan	Eardinet
Wholesale	45.94	46.34	44.58	44.58
Trade	50.90	50.40	48.36	48.70
Retail including VAT	65.04	61.44	58.32	58.92

*Although these figures include maximum published discounts, heavy promotional allowances are given by all suppliers.

Exhibit 9 *Characteristics and Consumption of Brandy Drinkers*

	All Adults	All Brandy		Heavy Brandy Drinkers[1]	Grape Brandy	
		Drinkers	Volume consumed		Drinkers	Volume consumed
	(%)	(%)	(%)	(%)	(%)	(%)
SEX						
Male	47	50	59	53	54	63
Female	53	50	41	47	46	37
SOCIAL CLASS						
AB	14	19	15	21	20	15
C1	21	23	27	21	19	14
C2	32	30	25	29	30	25
DE	32	28	33	29	31	46
AGE						
18—34	35	35	26	25	36	28
35—54	32	35	38	35	34	33
55+	33	30	36	40	29	39

1. Heavy drinkers account for 91% of brandy consumption.

Source: NOP '76

Exhibit 10   *Brand Profiles*

	Martell (%)	Courvoisier (%)	Hennessy (%)	Remy Martin (%)	Three Barrels (%)	Grand Empereur (%)
DRINKERS OF THE BRAND						
Male	50	52	61	63	52	55
Female	50	48	39	37	48	45
AB	17	31	17	35	14	22
C1	23	25	25	28	17	19
C2	29	27	31	22	22	25
DE	31	17	27	14	40	34
18—34	33	38	32	31	31	35
35—54	34	39	40	54	33	34
55+	33	23	28	15	36	31
ALL BRANDY DRINKERS						
Brand Awareness October 1977						
Spontaneous	65	35	28	12	17	5
Prompted	93	67	72	35	46	18

Source: NOP '76

Exhibit 11   *Use of Mixers*

At home, in pubs, visiting friends, over half the drinkers (especially C2DE women) use a mixer; only in restaurants does the majority (74%) drink it neat.

The main mixers used are ginger ale (15%) and Babycham (14%) outside the home; and ginger ale (10%) and water (10%) in the home.

Exhibit 12   *Nielsen Definitions*

Consumer Sales £ at RSP
Sales made to consumers computed at retailer selling prices and expressed in sterling. The market shares are shown beneath as percentages.

Consumer Sales
Sales made to consumers expressed in the units specified by the client. The market shares are shown beneath as percentages.

Retailer Purchases and Sales
Purchases and sales made by retailers expressed in the units specified by the client.

Stocks and Weeks' Supply
The total amount of stocks held by retailers in their shops and stockrooms expressed in the units specified by the client. Weeks' supply gives the number of weeks these stocks will last at the current rate of sale to consumers.

RSP
The average price paid in pence by consumers calculated from the prices observed in all shops on the day of audit, and weighted by volume.

Shop Handling
The percentage of shops handling the brand.

Sterling Handling
A qualitative figure showing the percentage of total annual turnover accounted for by the shops handling, out-of-stock and purchasing. Total turnover is used in the case of specialists, but total liquor turnover for all grocers.

Sterling Purchasing and Sterling Out-of-Stock ('00s)
The percentage of total turnover accounted for by the shops purchasing in the period and out-of-stock on the day of audit.

Definitions
Universe
All Licensed Grocers and Specialist Off-Licences. Off-Licences forming part of on-licensed premises are excluded. Tenanted outlets are included in the 'Independent Grocers' and 'Other Specialists' breakdowns as appropriate.

Licensed Grocer
A fixed retail outlet, licensed to sell Liquor, with 20% or more of its turnover in groceries and/or provisions which does not have a larger proportion of turnover in any other commodity unless it is one or a combination of Off-Licence trade, bakery goods, or tobacco.

Specialist Off-Licence
A fixed retail outlet which, not being a licensed grocer, has at least 20% of its turnover in alcoholic beverages for consumption off the premises and no greater proportion in any other commodity.

Multiple
A shop belonging to a group of ten or more retail outlets operated under common ownership.

Co-operative
A shop owned and operated by a Co-operative Society.

Independent
A shop not classified as a Multiple or Co-operative.

Major Brewery Owned Chains
These Specialist Chains are included: Arthur Cooper
                                         Bass Charrington/Galleon Wines
                                         Peter Dominic/Westminster Wines
                                         Whitbread/Threshers/Mackies
                                         Victoria Wines

Other Specialists
Remaining Multiple owned Specialist shops and all independent Specialist Off-Licences.

Exhibit 13   *Nielsen store audit data for the grape brandy market*

Sales - Grape Brandy - All Off Licences

Bottles (oo)

Y.AGO %CH	77	JJ (76)	AS	ON	DJ	FM	AM	JJ (77)	AS	ON
TOTAL	48886	4553	5357	8212	16175	6170	6235	6002	6189	8115
Grand Empereur	6.8%	4.5%	5.8	6.6	6.5	7.2	7.6	6.9	6.8	6.4
Three Barrels	37.0	34.5	35.6	34.5	39.7	33.2	34.2	35.8	36.1	38.0
White Swan	1.4	2.9	4.2	2.7	3.0	3.4				
Bordinet	9.2		10.9	12.5	9.7	11.4	9.9	8.8	7.8	7.9
All Other	45.6	58.1	43.5	43.7	41.1	44.8	48.3	48.5	49.3	47.7

£ (oo)

Y.AGO %CH	77	JJ (76)	AS	ON	DJ	FM	AM	JJ (77)	AS	ON
TOTAL	21689	1894	2259	3438	6770	2761	2844	2754	2842	3718
Grand Empereur	6.7	4.3	5.6	6.4	6.4	7.1	7.4	6.8	6.7	6.4
Three Barrels	38.5	36.2	37.5	36.4	41.3	35.1	35.9	37.7	37.6	39.3
White Swan	1.4	3.0	4.1	2.8	3.1	3.4				
Bordinet	8.5		10.1	11.6	9.0	10.3	9.1	8.2	7.3	7.5
All Other	44.9	56.5	42.7	42.8	40.2	44.1	47.6	47.3	48.4	46.8

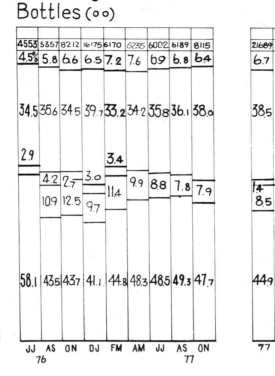
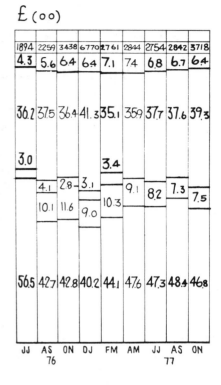

Sales - Grape Brandy - Grocers

Bottles (oo)

Y.AGO %CH	77	JJ (76)	AS	ON	DJ	FM	AM	JJ (77)	AS	ON
TOTAL	27196	2417	2777	4681	9636	3409	3413	3151	3217	4370
Grand Empereur	3.7%	3.3%	4.5	4.6	4.3	4.1	3.7	3.2	3.4	3.1
Three Barrels	45.6	44.7	44.7	42.3	49.1	40.0	41.8	43.4	45.7	46.7
White Swan	0.7	2.7	2.9	1.8	1.3	1.8				
Bordinet	15.1		16.9	19.7	14.7	18.8	16.7	15.4	13.4	13.2
All Other	34.9	49.3	31.0	31.6	30.6	35.3	37.8	38.0	37.5	37.0

£ (oo)

Y.AGO %CH	77	JJ (76)	AS	ON	DJ	FM	AM	JJ (77)	AS	ON
TOTAL	11824	983	1149	1921	3963	1489	1526	1417	1458	1971
Grand Empereur	3.7	3.2	4.3	4.4	4.2	4.0	3.6	3.1	3.3	3.1
Three Barrels	47.8	47.6	47.2	44.6	51.4	42.7	44.1	45.9	47.9	48.5
White Swan	0.7	2.8	3.1	2.0	1.4	1.9				
Bordinet	14.1		15.6	18.4	13.8	17.3	15.6	14.7	12.8	12.6
All Other	33.7	46.4	29.8	30.6	29.2	34.1	36.7	36.3	36.0	35.8

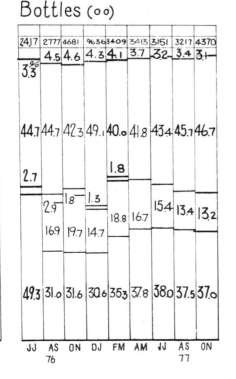
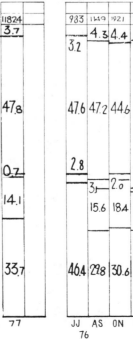
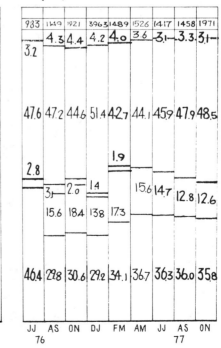

Sales-Grape Brandy-Specialists
Bottles(oo)   £(000)

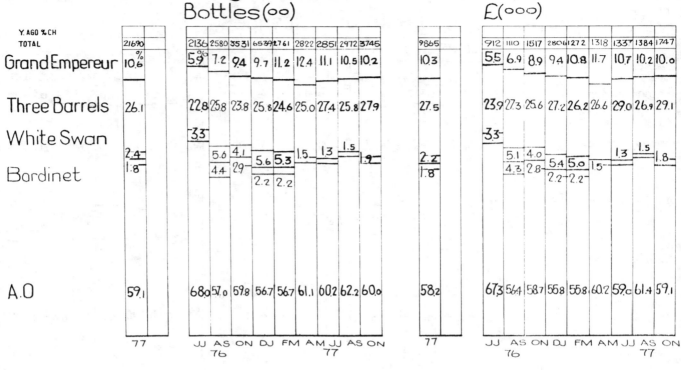

	Y.AGO %CH																					
TOTAL	21690		2136	2580	3531	6539	2761	2822	2851	2972	3745		9865		912	1110	1517	2806	1272	1318	1337	1384	1747
Grand Empereur	10.6 %		5.9%	7.2	9.4	9.7	11.2	12.4	11.1	10.5	10.2		10.3		5.5	6.9	8.9	9.4	10.8	11.7	10.7	10.2	10.0
Three Barrels	26.1		22.8	25.8	23.8	25.8	24.6	25.0	27.4	25.8	27.9		27.5		23.9	27.3	25.6	27.2	26.2	26.6	29.0	26.9	29.1
White Swan	2.4		3.3	5.6	4.1	5.6	5.3	1.5	1.3	1.5	.9		2.2		3.3	5.1	4.0	5.4	5.0	1.3	1.5	1.8
Bordinet	1.8			4.4	2.9	2.2	2.2						1.8			4.3	2.8	2.2	2.2	1.5		
A.O	59.1		68.0	57.0	59.8	56.7	56.7	61.1	60.2	62.2	60.0		58.2		67.3	56.4	58.7	55.8	55.8	60.2	59.0	61.4	59.1

77   JJ AS ON DJ FM AM JJ AS ON   77   JJ AS ON DJ FM AM JJ AS ON
     76   77   76   77

Grand Empereur-All Off Licences   Equiv Bottles(oo)

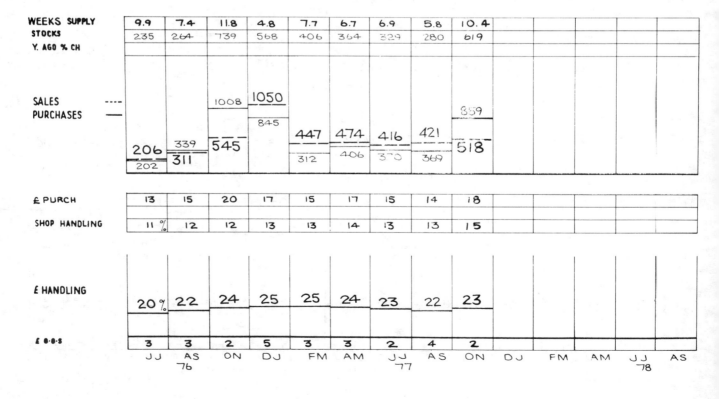

WEEKS SUPPLY	9.9	7.4	11.8	4.8	7.7	6.7	6.9	5.8	10.4				
STOCKS	235	264	739	568	406	364	329	280	619				
Y. AGO % CH													
SALES ----			1008	1050					859				
PURCHASES ——				845	447	474	416	421	518				
	206	339	545										
	202	311			312	406	370	369					
£ PURCH	13	15	20	17	15	17	15	14	18				
SHOP HANDLING	11 %	12	12	13	13	14	13	13	15				
£ HANDLING	20 %	22	24	25	25	24	23	22	23				
£ O·O·S	3	3	2	5	3	3	2	4	2				

JJ AS ON DJ FM AM JJ AS ON DJ FM AM JJ AS
     76   77   78

Av R.S.P-All Off Licences

Pence per Equiv Bottle

Grand Empereur

Three Barrels

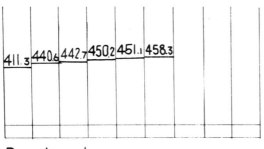

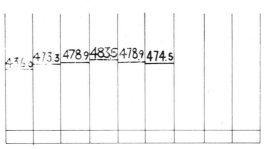

Bardinet

All Others

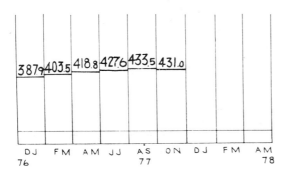

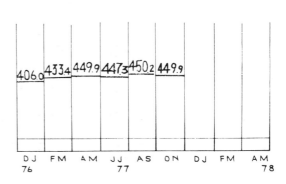

	D J	FM	AM	JJ	AS	ON	D J	FM	AM
	76		77						78

All Off Licences

Bottles (00(

Three Barrels

Bardinet

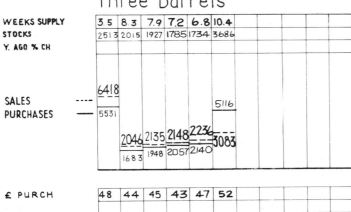

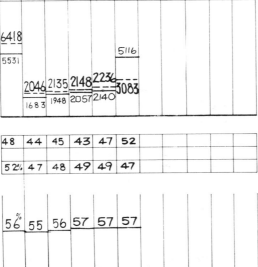

WEEKS SUPPLY	3.5	8.3	7.9	7.2	6.8	10.4	1.4 1.5 1.6 1.5 1.6 2.0
STOCKS	2513	2015	1927	1785	1734	3686	240 120 111 92 87 146
Y. AGO % CH							

SALES PURCHASES	£ PURCH	SHOP HANDLING

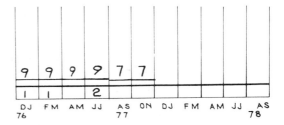

	D J	FM	AM	JJ	AS	ON	D J	FM	AM	JJ	AS
	76		77								78

*Insufficient Data

Sales-Grape Brandy-Co·ops   Grocers Equiv. Bottles (oo)

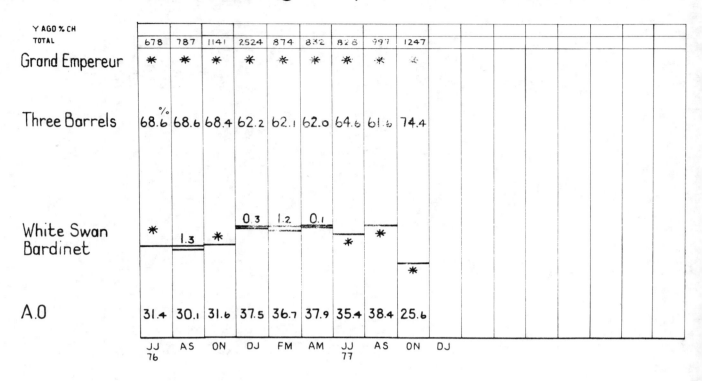

Y AGO % CH TOTAL	678	787	1141	2524	874	832	828	997	1247
Grand Empereur	*	*	*	*	*	*	*	*	*
Three Barrels	68.6%	68.6	68.4	62.2	62.1	62.0	64.6	61.6	74.4
White Swan Bardinet	*	1.3	*	0.3	1.2	0.1	*	*	*
A.O	31.4	30.1	31.6	37.5	36.7	37.9	35.4	38.4	25.6

JJ 76   AS   ON   DJ   FM   AM   JJ 77   AS   ON   DJ

Sales-Grape Brandy-Mults   Grocers Equiv. Bottles (oo)

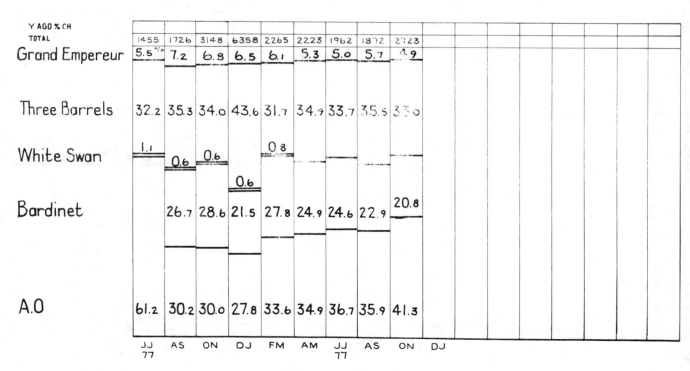

Y AGO % CH TOTAL	1455	1726	3148	6358	2265	2223	1962	1872	2723
Grand Empereur	5.5%	7.2	6.8	6.5	6.1	5.3	5.0	5.7	4.9
Three Barrels	32.2	35.3	34.0	43.6	31.7	34.9	33.7	35.5	33.0
White Swan	1.1	0.6	0.6	0.6	0.8				
Bardinet		26.7	28.6	21.5	27.8	24.9	24.6	22.9	20.8
A.O	61.2	30.2	30.0	27.8	33.6	34.9	36.7	35.9	41.3

JJ 77   AS   ON   DJ   FM   AM   JJ 77   AS   ON   DJ

*Insufficient Data

Sales-Grape Brandy-Inds   Grocers Equiv. Bottles (oo)

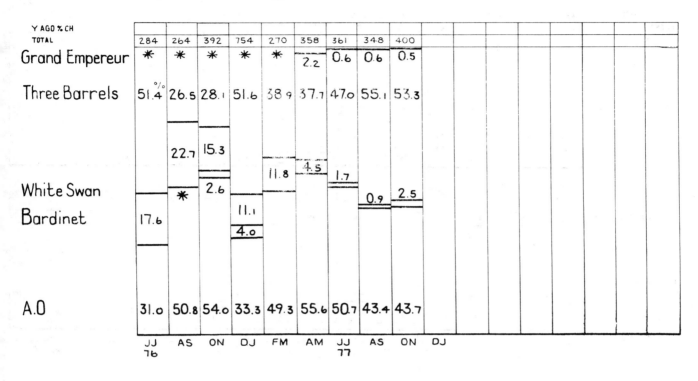

Y AGO % CH TOTAL	284	264	392	754	270	358	361	348	400
Grand Empereur	*	*	*	*	*	2.2	0.6	0.6	0.5
Three Barrels	51.4%	26.5	28.1	51.6	38.9	37.7	47.0	55.1	53.3
		22.7	15.3		11.8	4.5	1.7		
White Swan		*	2.6					0.9	2.5
Bardinet	17.6			11.1					
				4.0					
A.O	31.0	50.8	54.0	33.3	49.3	55.6	50.7	43.4	43.7

JJ 76   AS   ON   DJ   FM   AM   JJ 77   AS   ON   DJ

*Insufficient Data

Grand Empereur-Grocers   Equiv Bottles (oo)

Co-ops   Mults

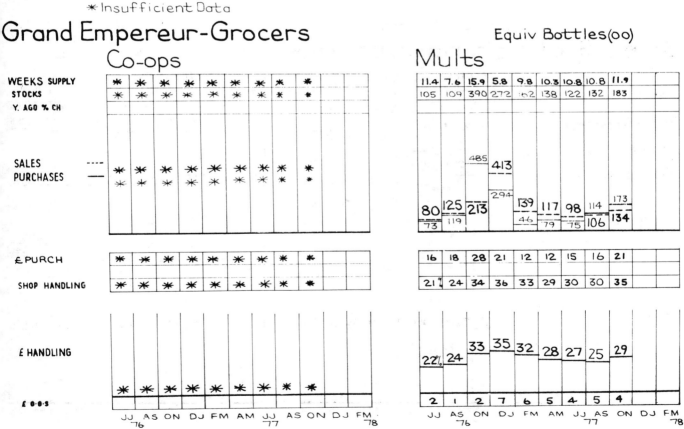

	Co-ops									Mults								
WEEKS SUPPLY	*	*	*	*	*	*	*	*	*	11.4	7.6	15.9	5.8	9.8	10.3	10.8	10.8	11.9
STOCKS Y. AGO % CH	*	*	*	*	*	*	*	*	*	105	109	390	272	62	138	122	132	183
SALES	*	*	*	*	*	*	*	*	*	80	125	213	485 413 294	139	117	98	114	173
PURCHASES	*	*	*	*	*	*	*	*	*	73	119			46	79	75	106	134
£ PURCH	*	*	*	*	*	*	*	*	*	16	18	28	21	12	12	15	16	21
SHOP HANDLING	*	*	*	*	*	*	*	*	*	21%	24	34	36	33	29	30	30	35
£ HANDLING	*	*	*	*	*	*	*	*	*	22%	24	33	35	32	28	27	25	29
£ O.O.S										2	1	2	7	6	5	4	5	4

JJ 76 AS ON DJ FM AM JJ 77 AS ON DJ FM 78   JJ 76 AS ON DJ FM AM JJ 77 AS ON DJ FM 78

Grand Empereur-Inds-Grocers

Equiv Bottles(oo)

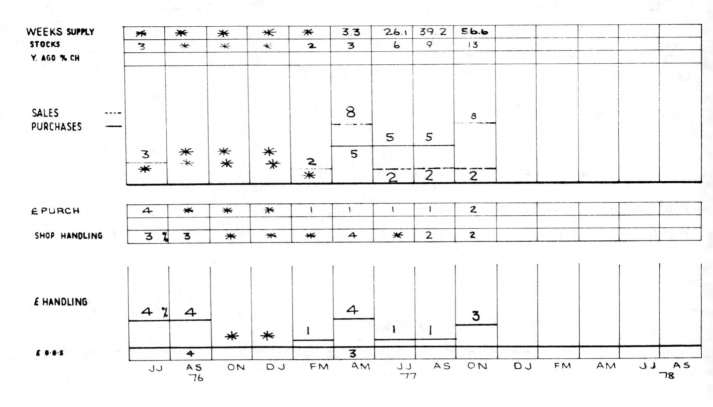

	JJ	AS 76	ON	DJ	FM	AM	JJ 77	AS	ON	DJ	FM	AM	JJ	AS 78
WEEKS SUPPLY	*	*	*	*	*	3.3	26.1	39.2	56.6					
STOCKS	3	*	*	*	2	3	6	9	13					
Y. AGO % CH														
SALES ----						8			8					
PURCHASES —						5	5	5						
	3	*	*	*	2	5								
	*	*	*	*	*		2	2	2					
£ PURCH	4	*	*	*	1	1	1	1	2					
SHOP HANDLING	3 % 3		*	*	*	4	*	2	2					
£ HANDLING	4 % 4		*	*	1	4	1	1	3					
£ o·o·s		4				3								

*Insufficient Data

Sales-Grape Brandy-Specialists

Equiv Bottles (oo)

Major Groups

Others

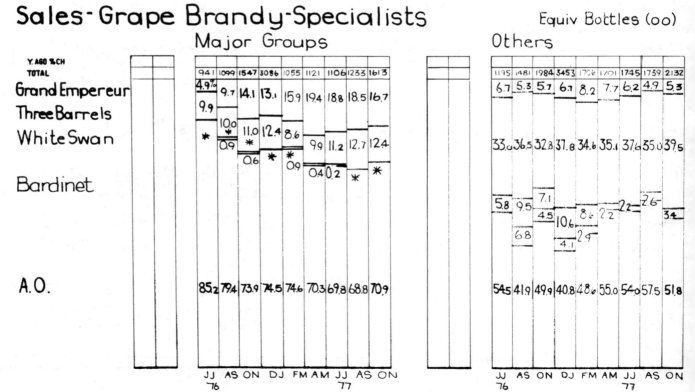

	JJ 76	AS	ON	DJ	FM	AM	JJ 77	AS	ON
TOTAL	941	1099	1547	3086	1055	1121	1106	1233	1613
Grand Empereur	4.9%	9.7	14.1	13.1	15.9	19.4	18.8	18.5	16.7
Three Barrels	9.9		10.0						
White Swan	*	0.9	11.0	12.4	8.6	9.9	11.2	12.7	12.4
			0.6	*	0.9	0.4 0.2	*	*	
Bardinet									
A.O.	85.2	79.4	73.9	74.5	74.6	70.3	69.8	68.8	70.9

	JJ 76	AS	ON	DJ	FM	AM	JJ 77	AS	ON
TOTAL	1195	1481	1984	3453	1706	1701	1745	1739	2132
Grand Empereur	6.7	5.3	5.7	6.7	8.2	7.7	6.2	4.9	5.3
White Swan	33.6	36.5	32.8	37.8	34.6	35.1	37.6	35.0	39.5
Bardinet	5.8	9.5	7.1			2.2	2.6		
			4.5	10.6	8.6	2.2			3.4
		6.8		4.1	2.9				
A.O.	54.5	41.9	49.9	40.8	48.6	55.0	54.0	57.5	51.8

Grand Empereur - Specialists

Major Groups

Equiv Bottles (oo)

Others

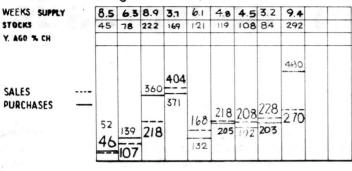

	JJ	AS	ON	DJ	FM	AM	JJ	AS	ON		
WEEKS SUPPLY	8.5	6.3	8.9	3.7	6.1	4.8	4.5	3.2	9.4		
STOCKS	45	78	222	169	121	119	108	84	292		
Y. AGO % CH											

SALES ----
PURCHASES ——

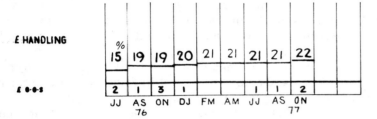

	JJ	AS	ON	DJ	FM	AM	JJ	AS	ON		
£ PURCH	11	16	18	19	19	19	18	18	21		
SHOP HANDLING	22%	27	27	29	31	31	31	30	32		

	JJ	AS	ON	DJ	FM	AM	JJ	AS	ON		
£ HANDLING	%15	19	19	20	21	21	21	21	22		
£ O-O-S	2	1	3	1			1	1	2		

JJ AS ON DJ FM AM JJ AS ON
76 / 77

	JJ	AS	ON	DJ	FM	AM	JJ	AS	ON		
WEEKS SUPPLY	8.9	8.5	9.7	4.8	7.3	6.9	7.5	5.6	10.2		
STOCKS	72	77	127	127	121	104	93	55	131		
Y. AGO % CH											

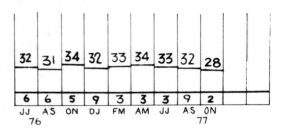

	JJ	AS	ON	DJ	FM	AM	JJ	AS	ON		
£ PURCH	17	20	26	20	22	26	19	17	22		
SHOP HANDLING	21	21	21	23	23	24	24	23	25		

	JJ	AS	ON	DJ	FM	AM	JJ	AS	ON		
£ HANDLING	32	31	34	32	33	34	33	32	28		
£ O-O-S	6	6	5	9	3	3	3	9	2		

JJ AS ON DJ FM AM JJ AS ON
76 / 77

This case was prepared by Kenneth Simmonds of the London Business School.
© Kenneth Simmonds, 1980.

CASE C4
Chalfont Bedspreads

John Blore, the new Commercial Manager of Chalfont Bedspreads Ltd of Manchester, had concluded that the best way to increase Chalfont's static sales of patterned cotton bedspreads was to extend sales coverage to large retail furniture stores. Blore's investigation of the United Kingdom market figures had disclosed that more than twice as many mattresses were sold annually as bedspreads. Blore was certain that many people did not use bedspreads and that there was an unfilled demand that could be reached by selling bedspreads at the time people were buying bedroom furniture. Already a few furniture firms were selling household textiles, including sheets, blankets, duvets and bedspreads; moreover, retail furniture salesmen were generally paid an incentive commission of around 2% and bedspread sales would add to their earnings.

All Chalfont's £3 million sales were made through the Crane Sales Agency whose 15 salesmen called on some 450 wholesalers, multiples and large department stores, representing the lines of a number of textile manufacturers. Crane received a normal commission of 5% on Chalfont turnover, but Blore realised that some incentive would be needed to compensate for the cost of breaking into the new outlets. He was prepared to increase the commission to 7½% for the first year's orders from new outlets. Some of the increase would presumably be paid as an additional incentive to the Crane salesforce who received a straight 2% commission on sales, yet the remainder would make a significant contribution to Crane's profit. Chalfont already represented 25% of Crane's turnover.

Blore was also contemplating a television campaign. Chalfont bedspreads presented a very colourful range that, allowing for retail store margins of around 30% on sales, retailed from £14 to £36 each. He could envisage a kaleidoscope of colour in short spot advertising on national TV. Competing mattress firms regularly advertised their brands, but to date no bedspread firm had mounted a campaign.

This case was prepared by Kenneth Simmonds of the London Business School.
© Kenneth Simmonds, 1978.

CASE C5
Alabaster Soap

It seemed a natural step up for David Brandon when an invitation came through an executive search firm to join Marcelin Greene Ltd of Uxbridge as Marketing and Sales Director. At age 36, he was already one of four national line sales managers for a leading branded food firm and he was ambitious to take full responsibility for the sales and marketing of a single company.

Greene's was a sleepy one-product firm selling its 'Alabaster' soap in toilet and bath size packages throughout Britain. Net turnover was about £1.6 million per annum, giving Alabaster around 2% of the national market for toilet soap in tablet form. By using the retail price index as a deflator, David calculated that in real terms Greene's sales seemed to have been decreasing around 5% per annum over the past four years. Nevertheless, the Alabaster brand, with its distinctive white emblem of a Grecian urn, was widely recognised and the firm made a profit before tax of 6% on sales. The brand had been sold for sixty years and had a good quality image. David was confident he could reverse the trend with an energetic sales campaign. He was on a first-name basis with many of the buyers for national supermarket and retail chains, came into frequent contact with them to arrange special deals and promotions, and had entertained and been 'out on the town' with a number.

One of David's first actions on joining Greene's was to commission a special Nielson-type study of Alabaster representation in different outlets and its share of the market through those outlets. The figures are summarised in Exhibit 1. There was some difference from region to region not shown in this summary, but David concluded that a national sales drive aimed at selected supermarket chains where Alabaster was weakest should be his first priority. He would have to build a national sales force, however, to replace Greene's current manufacturers' representatives.

During the Second World War, Greene's had been forced to use general manufacturers' representatives working on commission to cover its accounts. Thereafter, Greene's had never fully returned to an employee salesforce. The firm now operated through representatives in six regions, although its own Sales Director covered a seventh — London Western — operating from the Uxbridge offices. The representatives worked on a 2% commission for all orders from their regions, including national wholesale and retail chains who purchased for delivery to other regions. Greene's then supplied the orders from bulk warehouse stocks which they maintained at four sites and replenished from Uxbridge. The six regions covered by the representatives were London Eastern, Southwestern, Midlands, Northern, Scotland and Northern Ireland.

The recommended retail price for a standard Alabaster toilet bar was 20p. This placed the brand in the upper third by price, among the quality brands, although some soaps were considerably more expensive. For a standard toilet bar, prices ranged from 5p for a very cheap supermarket soap, through 14p for a typical leading national brand, to 25p for a high-quality name brand. Six brands dominated the market with Lux, Palmolive and Imperial Leather enjoying shares of around 11% and Camay, Fairy and Lifebouy shares of about 8%. Fresh and Knight's Castile followed with 4 or 5% each and the remainder of the market was divided equally between 'own brands' and 'others'.

The total marketing expense for Greene's was 15% of its invoiced sales figure net of discounts. Wholesalers were invoiced at list prices less 20% less 10% and the 20% margin was expected to be passed on to the retailer. Very large chains buying directly received both discounts. Warehousing and distribution represented the

Exhibit 1   *Market Audits Limited Summary Distribution Study*

Client: Marcelin Greene Limited

Retail Segment	Estimated Total Outlets ('000s)	Proportion of Sample Stocking Alabaster (%)	Alabaster Share of Total Sample Outlet Sales of Toilet Soap in Tablet Form at Retail Prices (9 months) (%)
Grocery Outlets	98	31	1.3
Chemists	13	47	3.9
Other	5	64	2.1

largest share of marketing expenses, averaging 10% of sales. Advertising took another £40,000 per annum and was spent largely on displays in women's magazines.

Several competitors spent double the Alabaster percentage on advertising, but David was not impressed with advertising as a strategy for increasing share. He referred to the heavy advertisers as 'men of the sixties'. Virtually all housewives bought toilet soap and some 9% — disproportionately grouped in the 35 to 44 age bracket — were classified as heavy users. To get at these heavy users, David argued there was no substitute for supermarket display. Two-thirds of all soap sales went through this segment when Boots, with 14% of the market, was included with supermarkets and self-service groceries. This left only small shares of 14% from the remaining grocery outlets, 8% from other chemists and 12% from departmental and variety stores.

For the longer term, David had more ambitious goals. He planned to introduce a 'bath gel' under the Alabaster brand. He could see that the use of bath gels was still in its early stages in the United Kingdom. Badedas, owned by Beechams, was a widely recognised brand and sold at a very profitable price to a small percentage of the population. Its normal price of 66p for 64 fl ozs gave it by David's estimate over 1,000 per cent margin on production cost. While there were also some less well-known brands sold, widespread use of gel as a soap replacement in bath and shower, as had developed throughout France and Germany, was yet to come.

David had seen a recent survey which disclosed that six per cent of the English population put washing-up liquid into their baths; thus many were not averse to the use of liquid gels. Most of the United Kingdom population, however, were not yet aware that gels could replace soap and were more than just liquid bath additives. Some even associated use of Badedas with upper-class pretensions because of its advertising approach. David retold the story with great glee of the woman who asked in the chemist's for 'Baa-dee-dah'.

David's idea was to launch his new gel as 'Alabaster Gold', thus building on the Alabaster name. The new gel would be a rich golden liquid in a golden container with the familiar white emblem. The launch would be based on widespread coverage of supermarkets with a massive introductory point-of-sale display backed up with considerable media advertising. By such a dramatic move within the next year, David believed that he would put Greene's in on the ground floor of the trend towards gels and could establish Alabaster Gold as a generic name for liquid gel.

Advertising and promotion for the initial launch would require a budget of £250,000, but the high margins from a gel would quickly repay the initial investment. A temporary bank loan would be required, but David was sure that there would be ample security from the Uxbridge property. Land values in Uxbridge had escalated a thousandfold since Greene's had purchased their site and the firm was sitting on an investment worth over £3 million.

This case was prepared by Kenneth Simmonds of the London Business School. © Kenneth Simmonds, 1971.

CASE C6
Rediplant

Early in 1971 John Bryant, owner and Chairman of a successful English timber products firm, was asked by his close friend Martin Nievelt whether he would consider becoming a Commissar of Rediplant NV — a company being formed to exploit the new Rediplant method for packaging bulbs. Commissars of Dutch corporations are outside directors appointed by the shareholders to oversee the employee directors. They have a number of specific powers and their consent must be obtained for all borrowing by the company. Martin also wanted John's opinion on the number of sealing machines that should be purchased in advance of the first full season of Rediplant sales. This was a particularly difficult decision, as there was little guide to the volume of sales that could be expected and most of the packaging would have to be carried out during the month of August.

Martin Nievelt and Walter Praag were owners and joint Managing Directors of Hans Praag & Co, an old established Dutch bulb exporter and based in Hillegom, Holland. Before the Rediplant development, Praag had concentrated on bulb sales to France, United Kingdom, Switzerland and Germany, selling to nurserymen, wholesalers and large retailers as well as directly to the public through mail order catalogues. There were two seasons each year. The larger was for spring bulbs which were lifted from the bulb fields and distributed in the autumn for planting up to mid-winter. This season represented 70% of the bulb market and covered tulips, crocuses, narcissi and hyacinths.

Performance of many firms in the bulb business had been poor and there had been numerous failures over the previous two years. There were some 600 exporting houses and, although they belonged to an industry association and argued the need to hold price levels, competition amongst them resulted in continual margin cutting. Praag had recorded losses both years, mainly because of low response to their mail order catalogues, attributed by Martin Nievelt to cold, wet weekends discouraging customers from thinking about gardening. While substantial profits could still be made in a good mail order season, the response rates had been dropping at an average rate of 8% per year and increased order size had not grown in step. The development of the Rediplant system therefore came at a particularly opportune time and gave Praag an opportunity to differentiate its product and increase its margins. Praag decided to withdraw from the direct mail order side of the business and concentrate on building the broadest possible sales of Rediplant packed bulbs. Sale of the mail order lists, moreover, would provide finance for the new effort and avoid surrender of ownership interest which was usually required in order to obtain long-term bank lending for small private companies.

*The standard abbreviation for a Dutch guilder, or florin, is Fl. Exchange rates in January 1971 were:
$1 (US) = Fl.3.60
£1 (Stg) = Fl.8.60
1 Deutsche Mark = Fl.1.00*

The French, German and Swiss mailing lists were sold to Beinum & Co late in 1970. Beinum was the largest Dutch bulb merchant with a turnover of around 50 million guilders (Fl.50 m.)[1] and a mailing list of 5 million catalogues. Praag's United Kingdom mail order list and the UK wholesale business were sold to Sutcliffe Seeds Ltd of Norwich. Sutcliffe were moving into the bulb market as an extension to their traditional seed activities and the agreement provided for Praag to supply all Sutcliffe's requirements for Dutch bulbs, whilst retaining the right to go directly to a selected list of retail chains and large stores in the United Kingdom.

Development of the Rediplant System

The idea for Rediplant was first conceived in November 1969 by Walter Praag, who concentrated on the engineering and production side of the business, leaving

203

the commercial side to Martin Nievelt. Rediplant was basically a transparent plastic strip moulded to hold bulbs in equally-spaced blisters open at the top and bottom. It was designed as a usage container that could be planted directly in the soil without removing the bulbs, giving them protection from frost, birds, rodents and slugs, and enabling the bulbs to be easily retrieved for planting in subsequent seasons.

Walter Praag explained the development in this way: 'I got the idea at the end of 1969 and aimed only to make our competitive position easier and to solve planting problems for the buyer. We ran trials and found that it made not only for easier planting but also gave protection and a better flower, though it was not invented for that purpose. We tested a great quantity with a sensitive control test and the packaged bulbs showed up better than bulbs planted by hand. We limited our tests to hyacinths, tulips, narcissi, crocuses and gladioli, because the others have extra difficulties for packaging and these are the main selling items. With gladioli we had some trouble and I had to redesign the pack as the sprouts came out of the side of the bulb rather than the top. We make our own prototype wooden moulds and have our own cabinet maker for this. When we told people the name of our new pack was Rediplant many remarked that it was not a very good name — but minutes later they would all use the name without any prompting. We decided it must be a very good name'.

The bulbs were packed automatically into previously formed plastic strips which were then sealed and fitted into a cardboard sleeve printed with details of the bulbs and planting instructions. After considerable experimentation the new pack was ready for launching and in May 1970 a vacuum forming machine was purchased to make quantities of the strips. At this stage the pack was comparatively crude, with a single coloured cardboard sleeve which totally enclosed the plastic strip which was in turn stapled together to hold the bulbs.

Mr Nievelt did his own market research by asking friends, acquaintances and the general public what they thought of the packs and if they would buy them. On his frequent sales trips to England, for example, he asked customers in garden centres and large stores he visited whether they would buy the packs and they all said they would. The packs contained six tulips with a suggested retail price of 32½p, as against a price of 25p for similar loose bulbs. Martin also asked retailers in England what they thought of the packaging. He recalled: 'Large retail chains, Woolworths, Boots, Debenhams and John Lewis liked it and after a while the larger garden centres would say that they would buy it. Small centres and garden stores, however, generally said they did not like Rediplant. They gave few reasons but they seemed worried that it would mean other types of stores would find it easier to sell bulbs . Martin also persuaded three different outlets to test market the strips — a store on a US air force base at Woodbridge, a seedshop in Ipswich and a garden centre at Ramsey, Essex. Each received one hundred strips, without charge, and each quickly sold the entire assignment at 32½p.

Rediplant packaging was next featured in Praag mail order catalogues for spring bulbs sent out in autumn 1970. These were mailed to some 300,000 customers in England, France and Germany at a cost including postage of £0.05 each. Prices for a Rediplant package of six bulbs were set about 30% below the catalogue prices for a standard quantity of 10 loose bulbs, making the price for a Rediplant bulb 15% higher than an equivalent loose bulb. Rediplant packaging featured on the cover and the catalogue started with a two-page spread outlining the Rediplant system and offering a 200% guarantee to replace every non-flowering Rediplant bulb with two new bulbs. The spread also showed how Rediplant strips could be planted in evenly spaced rows or in cartwheel or zigzag patterns. Walter Praag commented that this sort of thing seemed to appeal particularly to the German market, who were also much more concerned with rodent and insect damage than other nationalities. He thought the British tended to be keener gardeners and more knowledgeable about bulbs, while many more potential customers in France and Germany would avoid buying loose bulbs that they did not understand, or else buy some and plant them upside down. With Rediplant packages these customers would find it much easier. Praag experience had been, too, that the British tended to be much more price conscious than the others, while the French tended to identify value with the price charged.

As orders began to come in during the early winter months, Praag were very encouraged by the high proportion of Rediplant sales. Final figures were as follows:

Country	Catalogues Posted	No. of Orders Received	Average Order Size	% of Total Ordered in Rediplant Packs		
				Tulips	Hyacinths	Narcissi
UK	150,000	8,056	£3.50	18	20	10
France	101,000	5,581	£5.20	27	32	13
W. Germany	50,000	2,091	£5.45	44	39	39

Examination of 160 UK orders at random showed the average order for Rediplant to be £2, representing an average 50% of the customer's total order.

Walter Praag continued work on the Rediplant design and at this stage employed a local firm of two young design consultants with excellent reputations in the textile and packaging markets. The cardboard sleeve was redesigned with full colour pictures of the blooms and better instructions, and the strips were made narrower and extended to include seven bulbs rather than six in a new pack measuring 40 centimetres. Martin Nievelt thought this might discourage price comparison with loose bulbs sold in dozens. These new strips can be seen on the display stand in Exhibit 1.

For sale through retail outlets, special units of 90 and 180 strips were designed with wire pegs for each six strips. These pegs could be fitted onto pegboards or specially designed Rediplant display stands for floor or counter displays. The mix of varieties for the units was based on a statistical analysis of the historical proportions of bulb sales and would not be varied for individual orders. The '180' unit contained 112 strips of tulips in 14 varieties, 24 strips of hyacinths in 4 varieties, 12 strips of narcissi in 2 varieties and 32 strips of crocuses in 4 varieties. Large display posters illustrating the planting of Rediplant strips were designed to accompany each unit, which would be boxed with or without a display stand as required.

Patents for the Rediplant system of packaging were applied for and obtained in the Benelux countries, the United Kingdom, France, Germany, Canada and the USA. This patent was granted for a 'usage' package and competitors would find it difficult to break through simply by altering the design. Moreover, anyone wishing to compete would find it essential on a cost basis to package in Holland, rather than to ship, pack and then redirect the bulbs — and Praag were sure that they would be advised by the Dutch Customs if their patent was infringed.

Partnership with Van Diemen Bros

In early 1970 when the new designs were being developed Praag were approached by Van Diemen Bros who had seen the packages and wanted to explore ways by which they too could use the new packaging method. Discussions led to the idea of a partnership for developing the system. Van Diemen had the largest sales force in the Dutch bulb industry, owned their own bulb fields and research laboratories and were suppliers by appointment to the Netherlands Royal Family. 'The idea went against the mentality of the industry that it is not right to work together', said Martin Nievelt. 'We had the idea but the other firm had forty sales people against Praags' two, as well as contacts with wholesalers all round the world. A partnership would provide resources and backing at the same time as it removed one of the major sources of potential competition. Another reason was that the product had to be kept secret while patents were applied for and Van Diemen was one of the few companies with its own laboratories'. Nievelt believed that the fragmented nature of the industry and the lack of product differentiation were the prime causes of low prices and small or non-existent profits and he hoped that the combined strength of the two firms would enable them to make a much larger impact on the bulb market and eventually claim a significant proportion of Dutch bulb sales at higher margins.

Exhibit 1

Assortment 180 s

An exclusive new pre-assembled
Assortment for You!

112 packs of tulips in 14 varieties
    7 bulbs per pack

 24 packs of hyacinths in 4 varieties
    5 bulbs per pack

 12 packs of narcissi in 2 varieties
    5 bulbs per pack

 32 packs of crocus in 4 varieties
    14 bulbs per pack

180 packs in 24 well-chosen varieties

Floor space:	15" × 33"
Height display:	63"
Size display poster:	31½" × 18½"
Weight case:	59 lbs.

This display offers an easy and fast
set-up with a minimum of floor
space

Advantages:

REDIPLANT is unique (patent
pending)
Honest presentation in see-through
packs
Optimal ventilation preserves the
quality of the bulbs
Packs are delivered on pegs, saving
labour in setting up display (except
assortment 180 and 90)
REDIPLANT has been successfully
tested
Over a century of successful bulb-
growing experience guarantees a
high quality product
Your Department as well as the
Dutch Dept. of Agriculture inspects
all bulbs before they are exported

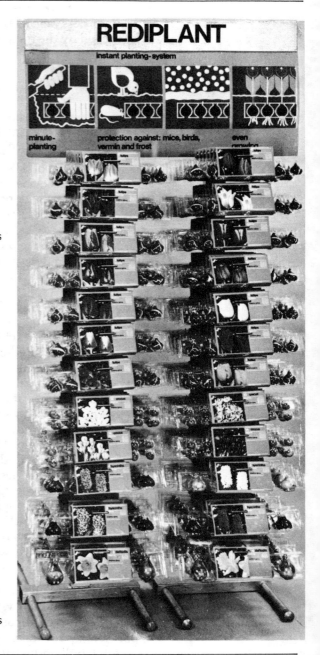

The arrangement worked out on a friendly basis with Van Diemen was that
Rediplant NV would be formed as a limited company, with Hans Praag & Co and
Van Diemen Bros each owning 50% of the equity. Rediplant would lease Praag's
storage and packing facilities in Hillegom and manufacture for the two sales companies, invoicing them at cost after payment of a royalty to Praag of Fl 0.02 per
strip. Praag would retain the right to all sales anywhere in the world destined for
customers via mail order and also to wholesale sales in the United Kingdom,
Holland and Switzerland. Van Diemen would cover wholesale sales in all remaining countries. This arrangement meant that there would be little change from past
concentration because Praag had had very little wholesale revenue from France or
Germany. The direct mail market, moreover, accounted for some 20% of Dutch
bulb exports for dry sales. Martin Nievelt and the senior Van Diemen agreed to act

as commissars for the new firm and to ask John Bryant to act as a third neutral commissar. Solicitors were asked to draw up formal agreements and as at the end of February 1971 the drafts had not yet been received.

Meanwhile, Walter Praag and Dik Van Diemen, son of the Van Diemen President, had agreed to become joint Managing Directors of Rediplant and had become immersed in detailed planning of the production requirements for the 1971 spring bulb season. The elder Van Diemen had also applied to the Dutch government for a grant to develop the invention — on the basis of its potential contribution to Dutch exports — and Rediplant had received a non-returnable grant of 65,000 guilders.

Meeting the Demand   The period for selling spring bulbs to intermediate outlets ran from January through August, but delivery requirements would be very tight. Excluding mail order business, 55% of all sales must be packed by 17th August, the next 30% by the end of August and the last 15% by the end of September. All United States sales were included in the initial 55% because of the need to meet shipping dates, but another week could be saved by air freight although it would increase the freight cost for a standard shipment from $6 per '180' unit to $18. After September, mail order business could then be supplied fairly evenly until early December. Delivery commitments were regarded as very important by all the Rediplant executives. The retail buying season was concentrated and a supplier who failed to meet his commitments would ruin his chance of repeat business. Martin Nievelt considered it would be better to take a limited amount of Rediplant orders in the first season rather than run the risk of not being able to meet orders on time and ruining the Rediplant name.

The supply of bulbs themselves presented few problems. Most bulbs were bought from the growers on a contract basis in the spring while still in the ground. A buyer would contract to buy all the production of a given acreage at a fixed price per bulb. As he sold to his customers before he knew how many bulbs he would receive from this acreage, he had to buy any additional requirements or sell any excess on the free market where the price could fluctuate wildly depending on whether there was a glut or a poor season. Although the average price of bulbs could usually be predicted within 10%, a given tulip had fluctuated in price between Fl 14 and Fl 22 per hundred over the previous few years. By industry agreement, payment to growers was required promptly on 1st November and for a merchant to retain a good name amongst suppliers this could not be delayed.

The real problems in supply stemmed from the short packaging season after the bulbs were taken from the fields. Crocuses might not be ready to be packed until 25th July, narcissi and hyacinths until the end of July, and tulips between the 25th July and 10th August depending on the variety. Packaging, therefore, had to be very carefully planned.

When the bulbs arrived for packaging they would be inspected and sorted before being placed in the PVC strips by semi-automatic filling machines. The strips would then pass along conveyors to an automatic radio frequency sealing machine and from there to a station where they would be fitted with the cardboard sleeve and packed into cartons. While the vacuum-forming machine making the PVC strips could produce only 900 strips per hour, stocks could be built up well before packaging began. The sorting machine worked rapidly and could take large quantities of bulbs so they did not limit the output in any way. The speed of the filling machines could also be increased if needed. Four filling machines, moreover, had been built and these could keep at least four sealing machines busy. The limiting factor, then, seemed to be the number of sealing machines. These operated with an output of 900 strips per hour and at Fl 16,500 were the most expensive items. One machine had been specially designed for Rediplant and modified after tests. Orders for further units would have to be placed immediately as there was a three month delivery time and orders placed after the beginning of March might not be received in time for the packaging season if there was any delay. The machines were believed to be reliable, but if an electronic component should break down an engineer from the manufacturer would be required.

Praag and Van Diemen were annoyed that the manufacturer of the sealing machine was insisting on payment before delivery, had raised the price to Fl 16,500 from a verbally agreed figure of Fl 12,500 and would not make any effort to schedule shorter delivery. They had, therefore, investigated other methods of sealing that did not require expensive equipment. All had major disadvantages. Adhesives and stapling were much slower and stapling spoilt the look of the package while adhesives attracted the dust from the bulbs and were not 100% effective.

Martin Nievelt argued that only one further sealing machine should be ordered. He pointed out that there was no guarantee that huge volumes of Rediplant could be sold in the first season when the buyers knew it to be experimental; moreover, financial difficulties could limit the opportunity to expand in later years. Hans Praag & Co had little finance available and this had been a further reason for the partnership with Van Diemen. The total requirement for subscribed capital had to be kept to 200,000 guilders (see Exhibit 2) if Praag's share in the partnership was not to fall below 50%. There was no chance of credit from the machinery supplier and at this stage banks would only advance capital if there was a surrender of some of the ownership equity.

During the busy season it was usual to work two shifts, seven days a week, using mainly student labour. For the peak period from 27th July until 17th August, Martin calculated that two sealing machines would enable a production of 605,000 strips (21 days × 16 hours × 900 strips × 2 machines). As this period would represent 55% of the season's activity this would mean a total production limit of 1.1 million strips. To be on the safe side he set a first tentative limit of 4,750 units (855,000 strips) for the season's selling activity.

Exhibit 2 *Rediplant Costings*

	Fl	Fl
Equipment		
Vacuum Forming Plant	42,000	
Transformer & electrical installation	10,000	
Moulds	20,000	
Sorting Machines 5,000 × 4	20,000	
Filling Machines 3,750 × 4	15,000	
Transport Lines	10,000	
Sealing Machines 16,500 × 2	33,000	150,000
Packaging Cost		
Electricity & Maintenance	5,000	
Rent	20,000	
Labour (25,000 hours @ Fl 6)	150,000	
Other Overheads	50,000	
Depreciation @ 20%	30,000	
Interest : on Equipment	15,000	
on Materials and Working Capital	10,000	280,000

		Per Unit
Packaged Cost (Excl. display stands)	*Per Strip*	*(180 Strips)*
Bulbs	0.62	111.6
PVC	0.04	7.9
Sleeve	0.06	10.8
Royalties (all sales)	0.02	3.6
Packaging (@ 1m strips)	0.28	50.4
Carton Packaging including labour	0.04	7.0
Point of Sale Advertising (display posters and pegs)	0.03	4.3
Packaged cost	1.09	195.6

Rediplant Sales While Walter Praag and Dik Van Diemen concentrated on the production planning, Martin Nievelt took on the task of coordinating the Rediplant sales commitments. With Van Diemen's agreement, he had in January allocated the tentative target limit of 4,750 units on the following basis:

1,500	United Kingdom
1,000	United States
1,000	Germany
500	Sweden
250	France
250	Holland
250	Switzerland

Martin was quick to admit that these were little more than rough guesses based on what he thought the salesmen would achieve but he felt that the overall demand figures offered even less help. These are shown in Exhibit 3.

By the end of February the sales force was just commencing its main effort and there was still very little sales feedback to go on. One large order of 1,000 units without stands, however, had just been confirmed by the largest garden supply wholesaler in Germany who had placed this initial order against a request that he be the sole German distributor next year. This firm employed a sizeable sales force calling on both garden supply outlets and major retail chains. The price negotiated by the Van Diemen sales force was Fl 1.33 per strip net ex Praag warehouse. The retail price the wholesaler would aim for was not known but the German retail mark-up was usually 35% on sales and the Van Diemen sales representative had gained the impression that the wholesaler himself would take a 20% mark-up on retail price. Transport costs to be met by the wholesaler, moreover, would be small and there was no duty into Germany.

There had also been other enquiries for large volume supplies but Martin Nievelt had argued against pursuing these for 1971. For example, Beinum, the mail order house who had purchased Praag's mailing lists, had enquired about Rediplant. They would supply their own bulbs and purchase only the packing — but the volumes required could be very large indeed. After initial discussions that ranged around a figure of Fl 0.6 per strip it was decided not to do anything until the following season. A very large USA mail order firm, Henry Field Seed Nursery Co of Iowa, also showed interest, but would have required delivery for September when their mail order packing commenced. Several of the large US retail chains had expressed interest. Other than arrangements for a modified test by A & P, the supermarket chain, however, these were not followed up because this one firm

Exhibit 3 *Dutch Bulb Exports 1969*

	Total Exports (Fl millions)	Exported for Dry Sales* (%)
Germany	118	31
USA	48	70
Sweden	35	35
United Kingdom	34	64
France	31	59
Italy	21	42
Switzerland	8	68
Canada	6	64
Austria	5	55
(All other markets less than Fl 5m)		

* Dry sales refer to the proportion of the sales going to the general public either directly or through outlets. Wet sales refer to sales to nurserymen for forcing cut flowers.

alone could absorb all Rediplant output in just one of its regions. Van Diemen's United States salesmen were instead concentrating on the suburban garden centres who mainly purchased loose bulbs. One of them had reported that, by chaining the size of the Rediplant order he would accept to the amount of loose bulbs ordered, he had been able to gain a substantial increase in his sales of loose bulbs.

Martin Nievelt felt that he could safely leave the Van Diemen sales effort to the Van Diemen management. They were well organised, with a world-wide sales director and four area managers. He had, however, provided sets of Rediplant brochures and price sheets drawn up in five languages. The prices Van Diemen chose were set to allow them around 20% on sales and meet the usual trade margins in the particular country. In the United States, for example, their standard price for a strip had been set at US $0.46 (Fl 1.65) to cover such a margin, 12½% duty, and delivery costs.

Van Diemen salesmen were paid a basic salary of Fl 12,500 plus a commission of 2% for the first Fl 400,000 increasing by ½% for each additional Fl 100,000. A detailed technical training was given and maintained on all aspects of bulb culture, although there was no special sales training. A geographical breakdown of Van Diemen's sales is shown in Exhibit 4, together with the numbers of salesmen concentrating on each country. Scandinavia, with a 5% growth rate, was the fastest growing market as well as bringing Van Diemen its largest sales.

United Kingdom Market

Having reserved 1,500 units for the United Kingdom market, Martin Nievelt was anxious to meet this figure and was awaiting news from Jan Straten, Praag's only other salesman, who was currently on a sales trip in England. Martin expected him to come back with some good orders for Rediplant, some of which would be test orders from the major chains.

Praag's United Kingdom bulb turnover in 1970 had been £90,000, of which £40,000 was direct mail. Martin Nievelt had built this turnover steadily since the end of World War II, even shifting his home to England for the first few years in order to get a good start. At this level of activity Praag was 6th or 7th in the ranking of about 300 Dutch bulb exporters to the United Kingdom. It was this entire turnover that Praag had sold to Sutcliffe Seeds Ltd at the end of 1970. As part of the agreement Sutcliffe undertook to purchase all their Dutch bulbs from Praag at an agreed

Exhibit 4   *Van Diemen Bros — Geographical Performance*

	% of 1969 Turnover	No. of Salesmen
Sweden	20.1	4
W. Germany	19.7	4
Finland	16.7	1 + 1 agent
France	10.7	6 + 3 agents
Italy	8.2	1
Norway	7.0	1 + 6 agents
USA	4.5	5
Denmark	3.8	1
Switzerland	3.0	1
Canada	1.4	—
Austria	1.2	1
Persia	1.1	—
England	0.9	1
Greece	0.4	—
South Africa	0.4	—
Belgium	0.4	—
Japan	0.1	—
Portugal	0.1	—
Hong Kong	0.1	—
Rest	0.1	—

formula, whether sold by direct mail or through outlets. Prices were to be set to cover packing and shipping costs and give Praag a 20% mark-up on the packaged cost. The suggested retail price would then be set at a 100% mark-up on the price to Sutcliffe (50% on sales). Sutcliffe would give its outlets a discount of 33.3% off this suggested retail price plus an additional 5% for payment within 30 days.

Praag's agreement with Sutcliffe had been reached at a time when Sutcliffe were actively looking for ways of expanding their sales of bulbs. Sutcliffe had recently taken over the garden seed division of Charles Gibb & Sons and now held over 30% of the retail seed market in the United Kingdom. With a total UK seed market of only £6 million, however, further growth would be difficult. Against this the UK bulb market of around £10 million offered more opportunity and Paul Duke, Managing Director of Sutcliffe had set his sights on 10% of this market by 1975. Although Sutcliffe had bulb sales of only £40,000 at this time and there were a great number of competitors, Duke planned to develop into the quality end of the market using Sutcliffe's name and selling only the best Dutch bulbs. Local bulb growing had expanded considerably in recent years and Dutch mail order firms had been undercut by local suppliers, but there were still many bulb varieties better provided from Holland and direct container shipment in bulk could offset almost all the location advantage.

Paul Duke had also asked if Sutcliffe could have an exclusive distributorship for Rediplant in the United Kingdom. Martin Nievelt knew that Praag would not have the resources to set up a significant sales force and had agreed to Duke's proposal, subject to Praag retaining the right to visit a number of their existing outlets and 20 of the largest chain stores and department stores in the United Kingdom. Martin undertook not to sell to these outlets at a price lower than Sutcliffe's net price to its outlets less 2% cash discount, on the understanding that Sutcliffes would use the same mark-ups as for loose bulbs.

Nievelt was very pleased with the agreement made with Sutcliffe. He thought that in the first year Sutcliffe's sales force of 60, which called on all the garden centres and hardware and garden stores in the UK, would take orders for somewhere in the vicinity of 600 units. The top salesmen sold between £50,000 and £60,000 of merchandise each year. Sutcliffe planned, moreover, to spend £20,000 on advertising their bulbs in the ensuing year and were planning to hold a cocktail and dinner party to announce their venture which would be widely covered in the trade papers.

With the major demands of the Rediplant development, Martin had been unable to manage a selling visit to the major outlets he had retained for Praag, and had sent Jan Straten in his place. Jan Straten had started with Praag eight years ago at the age of eighteen and with the exception of a two-year spell in the Dutch army had worked with them ever since. He was paid a fixed salary of Fl 12,000 and received £6.50 a day to cover his expenses while in the UK. He retained his home in Hillegom, seldom being away from home for more than a month at a time, and had sold £25,000 last year which Martin Nievelt thought was fairly good for a younger man.

The price at which Jan was seeking Rediplant sales in the United Kingdom was 22p per strip delivered to the customer, less 2% discount for payment within 10 days. This price was based on a suggested retail selling price of 33p per strip, which Martin had decided would be necessary to give Sutcliffe the same mark-up as for loose bulbs and still leave a reasonable profit for Praag. Costs of packing, freight, insurance, duty (10%), delivery, etc. would amount to about 20% of the packaged cost although this percentage might be reduced for full container deliveries. Martin would have preferred the retail price to be 29p which would have about equalled the price for similar loose bulbs in garden stores, but was convinced that at 33p Straten should be able to persuade several of the chains to place orders.

This case was prepared by Charles B. Weinberg, Faculty of Commerce and Business Administration, University of British Columbia, as a basis for class discussion. It is not intended to illustrate either effective or ineffective handling of an administrative situation. The location, setting and internal operating data are disguised.
© *Charles B. Weinberg, 1980.*

CASE C7
The Mancunian Cooperative Building Society

The managers of the Mancunian Cooperative Building Society were trying to determine an appropriate strategy for expansion of their branch network. The Mancunian had £2,500 million in deposits, which is about 7% of total building society deposits in the UK. In recent years the Society had followed an aggressive branch development strategy as had many other building societies. Mancunian currently had branches in areas accounting for 50% of total deposits. Unfortunately, not all the new branches had been as successful as management had hoped they would be. The management had allocated an annual budget of £1,500,000 for consumer marketing which included market research, branch expansion and advertising.

A market research team had done a thorough analysis of the country and had developed a list of 40 potential sites for major building society branches. These sites consisted of main-street shopping areas, locations in existing or planned shopping centres, and possible locations in suburban communities or new towns. The market researchers had not included downtown sites in major cities such as London and Birmingham, because these were largely oriented to commercial banking as opposed to building societies. For each site the market researchers had delineated the trading area from which that branch would draw deposits. By projecting population and income trends, the market researchers had also developed estimates of deposits five years ahead. Of course, the deposit level would also be sensitive to national economic factors. The results of this research project, with some additional data on the number of building society branches in the area, are given in Exhibit 1.

The management was concerned with the market share potential as well as the total deposit potential in each area. At first the Society had hoped that it could be assumed that market share was approximately equal to share of branches; that is, if the Society had two of the eight branches in an area, it would have a 25% share of deposits. Unfortunately, this turned out not to be a very good rule of thumb; it explained less than 20% of the variation in deposit share.

Consequently, management tried to generate other reasons for variations in market share. Among the reasons were the following:

1) Newness of the branch. It took about four years for a branch to build its market share to its mature level. In two years a new branch reached 70% of its mature potential.
2) Specific features of the branch, e.g. whether or not the branch had a large premises, a corner site, had large passing traffic etc.
3) Reputation, service, image and other characteristics of the parent society. For example, one society had a particularly strong advertising campaign. Another operated a widely-advertised build-up share scheme.
4) Skill of branch manager and his competition.

Exhibit 1

Area No.	All Building Societies: 5 Year Deposits Forecast (Current £'000s)	All Building Societies: Current Deposits (£'000s)	Total Number of Branches	Mancunian Branches
1	115,700	76,700	3	2
2	341,450	294,000	6	3*
3	143,820	87,200	4	2
4	235,500	159,700	5	1*
5	226,575	158,900	3	1
6	131,580	106,040	4	2
7	67,300	39,985	2	0
8	97,100	75,900	3	1
9	344,100	229,800	4	0
10	75,400	54,600	2	1*
11	268,200	195,200	6	2
12	366,000	292,300	7	0
13	294,400	230,200	5	2
14	646,600	593,300	10	1
15	328,400	260,000	4	0
16	194,600	142,500	4	1
17	44,600	18,200	2	2*
18	107,700	63,100	2	1
19	261,000	189,100	4	2
20	253,600	187,800	2	0
21	40,000	90,000	2	2
22	125,100	90,800	2	1*
23	413,300	343,100	5	2
24	379,500	415,000	6	1
25	332,800	242,900	3	0
26	438,100	347,700	7	3
27	143,900	77,800	3	2
28	79,900	59,700	3	1*
29	200,000	157,900	4	2
30	714,500	728,200	9	0
31	270,400	249,000	5	0
32	209,300	154,100	4	1*
33	676,500	516,900	16	0
34	313,400	238,500	5	1
35	495,300	337,900	11	3
36	254,200	245,100	4	0
37	190,400	135,800	5	0
38	542,130	476,700	10	1
39	128,500	72,600	5	0
40	230,200	170,900	5	0
TOTALS	10,700,000	8,600,000	196	44

*Office opened within past two years

Because these factors could not be evaluated individually, a multiple regression analysis was run.

The management had worked successfully with the market research group and had built trust in analytic procedures. The results were the following:

1) Newness. If a branch in the area was two years old or less, the Society's total market share in that area would be lowered by 4%.

2) The variable for specific features was not significant in determining market share. This was not because they were unimportant, but rather because in any area usually all or none of the societies had them.

3) If the parent society were either Society A or Society B, 8% should be added to the total share for that area. This was a very strong and surprising effect. Society A had a particularly strong advertising campaign and Society B continually advertised its build-up share scheme. There was neither a positive nor a negative effect for being a Mancunian branch, or a branch of the other two societies which made up the five largest building societies.

4) Outlet share was multiplied by 1.2 and then 0.07 was subtracted from the total.

5) No measure of branch manager's skill, especially for competitors, was available and consequently was not evaluated.

This analysis explained 70% of the variation in market share. All felt this to be a highly satisfactory result. To recapitulate, to predict market share in an area it was necessary to:

(a) Multiply branch share (in decimals) by 1.2. (b) Subtract 0.07. (c) If any branches two years old or less, subtract 0.04. (d) For the parent society being Society A or B, add 0.08.

The predicted market share was limited to a range of half of outlet share to twice outlet share.

Management had to design a branch development strategy for the next five years. To establish a major branch required, on average, a one-time cost of £300,000 and an annual cost of £350,000 for maintaining the branch. Assuming that all deposits could be loaned, each deposit contributed, after interest, 1.5% of its capital amount towards profit for the year.

The Mancunian's new advertising agency, on the other hand, had suggested a substantial advertising budget increase and a new campaign. The agency pointed to the Society A and Society B effect and claimed advertising could accomplish positive results for Mancunian. Instead of the rather subdued campaigns of the past, the advertising agency advised an aggressive campaign based on a 'reward' theme — 'Mancunian puts the Pounds into Savings'. An advertising campaign would cost £2,000,000 to £3,000,000 for a year, with the advertising agency asking for the higher amount to have the greatest probability of maximum effectiveness.

What branch development and advertising strategy should the Mancunian employ? The management was concerned with its plans for next year, as well as over the next five years.

This case was prepared by Kenneth Simmonds of the London Business School.
© *Kenneth Simmonds, 1974.*

CASE C8
Phipps and Company

Geoffrey Fanshaw, principal consultant with a small London consulting firm specialising in marketing management, had been asked for advice by Arthur Stanford of Phipps and Co in the first week of 1974. Early 1974 was a particularly worrying period for British managements who were faced with the world oil crisis, protracted union problems, and a government reduction of public sector investment in an attempt to stem inflation. Economic forecasters were predicting from zero to five percent reduction in gross national product during 1974. As building contractors dependent on continued investment, Phipps and Co could be severely affected. Stanford, Phipps' Managing Director, therefore asked Fanshaw for a rapid indication as to how much Phipps' prices should be lowered, as well as a general marketing assessment. The current supply shortage might lead to further cost increases for a period, but Stanford felt Phipps could cover itself adequately against supply shortages and further cost escalation.

Several days' investigation by Geoffrey Fanshaw confirmed that the marketing data available from Phipps was very sketchy. Phipps operated throughout the Southeast of England engaged mainly on apartment blocks, office buildings and small industrial plants. No market figures, however, were available for the area covered. Even within Phipps no usable records were kept of the volume of invitations received. Simon Grange, Phipps' Commercial Director, told Fanshaw that collecting market data would be a waste of money. He claimed that Phipps represented only one per cent or so of the total capacity in the area and although the firm went ahead with bids or negotiations on only two-thirds of the enquiries, it would not be difficult to get Phipps onto many more bidding lists.

From the firm's accounting records and Grange's records of bids submitted, Fanshaw was able to compile the comparative sales summary shown in Exhibit 1. Around one quarter of all orders were at negotiated prices some 2% above markups on orders obtained through bidding. For 1971 Phipps general and administrative overheads ran at £520,000, leaving a profit before tax of £286,000. Orders in hand were at a high level with sufficient work to stretch the work force through April. After that the loading fell off quite steeply at about 10% per month — but work from current bids could be commenced by April.

Phipps' prices were set at a weekly bidding meeting attended by Stanford, Grange, the chief estimator and the financial director. Stanford, a solicitor aged 60

Exhibit 1 *Comparative Sales Summary*

		1971	1972	12 mths	1973 Jan—Jun	Jul—Dec
Sales Invoiced	£m	9.7	10.7	11.1	5.3	5.8
Gross Margin	£00,000	650	740	706	316	390
Negotiated Work	£m	2.6	2.8	2.9	1.4	1.5
Average Markup on Cost	%	(9.8)	(8.4)	(9.7)	(8.3)	(11.1)
Bids Submitted	£m	47.0	44.0	49.0	20.0	29.0
Successful Bids	£m	8.9	7.7	9.7	3.6	6.1
Average Markup on Cost	%	(7.7)	(7.7)	(7.8)	(6.2)	(8.9)
Total Orders Obtained	£m	11.5	10.5	12.6	5.0	7.6
Average Markup on Cost	%	(8.2)	(7.9)	(8.3)	(6.7)	(9.3)

who represented a significant shareholding and had been appointed from outside three years previously, was very conservative in his pricing. He did not readily accept the more radical pricing recommendations advanced by Simon Grange. Grange had worked for the firm for nearly thirty years since leaving school at 17 and started as a trainee estimator. He held very definite views about the market and competition and he argued these forcefully. In the last six months of 1973, for example, Grange had argued that markups should be raised well above the 10% norm because conditions were good. He was currently arguing for a reduction to 5% in advance of the bad times.

Fanshaw had great difficulty in finding any competitor data on which to base his own pricing recommendations. After a lot of searching, however, he uncovered 13 bids made during 1973 for which competitor prices were available — five dating from before the summer and eight made more recently. The competitor prices recorded are shown in Exhibit 2. As far as Fanshaw could ascertain, these bids were a representative sample of the total in size, type of work and competition, although Phipps was successful on none.

Exhibit 2 *Bid Prices Available*

Bid No.	Date	Bids Submitted (£'00,000's) (* indicated Phipps' bid)									Phipps' Contribution on Cost %
703	Jan. 16	9.3	9.9*	10.1	10.1	10.2					5
709	Feb. 27	8.9	9.2	10.2	10.5	11.0	11.2	11.5*	13.6		5
715	Apr. 3	3.3	4.0*	4.1	4.1						10
716	Apr. 8	11.0	11.6	11.8*	12.0	12.6	13.0				6
723	May 19	8.8	8.9	9.0	9.6	10.2*					8
730	Aug. 20	1.5	1.6	1.6	1.8*						17
731	Sep. 3	6.8	7.1*	7.8							11
733	Sep. 11	6.2	6.4	6.8	6.9	6.9*	7.1	7.4	7.7		16
738	Sep. 19	10.4	11.7*								14
745	Oct. 23	18.2	19.1	19.4*	19.9						14
746	Oct. 25	6.4	6.4*	6.6	6.7	7.3					5
754	Nov. 8	26.5	29.3	30.0*	31.5	32.3	33.8	35.7	36.7	40.4	12
758	Nov. 30	7.5	7.8	8.2*	9.5	10.3					10

This case was prepared by
Kenneth Simmonds of the
London Business School.
© Kenneth Simmonds, 1971

CASE C9
Structon Engineers

On 13 November 1965 Structon Engineers of Glasgow received a letter from the head office of Chemica Internationale SA (CISA) in Brussels, announcing their intention to build an oil-seed extraction plant in Paran. Paran was the main port and second largest city of the West African nation of Astoria. An extract from this letter reads as follows:

> ... The work to be performed is the erection of the plant and its related facilities. All the necessary materials will be purchased by CISA and delivered at Paran harbour.
>
> We are preparing an erection specification in which the requirements for this project will be given and on the basis of which we intend to invite competitive lump sum bids. We should appreciate your letting us know on or before 19th November whether you would be interested in submitting a tender for the erection work. We will then send you our invitation to bid together with our erection specification and our proposed agreement.
>
> The tender should be submitted six weeks after the date of the formal invitation to bid. It is intended to award the contract about one month after the tender will have been received, and the construction of the plant will have to be completed on or before 1st June 1967.

Mr M. Bergen, Structon's Sales Director, knew that an expression of interest in this project would not bind the firm to submit a bid, but on the other hand, any later withdrawal or submission of an unreasonably high bid might prejudice CISA against Structon when selecting bidders for other projects. The background of the firm and the market conditions against which Mr Bergen had to make his decision on whether to tender are outlined in the following sections.

Structon's Background Structon was an international construction firm specialising in the design and construction of chemical processing plants. The firm had been formed shortly after the end of World War II and had quickly concentrated on plant that required an integration of mechanical, chemical, electrical, structural and civil engineering skills. Structon's headquarters were in Glasgow, and all the design and engineering staff were located there.

Exhibits 1 and 2 show the firm's sales pattern over the last five years broken down by type of contract and nature of the process, and according to the location of the construction. These figures represent the value of construction and engineering actually carried out during the year, not the value of orders recorded during the year. Demand was susceptible to changes in economic conditions and business investment, but demand for the type of construction the firm specialised in was projected to grow at a much faster average rate than total production, in almost every country.

Product Line Policy Two-thirds of Structon's business was made up of orders for which the customers provided Structon with information or designs concerning their own processes. This was divided again into work for which the customer arranged the engineering (construction only) and work for which Structon engineered the process based on the customer's data. Structon preferred to use its own engineers. Construction-

Exhibit 1   *Five Year Analysis by Type of Contract and Process*

	£ ('000s)				
	1961	1962	1963	1964	1965 projected
Structon Processes					
Industrial Chemicals	530	510	560	850	910
Agricultural Chemicals	500	630	840	1,020	1,110
Petro-Chemical Processes	80	120	120	30	180
Other (Sugar refining, salt plants, textile treatment, etc.)	610	670	770	900	1,000
Clients' Data					
Engineering and Construction:					
Industrial Chemicals	1,520	310	790	1,120	900
Argicultural Chemicals	290	1,390	770	860	1,040
Petro-Chemical Processes	130	60	90	—	—
Other	710	1,200	2,010	1,030	1,170
Construction Only					
Industrial Chemicals	630	210	590	810	1,030
Agricultural Chemicals	—	—	—	—	—
Petro-Chemical Processes	1,400	30	370	800	1,200
Other	—	—	750	600	—
Total					
Industrial Chemicals	2,680	1,030	1,940	2,780	2,840
Agricultural Chemicals	790	2,020	1,610	1,880	2,150
Petro-Chemical Processes	1,610	210	580	830	1,380
Other	1,320	1,870	3,530	2,530	2,170
Total	6,400	5,130	7,660	8,020	8,540

only work did not add to the engineering capabilities that the firm wanted to build up, and when engineering and provision of materials were in the customer's hands Structon had little opportunity to make economies in design or scheduling. Customers who arranged the engineering separately, however, were mainly very large firms or public authorities with a considerable volume of work, not all of which might be already engineered. Large firms were also in a position to license construction firms to build plants using their processes, for other customers. Construction-only work could also add to the firm's output at a time when engineering staff were occupied on other work.

The remaining third of Structon's business was represented by plants and ancillary installations for which Structon provided all the technological knowledge. Structon wished to extend this side of its operations, hoping to get to the stage of being able to offer developing nations and less sophisticated customers inexpensive well-designed plants. Orders for this class of work were less subject to fluctuations and helped to smooth out the troughs between major, one-off contracts. Tender and selling costs were higher but this was offset by the higher success rate and higher mark-ups, although the firm had to invest in research and development in anticipation of a market for a particular process.

A preponderance of Structon's production had been in chemical processes, providing industrial chemicals and gases and agricultural chemicals for fertiliser except where these were processed from petro-chemical by-products. Although Structon had erected a number of plants in the petro-chemical field, it was not a major contractor here. No contract for the complete design, engineering and erection of a major petro-chemical plant had ever been undertaken. Structon executives had realised that much of the growth in chemical processing plant would be centred

Exhibit 2   *Five Year Sales Analysis by Geographical Location   £ ('000s)*

	1961	1962	1963	1964	1965 projected	Estimated Average Rate of Growth of Market Over Next 5 years
Home Market	2,570	1,930	3,810	2,410	2,920	8%
Western Europe	2,210	1,420	1,320	910	1,500	15%
Eastern Europe	—	310	—	2,090	1,640	20%
Middle East	—	190		1,410	1,170	5%
North Africa	640	—	1,450	—	—	10%
Rest of Africa	—	560	—	—	—	10%
Asia	360	—	810	—	—	10%
Australasia	—	720	270	1,200	1,310	10%
Central & South America	620	—	—	—	—	?
Total	6,400	5,130	7,660	8,020	8,540	

round petro-chemicals, and had decided that Structon should begin to move more strongly into this field. With this in mind an agreement had been entered into, in 1965, with an American petro-chemical contracting firm, to draw on their engineering experience for work outside the North American market.

Some Structon executives considered that the firm should immediately take steps to enter the bidding on contracts for the complete engineering and construction of major petro-chemical plants. Others were against this plan. They pointed out that there were many larger firms already experienced in engineering and erection of petro-chemical plants against whom Structon would have to bid. One executive claimed that even with the engineering know-how of the American firm, two or three major contracts might have to be taken at a loss for each type of process before Structon could build up the experience to compete with established firms. Also, the technology was relatively developed and profitability would therefore be quite low. Structon might never recover the initial investment in lost profits. The executives who were against bidding on complete major plants were generally agreed that the firm should put its efforts into less developed areas of petro-chemical processing for which Structon could eventually develop its own processes, and which were not confined to large, sophisticated chemical firms as customers.

Geographical Policy   Mr Bergen had summarised Structon's geographical policy in his forecast for 1965 by claiming, 'Structon is prepared to undertake the right sort of job almost anywhere in the world, provided it fits into the work schedule and the risk is adequately covered.' There were, however, advantages from building up contracts and experience in a particular country or area and as a guide for focusing the firm's selling effort, rather than diluting it by attempting to cover the whole globe, Mr Bergen had drawn up a list of geographical priorities.

After its home market, Structon was particularly interested in Eastern Europe where it held a political advantage over American, German and Japanese firms. In most Eastern European countries, however, very little of the actual construction was let to foreign firms. Other West European countries were next on the list, although local competition was generally too strong in Holland and Germany. European countries were developing rapidly, not too distant geographically and relatively stable. They offered immense scope for plant erection over the next five years.

Structon had recently established a resident branch in Australia and wished to give work there a priority. With a resident construction force it was considered particularly important to develop a steady volume of business, whereas in other countries it was the policy to operate on a job basis and withdraw all resident staff when a major job was completed.

In the Middle East a considerable number of contracts had been undertaken in Iraq and Iran, mainly in fertiliser and refinery plant, but finance was now a major problem for this area. Egypt and Libya were also listed high on the priority list because they offered much opportunity for petro-chemical plant, and Egypt in particular was extending its production capacity in many fields. Elsewhere in Africa there was little to attract specific concentration by Structon, except for South Africa, and a policy decision had been made to avoid work there.

India and Pakistan were considered worthy of further attention and although little work had been undertaken in the past in these two countries, Mr Bergen was actively following all opportunities to bid there. Structon also had little experience in South America. Political conditions had discouraged the management and no priority was placed on expansion there. Opportunities to bid in Venezuela, Colombia and Peru would be considered, but not actively sought.

The Customer CISA was a large and widely diversified chemical firm operating many chemical process plants in Western Europe, Africa, the Middle East, South America and Australia. All new CISA investment was administered from Brussels and the majority was currently being funnelled into Common Market countries.

CISA normally invited only three or four firms to tender on its plant investments. This brought advantages to both the tendering firms and to CISA. Costs of allocating an order reduced with the number of firms bidding, particularly when those chosen were all experienced and CISA could be relatively certain of their competence. CISA could also ensure effective competition by inviting only those firms that needed the work. A limited number increased the probability that any one competitor would be successful, and made it likely that each firm would be keener to submit its best price and perhaps spend more on pre-acceptance costs.

Structon had not been invited to tender on a major job for CISA for the past ten years, although many attempts had been made to get onto the list of invited firms. In October Mr Phillips, Structon's Managing Director, had visited Brussels to discuss a conflict of interest with the CISA management, and the plans for the Paran plant had been mentioned during the conversation. When asked if Structon would be interested, Mr Phillips had replied that Structon would certainly like to take a look at it. Having expressed an interest and received an invitation to bid, it seemed unwise not to take advantage of it. Even if the bid were unsuccessful, co-operation now might lead to further opportunities later.

Structon also knew that CISA would shortly be building a plastic resins complex alongside a refinery in Australia and successful construction of the Paran plant would be a mark in Structon's favour when it came to getting this Australian order.

There were many advantages in working for CISA. It was a reliable firm and payment was certain. Work would not have been opened for bidding without an intention to proceed, and the engineering plans would be of a high standard. Structon executives were fairly confident that once CISA had made sure that bidders understood the specifications and were in a position to carry out the work at a high standard and within the specified time, the lowest bid would normally be accepted. A contract with CISA would enable Structon to establish itself in a new country without the risks and investment normally associated with working in a developing territory.

Astoria Structon had never previously carried out work in Astoria. There was a possibility, however, that the firm would obtain a contract to design, engineer and erect a fertiliser plant in Capitalia, the capital of Astoria, some 500 miles inland from Paran.

This contract might reach £2 million in value. The customer would be the Astorian government, but the successful tenderer on the oil extraction plant would not receive any preference for the fertiliser plant, as the nationalism of the government contrasted sharply with the foreign entrepreneurship of CISA. It was possible that Structon might obtain the government order without competitive bids being called. Some initial negotiations had been entered into with the Astorian government authorities concerning this plant, so Structon already knew something of the general conditions in Astoria.

Paran was the only seaport in Astoria and it handled a considerable tonnage. The cranes available at the port would be adequate for handling the materials for the oil extraction plant. The transport of equipment and material to the site presented few problems, although Structon's commercial section reported that 'commissions' were becoming more and more prevalent and some expense of this nature might have to be incurred to facilitate clearance.

Generally speaking, the political conditions were stable and little political involvement would be necessary, particularly as CISA had a resident company. There had been an army coup three years previously and the government was now backed by the military. The country had a sound development policy, but Structon did not expect any further major projects over the next three or four years.

There were conflicting reports as to the availability of local labour. It was fairly definite that there would be inadequate labour in Paran itself, but it was claimed by those who knew Astoria, and by the local labour office, that men could be brought from Capitalia. On the other hand, the volume of civil and industrial construction planned for Astoria would call for a greater number of production hours than had ever before been achieved. The labour office stated that a contractor would be given every facility to engage expatriate technicians for 'highly technical or other jobs for which he cannot find qualified Astorians.' Artisans and tradesmen were already scarce and it was feared that those available, if any, would be men found unsatisfactory by other contractors.

Labour troubles had been relatively unknown. Unions existed, but they were not strong nor nationally organised. Unions were company unions including all employees regardless of trade, so labour troubles would not be caused by issues outside the control of the employer. There were no regulations or difficulties regarding firing.

In Paran the hot months were July to August, when average temperatures were around 110 degrees Fahrenheit with humidity up to 98%. The rainy season, when flooding could interrupt construction, was from November to January.

The Competition

Structon knew that CISA would follow its usual policy of inviting three or four firms to tender. For many years the Belgian firm of Meerdonk had carried out a considerable amount of CISA's new plant construction and it was highly probable that they would be one of the bidders. Their bids had always been very competitive and their close liaison with CISA might bring them some preferential treatment, but this would be hard to gauge.

A large British firm with a chemical engineering division, Weybridge Limited, was also expected to be amongst the bidders. No special advantage was held by Weybridge.

Structon's Current Order Book

In November 1965 Structon had no major overseas construction project scheduled to start in 1966. If the firm was to continue to build up its reputation as an overseas constructor, at least one project was essential. Structon was nearing completion of a major series of construction contracts in the Middle East and would have supervisory staff available from these projects. If the CISA order were not obtained, however, most of these men could be absorbed as advisors in the erection of cotton-finishing, detergent and weed-killer plants that had been sold to Russia, exclusive of erection.

Exhibit 3   *Order Book as at 31st October 1965 £('000s)*

	1966				1967		
Quarters in which work is programmed:	Jan Mar	Apl Jun	Jul Sep	Oct Dec	Jan Mar	Apl Jun	Jul Sep
Structon Processes							
Orders on hand, 31 Oct.	630	620	540	370	220	160	200
Outstanding Bids[1], 31 Oct.	190	460	860	520	710	420	500
Clients' Data							
Engineering & Construction:							
Orders on hand, 31 Oct.	910	870	940	420	500	320	70
Outstanding Bids, 31 Oct.	360	750	280	1,690	730	410	210
Construction only:							
Orders on hand, 31 Oct.	430	420	—	—	—	—	—
Outstanding Bids, 31 Oct.	—	520	390	210	—	—	—
Total							
Orders on hand, 31 Oct.	1,970	1,910	1,480	790	720	480	270
Outstanding Bids, 31 Oct.	550	1,730	1,530	2,420	1,440	830	710

1. Outstanding Bids include estimated figures for bids under preparation, but not yet submitted. All work is apportioned over the quarters in which it would be carried out.

Exhibit 4   *Bidding Statistics: Bids submitted 1961—64*

| | Structon Processes | | Clients' Data | | | | | | | |
			Under £200,000		£2—500,000		£500,000 to £1m		Over £1 million	
No. of opportunities considered	103		583[1]		139		238		31	
	Bids Made	Orders Recd.	Bids Made	Orders Recd.	Bids Made	Orders Recd.	Bids Made	Orders Recd.	Bids Made	Orders Recd.
No. of bidders										
2			12	5	—	—	—	—	—	—
3			98	20	10	2	33	5	2	1
4			104	17	27	6	35	5	4	1
5			57	6	25	4	20	2	3	1
6			13	1	20	2	9	—	4	—
7			—	—	4	—	2	—	—	—
	75	39	284	49	86	14	99	12	13	3
Average Value of Bid (£'000s)	210	240	90	90	310	300	710	710	1,410	1,370
Average Mark-up on Prime Cost + Contingency Estimate (%)	14.8	13.3	13.3	9.7	13.1	11.9	11.9	9.5	9.6	9.1
Average Cost of Submitting Bid[2] (£)	2,000		670		1,520		3,100		5,570	

1.   Structon had a policy of rejecting all opportunities to bid on clients' data which after initial consideration were shown to be under £50,000 in value.

2.   The cost of submitting a bid is not included in the prime cost. This average cost of submission includes an allowance for administrative time and associated overheads. Of these submission costs, 70% are fixed, and the firm's expenditure on these does not vary with short-run fluctuations in the number of bids.

Exhibit 3 shows the state of Structon's order book as at 31st October 1965, Exhibit 5 the budgeted work load for firm orders and bids being prepared, and Exhibit 4 sets out various statistics concerning Structon's bidding over the previous four years. Structon's estimating section advised Mr Bergen that erection of the CISA plant would require up to fifteen months from commencement, with manhour requirements spread fairly evenly across months three to thirteen of the erection programme.

Mr Bergen knew that there would be other opportunities for construction work in 1966, but there was no indication as to when and where these would arise. It would be unlikely that any major work for 'construction only' could be tendered for and commenced before September 1966.

Profitability of the Order

Structon's estimating section estimated the prime cost of the contract would be roughly £1 million. It was thought that an overhead and profit margin of 10% might be expected. This £100,000 mark-up would be after depreciation on plant, but before meeting interest on the capital required. The firm would probably require to spend £250,000 on new plant at the commencement of the project, but the total amount of capital tied up by the project would probably average only £125,000 for 15 months. Structon used an interest rate of 6% per annum in calculating the cost of finance, and at this rate could obtain the necessary funds.

The accounting section had calculated that only two-thirds of the firm's overheads were applicable to construction work where no engineering was involved, and included in this were the pre-acceptance overheads for estimating, selling and tender presentation. Mr Bergen estimated that it would cost the firm around £6,000 to prepare a bid to CISA. Structon's flexible overhead and profit budget over its likely range of turnover is shown in Exhibit 6.

Exhibit 5   *Budgeted Load on Engineering Staff as at 31st October 1965*

	Percentage of Capacity Committed to Firm Orders and Bids Under Preparation					
	Nov	Dec	Jan	Feb	Mar	Apl
Engineering Section:						
Mechanical	100	100	120	90	80	60
Structural	90	80	70	70	40	40
Electrical	80	90	90	80	50	30
Chemical	95	100	70	65	40	30
Instrumentation	80	75	60	30	20	10

Exhibit 6   *Flexible Overhead and Profit Budget 1966 £ ('000s)*

Sales	5,000	6,000	7,000	8,000	9,000	10,000	11,000
Overhead and profit Margin — 10% of Sales	500	600	700	800	900	1,000	1,100
Overhead Cost	500	500	525	550	550	575	600
Profit before tax	—	100	175	250	350	425	500
Taxation (at 40%)	—	40	70	100	140	170	200
Profit after taxation	—	60	105	150	210	255	300

*This case was prepared by
Shiv Mathur and Kenneth
Simmonds of the London
Business School. It is not
intended to illustrate the
policies or practice of any
particular firm. Financial assistance was provided by the
British Overseas Trade Board.
© London Business School,
1976.*

CASE C10
Glassfibres Ltd

In July 1974 Mr Wong Lee, Managing Director of Glassfibres Limited of Singapore, a member of a large UK group of companies, was concerned about the steep decline in the sale of glassfibres in the wake of the recent hike in oil prices. The drop in sales to the island republic of Sri Lanka was the most serious and of particular concern.

Glassfibres Limited was the sole manufacturer of glassfibre in Southeast Asia and for all practical purposes the only supplier to the countries surrounding Singapore. European and Japanese manufacturers found it difficult to compete, owing to the high cost of freight, strict quotas and differential tariffs on imports from outside the region.

Glassfibre was a recent introduction to Southeast Asia and was used almost entirely in the fabrication of glassfibre reinforced plastics (GRP). Over the last 5—7 years GRP had experienced a very dynamic growth in Southeast Asia and Mr Wong's company had performed very satisfactorily until the 1973 hike in oil prices.

Glassfibre Reinforced Plastics

GRP had been developed on a commercial scale towards the end of the Second World War and had since been used extensively in the developed countries of the world to replace metals in various applications. In most of these applications GRP had substantial advantages over many metals — it was cheaper, lighter and was more resistant to chemical and atmospheric corrosion. These properties had resulted in a very steady growth for the new product. GRP had soon not only become a replacement for the more expensive metals and plastics, but was also recognised as a structural material in its own right. In industries like transportation and chemicals it was obvious that GRP had come to stay, and by the middle of the sixties the fabrication and maintenance of glassfibre reinforced plastics was considered an integral branch of plastic engineering.

Though the actual technology of GRP was quite involved, the basic principles were fairly simple. Strands were drawn from molten glass and this constituted the essential ingredient. These strands could then be laminated with the help of chemical resins directly into various forms of GRP; or, what was more common, the strands were chopped up and chemically bonded together into fibrous mats. The mats could then be laminated by intermediate processors and moulders, at their own premises, to form GRP.

There were many ways of converting glassfibre mats into GRP. The most basic and extensively used was known as the 'hand lay-up technique'. This required a wooden, plastic or steel mould. On this mould a chemical separator was applied and then a coat of activated thermo-setting resin. When the resin became tacky and was beginning to set, it was covered by an appropriately cut piece of glassfibre mat. The strands of glassfibre became incorporated in the resin base and reinforced it, thus giving the end product its name. When the resin had cured, it was possible to separate the GRP laminate from the mould; or alternatively another coat of resin and then glass could be applied, thus building up the thickness of the laminate to the required level. By this simple and laborious process it was possible to construct various industrial and commercial vessels and equipment which were light, corrosion resistant and had very desirable structural properties. By avoiding the use of a separator, it was also possible to 'line' metal pipes and structures thus protecting them from corrosion and, to an extent, reinforcing them structurally.

In the developed countries of the world many improvements had taken place in glassfibre technology. For large volume production of a popular item it was now possible to use special presses that did away with the laborious hand lay-up technique. The introduction of mechanised forms of manufacture had made many GRP consumer durables competitive with mass produced metal ones and GRP technology in many countries had advanced to the level when, for many products, it was no longer necessary to make the intermediate mats from glassfibre strands, but the strands themselves could be fabricated directly into GRP. This was especially convenient when fabricating cylindrical vessels like pipes: the strands coated with resin could be wound directly onto a rotating mandrel — a technique known as filament winding.

Sri Lanka GRP Industry In developing countries the hand lay-up technique was still the most popular form of fabrication. In Sri Lanka GRP had found the local industrial market very receptive and many businesses had started hand moulding operations. The growth of GRP had not only been a welcome addition to the small-scale sector of the economy — a group that the government was making every effort to develop — but also for the larger industrial houses. The availability of locally fabricated equipment had considerably lowered the economy's dependence on imported items and geographically distant suppliers — occasionally with considerable savings in time and capital outlay.

By the end of 1973 there were altogether about 50 small moulders down the length and breadth of the country, who placed orders directly with Glassfibres Singapore for their requirements. A large number of the moulders were very small operators, each employing about six or seven people; only nine of the moulders were of any size. Glassfibre's marketing department estimated that these nine accounted for about 60—65% of the island's GRP business.

Most of the demand for GRP was confined to the industrial sector of the economy and even then confined in the chemical processing industry. The larger moulders had close business connections with the bigger industrial houses and were able to take on many technically demanding assignments.

All over Southeast Asia Glassfibres Limited was very concerned about the technical quality of the end product. Though the final product was the result of many variables, like the quality of resin and moulding expertise, in the company's experience the fact that they were the dominant suppliers of glassfibres led customers to regard them as final guarantors of quality. Glassfibres Limited realised this and to an extent welcomed this responsibility, as it gave them a hold on the market which may not otherwise have been possible. To discharge this responsibility, the company had set up a separate technical services department at their headquarters in Singapore that gave advice to prospective customers and moulders on the most effective use of GRP laminates. If a particular moulder required technical assistance of a complex nature, an expert would be flown out for detailed consultation. Often the department had been able to influence customers to use GRP instead of other materials and occasionally was able to design complete facilities using composite laminates of GRP and other materials.

The smaller moulders, unlike their bigger counterparts, were largely involved in small repair and 'lining' work. The nature of their assignments did not often bring them into contact with the technical services department of Glassfibres Limited and their technical competence had been the cause of anxiety to the company. However, with the growth of the GRP industry and the movement of trained and experienced personnel, the problems of the small moulders were becoming less obvious.

The smaller moulders, besides being of varying technical capabilities, were also of uncertain financial strength. They seemed to live on a financial precipice and the business scene was in a state of constant flux. Small companies would often vanish under the strain of a misjudged quotation or the inability to meet their debts, and new organisations, often with the same people involved, would appear on the business scene. The changing portfolio of moulders was in sharp contrast to the firmly established resin manufacturing facilities on the island.

Resin Manufacturers   Prior to the introduction of GRP in 1968, there was only one resin manufacturing plant to cater for the limited requirements of the local button manufacturing industry. With the introduction of GRP, the industry had grown almost overnight and by late 1973 there were three plants manufacturing resin. The introduction of new capacity was not a very difficult task and basically involved the erection of 'reaction kettles' at the expense of a couple of hundred thousand rupees; this gave an average increment in production capacity of 30—50 tonnes of resin a year. Though some of the raw materials required for the manufacture of resin were locally available, most of the petroleum based products, which constituted a major portion of the inputs, had to be imported against government-issued import licenses and foreign exchange permits. With import duties running at about 90% of the c.i.f. prices of petroleum products, local production was an expensive business, though still possible owing to the outright ban on imports of resin manufactured overseas.

The government was not only very strict about imports, but also wary of foreign involvement in the nation's economy. Foreign equity investment in most industrial sectors was discouraged and in the small-scale sector, which incorporated both the manufacture of resin and fabrication of GRP, was completely banned. The three resin manufacturers had, however, been able to produce under license from foreign producers of resins and the quality of their product, though not always uniform, was generally satisfactory.

By the third quarter of 1973 the three resin manufacturers were working at about 80% of capacity, supplying between them about 300 tonnes of resins to the local GRP industry. The largest of them had, at 200 tonnes, the dominant market share and the other 100 tonnes was split about equally between the other two.

Glassfibres had maintained close contact with the resin manufacturers and had often participated with them in technical seminars and training programmes. Though the resin manufacturers did not always get on with each other, their relationship with Glassfibres Limited was fairly cordial. In Mr Wong's opinion this was only to be expected, as they had done very well out of the sale of resin to the local GRP industries, pricing very close to each other to give them a margin of about 60—65% after direct costs had been deducted.

The Oil Price Rise   In October 1973 the steep increase in the price of petroleum products had considerably altered the business scene. The landed cost of petroleum-based raw materials had risen 2½ times and the resin manufacturers had doubled their prices to reflect this change in production costs. Burdened by this increase and the fact that the landed price of glassfibre had gone up from Rs 16/kg to Rs 20/kg, the GRP industry took a sharp dive. By April 1974 it was clear that the current year's sales were running at half the level for the previous year.

In May 1974 Mr Wong, alarmed by the situation in Sri Lanka, had commissioned Mr John Holden, Glassfibres Export Manager, to submit a report and recommendations. Mr Holden submitted his report in July; extracts from it are reproduced below.

Glassfibres Sales in Sri Lanka
by
John Holden
1.7.74

Background

From a level of about 50 tonnes a year of GRP in 1968, consumption had grown to about 250 tonnes in 1971 and about 500 tonnes a year by early 1973. This implied glassfibre sales at about 200 tonnes per annum. Sales of glassfibre during the period October 1973 to February 1974 was a total of 45 tonnes, which indicates a level of GRP activity of about 112.5 tonnes for the six-month period. It seems that though the level of ordering will not fall further, it is unlikely to recover significantly. Till the end of September 1974, it is estimated that a total of around 100 tonnes of glassfibre will be sold in Sri Lanka.

GRP Market

The steep rise in the price of resin and glassfibre has completely altered the competitive position of GRP in the local market. Equipment fabricated from GRP is no longer as competitive as it used to be, with the result that consumers are gradually drifting back towards the use of conventional materials. The industry has shrunk to the stage where GRP is now only being used for application where metals and other materials are either too expensive or unsuitable. This implies that all applications where GRP had marginal cost advantages have already been lost to competitive structural materials.

The recession has hit the GRP industry harder than other industrial sectors because of the unique role it plays in the Sri Lankan economy. For it is always easy to forgo capital equipment projects and routine maintenance in times of economic crisis — industrial applications where GRP had made significant inroads.

It is difficult to forecast for the next year and a great deal will depend on the prevailing price. The following is an estimate of sales at various price levels:

Price of GRP (Rs/kg)	Total GRP Requirements (Tonnes)	Glassfibres Requirements (Tonnes)
40	100	40
39	150	60
37	200	80
35	290	115
33	325	130

Moulders and Product Quality

The effect of the reduced demand levels on the smaller moulders has been quite traumatic. The smaller companies had, even at the best of times, made only a marginal living. The sharp drop in business — especially in repair and maintenance work — has meant that many small moulders have disappeared from the face of the earth. However, in their dying throes they have done their utmost to wreck the existing GRP industry. The disappearance of moulders was preceded by a very disagreeable fight for a shrinking market. Initially, profit margins were cut back, but there was little room for manoeuvre and there was consequently a sharp deterioration in the technical quality of the work done. Laminates of indifferent workmanship and insufficient thickness have become prevalent over the last six months. These business practices are still continuing and are a cause for concern. The problems that this will create for the long-term development of GRP are obvious.

As the position is deteriorating every day we shall have to make up our minds at an early date on how to deal with this situation. In Exhibit 1 I have attempted to illustrate how the rise in the price of raw materials has affected the price of GRP products. The figures are, of course, just estimates and do not take into account any adjustment in profit margins made by the moulders or the particular variations of a project.

Government Attitude

The government in Sri Lanka has been greatly concerned about the havoc that has broken loose in the moulding community. In the same way as our company had been thought to be the force behind the dynamic growth of the industry, we are being held responsible for its downfall. When I last visited Sri Lanka and paid a visit to the Permanent Secretary, he was very concerned about the effect of the recent recession on the moulders. A great deal has been made of the increase in the landed price of glassfibres from Rs 16/kg to Rs 20/kg. There is a lobby on the island that sees this increase as uncalled for and blames Glassfibres Limited for the decline in the industry's prosperity. I did not have the figures at the time to point out the justification for the price increases, but I did make clear to the Permanent Secretary that our ex-Singapore prices were half the landed costs, the rest being attributable to freight and a 75% custom duty on imported goods. The small increase in our own prices from Rs 8/kg to Rs 10/kg ex-Singapore was attributable to our own increased costs, and consequently higher transfer prices that the marketing division had to pay the production unit. There is, in my view, a case to be made for the reduction of import duties on glassfibres and I have suggested to the leading local moulders that they should make a representation to the Government Tariff Committee.

I have since received from the Works Accountant a clearer analysis showing the reason and justification for the increase in our costs, and thus transfer prices, and this is reproduced in Exhibit 2.

Marketing Viewpoint

The general decline in sales for the whole of Southeast Asia and Sri Lanka in particular is distressing, but there are a few definite benefits that might come out of these ashes. The sharply competitive market has meant that a few marginal moulders have been phased out of the industry completely. This is not such a bad thing. It should now be possible to ensure that the remaining moulders meet the required technical standards more carefully, and this could be the opportunity to organise the marketing effort along more clearly thought out lines. There are various short and long term issues that need to be discussed and I have listed some below:

Short Term: Should we alter our marketing strategy? Is there any reason for re-pricing our product? Freight cost quotas and preferential tariffs still provide an effective barrier to imports from European and Japanese exporters. However, the barrier has been significantly eroded and if other countries decide to dump, in the short run it could mean the end of our dominant position. The continuance of quotas and hence government good-will is important.

The technical reliability of GRP is being increasingly questioned. The proliferation of 'mushroom' moulders has created technical problems. We shall have to decide what to do to safeguard the technical quality of GRP products.

In the immediate future we will have to take measures to stem the sharp decline in sales and decide on a corrective strategy.

Long Term: Over the next few years we shall have to decide whether our organisation as it presently stands, with product managers responsible for developing projects and looking after technical requirements and a sales function performed by another arm of the organisation is adequate for our objectives.

Exhibit 1   *The Rising Production Cost of GRP*

	Mid 1973 (Rupees)		Early 1974 (Rupees)
1 kg of glassfibre (at Rs 16/kg)	16	(at Rs 20/kg)	20
1.5 kg of resin (at Rs 10/kg)	15	(at Rs 20/kg)	30
Activators and ancillary materials	2		3
Labour at Rs 15/2.5 kg of GRP	15		15
Total direct cost of 2.5 kg GRP	48		68
Moulders' overhead and margin at 1.6 times labour costs	24		24
Total cost of 2.5 kg of GRP	72		92
Cost/kg	29		37

Exhibit 2 *Analysis of Cost Increases*

	Mid 1973 (% of variable costs)	January 1974 (% increase in cost as compared to mid 1973)
40% increase in cost of materials and fuel	50%	20.0%
10% increase in labour cost	20%	2.0%
10% increase in indirect wages, maintenance, packing etc	20%	2.0%
10% increase in ancillary costs	10%	1.0%
	100%	
Total increase on mid 1973 variable cost of Rs 4/kg		25.0%
Increase in allocated costs owing to 20% reduction in volume from normal of 2,000 tonnes/annum (mid 1973 volume allocated costs of Rs 2/kg)		25.0%
Increase in total costs		25.0%
Pre-oil-hike transfer prices charged to Marketing Department		Rs 6/kg
After 25% increase		Rs 7.50/kg

It is clear from the industry's experience in other countries that there is overall an increasing trend toward mechanisation of GRP fabrication. In Sri Lanka it is estimated that if pipes could be manufactured by the less resin-intensive filament winding process, this would completely revolutionise the tubewell industry, replacing the mild steel product now in use. A conservative estimate of 1980 requirements is about 1000 tonnes of glassfibres. The questions that arise are whether we wish to encourage a move towards mechanisation and if so how, in terms of restructuring of resources and organisation, should we go about this? This question becomes especially relevant if it is assumed that petroleum-based products are likely to retain their exorbitant prices and GRP must therefore be fabricated in more mechanical ways using less resin.

It seems that quite a few of the above questions should have been part of an on-going evaluation of the company and its direction. Like always, however, it is a crisis that has been required to bring them into focus.

Mr Wong agreed with a lot of the questions that Mr Holden asked and he realised that he had as much information as he would ever get to make up his mind. He agreed that the long term would require a fairly fundamental re-thinking, but he still did not have a clear idea of what to do next month about the shrinking Sri Lanka market.

CASE C11
Water Hyacinth

For issue to both parties

Note: This is a negotiation case study, intended for two teams each representing the principal parties. The material in this paper is common to both parties; certain additional material will be issued by the directing staff to each team or to individuals in the teams.

As indicated in this text, the teams should meet separately to consider their negotiating position, prior to their first joint confrontation.

During the five years following the dramatic OPEC oil price rise in 1974, Constructors of Britain, a process engineering and contracting company, had been, like so many others, looking for alternative sources of energy.

One direction of their search had been into Biomass, or renewable energy sources. One such source was the water hyacinth, a plant which flourished in semi-tropical swamp; up till now the problem had been finding a method of preventing the water hyacinth from multiplying rather than encouraging it to renew itself. It was capable of covering a square mile of swamp in three months from the first introduction of a few plants.

Constructors of Britain (COB) had developed a process capable of converting water hyacinth into prethanol using a catalyst K5, which they had patented and for which they had developed production facilities. Prethanol was a liquid capable of being mixed with oil 50/50 by volume, and the resulting refined mixture gave as satisfactory a performance in motor vehicles as petroleum, without requiring any alteration to the carburation system.

In 1979 COB had constructed a demonstration plant which adequately confirmed their study work on the process both from the technical and cost viewpoints. However, costs were higher than the oil equivalent, and the environments in which the water hyacinth flourished tended to be specialised and inhospitable to man. Consequently Prethanol had not turned out to be the hoped-for 'breakthrough' and no full-scale plant had so far been built.

One country where the water hyacinth was highly prolific was San Feriano, a Latin American republic of some 5 million inhabitants, governed by a military junta. San Feriano not only had to import all its oil requirements, but had little to export in order to earn hard currencies — or at least harder currencies than its own — in order to pay for its oil needs. However, LDC Credit Bank, an institution supported by OPEC funds, had offered San Feriano a loan of £50 million, with interest payments at 5% to start no earlier than 10 years after the date of the loan.

The money would be available only for an approved project. The water hyacinth scheme, or a possible hydro-electric project, had been provisionally approved. The government of San Feriano favoured water hyacinth for several reasons : it was more glamorous, it would employ unskilled labour and political prisoners in harvesting the plant, and would keep the security forces mobile — which the hydro-electric scheme would not.

The San Feriano energy minister had contracted COB and requested a study on a Prethanol project. COB knew that San Feriano had exhausted their borrowing power in the international commercial market, but became more enthusiastic when the LDC Credit Bank confirmed the offer they had made.

This was the outcome of the study, presented in May 1980:

(a) Plant to produce 1,125,000 barrels of Prethanol, oil equivalent, per annum. Estimated overall cost £50 million.
(b) Estimated cost of engineering, procurement of equipment, offsites and services; supervision of construction £45 million.

(c) Construction to be undertaken by a local organisation S F CoCo, by direct contract betwen the government and S F CoCo, as stipulated by the government. Estimated cost £5 m; estimate to be checked locally.

(d) Estimated time to complete: 2 years 5 months from date of signing contract.

(e) Operating economics:

	£ per barrel
Depreciation, straight line 10 years, £5m p.a.	4
Feedstock delivered to plant (figure supplied by Minister for Agriculture)	6
Processing of Water Hyacinth, conversion into Prethanol at rated output of 160,000 tonnes p.a., using expatriate management and supervision, local skilled and unskilled labour. Plant overheads and energy consumption estimated from equivalent petrochemical plant	5
K5 Catalyst, delivered to plant	1
Total cost per barrel	16
Suggested realisable price per barrel	20

(160,000 tonnes $\cong$ 1,125,000 barrels $\cong$ 40 million imperial gallons)

The San Feriano government considered the study sufficiently interesting to request immediate talks, in detail, with a view to settling a contract. However, they indicated straightaway that the time to complete was unacceptable, even if attained. It was essential that the plant be on stream in time for the 10th anniversary of the coup which brought the military junta to power, i.e. October 1982.

Moreover, although the terms of payment had not been mentioned in the study, the government declared that *produit à main* would be expected, i.e. the cost of the plant should be met from the revenues it generated from its operations.

COB replied diplomatically that the time to complete could not be improved upon, and that *produit à main* was a universally unacceptable condition, but agreed to meet a government team in San Feriano on June 16, 1980.

Both COB and the San Feriano government realised that they would need to spend some time, prior to the agreed meeting, in determining their own positions. To this end each had prepared a note of the sorts of issues which would need to be determined. By coincidence, the lists were identical, and a copy is reproduced below, as Exhibit 1.

Exhibit 1   *Issues for determination*

Definition of the project : plant performance commitments & limitations
Liabilities: main contractor
Liabilities: sub-contractor
Price
Terms of Payment
Guarantees
Catalyst supply and price
Penalties: main contractor
Penalties: sub-contractor

In preparation for the June meeting both sides informed each other of the composition of their negotiating teams. They were as follows:

Constructors of Britain	Sales Director	Anthony Absolute
	Project Director designate	Basil Bartram
	Finance/Commercial Director	Charles Chandos
	Operations Director	David Dunkley
	Production Director, Chemicals	Ernest Elder
	Managing Director	Frank Fearless
Government of San Feriano	Energy Minister	General Geronimo Garcia
	Finance Minister	Ippolito Italo
	Agriculture Minister	Jose Jimenez
	Chief of Police	Colonel Konrad Kapstadt
	Prospective Plant Operator	Leonardo Little
	Prime Minister	General Massimo Montonero

This case was prepared by J.R.C. Wensley of the London Business School, with assistance from Johnson's Wax and McCann-Erickson, as a basis for discussion rather than to illustrate either effective or ineffective handling of a business situation.
© J.R.C. Wensley, 1976.

CASE C12
Pledge

[handwritten: what should McCann Erickson propose?]

On 13 February 1972 account executives at McCann-Erickson, a large London advertising agency and a subsidiary of the American Interpublic Group, sat down to discuss the design and approach they should follow for the agency presentation the next day on the potential new account from Johnson's Wax for their major product 'Pledge'.

Just under a month earlier, McCann's had been briefed by executives of Johnson's Wax on the problems that Pledge faced and asked for recommendations on advertising copy, advertising and promotion expenditure and brand share targets.

Johnson's Wax Johnson's Wax, previously S.C. Johnson, is a UK subsidiary company of S.C. Johnson & Son Inc (USA). The UK company is located at Camberley, Surrey. Johnson's Wax had a turnover of £7.28m in 1971 (1970 — £6.46m) and a net profit of £71,500 (£330,000). At the end of 1971, current assets were approximately £3m and current liabilities £2.3m, and fixed assets £3m.

The UK company is a manufacturer of polishes and cleaners for household, industrial and automotive use, and also industrial floor cleaning equipment. They also make and supply disinfectants, insecticides and personal care products, employing approximately 700 people. The American parent company has an extensive operation in the USA and owns other subsidiaries in Belgium, France, West Germany, Holland, Italy and Switzerland.

Aerosol Wax Market In 1959 Johnson's launched Pledge onto the furniture polish market. It was the first aerosol polish; all the previous products were either pastes or liquids. Johnson's were well represented in both the paste and liquid markets. The technology of aerosol furniture waxes simply involved a standard propellant and stable wax/water suspension containing various cleaning agents. It was possible to adjust the wax/water proportions to generate either a wax-rich suspension (usually referred to as 'oil out') or a water-rich one (usually referred to as 'water out').

In 1966 Lever Bros introduced a competitive product 'Sheen' into a regional test market. Johnson's responded with heavy pressure both in terms of advertising and promotion, with the effect that Lever's finally withdrew Sheen from the test in 1967.

In 1967 Johnson's launched Favor into a test market and went national in 1968. At the same time the Pledge formulation was changed to 'oil out' and the advertising strategy redirected to 'richer in wax' and away from 'dusting aid'.

Mr Sheen In 1970 Reckitt & Colman introduced Mr Sheen in London, the Midlands and the South. Mr Sheen was already a successful product for Reckitt's in the Australian market. Mr Sheen had a 'water out' formulation and was launched on a versatility strategy of cleaning glass, tiles and other surfaces. At this time Pledge was being advertised on a 'cleans, shines and waxes' strategy. Johnson's reacted to the threat posed by Mr Sheen to Pledge by a number of measures including 'improved formulation', increased advertising budget, an '18% more free' pack, 15 for 12 trade deal, commando salesforce, and a money-off coupon drop. These actions did not, *[handwritten: reaction to Mr Sheen]*

233

Exhibit 1 *Pledge Performance to the end of 1971*

All Polishes Market Shares by Product Category (%)

	1966	1967	1968	1969	1970	1971	Oct/ Nov 1971
Pastes	30.9	28.6	27.4	24.2	23.7	18.8	17.2
Furniture Liquids & Creams	10.7	10.2	9.4	8.4	7.3	5.8	5.3
Aerosols	23.0	27.6	33.7	38.8	44.2	55.1	58.9
Floor & other polishes	35.4	33.6	29.5	28.6	24.8	20.3	18.6

Pledge's Market Position: Brand Shares (%)

	1966	1968	Jun/ Jul 1969	Jun/ Jul 1970	Feb/ Mar 1971	Oct/ Nov 1971
Pledge	80	70	66	64	64	42
Favor	—	13	17	10	11	7
Sparkle	—	—	—	—	—	19
Mr Sheen	—	—	—	—	12	23

Source: Market Research

Bi-Monthly Brand Shares

		Pledge (%)	Sparkle (%)	Mr Sheen (%)	All Brands Sales (Index)	All Brands Advertising (Index)
1970	Jun/Jul	64	—	—	100	100
	Aug/Sep	54	—	15	119	769
	Oct/Nov	56	—	18	122	450
	Dec/Jan	58	—	13	110	206
1971	Feb/Mar	64	—	18	136	556
	Apr/May	54	13	18	168	1250
	Jun/Jul	41	22	21	166	625
	Aug/Sep	39	19	24	154	663
	Oct/Nov	42	19	24	164	681

Source: Market Research

Pledge Sales, Advertising and Deals

	Sales (£m)	Advertising (£m)	Deals (£m)
1966	1.10	0.196	0.025
1967	1.39	0.211	0.040
1968	1.28	0.238	0.045
1969	1.47	0.199	0.050
1970	1.65	0.215	0.085
1971	1.46	0.394	0.195

Source: Company Data

Advertising Expenditure (% to sales)

	1970	1971
Pledge	15	17
Favor	20	35
Sparkle	—	44
Mr Sheen	53	35

Source: Market Research

however, stop Mr Sheen gaining a substantial market share and gradually going national.

In 1971 Johnson's introduced a new aerosol product 'Sparkle' formulated and positioned to compete directly with Mr Sheen. Pledge advertising was developed to suggest at least limited versatility and the can size was increased. Then in September a reformulated Pledge was introduced as 'Instant Shine Pledge', emphasising the fast, easy, superior shine.

At the end of 1971, Johnson's had been in a position to assess the results of the rather hectic activity in 1970—71. Their summary of the situation as presented to McCann's is given below and their figures on Pledge performance are set out in Exhibit 1:

a) Consistent erosion of share since the launch of Mr Sheen.

b) Unit sales are static, whilst the aerosol polish market is expanding rapidly. The total 'all polishes' market has remained fairly static around £6m, but aerosol share has risen from 23% in 1966 to 58.9% by the end of 1971.

c) The cost of being competitive in the market has increased substantially for Pledge, reducing profitability. In 1966 advertising and promotion represented 20% of sales; in 1971 this figure has more than doubled with over 10% in deals alone.

d) Pledge's versatility strategy has not been successful in increasing the brand share in an increasing market.

Product Positioning McCann's account group prepared the following summary of Pledge positioning for their internal meeting:

There are three main segments in the furniture polish market:
  i)   Paste Polishes
  ii) Liquid Polishes
  iii) Aerosol Polishes: wax furniture polishes
                        cleaner/polishes

Consumers of products in the first two segments of the market are generally people who believe that polishing requires a lot of rubbing and a lot of effort. They are likely to find it hard to accept that aerosol furniture polishes can do as good a job as the products they are currently using, and continue to use their current products through force of habit. However, both these segments are declining steadily in terms of sterling value, as trial of aerosols increases.

Johnson's Wax and Goddard together have a reasonably steady 26% unit share of the paste polish sector, while Johnson's Pride holds a unit share of 18% in the liquid polishes sector and is losing position slowly.

Consumers of aerosol polishes are extremely happy with the end result that they receive, and take a pride in the fact that they have found a product which offers convenience as well as a good finish. This segment incorporates both wax furniture polishes which are used by women who are concerned about their home and furniture appearance, and cleaner/polishes which are purchased by women concerned about versatility and a 'quick job' enabling them to be free to concentrate on other activities.

There are four main branded products in the aerosol sector: Favor, Pledge and Sparkle (all three from Johnson's Wax) and Mr Sheen.

Favor and Pledge are seen as being very different products from Mr Sheen and Sparkle. Favor is seen as being a good wax polish with Beeswax for furniture, although many of its users have extended its usage onto other surfaces.

Mr Sheen and Sparkle users require versatility as well as convenience, and they consider that neither Favor nor Pledge meet their needs, mainly because both products contain wax which causes smearing on surfaces other than furniture. Sparkle is seen as being just a little more versatile than Mr Sheen, whereas Pledge is seen in the furniture care area.

Advertising
Development Prior to the January briefing by Johnson's Wax, McCann-Erickson had carried out in depth interviews during December among aerosol polish users. Further results

Exhibit 2   *Background Research Information*

The following are the results of relevant pieces of research carried out on behalf of either Johnson's Wax or McCann-Erickson, both before and after Johnson's Wax briefed the Agency:

1. *Pledge and Mr Sheen Group Discussions*
Eight group discussions were carried out during December 1970. Generally these discussions confirmed that Pledge had an established, conventional and reliable image, whereas Mr Sheen was brighter and more versatile.

2. *Pledge Usage and Attitude Survey*
101 interviews were conducted with housewives in London and 100 with housewives in Sheffield during December 1970 to investigate possible regional differences.

3. *Pledge Attitude Profile*
448 interviews with housewives were carried out around London, Manchester and Yorkshire during January 1971 to investigate attitudes to Pledge amongst users of the product. Pledge was seen as a good value, cleaning, shining product.

4. 1,535 interviews were held through 40 sampling points in the UK between 28th June and 8th July 1971. Results related to Pledge generally confirmed previous research. but also indicated that wooden furniture was still the major usage area for main brands.

5. *Group discussions with Pledge and Mr Sheen/Sparkle Users*
Two group discussions were carried out in January 1972. The general indication was that Pledge users were concerned with preserving, while Mr Sheen/Sparkle users wanted speed/convenience.

6. *McCann-Erickson Preliminary Brand Image Research*
Conducted on behalf of McCann-Erickson during December 1971 in the form of eight unstructured interviews. Results confirmed previous research, particularly (1) above, and also indicated that each usage groups' perception of the other was as expected, given the relevant images.

7. *McCann-Erickson Depth Interviews*
Two group discussions were held at the end of January 1972 by an independent psychologist on behalf of McCann-Erickson to test four concepts. Among the concepts discussed, users liked the 'Come-Alive' one most (see Exhibit 3). During this time, ten depth interviews were also conducted on behalf of McCann-Erickson at the end of January 1972.

8. *McCann-Erickson Based Proposition Testing*
285 interviews were conducted for McCann-Erickson during the first week of February 1972, to test the four propositions indicated in the test. The results (representative but NOT actual figures) were:

Overall Propensity to Buy	%
Care (including Care + Wax)	50
Shine (including Shine + Wax)	30

9. *Screening of Four Film Storyboard Commercials in Three Group Discussions*
Three group discussions were carried out on behalf of McCann-Erickson on 12th February 1972. Two of these groups were of Pledge users and one was drawn from users of other aerosol polishes. This research indicated overall preference for the 'It shows you've cared' commercial, which was seen as highly effective and appealing. Some minor improvements were suggested.

---

on several research studies conducted on behalf of Johnson's Wax Limited were also made available to McCann's after the briefing. Summarised findings from these sources are included in Exhibit 2.

On the basis of the research information at their disposal, McCann's decided that Pledge had three main advantages in relation to its competition:

Exhibit 3

Another Come-Alive Shine from Pledge

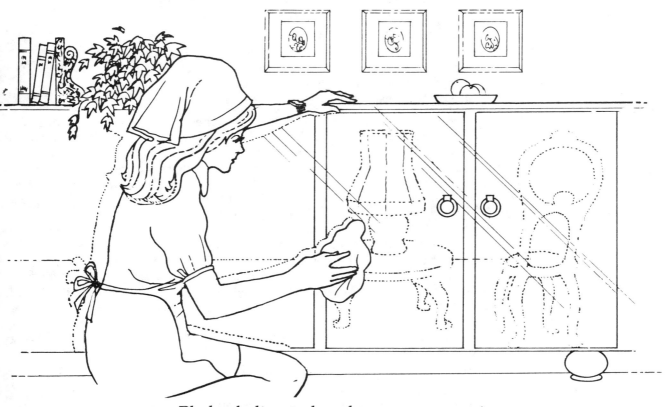

Pledge believes that the more we put into
your furniture, the more you get out of it.
So Pledge is careful to deep-shine while it cleans.
It has a fast acting polish that gives a deeper
lonmger-lasting shine. Doesn't your home deserve Pledge?
Pledge brings out the best in your furniture.

1) a higher wax content than the competition
2) a brighter shine when used on wooden surfaces
3) the fact that it looks after furniture better than the cleaner/polishers.

Bearing these advantages in mind, McCann's then developed a selection of advertising concepts. From these they selected four for concept testing on 25th January with a group of Pledge users and a group of Sparkle and Mr Sheen users. The four concepts were:

Concept 1: A cleaner, a protector, and a wax polisher.
Concept 2: Special waxes to add a new richness and shine.
Concept 3: Special furniture wax shine.
Concept 4: Johnson's Pledge in the family rooms.

The concepts varied in the way they presented Pledge. In one, Pledge was presented almost as a cleaner/polisher, while in another it was described as a polish which could only be used in certain rooms where there was furniture.

Pledge users immediately rejected the idea of Pledge only being used on furniture, because they had extended their use of the product. Wax seemed unimportant to them in comparison with shine and satisfaction in a job well done, and this caused McCann's to re-consider their overall approach.

Both the 'shine' and 'care' strategies were discussed at an Agency strategy review board meeting on 28th January, and it was then agreed to research both basic propositions, while they progressed with further creative work on each. In the meantime the results of further depth interviews carried out on behalf of McCann-Erickson, and group discussions held on behalf of Johnson's Wax, had been received. It seemed that they had two basic alternative concepts: 'care' against 'shine'. Another factor they had to consider further was 'wax'. Therefore, they conducted some straightforward proposition testing on 1st February with the following four propositions:

1) New Pledge's unique blend of ingredients are specially formulated to give better care to your furniture. (CARE)
2) New Pledge cares for your furniture better because it contains more wax. (CARE + WAX)
3) Nothing gives such a brilliant shine to your furniture as new Pledge because it contains more wax. (SHINE + WAX)
4) The special ingredients in new Pledge mean that it gives a more brilliant shine to your furniture. (SHINE)

The results of the research showed for Pledge that 'care' was more important to the housewife than 'shine'. The two other research reports received at the end of the previous week confirmed this.

While the research was taking place, thirteen more advertising approaches were developed incorporating various combinations of the elements they were examining. They did not consider all of them to be viable in the light of the research results and they held another meeting to discuss the thirteen approaches. A summary of these is set out below with McCann executives' comments against each:

1. *The good old-fashioned shine — instantly with Pledge*

This was discarded because it was felt that the theme and treatment might provide unfavourable associations for Pledge by 'dating' it and, perhaps, implying hard work. It was also felt that there was too much emphasis on shine and not enough on care.

2. *Introducing the Concentrated Shine. New formula Pledge is concentrated — to give your furniture a deeper, brighter shine*

We retained the idea of a concentrated polish in later development, but this particular treatment was abandoned as being too harsh and unsympathetic.

3. *Pledge does a little more — like you do. Some mums want to do a little more. That's why when it comes to taking care of their furniture, they use Pledge*

We felt this treatment was correct both in terms of approach and the strategy and we decided to take it further into development, but we thought that claims for the product had to be more competitive to be effective.

4. *The Deeper Shine. If you could measure a shine, you'd find that Pledge wins hands down*

The treatment relied on a rippling water effect to prove the point and we could not be sure if it would work. We decided to take the treatment no further because it communicated shine too strongly, and care not strongly enough.

5. *Get a Spring Clean Shine all the time with Pledge*

We were concerned that, unless this aproach was very carefully considered and communicated, we could encourage a more limited usage of Pledge.

6. *Another Come-Alive Shine from Pledge. Pledge believes that the more we put into your furniture, the more you get out of it*

We considered this to be a very effective, meaningful way of presenting Pledge, and agreed that it should be considered further. However, we did decide to emphasise care more at a later stage. (Exhibit 3 illustrates the standard of finish to which this and other concepts were taken at this stage.)

7. *Pledge — the more you use it, the more it shines*

This approach emphasised shine too heavily, and it was dropped.

8. *More of a Shine. (Demonstration of two pigs sliding down polished surfaces to communicate Pledge's superior shine)*

We discarded this approach because it was not consistent with the image of a superior, quality polish.

9. *Snow White — "All I did was dust with Pledge"*

This was an opportunity to exploit the 'easy dusting' idea, by linking Pledge with a classic of house-tidying as shown in the Walt Disney version of Snow White. We decided to take it no further because it contained no element of care.

10. *The care you give with Pledge brings a kind of shine that looks so good you find yourself touching it*

We felt that this was an area where we could explore futher.

11. *Testimonials*

We had many interesting comments from housewives on tape, and felt that this could be a method of communicating the complete Pledge message in a very creditable and convincing way. One thing we were concerned about was the possibility of identification resistance.

12. *Pledge: an aerosol that sprays real polish. Enough real polish for a real bhine*

This approach was thought to be highly competitive and worth exploring further. However, we thought it best to discard some elements of the treatment: we decided that the word 'aerosol' was superfluous, and we decided not to associate shine with slipperiness as we had in the treatment.

13. *Pledge: wherever it rains, it shines*

The only way to find out if this treatment worked was to shoot some test footage of film, and we decided to do this.

Following the January 28th meeting, scripts for four commercials were produced and discussed at a further meeting on 8th February. The scripts for these four commercials are included in Exhibit 4. Each script is discussed briefly below:

1. *Pledge — the one polish that cares a little more. Just like you do*

This is an attempt to gain the support of the housewife who likes to think she looks after her home and furniture. We offer her a product which is worthy of her efforts in polishing the furniture, because it makes it all worthwhile by caring for her furniture and bringing her home to life.

The script also supplies a very tangible reason why Pledge is a superior furniture polish: 'special New Formula has more real wax polish'.

Exhibit 4   *Scripts for Four Alternative Commercials*

1. Just Like You Do

VIDEO	AUDIO
Open on a mother straightening a little boy's tie before he leaves for school. She hands him an apple as he goes out of the door.	*1½ seconds silence* *Soft music under:* If you care a little more, you do a little more. That's why you use Pledge.
Cut to CU of woman's hand picking up a can of Pledge from kitchen counter — we see CU of Pledge label.	
CU, same angle, of Pledge as woman sprays the dining room table with polish.	Because Pledge cares a little more.
MCU of woman polishing table — we can tell that she is enjoying herself. After she has finished as an after-thought she reaches out and and gently runs her finger over the shine. It is a gesture of admiration.	Its special New Formula has more real wax polish. It goes to work the moment you dust to bring out the best in your furniture.
Cut to woman spraying a cabinet. As she polishes from left to right, we pick up the reflection of the woman and then a child holding a teddy bear. The woman pats the bear on the head in the reflection. The little girl laughs. And the woman turns to look at the child.	You can tell Pledge cares because every time you use it your home seems to come alive (with a shine).
Super pops on with Johnson's logo. Pledge cares a little more — just like you do.	Pledge — the one real wax polish that cares a little more — just like you do. And all you do is dust. *½ second silence*

2. It Shows You've Cared

VIDEO	AUDIO
Open on CU can of Pledge — hold on label long enough for name 'Pledge' to register.	*1½ seconds silence* *Music — Let the sunshine in — softly underneath* *Announcer:*
CU of woman spraying Pledge on sideboard.	
CU of woman polishing in continuous sweep from left to right. As the polish clears to a shine, we see reflections of various parts of the house — a table with a vase of flowers on it, a television, a little boy dragging a toy train behind him.	There's an old saying — the more you put into things, the more you get out of them. So we put more real wax polish in New Formula Pledge. Now the care you take with Pledge shows the moment you use it. And the nicest thing about Pledge is the more you use it the more it shows you've cared. And all you do is dust!

Cut to pack shot with super
and Johnson's Wax logo.

Pledge — it shows you've cared.

*Music builds to a crescendo
until the end*

Music stops

Announcer:

Pledge real wax polish — it shows
you've cared.

½ second silence

---

3. Testimonial

(Percussion cued to cuts)
VO:

A woman knows every stick of her
own furniture . . . how many
things need the care of real polish.

1st Quote:

If you take a pride in your home,
you worry, you've got to take care
of it with real polish.

2nd Quote:

Real polish guards the wood from
the fingermarks.

VO:

Pledge is real polish, in abundance.
Real polish in rich droplets.
Real care.

3rd Quote:

All you do is dust!

(Percussion cued to cuts)

VO:

Pledge. Real polish.

---

4. The Rain that Shines

VIDEO	*AUDIO*
A falling mist of white shining 'raindrops' against a dark background.	*(Music for falling droplets)*
Quivering droplets form from the falling mist on an unpolished wood surface.	VO: This is rain, rich, nourishing rain. Wherever it rains . . .
Hand with polishing cloth wipes a shining path across wood surface.	*(Music to herald the shine)* . . . it shines! You know the furniture in your house needs taking care of. So does Pledge. That's why Pledge puts proper wax polish, in such abundance . . .
Pack being sprayed. Move in on quivering droplet on wood.	. . . in every drop, that Pledge gives you easily the richest finish there is.
Another wipe of the cloth, more shining surface.	Wherever it rains, it shines . . . To show how much you care.
Pack. She replaces it with flowers. Freeze frame before pack goes.	Pledge — the rain that shines from Johnson's Wax.
	And all you did was dust!

The commercial should strengthen the loyalty of current Pledge users, and help to convince some non-users that they need to use Pledge.

2. *Pledge — it shows you've cared*

With this script we try to convince the housewife that all her efforts in looking after furniture can be just that little bit more worthwhile with the superior end result she can get from New Formula Pledge.

The commercial will reinforce the loyalty of current Pledge users by rewarding them for the care they take, and encourage lapsed or non-users to take a fresh look at Pledge.

3. *'Real Polish'/Testimonial*

This commercial uses a combination of voice-over and various consumer quotes to explain that Pledge is 'real' polish; the only polish that can look after furniture properly.

It allows for an extremely competitive approach and also enables us to cover a spectrum of attitudes which exist within the market.

4. *Pledge — the rain that shines from Johnson's Wax*

Here the richness and quality of Pledge is stressed in the treatment of the commercial. The elements of gentle 'care' and end result, shine, are also strong.

Again, the approach is very competitive in the claims it makes for Pledge.

On 9, 10 and 11 February, film storyboard commercials were produced and transferred to videotape for three group discussions on the afternoon of 12 February. These group discussions were amongst current Pledge users and non-Pledge users, including users of Mr Sheen/Sparkle, and distributors' own brands. Many of the so-called non-Pledge users were actually lapsed users of Pledge.

The purpose of the group discussions was to test the communication and relevant factors of each commercial prior to the presentation. The results of the group discussions are set out in Exhibit 2.

After the screening of the four film storyboard commercials with two groups of Pledge users and one group of non-users, the results for the commercial 'It shows you've cared' were reported as:

The commercial received a strong preference over the other three. One the strongest elements of the commercial was the music. They included the Beatles' song, 'Here comes the sun' as the backing track, and this reflected many of the deep feelings that women have about polishing.

Polishing is one of the things that a housewife derives real satisfaction from in the home. It is not a chore; she finds it easy work and receives a great deal of pleasure and pride from standing back and admiring the finished result.

Sunshine reflects both the shine of polished furniture, and her feelings of happiness and satisfaction with a room of polished furniture. Sunlight is also a very severe test of whether furniture has been polished properly, because it shows up dust and dirt. The song used in the commercial touched many of the housewives' emotional feelings about the home and polishing furniture, and, although we could not use exactly the same music in producing a finished commercial because of copyright, we know we would be able to commission a special arrangement which would be very similar to the Beatles' record for the final film.

The commercial was also linked because it showed the woman actuallly polishing and expressing satisfaction at a very good result. The housewives in the groups identified very strongly with this, and appreciated it because it showed that the woman in the commercial cared. They also liked the fact that the family had been included in the commercial.

It also effectively demonstrated removal of fingermarks, which are the most common marks a housewife has to remove from furniture, and communicated that Pledge had more real wax polish, which the groups realised protected furniture and gave a better shine.

Summarising, the commercial communicated effectively Pledge's product advantages and had a very strong emotional appeal with most of the housewives in the groups.

This case was prepared by
K-C Mun of The Chinese
University of Hong Kong and
Kenneth Simmonds of the
London Business School. It is
intended as a basis for class
discussion rather than to
indicate either effective or
ineffective handling of
administrative situations.
Names of companies and
people are disguised.
© K-C Mun and Kenneth
Simmonds, 1980.

CASE C13
Far East Foods Ltd

In August 1971 Mr Wong Wing-fat, General Manager of Far East Foods Ltd was reviewing the promotional strategy for Ruby, a soft drink resembling orange juice, which was the sole product of Far East Foods' Beverage Department. Mr Wong was well pleased with the growing popularity of Ruby; sales had grown from 7,500,000 bottles in 1967 to 16,000,000 bottles in 1970. However, Ruby occupied only about 5% of the total market and Mr Wong felt that his product had considerable potential for further growth; although with at least ten well-known products available to consumers, the Hong King soft drink market was extremely competitive.

Ruby was a proprietary soft drink made from an orange concentrate produced by Sunshine-Citrus Corporation of San Diego, California. Far East Foods Ltd purchased the franchise for bottling and marketing Ruby throughout Hong Kong in 1957 and the sales growth from that time is shown in Exhibit 1. As part of its franchise agreement, Sunshine-Citrus Corporation undertook to finance up to one third of the advertising expenses for promoting the sale of Ruby in Hong Kong, provided that total advertising expenses did not exceed 6% of total sales. Although the US company made advertising materials available at a reasonable cost, Far East Foods Ltd was allowed full freedom in planning and carrying out all local marketing activities.

Mr Wong took over as General Manager of Far East Foods Ltd in March 1966. At that time he was still in his early thirties. He had graduated from a well-known American university and had worked in the international marketing division of a large food products company. He immediately undertook a comprehensive review of the company's activities and past policies.

In common with other major bottling firms in Hong Kong, Far East Foods distributed Ruby to thousands of retail outlets, restaurants, hotels and canteens and tuckshops of schools and other institutions. Salesmen called directly on all

Exhibit 1 *Far East Foods Ltd Sales and Advertising Expenditure 1957 to 1970*

Year	Sales by volume (HK$ millions)	Sales by volume (cases '000s)	Advertising Expenditure (HK$ '000s)
1957	1.23	206	103
1958	1.45	218	251
1959	1.55	247	188
1960	1.47	235	215
1961	1.53	222	193
1962	2.09	253	257
1963	2.85	383	288
1964	2.57	266	226
1965	2.30	251	241
1966	2.67	309	285
1967	2.56	309	272
1968	3.25	398	370
1969	4.36	505	356
1970	5.44	653	514

customers and were paid a basic salary plus a commission on sales. In addition to replenishing customers' stocks of Ruby when they called, Ruby salesmen inspected 'Ruby' signboards and other promotional material on the customers' premises to see that they were presentable and prominently displayed. They also checked that cases of Ruby were placed on top of other drinks so as to be ready at hand when the retailer was filling his drink cooler. Of course, salesmen for other soft drinks did likewise.

Mr Wong summarised the problems he identified with regard to the Beverage Department as follows:

1. The sales staff had no well-defined responsibilities. When production in the firm's Candy or Biscuit Departments required additional temporary staff, salesmen would be re-assigned to this work and deliveries of Ruby in these salesmen's districts would be suspended until they could be released from their temporary work assignments.
2. The salesmen were not properly supervised or controlled.
3. Most of the company's delivery trucks were obsolete. The poor condition of the fleet resulted in much wasted time on the part of the drivers and salesmen.
4. Although Ruby had wide-spread advertising coverage in all media, Mr Wong believed that the advertising programme had had little or no effect on sales. Mr Wong felt that the company had relied too heavily on advertising materials supplied by Sunshine-Citrus Corporation and that these materials were not suitable for Hong Kong.
5. The company's efforts at sales development had been concentrated almost entirely on retail stores and shops.
6. The trade marks on many Ruby bottles had become illegible. Mr Wong believed that this gave potential consumers a poor image of Ruby and encouraged them to select other drinks.

Mr Wong firstly increased the number of trucks to improve the efficiency of deliveries. The responsibilities of salesmen were then made explicit. Each salesman was to call on every retailer in his district at least twice each day and a standard sales quota for each district was calculated from estimated sales potential. Sales supervisors were appointed to ensure that calls were made as planned and to take appropriate action whenever a sales quota was not being met. Every salesman was required to submit a daily written report to his supervisor listing each call, the sales made and problems encountered.

Bottles with illegible trade marks were replaced by new ones from the USA to guard against old bottles making a poor impression on consumers. Mr Wong also requested Sunshine-Citrus Corporation to revise its policy on advertising expenses to permit a more aggressive marketing programme for Ruby. When this request was refused, Mr Wong decided to go ahead with the programme anyway, even though Far East Foods would have to pay more than its two-thirds share of the cost. In fact, Mr Wong decided to plough all 1966 profits from Ruby into the advertising campaign.

Analysis showed that school children were the largest group of potential consumers of Ruby. Parents generally did not favour their children drinking too many carbonated beverages. Ruby was non-carbonated and it also contained the food and health value of natural oranges. Mr Wong decided, therefore, that the company's advertising should be directed towards school children and their parents. Advertising films for use in cinemas and on television were commissioned locally. These showed six and seven year old children sitting in first-class hotels and asking waiters for Ruby. Classical music formed the background for the soundtrack message. These films acutally carried two messages: 1) Children liked Ruby. 2) Ruby was a popular drink in high society.

Using these themes the firm undertook the sponsorship of a family-type television programme during prime evening hours. Although the company's advertisements were aimed primarily at children, teenagers were not entirely neglected.

Exhibit 2 *Cost Structure of Ruby, July 1971*

	Cost per bottle (cents)	(%)
Ruby concentrate & other materials	9.53	28.6
Labour and other production costs	4.02	12.1
Advertising (net)	2.08	6.3
Selling, including delivery	12.35	37.2
Administration	2.38	7.2
Depreciation	2.83	8.6
	HKc 33.19	100.0

The company sponsored a radio 'top of the pops' programme which promoted only Ruby. Mr Wong concentrated his advertising on television, radio and cinema, using other advertising media only to a minor degree.

Mr Wong believed that, in general, the advertisements of most soft drink companies were too ordinary and to avoid customer interest and awareness falling off with the high level of Ruby advertising, he developed a 'free gifts' strategy. Soft drink consumers were urged to collect Ruby bottle caps and to exchange them for drinking glasses made in shapes and designs that were quite out of the ordinary.

Added sales emphasis was also placed on school canteens and restaurants. Mr Wong had salesmen despatched to promote sales of Ruby in the canteens of primary, secondary and post-secondary schools throughout Hong Kong. By 1969 Ruby was being sold in the canteens of 2,000 of the 2,800 schools in Hong Kong. Salesmen were also sent to restaurants to pose as customers for Ruby. If the restaurant did not have Ruby, the salesman would express his unwillingness to order any other soft drink. He would then re-visit the restaurant the next day or several days later and ask for Ruby again. Thus in order to cater to their customers' requests, the restaurant would eventually stock Ruby even though it had not originally intended to.

During Chinese dinner parties it is a common practice for waiters to place a variety of soft drinks on the tables for the guests to choose from. Mr Wong instructed salesmen to maintain friendly relations with the waiters of leading restaurants so that Ruby would always appear on their tables at dinners and other occasions.

Under Mr Wong's management, sales of Ruby increased dramatically as shown in Exhibit 1. The average annual rate of growth in sales between 1967 and 1970 was 21.2%, whereas that between 1958 and 1966 was only 6.7%.

In March 1971, following a build-up in costs over a period of years, the Hong Kong soft drink industry posted a general increase in prices. The retail price of the regular 6-ounce bottles of the major brands was raised by 20% and the wholesale price from 35c to 40c per bottle, in cases of 24 bottles. As would be expected, most brands experienced reduced sales after the price increase. Ruby was no exception; its sales fell by approximately 10%. However, some of the other brands encountered much larger decreases in sales.

The increased prices provided much more satisfactory profit margins at both the retail and manufacturing levels. Costings of Ruby sales in July 1971, shown in Exhibit 2, indicated a profit per bottle of nearly 7c. Furthermore, following the recent installation of new bottling equipment, break-even volume was estimated at only 300,000 cases. Therefore, Mr Wong decided that the major emphasis should be on further increasing the sales of Ruby and he intended that the company's marketing strategies should be directed towards this objective.

As a basis for calculating the amount of advertising he should spend, Mr Wong fitted a curve by least squares regression relating his sales achievement to advertising expenditure, as shown in Exhibit 3. From this he concluded that further advertising should produce sales of around 12,000 cases for every HK$ 10,000 spent. Five-year projections of Hong Kong population shown in Exhibit 4 indicated that there

Exhibit 3

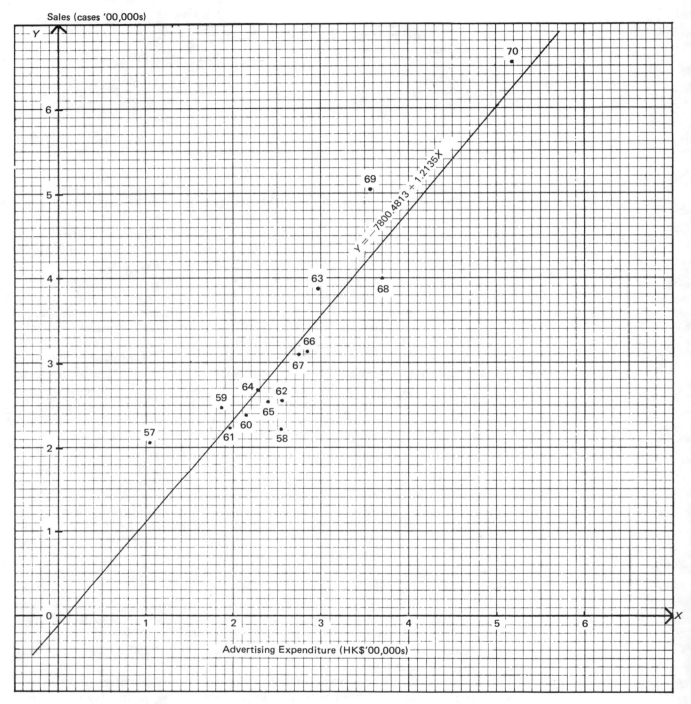

Sales (cases '00,000s)

Advertising Expenditure (HK$'00,000s)

The regression line is estimated as
$$Y = -7800.4813 + 1.2135X$$
where Y = sales volume in cases
X = advertising expenditures in HK$

Coefficient of determination: r^2 = 0.8295
Coefficient of correlation: r = 0.9217

would be 1.6 million within the 5 to 19 age bracket by 1981. At the modal drinking rate for Ruby estimated by the salesforce to be 20 bottles per annum, the potential sales would be 1.3 million cases or double 1971 sales. To achieve this target, annual sales growth would need to be about 130,000 cases, which had been achieved in 1971, and advertising expenditure then would need to increase by around $110,000 each year.

Exhibit 4   *Age Projection of Hong Kong Population, 1966 to 1981 ('000s)*

Age Group	1966	1971	1976	1981
0—4	533	501	573	673
5—9	528	534	501	573
10—14	448	532	537	504
15—19	385	452	535	539
20—24	201	390	456	538
25—29	211	207	394	460
30—34	245	217	211	397
35—39	260	248	219	214
40—44	234	260	248	220
45—49	192	232	258	246
50—54	166	188	227	253
55—59	117	160	181	219
60—64	91	109	150	170
65 & Over	121	178	240	324
Total	3,732	4,208	4,729	5,330

Source: Hong Kong Statistics 1947—67, Census & Statistics Department, Hong Kong, 1969.

CASE C14

Castle Crisps Ltd

In May of 1972 Mr Adrian Van Tassle, Advertising Director for Castle Crisps Ltd, tugged at his red moustache and contemplated the latest market share report. This was not one of his happier moments. "Blimey," he exclaimed, "I've got to do something to turn this market around before it's too late for Castle — and me. But I can't afford another mistake like last year . . ."

Indeed, Mr William Castle (the Managing Director and owner of 30 per cent of the shares of Castle) had exhibited a similar reaction when told that Castle's share of the market was dropping back towards 5.4 per cent — where it had been one year previously. He had remarked rather pointedly to Mr Van Tassle that if market share and profitability were not improved during the next fiscal year 'some rather drastic actions' might need to be taken. Van Tassle recalled a remark about 'a return trip ticket to Singapore' unless something good happened soon.

Adrian Van Tassle had been hired by Mr James Anthoney, Castle's Marketing Director, in the summer of 1970. Prior to that time he had worked for companies in the Netherlands and Singapore and had gained a reputation as a highly effective advertising executive. Now, in the spring of 1972, he was engaged in trying to reverse a long-term downward trend in the market position of Castle Crisps.

Castle's Market Position

Castle Crisps was an old established company in the crisps business, with headquarters in Staines, just outside London. Its market area included most of Southern England and the Midlands. The company had at one time enjoyed as much as 15 per cent of the market in these areas. These were often referred to as the 'good old days', when the brand was strong and growing.

The company's troubles began in the 1960s, when television became the primary advertising medium. Castle experienced increasing competitive difficulty as television production and time costs increased. Further problems presented themselves as several other old-line companies were absorbed by major marketeers. Finally, the advent of other snacks such as 'Chipitos' put additional pressure on Castle, which had no entry in product classes other than crisps. The downward trend in share was most pronounced during the early 1960s: the company had held 12 per cent of the market at the beginning of the decade but only about 5.5 per cent at the end. Market share had held fairly stable for the last few years. This was attributed to a 'hard-core' group of local buyers plus an active (and expensive) programme of consumer promotions and price-off deals to the trade. Mr Anthoney believed that the erosion of share had been halted just in time. A little more slippage, he said, and Castle would begin to lose its distribution. This would have been the beginning of the end for this venerable company.

Operation Break-out

When William Castle was elevated to the Managing Director's post in 1968, his main objective was to halt the decline in market position and, if possible, to effect a turnaround. His success in achieving the first objective has already been noted. However, both he and Anthoney agreed that the same strategy (i.e. intensive below-the-line promotion) would not succeed in winning back any appreciable proportion of the lost market share.

Both men believed that it would be necessary to increase consumer awareness

248

of the Castle brand and develop more favourable attitudes about it, if market positions were to be improved. This could only be done through advertising. Since the company produced a quality product (it was noticeably crunchier and less greasy than many competing crisps), it appeared that a strategy of increasing advertising weight might stand some chance of success. A search for an advertising director was initiated, which culminated in the hiring of Adrian Van Tassle.

After a period of familiarising himself with the Castle company and the British crisp market and advertising scene, Van Tassle began developing a plan to revitalise Castle's advertising programme. First, he 'released' the company's current advertising agency and requested proposals from a number of others interested in obtaining the account. While it was generally understood that the amount of advertising would increase somewhat, the heaviest emphasis was on the kind of appeal and copy execution to be used. Both the company and the various agencies agreed that nearly all the advertising weight should go into television. (There is some newspaper advertising for crisps, but this is usually placed by retailers under an advertising allowance arrangement with the manufacturer. Castle included such expenditures in its promotional budget rather than as an advertising expense.)

The team from Aardvark Associates Ltd won the competition with an advertising programme built around the theme 'only a Castle crisp is fit for a lord or a lady'. The new agency recommended that a 30 per cent increase in the quarterly advertising budget be approved, in order to 'give the new programme a fair trial'. After considerable negotiation with Messrs Castle and Anthoney, and further discussion with the agency, Van Tassle decided to compromise on a 20 per cent increase. The new campaign was to start in the autumn of 1971, which was the second quarter of Castle's 1972 fiscal year.* It was dubbed 'operation break-out'.

* The company's fiscal year began on July 1 and ended on June 30. For example, fiscal year 1972 included the summer and autumn quarter of 1971 and the winter and spring quarters of 1972.

Performance during Fiscal Year 1972

Castle had been advertising at an average rate of £30,000 per quarter for the last several years. Given the current level of promotional expenditures, this was regarded as sufficient to maintain market share at about its present level of 5.4 per cent. Castle's annual expenditure of £120,000 represented somewhat more than 5.4 per cent of industry advertising, though exact figures about competitors' expenditures on crisps were difficult to obtain. This relation was regarded as normal, since own brands accounted for a significant fraction of the market and these received little or no advertising. Neither Mr Van Tassle nor Mr Anthoney anticipated that competitive expenditures would change much during the next few years, whether or not Castle increased its advertising by 20, or even 30 or 40 per cent.

Advertising of crisps followed a regular seasonal pattern, which approximated the seasonal variation of industry sales. The relevant figures are presented in Table 1. Total sales of crisps in Castle's market area averaged 2 million cases per quarter and were expected to remain at that level for several years. Consumption in winter was about 15 per cent above the yearly average, while in summer the volume was down by 15 per cent. Advertising expenditures by both Castle and the industry in general followed the same basic pattern except that the seasonal variation was between 80 and 120 per cent — somewhat greater than the variation in sales. The 'maintenance' expenditure on advertising, shown in Table 1, was what the company

Table 1 Industry sales and Castle's advertising budget

Quarter	Industry ('000 cases)	Sales index	Maintenance Advertising (£'000)	(Index)	Planned Advertising for fiscal year 1972 (£'000)	(% increase)
1 Summer	1700	0.85	24	0.80	24	0
2 Autumn	2000	1.00	30	1.00	36	20
3 Winter	2300	1.15	36	1.20	43.2	20
4 Spring	2000	1.00	30	1.00	36	20
Average	2000	1.00	30	1.00	34.8	16

Exhibit 1　*Mr Figure's First Memorandum*

CONFIDENTIAL

Memo to: W. Castle, Managing Director
From:　　I. Figure, Controller
Subject:　Proposed 20 per cent increase in advertising

I think Adrian's proposal to increase advertising by 20 per cent (from a quarterly rate of £30,000 to one of £36,000) is a good idea. He predicts that a market share of 6 per cent will be achieved, compared to our currrent 5.4 per cent. I can't comment about the feasibility of this assumption: that's Adrian's business and I presume he knows what he's doing. I can tell you, however, that such a result would be highly profitable.

As you know, the wholesale price of crisps has been running about £2.40 per case. Deducting our average retail advertising and promotional allowance of 30p per case, and our variable costs of production and distribution of £1.35 per case, leaves an average gross contribution to fixed costs and profit of 75p per case. Figuring a total market of about 2 million cases per quarter and a share change of from 0.054 to 0.060 (a 0.006 increase), we would have the following increase in gross contribution:

Change in gross contribution = 75p × 2,000,000 × 0.006 = £9,000

Subtracting the change in advertising expense due to the new programme and then dividing by this the same quantity gives what can be called the *advertising payout rate:*

$$\text{Advertising payout rate} = \frac{\text{Change in gross contribution} - \text{change in advertising expense}}{\text{change in advertising expense}}$$

$$= \frac{3000}{6000} = 0.50$$

That is, we can expect to make 50p in net contribution for each extra pound spent in advertising. You can see that as long as this quantity is greater than zero (at which point the extra gross contribution just pays for the extra advertising), increasing our advertising is a good deal.

I think Adrian has a good thing going here, and my recommendation is to go ahead. Incidentally, the extra funds we should generate in net contribution (after advertising expense is deducted) should help to relieve the cash flow bind which I mentioned last week. Perhaps we will be able to maintain the quarterly dividend after all.

---

believed it had to spend to maintain its 'normal' 5.4 per cent share of the market in each quarter. Van Tassle had wondered whether this was the right seasonal advertising pattern for Castle, given its small percentage of the market, but decided to stay with it during fiscal year 1972. Therefore, the 20 per cent planned increase in quarterly advertising rates was simply added to the 'sustaining' amount for each quarter, beginning in the second quarter of the year. The planned expenditures for fiscal year 1972 are also shown in Table 1.

In speaking with Mr Castle and James Anthoney about the proposed changes in the advertising programme, Adrian Van Tassle had indicated that he expected to increase market share to 6 per cent or perhaps a little more. This sounded pretty good to Mr Castle, especially after he had spoken with the company's controller. (The controller's memorandum on the subject is presented in Exhibit 1.) Mr Van Tassle had, of course, indicated that the hoped-for 6 per cent share was not a 'sure thing', and in any case that it might take more than one quarter before the full effects of the new advertising programme could make themselves felt.

The new advertising campaign broke on October 1 1971, as scheduled. (October 1 was the beginning of the second quarter of Castle's fiscal year.) Adrian Van Tassle was somewhat disappointed in the commercials prepared by the Aardvark agency and a little apprehensive about the early reports from the field. The bi-monthly store audit report of market share for September/October showed only a fractional increase in share over the 5.4 per cent of the previous period. Nevertheless, Van Tassle thought that given a little time things would work out and that the campaign would eventually reach its objective.

The November/December market share report was received in mid-January. It showed Castle's share of the market to be 5.6 per cent. On January 21 1972 Mr Van Tassle received a carbon copy of the memorandum shown in Exhibit 2.

On Monday January 24 James Anthoney telephoned Van Tassle to say that Mr Castle wanted an immediate review of the new advertising programme. Later that week, after several rounds of discussion in which Mr Van Tassle was unable to convince Castle and Anthoney that the programme would be successful, it was decided to return to fiscal year 1971 advertising levels. The television contracts with the ITV companies were re-negotiated forthwith and by the middle of February advertising had been cut back subsantially toward the £36,000 per quarter rate that had previously been normal for the winter. (Aardvark Associates complained that the efficiency of their media 'buy' suffered significantly during February and March, due to the abrupt reduction in advertising expenditure. However, they were unable to say by how much.) The spring 1972 rate was set at the normal level of £30,000. Market share for January/February turned out to be slightly under 5.7 per cent, while that for March/April was about 5.5 per cent.

Planning for Fiscal Year 1973

Now, in mid-May of 1972, Adrian Van Tassle was faced with the problem of what to recommend as the advertising budget for the four quarters of fiscal year 1973. He was already very late in dealing with this assignment, since media buys would have to be upped soon if any substantial increase in weight were to be effected during the summer quarter of 1972. Alternatively, fast action would be needed to reduce advertising expenditures below their tentatively budgeted 'normal' level.

During the past month Van Tassle had spent considerable time reviewing the difficulties of fiscal year 1972. He had remained convinced that a 20 per cent increase in advertising should produce somewhere around a 6 per cent market share level. He based this partly on 'hunch' and partly on a number of studies that had been performed by academic and business market researchers with whom he was acquainted.

One such study which he believed was particularly applicable to Castle's situation indicated that the 'advertising elasticity of demand' was equal to about 0.5. He recalled that the definition of this quantity when applied to market share is:

$$\text{Advertising elasticity of demand} = \frac{\text{percentage change in market share}}{\text{percentage change in advertising}}$$

Exhibit 2 *Mr Figure's Second Memorandum*

---

20 January 1972

Memo to: W. Castle, Managing Director
From: I. Figure, Controller
Subject: Failure of Advertising Programme

I am most alarmed at our failure to achieve the market share target projected by Mr A. Van Tassle. The 0.2 point increase in market share achieved in November/December is not sufficient to return the cost of the increased advertising. Ignoring the month of October, which obviously represents a 'start-up' period, a 0.2 point increase in share generates only £3,000 in extra gross contribution on a quarterly basis. This must be compared to the £6,000 we have expended in extra advertising. The advertising pay-out rate is thus only −0.50: much less than break-even.

I know Mr Van Tassle expects share to increase again next quarter, but he has not been able to say by how much. The new programme projects an advertising expenditure increase of £7,000 over last year's winter quarter level. I don't see how we can continue to make these expenditures without a better prospect of return on our investment.

cc: Mr J. Anthoney
     Mr A. Van Tassle

Private postscript to Mr Castle: In view of our autumn 1971 performance, we must discuss the question of the quarterly dividend at an early date.

The researcher assured him that it was valid to think of 'percentage changes' as being deviations from 'normal levels' (also called maintenance levels) of advertising and share. However, he was worried that any given value of advertising elasticity would be valid only for moderate deviations about the norm. That is, the value of 0.5 he had noted earlier would not necessarily apply to (say) plus or minus 50 per cent changes in advertising.

Van Tassle noted that his estimate of share change (6.0 − 5.4 = 0.6 percentage points) represented about an 11 per cent increase over the normal share level of 5.4 points. Since this was to be achieved with a 20 per cent increase in advertising, it represented an advertising elasticity of 11 per cent/20 per cent = 0.55. While this was higher than the 0.5 found in the study, he had believed that his advertising appeals and copy would be a bit better than average. He recognised that his ads may not actually have been as great as expected, but noted that even an elasticity of 0.5 would produce 5.94 per cent of the market — within striking distance of 6 per cent. Of course, the study itself might be applicable to Castle's market situation to a greater or lesser degree.

One lesson which he had learned from his unfortunate experience the year before was the danger inherent in presenting too optimistic a picture to top management. On the other hand, a 'conservative' estimate might not have been sufficient to obtain approval for the programme in the first place. Besides, he really did believe that the effect of advertising on share was greater than implied by performance in the autumn of 1971. This judgement should be a part of management's information set when they evaluated his proposal. Alternatively, if management had good reason for doubting his judgement he wanted to know about it — after all, William Castle and James Anthoney had been in the crisps business a lot longer than he had and were pretty knowledgeable chaps.

Perhaps the problem lay in his assessment of the speed with which the new programme would take hold. He had felt it 'would take a little time', but had not tried to pin it down further. ('That's pretty hard, after all.') Nothing very precise about this had been communicated to management. Could he blame Mr Figure for adopting the time horizon he did?

As a final complicating factor, Van Tassle had just received a report from Aardvark Associates about the 'quality' of the advertising copy and appeals used the previous autumn and winter. Contrary to expectations, these ads rated only

---

Exhibit 3 *Theatre Tests*

In theatre testing an audience is recruited either by mail or by telephone to attend a showing of a test television programme. When the members of the audience arrive, they are given a set of questionnaires, through which an M.C. guides them as the session progresses. Usually, data on the audience's opinions of and preferences for the various brands in the product categories being tested are gathered before the show begins. The show consists of a standard television programme episode (or two or more such episodes) in which several television commercials have been inserted. At the close of the showing, audience members are again asked to fill-out questionnnaires, again asked to give their opinions and preferences regarding the various brands of the advertised products. In many cases the members of the audience (or some proportion of them) also record their interest in the show as it progresses by turning a dial as their interest level rises and falls, which permits the analyst to trace 'interest curves' for the programme.

The theatre test is one of the most versatile of the available test methods. It can be used to test television commercials in many different stages of development. To offset the high cost of this method, several advertisements for non-competing products are normally tested in a single session, thus splitting expenses among several advertisers. The method yields fair measures of attention-getting power, credibility, and motivating power. However, it is not very valuable for the diagnosis of specific problems with the commercials. To some extent interest curves can help to pinpoint weak spots, but the best way to obtain information that will point the way to improvement is to hold a group interview session immediately after the showing, using a few people selected from the audience.

about 0.90 on a scale upon which an 'average ad' was pegged at 1.0. (These tests were based on the so-called 'theatre technique', in which an advertisement was inserted into a filmed 'entertainment' programme and its effect on choices in a lottery designed to simulate purchasing behaviour was determined — see Exhibit 3.) Fortunately, the ads currently being shown had been improved slightly and now rated about 1.0 on the same scale. A new series of ads scheduled for showing during the autumn, winter and spring of 1973 appeared to be much better. Theatre testing could not be undertaken until production was completed during the summer, but 'experts' in the agency were convinced that they would rate at least as high as 1.15. Mr Van Tassle was impressed with these ads himself, but recalled that such predictions were far from perfect. In the meantime, a budget request for all four quarters of fiscal 1973 had to be submitted to management within the next week.

This case was prepared by Patrick Barwise of the London Business School as a basis for class discussion rather than to illustrate either effective or ineffective handling of an administrative situation. Figures have been disguised throughout.
© *Patrick Barwise, 1976.*

CASE C15
Ladbroke Holidays Ltd

Background

In September 1975 John Harounoff (Marketing Director of Ladbroke Holidays Ltd) was preparing his marketing plan for 1976. His main problem was media strategy. It was not a question of detailed scheduling, but rather of the broad issues like how much to spend on TV advertising, press advertising, direct mail and other activities, and how much weight to give the main opening campaign, as against subsequent follow-up. The 1975 season was drawing to a close, and for the first time Harounoff had a detailed computer record of advertising response and subsequent sales: he wondered how best to use this new information in planning for next year. The basic creative content of his 1976 advertising had already been determined and was reflected in the content and design of the 1976 brochures, now ready for printing.

Ladbroke Holidays Ltd

Ladbroke Holidays was part of the very successful Ladbroke Group, a major force in the UK leisure market. By 1975 the Ladbroke Group was making an annual pre-tax profit of over £12 million (a twenty-fold increase in just six years), and had significantly broadened its original base in betting shops. Activities now included casinos, bingo halls, nightclubs, hotels, racecourses and property development as well as holidays.

Ladbroke Holidays, started in 1972, owned eight seaside holiday villages in East Anglia, Cornwall and the Isle of Wight, all in Southern England. The accommodation comprised a total of 3,400 chalets and static caravans. Ladbroke Holidays also offered holidays in self-drive cabin-cruisers, touring caravans and camping sites. The boats were handled by a separate agency, however, and the touring and camping holidays were relatively minor profit contributors, so Harounoff's basic aim was to sell his holiday village capacity. At the same time, the main brochure gave some coverage to the other activities, partly to help the company get maximum return on all resources, partly because of a desire to promote a comprehensive range of holidays.

The Market

The most popular form of English summer holiday was a week at the seaside: 'seaside' was one of the most evocative words in an Englishman's vocabulary. Since World War II, a large slice of this market had been captured from the traditional small hotels and boarding houses by the operators of 'holiday camps', offering all-in holidays with dancing, cabaret, talent competitions etc. plus full board and lodging. By the 1970's the large camp operators (Butlins, Pontins, Warners) had themselves become as much an institution as the original boarding houses, and demand was shifting towards smaller, self-catering 'holiday villages', with more emphasis on freedom and less on organised entertainment. Over 90% of Ladbroke's capacity was 'self-catering'.

Ladbroke's share of the total holiday camp/village market was 5% to 10% (depending on definition), but Harounoff saw himself in the much broader market of holidays for the British public.

Holiday Industry: Christmas Campaign

Most Britons started seriously thinking about their next year's holiday(s) immediately after Christmas. According to conventional industry wisdom, publicity before Christmas would be largely wasted. The industry, including those selling

Exhibit 1 *Monthly Booked Occupancy as at the First of each Month; 1975 Season (000's unit weeks)*

Month	MAY	JUNE	JULY	AUG	SEP/OCT	TOTAL	Occupancy/Capacity (%) 1975	(%) 1974[1]
Weeks	4	4	4	5	5	22		
1 JAN	0.4	0.5	0.9	1.2	0.1	3.1	4	6
1 FEB	2.7	4.3	6.0	7.9	0.8	21.7	32	38
1 MAR	3.8	7.1	9.5	12.1	2.2	34.7	51	57
1 APR	5.5	8.5	11.3	14.0	3.2	42.5	62	65
1 MAY	6.1	9.3	12.1	15.0	3.8	46.3	68	71
1 JUN	6.4	9.6	12.3	15.2	4.2	47.7	70	73
1 JUL	6.4	10.1	12.8	15.4	5.0	49.7	73	76
1 AUG	6.4	10.1	13.1	16.3	6.8	52.7	77	80
1 SEP	6.4	10.1	13.1	16.7	8.8	55.1	81	83
Final occupancy	6.4	10.1	13.1	16.7	?	?	?	85
Capacity	9.3	13.6	13.6	17.0	14.6	68.1	100	100

1.   in 1974 total capacity was 61,000 unit-weeks.

overseas holidays, therefore burst into life during late December and early January — all the operators mounted heavy advertising campaigns during this period. The advertising was designed not so much to sell holidays as to generate coupon or telephone requests for brochures; it was then up to the brochure to sell the holiday — competing against (on average) two competitive brochures. Advertising was reckoned to be particularly effective if included in special holiday features or supplements produced by the media.

Review of the 1975 Season

By September Harounoff felt ready to look back at the 1975 season (now nearly over) and take stock. In round figures his promotional programme had been as follows:

December 1974:	brochure mailing to previous clients and enquirers
December/January:	£80,000 press + TV campaign
March/April:	£30,000 press + TV campaign
May—August:	£30,000 press campaign, spread through the season
January—August:	£15,000 direct sales effort, selling early and late season group bookings to social clubs

This was broadly similar to the programme for 1974, except that in 1974 it had not been necessary to mount such extensive late-season follow-up.

1975 Sales Performance

Exhibit 1 summarises how the booked occupancy for each month had built up through the season. By 1 September 1975 the bookings totalled 81% of total capacity. This compared with 83% by the equivalent date in 1974 (when the capacity had been about 10% less than in 1975). The eventual 1974 occupancy had been 85%.

Harounoff felt it was valid to give total figures for the eight centres, rather than showing each one separately. As a broad generalisation, a client who found one centre booked up was usually prepared to shift to another centre for the same week; he was less willing to change the date of his holiday in order to be at his chosen centre. Many of the early and late season occupancies corresponded to clients who were taking two holidays (usually of two different types) in the same year; 90% of bookings were for one week only.

Table 1 shows how the revenue and gross contribution per unit-week (accommodation plus sales of food, drink, etc.) varied through the 1975 season.

Table 1   *Unit Revenue and gross contribution by month: 1975 (average £/unit-week)*

Month	May	June	July	Aug.	Sep/Oct.
Accommodation charges	35	45	60	65	35
Sales of food, drink, etc.	15	20	25	25	15 (est)
TOTAL REVENUE	50	65	85	90	50
Less Marginal costs	(15)	(15)	(20)	(20)	(15)
GROSS CONTRIBUTION	35	50	65	70	35

Computerised Data Base

The December 1974 mailing. — the opening salvo of the sales drive for the 1975 season — had been the first *centralised mailing* done by the company. Previously each centre had used its own staff for addressing envelopes by hand. The system now was for stick-on labels to be prepared by the mailing house's computer.

The computer was also used in the *handling of enquiries* generated by advertising. Thirdly, *actual sales were* keyed into the system as they arose, and could usually be *matched to particular enquiries,* or to clients contacted in the December mailing. Thus the company was building a computerised data base whereby it could see how well the brochure was doing its job of converting enquiries into bookings. As of 1 September 24% of the 1975 brochures sent had resulted in bookings; each brochure had cost 10p and mailing it had cost about 10p more.

Just as important to monitor as the effectiveness of the brochure in producing sales was that of the advertising in producing enquiries. This was measured in terms of the cost per response (CPR):

$$CPR = \frac{\text{Cost of advertising}}{\text{No. of responses generated}}$$

The CPR measured the cost of getting the name of a prime prospect to whom to send a brochure; it did not include the 20p cost of then sending the brochure.

Exhibit 2   *Cost per Response by Publication, 1975 Christmas Campaign*[1]

Publication	Cost (£'000s)[2]	Replies ('000s)	CPR (£)
A[3]	0.3	0.7	0.44
B	3.5	6.9	0.51
C	4.4	7.9	0.56
D	3.6	5.9	0.61
E	6.5	9.6	0.68
F[3]	11.3	14.9	0.76
G	0.9	0.9	0.88
H	4.8	4.7	1.03
I[4]	0.1	0.1	1.48
K	0.4	0.2	1.95
L[4]	0.1	0.0	2.54
M	2.4	0.7	3.40
N[4]	0.2	0.0	5.80
O	1.3	0.2	7.52
P[4]	0.2	0.0	10.44
TOTAL	42.1	54.4	0.77

1. 1974 week 52, 1975 weeks 1—5
2. Net space costs plus production
3. Published anually
4. Included for research purposes

Exhibit 3   *Cost per Response by Publication, 1975 Spring campaign*[1]

Publication	Cost (£'000s)[2]	Replies ('000s)	CPR (£)
C	2.1	3.4	0.62
B	2.3	3.0	0.77
D	2.8	3.1	0.90
H	3.5	2.9	1.21
G	0.5	0.4	1.25
E	4.6	2.9	1.59
I	1.1	0.5	2.20
TOTAL	16.9	16.2	1.04

1. Weeks 13, 14, 15
2. Net space costs plus production

Exhibit 4   *Cost per Response by Month, 1975 Summer Follow-up*[1]

Month	Cost (£'000s)[2]	Replies ('000s)	CPR (£)
May	9.2	7.8	1.18
June	3.3	2.4	1.38
July	6.8	4.8	1.42
August	10.5	6.8	1.54
TOTAL	29.8	21.8	1.37

1. Publications B, C, D, H
2. Net space costs plus production

Direct Mail Advertising   Certain names were already on hand from previous years and cost nothing. Some of these had been mailed brochures, others had first been sent a reply-paid card, to be filled in by those who wanted a brochure. Totting up the numbers for the 1975 season, Harounoff found the following:

> *Brochures had been sent direct* to 48,000 clients who came in 1974, and 22,000 (unduplicated) 'friends' of 1975 clients; the latter were generated by a section in the booking form which invited clients to list up to three friends who might like a Ladbroke holiday brochure. For all these 70,000 names the effective CPR was zero.

> *Reply-paid cards had been sent* to 37,000 enquirers from 1974 and 21,000 clients from 1972-3 (these numbers were low because most centres had kept incomplete records). Of these 58,000 prospects, 15,000 filled in and returned the reply-paid card. The cost of this mailing was 9p per prospect, plus 6p per respondent (for the reply-paid card) giving an effective CPR of

$$\frac{(58{,}000 \times 9p) + (15{,}000 \times 6p)}{15{,}000} = 41p$$

Press Advertising   In the case of press advertising, all responses could be matched to individual insertions, because all coupons were coded. Exhibits 2 and 3 show the CPR by publication for the Christmas and Spring campaigns respectively; Exhibit 4 shows the CPR by month for the summer follow-up.

These exhibits show a steady increase in CPR through the year, from £0.77 in the Christmas campaign (December—January) up to £1.54 in August.

TV Advertising   For TV advertising it was not possible to relate individual enquiries to particular

Exhibit 5   *Cost per Response by TV Region and Week, 1975*

Week	Region X Cost[1] (£'000s)	Region X Replies ('000s)	Region X CPR (£)	Region Y Cost[1] (£'000s)	Region Y Replies ('000s)	Region Y CPR (£)	Total Cost[1] (£'000)	Total Replies ('000s)	Total CPR (£)
1	7.2	4.4	1.64	5.8	4.6	1.26	13.0	9.0	1.44
2	4.7	5.6	0.84	3.8	2.9	1.31	8.5	8.5	1.44
3	4.7	4.0	1.12	3.8	2.2	1.73	8.5	6.2	1.37
4	4.7	3.5	1.34	3.8	3.0	1.27	8.5	6.5	1.31
TOTAL XMAS	21.3	17.5	1.22	17.2	12.7	1.35	38.5	30.2	1.27
13	3.5	2.3	1.52	2.7	1.9	1.42	6.2	4.2	1.48
14	3.4	2.6	1.31	2.2	1.7	1.29	5.6	4.3	1.30
TOTAL SPRING	6.9	4.9	1.41	4.9	3.6	1.36	11.8	8.5	1.39
GRAND TOTAL	28.2	22.4	1.26	22.1	16.3	1.36	50.3	38.7	1.30

1. Net space costs plus production

'spots', but a reasonable week-by-week picture could be built up for each of the two regions used by Ladbroke Holidays (see Exhibit 5). Again, the CPR was higher in the Spring than at Christmas.

Way back in September 1974 Harounoff had written in his marketing plan for 1975:

> If our sole objective was to send out brochures to prime prospects, TV could prove to be an expensive medium. However, this must be weighed against the fact that the *TV Times* proved to be very cost-effective this year, and there is evidence that the response to other publications and to direct mail was also boosted by the concurrent TV coverage.
>
> Also, TV has a vital role to play in terms of long-term corporate awareness and image-building.

The 1976 Season   In planning for 1976 Harounoff felt he needed more than just an understanding of what had happened in 1975. The three other things he reckoned he needed were:
marketing objectives for 1976
an assessment of how 1976 might differ from 1975
some kind of framework for using the information now available to him to determine the best media strategy.
The first of these — the marketing objectives — had already been agreed.

1976 Marketing Objectives   Harounoff's main objective was to attain the *budgeted occupancy level of 85%*. He also had several subsidiary objectives:

(a) To increase spontaneous (i.e. unprompted) *awareness of Ladbroke Holidays*, already increased from 24% to 39% during 1975. The target was 50% by the end of 1976.
(b) To strengthen Ladbroke Holdiays' *reputation for value and reliability* : this aim was reflected in the planned investment in site improvements and in the 1976 pricing.
(c) To contribute to the *public awareness and image of the Ladbroke Group*, via (a) and (b) above, and through exposure of the corporate logo and slogan 'Ladbrokes — leaders in leisure'. TV advertising was felt to be particularly valuable in this respect.
(d) Wherever possible, *to help other companies within the Group*.

These longer-term considerations were stressed by Harounoff's boss, Managing Director John Jarvis, partly to increase the scope for future expansion.

Differences between
1976 and 1975   Harounoff and Jarvis had a long session together, reviewing what they reckoned might be different about 1976. Accommodation capacity would be unchanged, but the following other factors emerged:

(a) *Pricing:* Research had shown that the 1975 prices, especially in the early and late seasons, had produced some sales resistance and had not enhanced the company's reputation for good value. For 1976, high-season prices were being increased by 8% (the maximum allowed by the UK Government's Price Commission). Other prices were being only marginally adjusted. The net effect was a weighted-average increase of about 5% — versus annual UK inflation of 20% plus.

(b) *Economic Conditions:* 1975 had been a year of deep recession for the World economy, and the UK in particular was suffering a combination of high unemployment and high inflation. However, for Ladbroke's target market (except for the unemployed) wages had just about kept pace with the cost of living. Jarvis and Harounoff felt that 1976 would see a tougher government line, with an incomes policy in which wage increases were slowed down — most people would experience some reduction in their standard of living. In times of such uncertainty, the following responses might be expected:

down-trading and price-sensitivity — this would hit the overseas tour operators particularly, since the pound would presumably be weaker against most European currencies in 1976 than in 1975
less willingness to book a long way in advance
less second holidays — main holidays were expected to hold pretty stable (except for down-trading).

(c) *Advertising Cost Effectiveness:* Harounoff and Jarvis expected the volume of UK media advertising to start picking up again. Space rates would be up on 1975 and discounts one or two percentage points down — overall, every pound spent would buy maybe 10% less in 1976. In the case of printed media, however, Harounoff reckoned he could improve the cost-effectiveness by about the same amount, by reallocating resources in light of CPR data. Obviously, advertising effectiveness might also be influenced by the timing and level of competitive activity. Postal costs were increasing at 20% to 30% per annum, print costs by around 10%. Specifically, the design and print costs for 250,000 brochures (the same number as for 1975) would be £28,000, with a run-on cost of £70 per thousand additional brochures printed on the same run.

(d) *Direct Selling:* In 1975 Harounoff had spent a total of £16,000 on direct selling (including the cost of group discounts). This had sold 2,100 unit-weeks, all in the early and late season. For 1976 he could either keep this activity at the 1975 level, or increase it by up to, say, 50%, with a proportionate increase in the resultant sales (after due allowance for inflation). Beyond this point, direct sales would increase less than in proportion to expenditure.

(e) *Travel Agents* Almost all established operators in the holiday industry sold through travel agents (on a standard 8% commission basis), as well as by direct promotion. By 1976 Harounoff reckoned Ladbroke Holidays would be well enough established to gain widespread travel agent representation, if that was what they wanted. The question was what role, if any, agents should play in Ladbroke's long-term strategy. Harounoff felt it would be harder to control and motivate agents than his own resources; on the other hand, an agent who didn't sell anything also wouldn't cost anything.

Decision Framework   The key question was what financial criteria to use to evaluate different advertising strategies. This question had been bugging Harounoff for some time; he went to talk to Jarvis about it.

Jarvis: OK John, so why don't you want to use CPR? It's what the agency

	have always used, and they ought to know what they're talking about.
Harounoff:	Sure. The agency have done a lot of good work on CPR: they've shown that 2-column ads are better than 3-column, they've shown which publications we should drop. They've shown that the *cumulative* CPR was still dropping when we stopped advertising in January. They've also shown that we get a much higher CPR during the season than in the spring and in the spring than at Christmas.
Jarvis:	Which we already knew.
Harounoff:	Which we already knew. So they're now proposing a mammoth Christmas campaign for 1976 with very little follow-up — OK, with a big contingency reserve, because that's the business they're in. But I don't buy the CPR argument: I think it's adding apples to oranges and giving bananas!
Jarvis:	Could you please expand on that?
Harounoff:	Well, for a start, it usually happens that one's first sales effort in any field picks up the easiest prospects. One's later efforts have more work to do. Secondly, what you're selling depends on when you advertise. We know that 70% of the sales from our Christmas advertising are in July—August, with virtually all the rest in May—June. If we go into the same publications in the spring, the proportions are reversed — 70% May—June, 25% July—August. Finally, if we go in in August, it stands to reason that all the sales have got to be in September—October. What financial weighting should I be giving to all those different sales?
Jarvis:	Well, I guess the textbook answer would be to use gross margin. Isn't that what most people do — I mean, when they don't just take last year's advertising allocation and add 15%!?
Harounoff:	Right. And in a way that's valid — an August sale is worth twice as much as a late September one, and anyone in this business with empty chalets in August has real problems. But what's an August conversion worth once we've sold our August capacity? Nix, basically. Not you nor I nor anyone else can shift the sunshine and the kids' holidays from August to late September, just because that's when we've got spare capacity!
Jarvis:	Why so modest, suddenly? All right, maestro, what are you going to do about it?

PART D
Managing Marketing within the Organisation

Managing Marketing is essentially managing people, to recognise the demands of a marketplace and to act appropriately. It is not often an easy task. A changing market and competitive environment can mean that frequent changes are needed. Organisations have a tendency to resist change and to do so by ignoring or changing the messages from the marketplace.

This case was prepared by Kenneth Simmonds of the London Business School.
© *Kenneth Simmonds, 1980.*

CASE D1
The Equitable Building Society

It was one of those periods when demand for houses exceeded the supply, and prices were marching steadily upwards at 5% a month. Of course, David Thornton's search for a new post would be successful just at this time and require him to move from Manchester to London with no company backing to smooth the costs. Still, his four-year-old house had sold well and quickly, and he had placed a deposit on a new house on the outskirts of London, so he was covered against inflation. All he needed now was to arrange a mortgage so he could complete the purchase which would have to be done two months before he would be paid for his Manchester house.

Four years ago David had obtained a £15,000 mortgage from the Equitable Building Society, one of the nation's largest. He would need £25,000 now, but presumably the Equitable could arrange that. He was a reliable payer and a new house was always a prime risk, particularly with his equity over 50%. When David approached his local branch manager in Manchester, however, he was told that any such idea was totally out of the question. He would have to repay the current mortgage and apply for another in London. Moreover, the Equitable would not give him a second mortgage while he held the first one, as they frowned on rental ownership and two-house speculation. The manager's personal advice was to go to another building society. David found this hard to believe, but at the London branch the Manchester manager's comments were confirmed to the letter.

David came away from both visits with a feeling that he was *persona non grata*. Both branch managers clearly had less educational background and lower salaried posts than himself, but they had both treated him in an offhand, condescending manner as though they enjoyed saying 'no' to a nobody. He felt almost an enemy of his own building society, in which he had maintained a share deposit account for ten years.

Back at his bankers, David also learned that he would be given a bridging loan for his equity in the new house only if he produced a letter showing he had been offered a mortgage by a building society. There seemed no alternative but to approach other building societies. This was easier said than done. They all told David that their normal limits were £20,000 at the moment and, anyway, their entire office allocations were committed three months ahead.

Describing his problem to his new colleagues over coffee one morning, David was laughed at for his naiveté. "You're playing the system as though you're Joe Ordinary," said the Accountant. "I suppose they even have you believing that story about preference going to loyal depositors. Let me tell you, the world is made up of small savers and large borrowers. The modern world penalises the first and rewards the second. I'll tell you what to do. Call up Fred Spencer at the Head Office of Village National down the road and he will put you on their preferential quota. They always hold back 10 or 15% of their funds for allocation by Head Office. If they didn't, they would be asking favours of branch managers beneath them every time they were approached for Head Office influence in getting a loan. Their personal power as top men would disappear."

So David called up Fred Spencer, mentioned his firm, and indeed the loan letter offering £25,000 floated through like clockwork. So, too, did the bank bridging loan of £40,000.

Some months later the sale of David Thornton's Manchester property was completed and the solicitors paid off the Equitable Building Society mortgage. When the solicitors' statement arrived, David was amazed to find that the Equitable branch had charged an additional three months' interest beyond the period the mortgage was outstanding. The additional interest was levied under article 27(1)(a) of the Society's Rules, and on looking up the rule David read:

> . . . if the repayment is made within a period of five years from the date of the mortgage then whether notice of the intended repayment is given or not the mortgager . . . may be required to pay the Society such a sum of money not exceeding three months' interest on the principle . . . calculated at the rate at which interest is payable under the mortgage.

The additional interest amounted to £450, so David immediately wrote off suggesting that with the current shortage of funds and current high interest rates, the penalty should be reduced. After all, the rule was probably to protect the Society in times of severe depression. At the moment, The Equitable presumably lent the money out immediately and gained double. The manager's reply was a circuitous negative claiming:

> On the question of the payment of interest on redemption of capital, the provisions of the legal charge are specific and I would respectfully suggest that whether at any particular time a society welcomes, or not, the repayment of capital is quite another issue. Circumstances alter, rates of interest vary and it would be out of the question to alter the Society's practice to accord to circumstances at any particular time.

Almost in the same mail David received a very similar letter of rejection following a query about whether he would receive a refund of some of the mortgage insurance premium he had paid four years previously. At the time he had arranged his Manchester mortgage with the Equitable, they had claimed that even though the mortgage of £15,000 represented only 65% of the purchase price of the property, their security was inadequate. As a condition of the mortgage, they required a cover with the General and Commercial Insurance Company at a one-off premium of nearly £100 to cover the 30-year life of the mortgage. Since only four years had elapsed, David had asked about the unexpired portion of the premium. The General and Commercial manager replied:

> The premium was a single payment to cover the risk of inadequate security and where this cover has been extended for a significant period, as in your particular case, it is not the policy of the company to refund any of this premium. The substantial costs of extending this cover fall entirely in the initial years.

This case was prepared by Kenneth Simmonds of the London Business School.
© Kenneth Simmonds, 1980.

CASE D2
General Foods

21st November

Director of Marketing,
BIRDS EYE Division,
General Foods Corporation,
White Plains,
New York 10602.

Dear Sir,

My wife discovered a large black beetle in a packet of BIRDS EYE frozen spinach last week. The beetle and the packet wrapping are enclosed should you wish to investigate. Please return them to me, however.

As you can see, the beetle is almost a meal in itself. For my own peace of mind, I should like to know from you how it is possible for insects to escape your cleansing process, and if the process does permit some to be included with food, what the statistical probability is of this happening.

Yours faithfully,

CEDRIC CONSUMER

Enc.

3rd December

Dear Mr Consumer,

Thank you for telling us about your recent experience with BIRDS EYE Frozen Vegetables.

Because we know that insects sometimes attach themselves to leafy vegetables, extreme care is taken with our processing. Each vegetable load, as it is received from the grower, is inspected and graded by a federal-state inspector. The entire load is then passed through a large screen reel to shake out any foreign material and is immediately inspected in the dry state. The load is then passed through three concentric washers and again is inspected in the wet state.

The vegetable is then blanched in hot water and cooled in a cold water bath, after which it receives a final inspection. At these several points of processing, our quality control technicians examine samples of the product to check out the efficiency of these inspections.

All we can tell you is that this particular insect became rolled up in a leaf and escaped notice. We are extremely sorry and concerned but would ask you to give our product another chance. The enclosed BIRDS EYE certificate will be honoured by your grocer and we hope you will have no further reason to question any of our frozen food items.

Sincerely,

PEGGY KOHL
Vice President Consumer Affairs
General Foods Corporation

11th December

Dear Miss Kohl,

Thank you for your informative letter about the cleansing process for your spinach. What I was interested in knowing in addition was the statistical probability of impurities. Could you tell me what percentage of impurities is tolerated in the quality control samples?

It was thoughtful of you to enclose the certificate to replace the package. This is not necessary, however, and I am returning it with this letter.

In my letter to you of 21st November, I asked specifically if you would return the large black beetle and packet wrapping after you had viewed them. Would you ensure that they are returned?

Yours sincerely,

CEDRIC CONSUMER

17th December

Dear Mr Consumer,

Your recent letter to Miss Kohl has been referred to me for responding to your recent problem with our BIRDS EYE Five Minute Spinach.

We would like to point out to you, that in an effort to identify any problem areas with our products, all exhibits are forwarded to our Quality Assurance staff in an effort to further investigate the problem. We ask for your cooperation in following this procedure, and hope that you will understand why this method of operation is so vitally important.

In reference to your question concerning these statistical probabilities of impurities in our products, we are unable to give you exact figures. Our plant does have tolerance levels for each product and statistics involving foreign materials or additional impurities are unavailable to consumers.

We appreciate the interest you have shown in General Foods and for our products, and hope you will call on us again if we may be of further assistance.

Sincerely,

SUSAN DENMARK (MRS)
Consumer Representative
General Foods Consumer Centre

30th December

Dear Mrs Denmark,

I am not at all happy with your letter of 17th December. This is my third letter to General Foods and I still do not know how unlikely it is there will be further impurities in your spinach. Why have you adopted a policy not to tell this to consumers?

You ask for my cooperation concerning the large black beetle I forwarded. I cooperated tremendously by sending you the beetle and the package so that you might investigate. In return I expected your cooperation to forward the beetle and package back to me as I clearly and specifically requested. Would you please do so?

Yours sincerely,

CEDRIC CONSUMER

15th January

Dear Mr Consumer,

Your letter of 30th December, was forwarded to me by Mrs Denmark because our department is directly involved with quality control issues of BIRDS EYE Vegetables.

Mrs Denmark explained to you the steps that are taken to insure a quality and unadulterated product, from the raw material in the field to the inspection of the finished product.

Our quality control procedures specify that if any sample is found with an insect similar to your exhibit, the entire production lot must be restricted from shipment until it can be carefully checked. Rechecking is done at a frequency five times that stated in the current defect action levels published and used by the Food and Drug Administration.

The preamble to those defect action levels sums up the situation:

> 'The action levels are set because it is not now possible and never has been possible to grow in open fields, harvest and process crops that are totally free of natural defects.
> The alternative to establishing natural defect levels in some foods would be to insist on increased utilisation of chemical substances to control insects, rodents and other natural contaminants. This alternative is not satisfactory because of the very real danger of exposing consumers to potential hazards from residues of these chemicals, as opposed to the aesthetically unpleasant, but harmless natural and unavoidable defects.'

Although it is impossible to assure zero defects to the consumer, it is, however, our objective. In measuring our progress toward that objective, our quality control data is of little use. We take thousands of samples during a typical spinach pack, but the actual incident rate is too low to make meaningful comparisons between packs or manufacturing facilities. Instead, we have found that the letters we receive from consumers such as yourself provide much better information in assessing progress toward our objective.

You asked us to return the package wrapper and insect exhibit. It is attached. We appreciate the use of exhibits such as this one as explicit examples for our manufacturing facilities. They provide considerable incentive in our continuing pursuit of the highest possible quality. We have also attached pages from the FDA publication quoted above.

Sincerely,

CARL L. FARNER
Associate Quality Assurance Manager

Encs.

(The extracts from the FDA publication are shown in Exhibit 1)

Cedric Consumer opened the plastic envelope containing the big, black beetle. It was the same envelope he had sealed the beetle in when he sent it off — and it had not been opened. He measured the beetle. It was an oval shape 17 mm by 11 mm. Cedric wondered why he felt so annoyed and antagonistic towards General Foods. After all, he was a businessman and he should have expected a polite and beautifully polished stonewalling. But, then again, they had gone too far and if he did nothing further, their policies would continue. He listed down some points he could develop in a stiff complaint to the General Foods' President:

1) It is an insult to a complainant to use anaemic form letters with minor adaptations to the particular case.
2) It is a direct deception to fob off a first complaint that is basically being ignored by the Corporation with a signature from a Vice-President.
3) It is an insult to genuine complainants to buy them off with vouchers.
4) The firm should, at least, acknowledge the specific aspects of a complaint — call a beetle a beetle.
5) The firm should look into all genuine complaints properly and write explaining what is being done and the eventual outcome.
6) If the focus of the complaint clearly falls outside permitted statutory limits, the firm should point out those limits and advise the consumer as to the action alternatives.

Exhibit 1

DEPARTMENT OF HEALTH, EDUCATION AND WELFARE
Public Health Service
Food and Drug Administration
Rockville, Maryland 20352

CURRENT LEVELS FOR NATURAL OR UNAVOIDABLE DEFECTS IN FOOD FOR HUMAN USE THAT PRESENT NO HEALTH HAZARD

The food defect action levels contained in this list are set on the basis of no hazard to health. Any products that might be harmful to consumers are acted against on the basis of their hazard to health, whether or not they exceed the action levels.

In addition, poor manufacturing practices by a manufacturer will result in regulatory action, whether the product is above or below the defect level.

The actions levels are set because it is not now possible and never has been possible to grow in open fields, harvest and process crops that are totally free of natural defects.

The alternative to establishing natural defect levels in some foods would be to insist on increased utilization of chemical substances to control insects, rodents and other natural contaminants. This alternative is not satisfactory because of the very real danger of exposing consumers to potential hazards from residues of these chemicals, as opposed to the aesthetically unpleasant, but harmless natural and unavoidable defects.

The fact that the Food and Drug Administration has an established defect level does not mean that a manufacturer need only stray below that level. The action levels do not represent an average of the defects that occur in any of the food categories. The averages are actually much lower. The levels represent the limit at or above which FDA will take legal action against the product to remove it from the market.

The defect action levels on this list are under constant review and are periodically lowered as technology improves. FDA will continue to attempt to lower the action levels as technology permits.

The Food and Drug Administration emphasises its position that:

a) Compliance with defect levels will not prevent FDA from acting against a manufacturer who does not observe current good manufacturing practices. Insanitary plant conditions, for example, is a violation of good manufacturing practices and renders the food unlawful. This applies even though the defect levels may be below the FDA's action level.

b) The mixing of a food containing any amount of defect at or above the current defect level with another lot of the same or another food is not permitted and renders the final food unlawful regardless of the defect level of the finished food.

PRODUCT	DEFECT ACTION LEVEL
Spinach (canned or frozen)	Average of 50 aphids, thrips and/or mites per 100 grams.
	2 spinach worms (caterpillars) or fragments of 3 mm in length have an aggregate length of 12 mm per 24 pounds of spinach.
	Average of 8 leaf miners of any size per 100 grams; or an average of 4 leaf miners 3 mm in length per 100 grams.
	Average of 10% leaves by count or weight show mildew or other type of decomposition ½ inch in diameter.

This case has been prepared by Philip Law of the London Business School from published material. © London Business School, 1981.

CASE D3
What Price the XJ 12?

In November 1972 the black market price of an ever-so-slightly-used Jaguar XJ 12 was hovering around £5,300. For delivery of the standard XJ 12 at the list price of £3,726, dealers were quoting a two or three year wait and reporters masquerading as customers, to test the market for evidence of renegade dealers, drew comments that ranged from "We're pure" to "I do know where there are a couple of XJ 12's that might be bought at £5,500". British Leyland's advertising advised 'Keep Smiling: It's Worth Waiting For', while across the dinner tables of the gin-and-Jag set, executives took sides for and against British Leyland's pricing policy. The Motoring Columnists had a hey-day.

The XJ 12 had been unveiled in July, but output was immediately halted by a 10-week strike over piece rates at Jaguar's Coventry works. Although 500 cars had already been assembled, the strike prevented delivery to dealers; and road tests for the Motoring Press had to be carried out under cover, using four cars smuggled out through the picket lines. It was not until the end of September that the XJ 12 reached a production level of 100 cars a week.

The XJ 12 was assembled alongside the basic XJ 6 and total output of Jaguars was planned at 50,000 for 1973, although eventual expansion to 90,000 was hoped for. Of the 50,000, roughly 20,000 would be XJ 12's. Jaguar had invested £3 million in an automated line for the 12-cylinder engine, to bring its assembly cost to under £100 more than for the six-cylinder engine. At a price of £3,726 the XJ 12 would thus be much more profitable than the XJ 6, which was now sold at £3,071. Yet even at this price the XJ 6 could earn quite handsome profits.

The pricing policy for the XJ 12 seemed to be repeating Jaguar's experience with the launch of the XJ 6 four years previously. A lively black market had developed in 1969 when the 4.2 litre XJ 6 had been introduced at a £2,000 price. Even now delivery of the XJ 6 took four months. In 1969, too, unions had interrupted output with go-slow policies. The idea was getting around that Jaguar always under supplied and underpriced its cars as a matter of policy. Further evidence for underpricing came from comparison with the Mercedes. At £3,726 the XJ 12 was comparable in price with the Mercedes 280E, yet in engineering and performance more on a par with the Mercedes 300 SEL which sold at £8,500.

The price of the XJ 12 had been set by the British Leyland Board, with Lord Stokes himself and John Barber, the Finance Director, taking a significant part in the decision. Knowing that demand would certainly exceed supply for the first few months and that production delays were highly probable, the pricing decision had not been straightforward. But to charge a scarcity price of say £5,000 to remove the black marketeers could have meant a price reduction later when supplies caught up with demand, and would also have opened the company to charges of profiteering. There was a widespread belief in marketing that price reductions for cars could induce a reduction rather than an expansion in sales. Furthermore, the supply and demand for the XJ 6 were beginning to stabilise at £3,071 and a price of £5,000 would have placed the XJ 12 well out of line with the XJ 6. The £3,726 price seemed to be the level at which, adjusted to current prices, Jaguar would be able to sell perhaps half its output as XJ 12's when it finally reached the 90,000 annual production target.

The general public quickly picked up their pens to defend and chastise Lord Stokes through the correspondence columns. One railed at the abysmal failure of the British motor industry to take a global view and to build its capacity early and determinedly in order to grasp and supply a global market. Deficient supply constantly irritated overseas agents. Another asked, "Is the fundamental purpose of industry to serve the community or not?" This correspondent lauded decisions to produce fine British cars at prices which made them available to a reasonable section of the community, thereby achieving a social purpose as well as building a prosperous company. He thought any short-sighted action of using Jaguar to prop up British Leyland's general inefficiency by milking the public and consequently reducing the number of people who could indulge in a fine car, as likely to bring industry into general disrepute and sow the seeds of destruction of the whole system. Similar thoughts were advanced by others:

> Sir — regarding the selling price of the Jaguars . . . not a single mention is made of 'fair profit'.
> If Jaguars can manufacture, include a just and reasonable profit and sell such a superb car at its current price, then that is its moral duty. This may be a utopian ideal which only the great Henry Ford, Sir William Lyons and Lord Stokes have realised, but all praise to them, and if a few other British manufacturers, builders, financiers and speculators would take note, perhaps Mr Heath would not now be forced into curbing price rises which have become so manifestly intolerant of the interests of the consumer.

Despite the plethora of 'advice' to the manufacturer, however, there was little guidance tendered to the dealers. The public seemed to see them as already condemned to the grey world of dealing — a world into which one would not want a daughter to marry. But perhaps one might just buy a slightly used car?

This case was prepared by Kennth Simmonds of the London Business School.
© *Kenneth Simmonds, 1981.*

CASE D4
Stationery Supply Corporation

Every Christmas Stationery Supply designed and had specially manufactured a selection of expensive pieces of desk and office furnishings such as paper weights, clocks, letter knives, barometers, book ends, statuettes and reading lamps. These were despatched as gifts to the firm's contacts in customer or potential customer firms. The items were frequently as expensive as one hundred dollars each and consequently a great deal of attention was paid to the compilation of the mailing list, with the final approval coming directly from Albert Wyskiel the Sales Vice President.

Albert had told the staff who compiled the list for approval that the objective was to build up 'goodwill towards the firm', and the gifts should not become a general handout to include many who would have no say in dealings with SSC. At the same time, Albert pointed out that it was important not to limit the list to buyers already placing large orders with the firm. Younger men rising in customer firms should be added if they looked to be going places, and changes in the staff of firms that generally placed most of their business with other suppliers should be particularly noted.

Although he continued to stress the need to build goodwill with new men, Albert had developed over the years a policy of discontinuing the expensive gifts to buyers who never placed significant orders with SSC. He reasoned that if buyers knew that gifts always went to everyone, less goodwill would be built up as far as sales achievement was concerned. On the other hand, Albert thought that an executive might get upset at not being remembered, perhaps reinforcing his tendency not to patronise Stationery Supply Corp. Al therefore had instituted a second list, on which were placed contacts who had received a gift in previous years but shown no interest in the firm or its salesmen. Those on this list received a small token gift costing under five dollars.

On November 30, 1975 George Brown, SSC's President, received the following letter from Global Stores Inc, a large retail chain with head offices in New York:

November 29, 1975

Mr. George Brown
President
Stationery Supply Corporation
E. 58th Street
New York, New York

Dear Mr. Brown,

It came to my attention last year that a number of our employees had been receiving quite expensive items as Christmas gifts from suppliers and others.

While this practice is undoubtedly well-intentioned, we have recently adopted a company policy that no gifts of significant value shall be accepted by our staff. This formal policy makes it clearer and fairer to all involved.

I am writing this letter so that all our suppliers will know of our policy, and in the case that your own Christmas gift plans would conflict with it I hope that you will adjust them accordingly.

Sincerely yours,

Frederick C. Dinsmoor
President
Global Stores Inc.

George Brown had taken over the presidency of SSC two years earlier, following a proxy fight for control, and had previously had little experience in the stationery field. He held only five per cent of SSC's stock himself, but was backed by a syndicate that held a further twenty per cent. The syndicate had apparently decided that the ample resources and potential for major expansion would lead to considerable stock appreciation. While George had succeeded in increasing turnover by sixty per cent through addition of new lines and acquisition of several smaller firms, he had not made much headway in increasing the firm's return on investment. Unless he could improve results significantly over the next year, he would be in danger of losing his backing. Increased volume seemed to George to be the answer, rather than paring expenses, and currently he had instituted a major programme for new business.

Prior to receipt of the letter from Global Stores, George had not given any thought to the details of the Christmas gift scheme. He called Albert, who told him about the two lists: that he had Global's top three buyers on the first list, knew each of them well, and the previous year had received expressions of appeciation from each about the thoughtful gift. Moreover, the chain placed orders amounting to many hundreds of thousands of dollars annually. "If we give anyone gifts, it should be these men," said Al. "After all, they are simply tokens of appreciation not bribes. You know, many of the men on the list are principals of their own firms. I think we should just ignore the letter and send something to their home addresses."

CASE D5
Gulf Oil Corporation

In December 1975 the Special Review Committee of the Board of Directors of Gulf Oil Corporation submitted its report to the United States District Court for the District of Columbia and the Securities and Exchange Commission.[1] This report was prepared by a special review committee which was established after a number of inquiries and proceedings had led to the public disclosure of substantial and illegal political contributions or payments from Gulf's corporate funds.

Part Three of the report is devoted to Gulf's foreign political contributions. At the outset of its investigation the committee was formed that Gulf, in response to demands on the part of political figures in South Korea, and made a $1 million contribution to the Korean Democratic Republican Party (DRP) in 1966 and another contribution of $3 million in 1970. These payments were authorised by Bob Dorsey, Chairman of the Board and Chief Executive officer of the Gulf Oil Corporation. The committee in its report of the background of these payments made the following comment about the circumstances under which the demands and the payments were made.

(a) The Korean Evolution from Agrarian Autocracy to Industrial Democracy

It is difficult to conceive of a country anywhere in the world whose rule in the last century has been more disturbed than that of Korea. It is an Asian country wedged in between the mass of China and the Soviet Union on the north and the power and strength of Japan to the east. The peninsula in the earlier part of the century was under a long dictatorial rule and, so far as its industrial and political development was concerned, a repressive foreign occupation, resulting in a largely agricultural and authoritarian society. More recently, due to the failure of the Soviet Union and the United States to agree on a plan for the reconstitution of the government of the whole country following the defeat of Japan in World War II, it was arbitrarily torn apart and divided. Thereafter, the southern half of the country was invaded by forces from the north and the country was ravaged by what turned out to be, in terms of the number of casualties and devastation suffered, one of the greatest wars in history. The war was marked by the steadfastness and fighting qualities of a rapidly organised ROK Army which, in conjunction with strong American forces aided by important United Nations contingents, fought off the invasion and finally restored the territorial integrity of South Korea.

Military rule in South Korea was followed by attempts to install democratic processes in an area where the traditions and the experience of representational government were largely non-existent. Following the war, American advisors, educated in traditional American constitutional doctrine and procedures, helped the South Koreans set up what was to them a relatively novel form of government. At the same time, the Korean government undertook an ambitious and serious attempt to expand greatly the country's industrial base. Theretofore, such industrialisation and economic strength as the country had enjoyed was in the north. In spite of many vicissitudes, limited funds and sparse natural resources, South Korea did succeed in creating an imposing political and economic post-war development. The Korean development was not accomplished without strong and resolute leaders at the top. In the course of it, the security of South Korea became a significant commitment in American foreign policy.

It was with this background that Gulf in 1963 and 1964 made its first, rather heavy, investments in the petroleum industry of South Korea, where the need and demand for energy was becoming very great. Gulf, in seeking an outlet for some of its Kuwait crude at a time when crude was in long supply, saw an opportunity in Korea where this industrial development, based on a limited supply of petroleum products, was taking place. According to Gulf officials who took part in the Korean venture, the idea of developing the industry of Korea appealed greatly to Whiteford, then Chairman of Gulf. He saw it not only as an immediate outlet for a part of Gulf's Kuwait crude, but he also became actively interested in the efforts being made to expand Korean industry. Other foreign interests began to see the possibility of Korean development, but the Gulf investment was undoubtedly the most significant private investment by any foreign company in Korea at the time. Certainly it was the most important private United States investment.

A refinery at Ulsan (known as the 'Pittsburgh of Korea') was started in 1963 and completed and inaugurated in 1964. It was later expanded. In this period Gulf made its original investment of $25,000,000 in the Korean Oil Company (KOCO), which was and is jointly owned with the Korean government. What turned out to be successful plastic and fertiliser plants were built by Gulf on a joint venture basis with the Korean government, and altogether Gulf officials estimate the company's Korean exposure grew in a few years to some $200,000,000 if not more. In the meantime, Gulf was steadily increasing the daily flow of oil into the refinery until it reached as much as 150,000 to 200,000 barrels of oil a day. In the Committee's interviews with Mr Herbert Goodman, now the head of Gulf's shipping interests and in the mid-sixties an important factor among Gulf executives operating in the Far East, including Korea, he stressed that Gulf had not only an interest in what was becoming a very profitable venture, but also a sense of commitment to Korea as an active partner in its industrial development.

While this industrial expansion was occurring, political developments were also moving forward. Operatives from United States government agencies then functioning in Korea were, according to Goodman, constantly pressing the then Korean leaders for the creation and maintenance of an electoral system which could serve as a base for a stable form of representative government for the future. Efforts were made by United States government personnel to instruct the Koreans in election forms, such as registration and election procedures, and in how to create the other machinery of an elective system. Goodman and others referred to the fact that the Korean government was poor and had little, if any, money to carry on the usual electoral processes associated with representative government. It was emphasised that it took a great bit of money on the part of the Koreans to establish these procedures and the mechanics by means of which an electoral system could be made to function.

The driving force of the new Korean development was President Park Chung Hee, the former leader of the Revolutionary Council which had ousted Syngman Rhee. As President, he became intensely interested in the economic development of the country. He himself directed much of the effort being made toward Korea's industrial expansion. Gulf officials and President Park and his representatives at times, according to Goodman, jointly participated in planning for the expansion of the country's industry. Other American companies entered the country — some, according to Dorsey, with the encouragement of Gulf — and they also became a part of the industrial development.[2]

2 Source: Report, pp. 95—8.

The committee's report on the two contributions is duplicated in its entirety in the following section.

(b) The 1966 Contribu-
tion
The Committee's investigation showed that in 1966, with this background of national development but otherwise out of a clear sky, a substantial political contribution was requested of Gulf to help meet the expenses of a coming election campaign. Goodman was approached by a high official of President Park's Secretariat, who told him that the government felt a contribution should be made by Gulf to the Democratic Republican Party (DRP) in the amount of $1,000,000 for the coming election campaign. Goodman promptly reported the matter to Messrs E.D.

Loughney, a Gulf Vice President, and Dorsey, in Pittsburgh. Goodman did not suggest in his interview with the Committee that the request was in the nature of a threat, and Loughney's recollection is consistent with Goodman's in this respect. Loughney told the Committee that Goodman did not report that any specific reprisal would occur if no contribution were made. Loughney does recall that Goodman said that most other companies had been or would be asked to make a contribution.[3] Loughney was aware that an election in Korea could be expensive, that the Koreans were poor, and that the DRP had to depend largely on industry and business for political contributions.

3 Goodman did not state that
he had knowledge that any
other companies had in fact
made contributions, but he felt
certain that others had been
approached and had complied.

There was no question in the minds of the Gulf officers then on the ground of the identity of the government with those officials who were making the request.

There is another element which recurs in the Committee's examination of the atmosphere in which the first Korean contribution was made by Gulf, and that is the persistent encouragement, if not pressure, on the part of American government officials on the Korean government toward the institution of American-style elections. The Koreans who approached Gulf for the contribution believed that to respond to this 'encouragement' or policy would involve heavy expenses which they could not meet, and it was thought natural on their part to turn to the foreign investors, particularly the Americans, as a source of funds for the purpose. The Gulf representatives involved viewed the 1966 contribution as supportive of the developing democratic process in Korea, and they communicated this attitude to Pittsburgh.

In regard to the 1966 payment, Dorsey testified before the Senate Foreign Relations Subcommittee on Multinational Corporations as follows:

> Our investigation indicates that the demand was made by high party officials and was accompanied by pressure which left little to the imagination as to what would occur if the company would choose to turn its back on the request. At that time the company had already made a huge investment in Korea. We were expanding and were faced with a myriad of problems which often confront Amreican corporations in foreign countries. I carefully weighed the demand for a contribution in that light, and my decision to make the contribution of $1 million was based upon what I sincerely considered to be in the best interests of the company and its shareholders.

Dorsey also stated to the Review Committee his recollection of the 1966 request. He recalled obtaining information about the request only from Goodman saying:

> . . . it was a very strong approach indeed; not threatening, but with implications that if you really want to do well and if you really want to survive, we appreciate what you have done, but now — now, it's time that friends stand together. It's a critical situation with us. We are trying to adopt democratic processes after two thousand years of autocracy.
>
> Your government is encouraging us in this. We need money to do it, and you have fared well here. And in addition, in kind of an oblique way, made it rather apparent — rather clear to him that our — his continued well-being and our continued well-being depended on our doing what they wanted us to do, which was to give them a million dollars.
>
> He (Goodman) came to Pittsburgh and talked to me about it and we ultimately agreed — I ultimately agreed to give them the million dollars as a contribution to that party under the pressure — there was great pressure that existed to do it.
>
> I thought it was the correct thing to do. It was in the best interests of the corporation, so I did it.

Later in his interview, Dorsey again implied that a certain amount of coercion was involved in the 1966 request:

> But certainly, I was told by him (Goodman) that there were veiled threats of what — you know — threats that if you want to survive and do well — if you want to continue in the role you're in and prosper in this country, you had best do this.
>
> Now, the other side of that coin, obviously, if you don't do it, you don't prosper and stay here very long. But nothing more specific than that.

The Committee is satisfied that the documentation shown to its accountants in connection with the 1966 transfer of $1,004,000 charged against Bahamas Ex. related to the $1,000,000 contribution to the Korean DRP in 1966 and that the payment constituted a political contribution within the meaning of the Undertaking.

(c) The 1970 Contribution

In 1970 there came another demand in the face of a heavier political challenge to the DRP. This time it was $10,000,000 and it was attended by a much more blunt approach. Mr S.K. Kim, who is now deceased, made the demand. He was a sort of party head, close to the administration and a man of great determination and vigour. Gulf officials who knew him speak of him as a rough customer. Kim made his demand by summoning to his office a Mr Nam, a Vice President in charge of government relations of Korean Gulf Oil Company (KORGOC, a wholly-owned Gulf subsidiary). Kim indicated that other concerns operating in Korea were being faced with similar demands. This demand also was immediately conveyed to Pittsburgh, but no action was taken on it pending Dorsey's visit to Korea which had been scheduled prior to receipt of the demand. When Dorsey arrived, he met with Kim. It turned out to be an unpleasant encounter, resulting in Dorsey's refusal to meet the demand for $10,000,000 and his departure from the meeting in anger. Subsequently, after temperatures had subsided, Dorsey agreed to pay the sum of $3,000,000, which he justified on the basis of the need for the continued goodwill and cooperation of the Korean government on which, in the newly-organised society, it was necessary for a foreign company to rely.

Dorsey described for the Committee his first encounter with Kim as follows:

> He (Kim) dived right into the matter and told me that we were doing exceedingly well out there and that basically, our continued prosperity depended on our coming up with a ten million (dollar) political contribution to the party.
>
> And I, politely as I could, demurred and told him I thought we had been helpful before; we had been pleased to, because we believed in it — believed in his country; we knew the necessity for election, and there was no — almost no way of raising popular funds in Korea for these things, and we had done it out of a sense of obligation before. But the question of ten million dollars, there was no way I could do anything like that; that it was almost preposterous. And at that point, he became exceedingly angry with me and exceedingly irritated and talked to me just about as roughly as he could; in effect, saying, you know, 'I'm not here to debate matters. You are either going to put up the goddamned money or suffer the consequences,' although he said it substantially more roughly than that.
>
> I was very angry. I was very upset, and I told him that I was not going to be talked to that way. And that was the end of the conversation. I walked out of his house and he made no attempt to restrain me or apologise or anything else.

The figure of $3,000,000 was reached in the following manner:

> So, in effect, we then sort of negotiated the matter down. He had impressed on me that the needs were infinitely greater; this was a serious campaign; real opposition and a real need for getting out the votes and talking to people.
>
> So, somehow or other, we arrived at the amount of three million dollars and I was agreeable.

Dorsey summarised his reasons for making the payment as follows:

> So you really are there at the mercy of the government and you are there at the sufferance of the government; if you're going to prosper and do well, you need the government on your side. You need that kind of an environment, unlike any Western country.
>
> *Mr Jackson* (for the Committee): Did you fear that if you didn't make the contribution there might be nationalisation of assets of your company?
>
> *Mr Dorsey*: No. I don't think I — I don't think I thought that, at all. I just thought that the opportunity to continue a profitable business, without unwarranted and inhibiting government interference, required it.
>
> I think that I felt that there were further opportunities to — or, for further investment to expand and to do other things there. And that our ability to do them again

depended on ministers and government officials that really made the decisions in the end.

(d) Motivations and Mechanics of the Two Contributions

Whatever the nuance behind the 'requests' in terms of pressure may have been, it is quite clear that Gulf was in no sense a volunteer seeking to suborn favours by means of largesse. Neither the first nor second payment was in any sense initiated by Gulf or treated by Gulf as anything other than a distasteful effort on the part of the government or the party to obtain a contribution which Gulf had no desire to make.

Dorsey, after thoughtful consideration, ordered the payments made, and according to him he took no part in arranging the details involved in carrying them out. Such arrangements were made by the Comptroller's and Treasurer's offices which used Gulf funds in the United States, booked them to Bahamas Ex. and transferred them to a Swiss bank account.[4] Goodman recalls that Henry, Executive Vice President, advised him that the employment of such methods of payment was due to a desire to avoid any handling of the matter in Korea by Gulf personnel stationed there. Although there was some discrepancy between Henry's and Goodman's recollections as to what took place in connection with the routing of the money to Switzerland for payment, this discrepancy does not appear to be significant.

In testifying before Senator Church's Subcommittee, as previously noted, Dorsey unsuccessfully endeavoured to withhold the identity of the country involved through agreeing to disclose the fact of the payments. This, he later stated to the Committee, was due to his desire to avoid any embarrassment to the South Korean government or its leaders at a time when sharp political attacks were being made on the administration of President Park.

The Committee has found it most difficult to arrive at a satisfactory conclusion in regard to the legality or illegality under then existing Korean law of the political contributions made by Gulf to the DRP in the 1966 and 1970 campaigns. The opinions of Korean counsel which the Committee has been able to obtain cannot be said to be conclusive of the question in the circumstances of this case under Korean law. Neither Dorsey nor Goodman seemed to have given any thought at the time as to whether the contributions were legal or illegal under Korean law. They seemed to have treated it as either a request or a demand from the Korean government to be acceded to or not as the interests of the company appeared. Dorsey met the request for the first payment which only led to a more peremptory demand for an even greater sum of a few years later. He stated that he acted reluctantly but with the conviction that what he did, considering all the circumstances, was in the best interests of the company and its stockholders.

The reason given by Dorsey for the failure to disclose the payments or the demands therefore to the Gulf Board of Directors at or about the time of the payments is best stated in his own words:

> First, I didn't need the authorization of the Board to make the — to make the payments. So it was clearly within my authority to do it.
>
> As to why I didn't — and it is very difficult to go back and reconstruct one's mental processes that far back — but I suppose in a sense, my reasoning was that — my reasoning grew out of a deep conviction — personal conviction that what I was doing was in the best interest of the corporation — something I believe in as strongly now as I believed in then.
>
> That being true, and the matter being rather delicate, and recognising that any revelation of this would be both embarrassing to Gulf and embarrassing to the party to whom the payment was made, that I simply decided that the better course was not to tell them.
>
> If there was any risk being run, I was quite willing to assume that risk myself. It was just my judgment that I should not involve these other people, because there was a potential risk of this being revealed and there being substantial embarrassment all the way around.
>
> That is about as near as I can come to my reasoning at the time.[5]

4 For example, in regard to the 1970 payment, the committee reviewed accounting documents dated July 20 and 31, 1970, supporting a disbursement (including a cheque request from Mr W.H. Burkhiser, assistant treasurer, to Deering, the comptroller), and an advice from the Mellon Bank indicating that a transfer of funds in the amount of $3 million was made from a Gulf account to the Union Bank of Switzerland, attention of Mr Robert Strebel. Documentation was reviewed which indicated that $3 million was disbursed from the Swiss bank, pursuant to instructions from Goodman, in the following manner:

9 cheques of $200,000 each Cash	$1,800,000
aggregating Bank	1,199,790
commission	210
	$3,000,000

5 Source: Report, pp. 98–105.

Questions

1. Do you agree with Bob Dorsey's conviction that the payments he authorised to the Korean DRP were in the best interests of the Gulf Oil Corporation? Why? Why not?
2. In what alternative ways might Dorsey have responded to the Korean 'requests'?
3. Formulate a corporate code of conduct that provides explicit guidance on how to respond to 'requests' for political contributions.

This case was prepared by Kenneth Simmonds of the London Business School. Persons, places and corporations are fictitious and the case is not intended to illustrate the policies or practices of any particular firms.
© Kenneth Simmonds, 1969.

CASE D6
John Marshall

Following the sudden death of the chief accountant of General Engineers Proprietary, John Marshall was promoted to fill the vacancy. The position reported directly to the firm's vice president of finance and entailed responsibility for the commercial side of the firm's operations, including invoicing, costing, accounts payments, and financial accounting, and full control of an office staff of over 100. John, who was only 29, was a chartered accountant and for two years previously had been an assistant accountant responsible for the development and installation of a new cost-control system.

General Engineers Proprietary carried out a range of engineering activities in Australia, operating from headquarters in Brisbane. In a section of its works on the Brisbane waterfront, some 300 men were regularly engaged in ship repair and maintenance work. This work was largely undertaken at cost plus a fixed percentage to cover overheads and profit. The fixed percentage was usually 8 to 10 percent and usually negotiated with the Australian offices or agents of the shipping companies owning the vessels.

Two days after taking up his new post, John was brought an invoice for signature by Bill Brady, the chief shipping clerk. It amounted to A$59,587 and was for repair work just being completed on the M. V. Hull. Bill explained to John that the invoice must be signed in quintuplicate by the chief accountant and then taken for countersigning by the captain and chief engineer before the ship sailed.

John immediately requested to see the cost sheets backing up the cost-plus invoice. Bill, who was an older man of over 60 and had always seemed to John to be reliable and helpful, if perhaps a little fatherly, was reluctant to bring the cost sheets. He first argued that Mr Knox, the previous chief accountant, had never bothered to check the cost sheets. Then he explained that the last two days' costs were not yet posted and had been taken from time records and material requisitions and purchase orders. Nevertheless, John insisted and Bill brought him the records and rapidly demonstrated the transfer of cost sheet totals onto the summary sheet shown in Exhibit 1. When these were checked, Bill left John with the summary sheet, suggesting he add it and compare the totals with the invoice.

Exhibit 1   *Cost Summary Sheet*

	Job No. and Particulars	Hours	Wages	Material and Supplies	Machinery and Transport Cost	Total Cost
8064	M. V. Hull—engine room	5,444	$10,009.64	$2,964.13	$1,167.79	$14,141.56
8065	M. V. Hull—engine room	2,939	5,123.15	822.65	756.29	6,702.09
8066	M. V. Hull—deck repairs	1,497	2,896.15	964.21	326.11	4,186.47
8073	M. V. Hull—pump and winch overhaul	2,329	5,093.60	1,064.22	3,421.61	9,579.43
8074A	M. V. Hull—shipwrights	1,261	2,939.20	1,745.50	491.27	5,175.97
8074B				405.00		405.00
8076	Electricians	2,413	4,762.79	980.73	1,731.32	7,474.84
		15,883	$30,824.53	$8,946.44	$7,894.39	$47,665.36
Above jobs	Unposted		515.00	2,175.25	165.00	2,855.25
			2,625.00			2,625.00
			$33,964.53	$11,121.69	$8,059.39	$53,145.61

As John added the summary sheet, the last entry for unposted wages caught his eye. He could not understand why the activity had jumped on the last day. He called the time office to check the figure and was told that the unposted cost was A$515, including an estimate for work still being completed.

When Bill came back to pick up the signed invoice copies, John raised this point:

John:	That's fine, Bill, but where do the unposted wages of $2,625 come from?
Bill:	Well, those are for ship's crew that helped us with the work instead of taking shore leave.
John:	How do we pay them?
Bill:	Well, I draw up a list of names and amounts, have it countersigned by the shipping manager, draw cash, and then make the payment when I take the invoice.
John:	Does anybody audit these payments?
Bill:	There is no need.
John:	Well, I would like to come down today.
Bill:	It's not really practical. You see, I usually give it to the chief engineer for distribution.
John:	But how do we know the right men get it?
Bill:	We don't — and it might be best for you not to worry further. What you have no cause to pursue can never hurt you.

It finally dawned on John that this was probably a payoff to ship's officers. He sat thinking for a while. Should he sign the invoice or should he push for more accurate particulars?

If he was not going to sign, he would have to take immediate action before the ship sailed — find out exactly to whom the amounts were paid, insist on an amended invoice and take whatever consequences the likely loss on the job would bring. With a rueful smile he signed the five copies and handed them to Bill, thinking as he did so that it would be best to take a few days to look into things and think it through.

That evening and the following day John considered the alternatives. He could do nothing and continue to sign invoices as the chief accountant had done in the past. Taking this approach he could always argue that he knew nothing of any payoffs, but then it was his responsibility to know what he was signing and to ensure adequte internal checking. Moreover, referring to the code of ethics of his accountancy institute he read quite clearly: 'No member shall make, prepare, or certify as correct any statement which he knows to be false, incorrect or misleading . . .' And John reasoned he would be no less unethical because no one could prove he knew what was going on. As a second alternative he considered the possibility of delegating responsibility for signing invoices to one of the accountants reporting to him. He felt they might have less ethical qualms than he, and everything work out much better. Third, he could acknowledge the practice and set up an occasional audit check to make sure the cash was actually reaching the ship's officers. And finally he might make an ethical stand on the issue and insist that the practice either be discontinued or he be formally exonerated in writing. He suspected, however, that neither would be done and he would have to leave or live with the situation. At the very least there would be considerable annoyance and embarrassment at what many would consider a youngster's Sunday School idealism.

The evening after this discussion with Bill Brady, John happened to enter the elevator with George Mitchell, the assistant shipping manager, so he suggested they call in for a drink on the way home. During the conversation John asked George what percentage of an invoice was usually paid ship's officers and how it was distributed, endeavouring to convey at the same time that he knew all about the practice. George explained that it varied with the officers, but rarely went as high as 10 percent, and that it might be distributed between as many as ten engineers on a large vessel. The arrangements as to percentage were part custom, part bantering negotiation over drinks, and part intuition by General Engineers' executives. George claimed that payoffs existed all around the world, although

Exhibit 2   *Ship Repair Section, 1964—69*

Year	Average No. of Men Employed	Ships Repaired	Total Invoiced ($'000s)	Markup On Total Cost	Payments To Ship's Crews ($'000s)
1964	351	108	$2,419	12.1%	$162
1965	337	101	2,386	11.8	157
1966	341	93	2,435	11.4	143
1967	331	99	2,264	11.3	127
1968	309	94	2,161	11.1	110
1969	305	85	2,216	11.0	102

some firms operated their own ship repair yards where they insisted on major overhauls being done. However, the ship's officers frequently had plenty of latitude for repairs and could always have storm damage, corroded pipes, winches, and refrigeration equipment repaired wherever it suited them. George also pointed out that most of the superintendents of the shipping companies knew all about the practice — having been ship's captains or chief engineers themselves at one time.

John could see that any action might affect the livelihood of the 300 men in the ship repair section. This was the biggest ship repair unit in Brisbane, and in all likelihood the work would go to another port, possibly outside Australia, if officers were not remunerated. The men employed could of course be absorbed over time in other work, but many were specially trained and had spent their working lifetime in ship repair. Before he made his final decision, John decided to have a look at the figures for ship repair activity to see what profits, volume, and payoffs were involved. The day after his conversation with George Mitchell, John had the tabulations shown in Exhibit 2 prepared for him.

This case was prepared by Kenneth Simmonds of the London Business School.
© Kenneth Simmonds, 1981.

CASE D7
Billie Daniels

As a district sales representative for Consumer Food Wholesalers Inc, Billie Daniels regularly called on some fifty supermarkets to check on promotion, turnover, ordering and inventory of the many lines handled by his firm. Billie had observed that in markets in which the management was poor, the staff were likely to over-order and have some of his lines clogging the storeroom; and likely to be very slack in checking the shelves and putting out additional supplies. He felt that many of the staff in these stores could not care less about hearing the standard comment that textbooks and sales manuals seemed to expect him to make about what this did to the store's profitability — and Billie knew from experience that any comments he made to a poor store manager would go in one ear and out the other.

Over the years Billie had become a strong believer in profit incentive and free enterprise and for the first time in his life had thrown himself actively into politics behind the Republicans' campaign. Billie himself worked on a straight commission. Following his belief in profit motivation, Billie had devised a scheme whereby he made a private arrangement to mail a quarterly cheque to selected head storemen of supermarkets in his territory, for keeping an eye on CFW lines. The payment was a small percentage of the store's orders from CFW and amounted to one-fifth of Billie's own commission.

Billie felt that the stores themselves benefited from this arrangement in several ways. The storeman was better remunerated, just as a waiter was rewarded for service through tips, and happier and more stable as an employee. He would work harder to make sure CFW lines were handled efficiently, which benefited the store as well as CFW, and inefficient selling pressure on store management was virtually eliminated.

CFW sales in Billie's territory improved significantly as he expanded his scheme to more stores. Two years after Billie had started his scheme, CFW named him 'Representative of the Year' and he received a handsome dinner service and was prominently featured in the house magazine. Shortly after the award, however, CFW headquarters received a complaint from the headquarters of a small chain with one store in Billie's district, claiming that there had been some allegations made by a new head storeman that his predecessor was known by his staff to have been 'paid off' by CFW's Mr Daniels. Although no firm evidence had been found, attention given to CFW products in the past seemed to confirm this.

The letter was received by Fred Harper, national Sales Manager for CFW, and he immediately called Billie to headquarters. Fred had been with CFW only eighteen months and prior to this time had been primarily engaged in marketing consumer durable lines. Before Billie arrived the following day, Fred had the one thought in mind that if Billie were paying off customer employees he would have to be let go, despite the difficulties and embarrassment in acknowledging the means by which Billie had become Representative of the Year. Perhaps dismissal might be smoothed over quietly. It was not until his secretary announced that Billie was in the outer office that Fred began thinking how to handle the interview. He decided to start by referring Billie to the company creed which was sent to all new employees. He pulled from his desk drawer a copy of the creed as his secretary showed Billie into the room. CFW's position concerning ethical behaviour was, it seemed to Fred, clearly set out in paragraph 5 of the creed:

It is our creed:

1. To fulfil our obligations to our *stockholders* by being outstanding in the achievement of profit potential.

2. To earn the respect, confidence and loyalty of our *customers* by serving them so well that they can attain maximum turnover of our products at a good profit.

3. To fulfil our obligations to *consumers* by distributing at all times products of highest quality and value.

4. To promote able and aggressive management and to give each employee a sound incentive for work and enterprise and reward for realisation of opportunity.

5. To conduct operations ethically, deal fairly with customers and suppliers, fulfil commitments, advertise fairly, cooperate with managements in the betterment of industry as a whole, and maintain our organisation as an outstanding example of the American free enterprise system.

Pointing to the copy of the creed after a few casual comments about the weather and business generally, Fred brought the conversation around to the purpose of Billie's visit.

Fred: I know you are familiar with section 5 of our creed, Billie. The reason I have asked you to come today was that we have had a complaint from a customer mentioning your name in connection with dealings with their personnel, that would be in direct opposition to all our creed stands for.

Billie: Did someone object to my bonuses to storemen?

Fred: Well yes, but . . .

Billie: Now, let me set the record straight here. I have voluntarily given bonuses of a proportion of my commission to storemen as an added incentive to efficiency. It has increased their turnover and ours — and everyone benefits. No storeman is under any obligation to me, nor expected to do anything detrimental to the interests of his employers. Besides, if any store management objects, I am perfectly willing to stop the arrangement — although only a short-sighted management would object.

As a matter of fact, I have been going to suggest to you a new scheme I am considering. I have arranged a source for Green Stamps. These stamps could be placed randomly in cartons before they are shipped to customers in my area. This will surely add a further incentive to open our cartons.

Fred: Why didn't you tell me about your other scheme?

Billie: Well, I started it before you came and you haven't come around to see us in the field since you took over.

Fred felt he had somehow to make a decision, but was not sure quite what his alternatives were. He had given no real thought before to the issue raised by Billie's candid acknowledgment, then defence, of his scheme. Billie seemed honest in his beliefs, and it suddenly seemed wrong to just fire a man on his own candid admission of what he thought was a good practice. After a few seconds thought Fred said: "Well, Billie, I am going to have to think this thing over. In the meantime I want you to stop any such schemes — and to make me a list of all stores affected, the names of the men involved and the amounts."

This case was prepared by Kenneth Simmonds of the London Business School.
© *Kenneth Simmonds, 1979.*

CASE D8
Crestlight Paper Company

The speed of David Farrel's management changes had surprised everyone. Aged 33, David was the first of the firm's graduate MBA recruits to reach the divisional general management level. He always seemed quiet and reserved, but interested in and understanding of others' viewpoints and his promotion from Assistant Manager in the Forms division to General Manager of the Education division had been a popular one. Three weeks after he took over from the retiring general manager, however, the Education division had a new personnel manager, a replacement for the accountant and two entirely new posts advertised for product managers. Now Farrel was calmly asking Andrew Smythe to take over as Divisional Sales Manager. "Wesley McFarlane expressed his interest in early retirement," said Farrel, "and we agreed that there would be little purpose in a drawn-out handover period. He will formally retire from Crestlight at the end of March, but hand over the reins of the sales force to you as from Friday week, 24th February. Unfortunately, I shall be away at the Group Conference all next week, but we can go over the situation in detail as soon as I am back — let's say the afternoon of Monday, 27th February."

Farrel's approach was so unexpected and his manner so direct, that in five minutes Andrew found he had accepted the promotion, agreed to clean up his outstanding commitments at Group Head Office within two days and to spend the next week, Wesley McFarlane's last, learning all he could from Wesley. As he walked back to his office, Andrew was elated with his new appointment; but he had a strange feeling of his future vanishing into a vacuum. Farrel had somehow stopped him asking about where he, Farrel, wished to head the Education division and had avoided any discussion at all about Wesley McFarlane's sales achievements. Had Wesley been good, bad or indifferent? Whatever the answer, this was the sort of opportunity Andrew had been waiting for. In fact, it was beyond his immediate expectations. He had believed his image in Crestlight to be that of a future 'comer' who would be given a year or two to prove himself in some assistant sales management post before he would be offered a senior divisional appointment. Farrel had certainly picked Andrew up and put him on the escalator.

Andrew Smythe   Andrew Smythe had joined Crestlight eighteen months ago, on completing his Master of Business Administration degree at Manchester Business School. He had been based at the Group Head Office as assistant to the Group Marketing Director and given a succession of non-repetitive problems to sort out — mainly concerned with matching supply and forecasts for Crestlight lines. Off and on over the past six months he had also participated as a member of a team sorting out a new group acquisition. But at 28 he was becoming restless in a staff position. He felt that he should get into some operating post. Operations seemed the only way to the top at Crestlight. At Business School he had positioned himself as a finance specialist, but then became disillusioned with capital asset pricing theory and rather low finance grades and, anyway, marketing had seemed from outside the function of the future in Crestlight. From within, he was not so sure. He had come to regard the Marketing Director as little more than the Group's senior sales person, with the added concern for investigating major foreign orders and new agency possibilities.

285

Prior to his two years at Business School, Andrew had been a sales management trainee with a branded food company. There, too, the position had been a misnomer — probably titled to attract graduates. The post had amounted to two and a half years as a field representative, calling on supermarket buyers and store managers and arranging special promotions. He supposed it was good experience, but he had not really enjoyed the job and he could see that his Bachelor's degree in Economics from Nottingham was not going to move him along in any way at all — he needed an MBA for that.

Andrew shared a flat in London with two other Business School graduates and led an active social life. He still played rugby, turning out for a team in Esher on Sundays, and for the last two years he had taken winter skiing holidays. He had no plans for marriage and the idea of settling into a Wates house in Croydon, as one of his friends had done, did not appeal to him; although he had toyed with the idea of buying a house in order to build up some equity.

Crestlight Education Division

Crestlight had grown from a small beginning in the late 1940s, based on a license from the US to manufacture and distribute throughout the UK a coated paper used in industrial drawing offices. Over the years the firm had added a whole range of photographic and reproduction papers and supplies, together with a line of equipment for reproduction of large size drawings. Then in 1964 Crestlight had moved onto the acquisition trail and added a speciality paper merchant and a major form printing house. A divisional organisation pattern had emerged almost without planning. There were now five principal divisions — Equipment, Supplies, Paper, Education and Forms — and four non-integrated subsidiaries.

The Education division had been formed in 1970 to give specialist attention to the increasing demand from the education sector for special paper and reproduction supplies and equipment. Nine years later the division carried a range of 1,000 items and sold directly to Local Education Authorities (LEA's), Central Supplies Departments (who usually supplied several authorities), universities, polytechnics and some large schools. Several education wholesalers were also supplied. Some of these carried a much broader line of education supplies than Crestlight — including, for example, scientific apparatus — and had very active salesforces calling on similar direct customers.

Profit margins differed from order to order. The standard gross margin for direct supply to Local Education Authorities and individual establishments was 40% of total sales value, while on sales to wholesalers and central purchasing stores the average margin was only 26%.

Learning from Wesley McFarlane

Wesley McFarlane was friendly and relaxed when Andrew moved in with him the following Monday. Tall and well-dressed, he reminded Andrew of a trained athlete as he seemed to flow around the office without effort. Although he was only 52, he seemed to have welcomed the early retirement and gave no hint at all that he felt he had been moved out. Andrew rather gauchely tried to sound him out about the internal politics behind the move by asking him whether he minded moving at this stage in his career. Wesley came back without any hesitation, "Should have done it years ago. Sales management will never get you anywhere against the engineers and accountants, and a safe middle-of-the-road salary is a living death in Britain today." He then went on to outline to Andrew his plans for a partnership with his brother in a caravan sales agency south of London. Now that his three children were safely through school and launched on their own careers, he could turn his sales skills to his own advantage without family demands requiring him to draw too much out of the business at the wrong times. Wesley was so convincing with the detail of his own plans that he spent an hour explaining to Andrew the 'ins' and 'outs' of the caravan business. Andrew couldn't help but feel it more fascinating than selling school supplies.

Wesley finally brought Andrew back to earth by starting on a comprehensive

Exhibit 1 *Crestlight Paper Company: Education Division Market and Sales by Product*
(£'000s)

	Market Estimates		Sales	
	1978	1977	1978	1977
Special Paper	3,600	3,050	696	560
Reproduction Supplies	2,200	1,850	401	337
Reproduction Equipment	1,300	1,100	363	311
Total	7,100	6,000	1,460	1,208

survey of the Education division salesforce. As Wesley talked, Andrew took his own brief notes and asked for photocopies of the annual sales figures and salesforce and territory details that Wesley showed him. Exhibit 1 shows the divisional sales figures and Exhibits 2 to 6 the territory and salesforce details and performance. Exhibit 7 sets out the notes on individual salesmen as Wesley pictured them — but, as Wesley said, Andrew would get a better picture by meeting them himself. He had, accordingly, arranged the next sales meeting for Wednesday, so that he could introduce the salesforce to Andrew before he formally took over.

The remainder of Monday vanished rapidly as Wesley outlined his overall sales philosophy to Andrew:

Last year's sales of one and a half million were just above a 20% increase over 1977. Most of this represented price increases rather than volume and by my guess market penetration has gone up slightly from 19.5%. When I say 'guess' I am basing this on my estimates of market size for the three product lines. These have been asked for each year for the annual plans and what I do is to identify all the competitors and place a sales figure against each. One or other of the salesmen is bound to have heard something about a competitor's sales levels, and I do some questioning around outside as well and check the competitors' annual reports and published estimates of educational purchasing. There are too many customers to build a figure up from their estimated annual order potential and industry figures don't coincide with our narrow line definitions.

They are all good men. There is not a bad egg among the nine and they work willingly if you don't push them too hard. Of course there are differences in sales performance, but these occur in all sales teams. Besides, you have to bear in mind the travel times some of them need to reach quite small accounts as well as the amount of work that has been done in the past to build up our accounts in a territory.

These same factors have to be taken into account in territory sizes. I think we have them about right now. As you can see from the territory variation in numbers of secondary and higher level pupils, the range between smallest and largest is only a factor of two — which is, in fact, very small. But each salesman has plenty of potential to uncover, no matter what his territory size.

The basic salaries can't be adjusted very much. You have to keep the basic high enough to attract new reps, who might not make much commission for a while, and yet not so high that they have an easy time. Actually, I had been thinking about raising the commission rates. I think the carrot works a lot better than any pseudo-analytical target that tries to push from behind. Commission rates are only 1½% and if we raised them a further 1% instead of a salary increase this year, I think we would get five times as much back in gross margin.

Expenses are pretty much under control; I get the daily call reports and I know who they are entertaining and where they are travelling. Harold Bindon spends more time away from home than any of the others and his entertainment goes up as a result, but if life were too dreary we would have problems with that territory.

Tuesday rushed quickly past as Wesley and Andrew waded through the files for each of the product groups in the Crestlight Education range. Eighty per cent of the sales came from internal production in the other divisions but the remaining

Exhibit 2 *Map of Sales Territories*

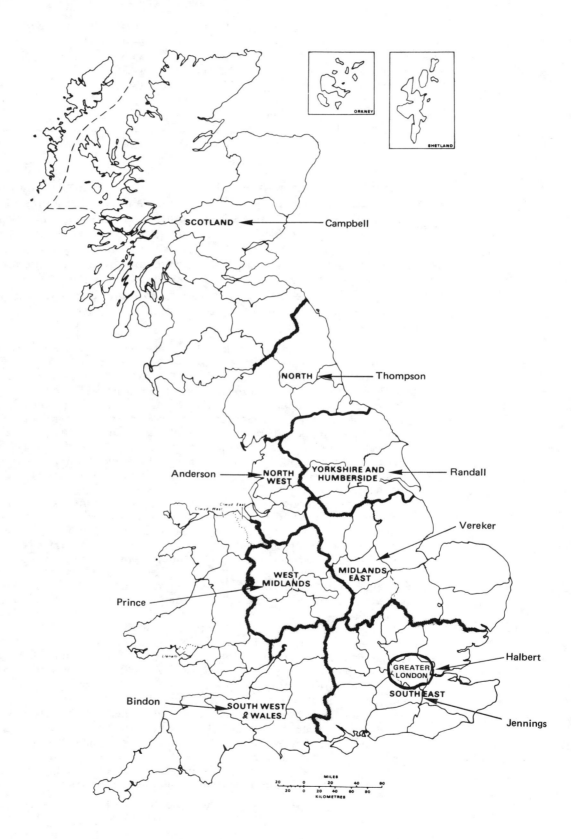

Exhibit 3 *Sales Territory Details*

	Territory	Salesman	Area ('000s sq km)	Secondary and Higher-Level Pupils 1978 (millions)	Estimated Potential Accounts	Home Base
1.	Greater London	HALBERT	1.6	1,60	570	Twickenham
2.	South East	JENNINGS	25.6	2.27	1,060	Bromley
3.	South West & Wales	BINDON	44.6	1.55	934	Cardiff
4.	Midlands East	VEREKER	28.2	1.18	653	Leicester
5.	West Midlands	PRINCE	13.0	1.24	566	Solihull
6.	North West	ANDERSON	7.3	1.65	699	Liverpool
7.	Humberside	RANDALL	15.4	1.16	531	Bradford
8.	North	THOMPSON	15.4	.83	423	Newcastle
9.	Scotland	CAMPBELL	78.8	1.32	529	Glasgow
Total			229.9	12.80	5,965	

Exhibit 4 *Sales Force Details*

	Salesman	Age	Year Joined Crestlight	Qualifications	Previous Experience	
1.	HALBERT, Russell	54	1965	—	Textile Salesmen Accounts Clerk	(10 years) (7 years)
2.	JENNINGS, Frederick	42	1973	H.N.C.	Post Office Teleprinter Salesman Equipment Maintenance	 (4 years) (16 years)
3.	BINDON, Harold V.	33	1971	B.A. (Geography)	Joined as Sales Trainee	
4.	VEREKER, John	29	1975	—	Head Storeman Despatch Clerk	(3 years) (3 years)
5.	PRINCE, Alan	57	1976	—	Salesman, etc.	(35 years)
6.	ANDERSON, Graham	37	1969	B. Tech.	Production Scheduling	(5 years)
7.	RANDALL, John	48	1951	—	Joined as Clerk in original Crestlight unit. Appointed Salesman 1964	
8.	THOMPSON, Herbert	33	1975	B.Sc. (Metallurgy)	Wallpaper Sales Rep. Research Technician	(4 years) (2 years)
9.	CAMPBELL, Ian	43	1971	B.A. (English)	Teacher	(12 years)

Exhibit 5 *Sales Force Performance*

	1978				1977			
	Sales £('000s)	Accounts Sold	Gross Margin £('000s)	Calls Made	Sales £('000s)	Accounts Sold	Gross Margin £('000s)	Calls Made
HALBERT	258	239	75	1,230	217	279	69	1,260
JENNINGS	239	509	79	1,168	198	539	69	1,194
BINDON	156	476	59	1,051	129	503	48	1,018
VEREKER	112	353	41	1,409	98	356	36	1,290
PRINCE	154	413	55	1,196	123	382	43	1,185
ANDERSON	112	398	39	1,450	97	412	34	1,410
RANDALL	142	202	50	1,171	125	198	42	1,293
THOMPSON	123	364	47	1,220	101	323	39	1,163
CAMPBELL	143	317	53	1,135	123	326	46	1,088
	£1,439		£498		£1,211		£426	

Exhibit 6   *Remuneration and Expenses, 1978 Education Division Sales Force*

Name	Salary 31.12.78	Commissions 1978	Total Remuneration	Expenses 1978
HALBERT	5,800	3,870	9,670	1,980
JENNINGS	4,800	3,585	8,385	2,810
BINDON	4,200	2,340	6,540	5,010
VEREKER	3,800	1,680	5,480	3,820
PRINCE	4,900	2,310	7,210	2,600
ANDERSON	5,100	1,680	6,780	1,940
RANDALL	5,200	2,130	7,330	3,400
THOMPSON	4,000	1,845	5,845	3,200
CAMPBELL	5,000	2,145	7,145	3,300
	42,800	21,585	64,385	28,060

Exhibit 7   *Wesley Macfarlane's Comments on Salesmen*

RUSSELL HALBERT — Our star salesman. Very experienced. Knows central area. Reacts well to new ideas and well liked by customers. Has a smooth, competent air about him.

FREDERICK JENNINGS — Very sound man, systematic and conscientious and well dressed. Moved across from equipment side, so knows the technical aspects. Had some marital problems last year but apparently straightened them out.

HAROLD BINDON — Very large area but really gets round it. Presents himself well. Sales coming along nicely. Could go a long way in the company.

JOHN VEREKER — Sales not really very high. Young man with a lot to learn. Probably as a young man about town is taking time off for other things.

ALAN PRINCE — Grandad of the team. An old sales lag. Joined only 3 years ago. Will not readily adopt new approaches, but you cannot teach an old dog new tricks. Will not be around for more than five years. No really formal education, so unlikely to make general impact on buyers in the education area. Nevertheless, doing quite acceptably.

GRAHAM ANDERSON — Has a degree, but very disappointing sales results. Technically competent and extremely conscientious in covering his territory. A good worker and a rather engaging personality.

JOHN RANDALL — Bright and attractive personality. Good salesman type. Always thinking up new ideas. A bit of a troublemaker. Fairly lazy and sales below what they might be. A good pep talk should move him along.

HERBERT THOMPSON — Only been with us a few years, but keen to perform. Will take time to develop the polish of the true salesman, but the material is there. Needs guidance from sales manager about sales technique.

IAN CAMPBELL — Very solid and unexciting. Always quiet at sales meetings. Suspect he will never make an outstanding salesman. Knows the Scottish educational buying scene very well. A chess player at competition level as a hobby.

twenty per cent included a very long list of products. In some of these cases, Wesley had been required as part of the agency agreement to provide quite detailed reports on the sales efforts and results.

The Sales Meeting The Wednesday meeting got underway in the conference room with a great deal of joking and laughter. As Andrew came in, Wesley was called away to the telephone, but the salesmen knew all about the management change and introduced themselves in ones and twos before drifting towards the table with coffee cups in hand. Wesley took the seat at the head of the long table and Andrew drew up a chair towards the other end, between John Randall and Ian Campbell.

Andrew could feel that Wesley was genuinely well liked and respected. He admired the way Wesley led the group smoothly through the agenda, starting with a discussion of the January sales figures and the effects that anticipation of a change in political party had had on educational spending. One foreign manufacturer of educational forms had been threatening to withdraw his line from Crestlight and this provoked a comparison of current buyers with those who had rejected the line. Wesley also had a spate of announcements concerning new items and replacements in the line. Under 'Other Business' a long discussion boiled up around order procedure problems that had stemmed from some abstruse ruling in the Department of Education.

As the meeting was drawing to a close, John Randall stood up and on behalf of the salesmen made a short farewell speech thanking Wesley for his years of leadership. Wesley acknowledged the round of applause, thanked them warmly and then everybody headed for the 'Three Feathers' where Wesley had booked a table for lunch.

The lunch went on rather a long time with numerous rounds of drinks and a series of wild sales stories directed at Wesley. John Randall and John Vereker were the most vociferous. Randall elaborated at great length about a female purchasing officer from a Local Education Authority who had him take her out until 3 a.m. every night for a week before placing an order for a gross of protractors — while Vereker seemed the authoritiy on landladies' daughters. At one point, Andrew ventured a story about clam digging that had been told with much hilarity at the Rugby Club. It went reasonably well, but was quickly lost in the stream of wisecracks and competing comments.

Finally, about 2.30 p.m., Wesley looked at his watch and the group began to break up. Andrew and Wesley were separated by the salesmen as they said their farewells. What struck Andrew as strange was that although each salesman used his own words, their message was the same: "If I can be of any help in showing you the ropes, don't hesitate to ask."

*This case was prepared by
Kenneth Simmonds of the
London Business School.
© Kenneth Simmonds, 1980.*

CASE D9
Arthur Lee & Sons Ltd

John Land, group Managing Director of Arthur Lee & Sons Ltd was faced with a final decision whether or not to divide the firm's salesforce into three product groups for strip, wire and bars. The change had been repeatedly requested by the general managers of the Strip and Wire, and Bar Divisions, but Lee's Sales Director, Nigel Barron, had always strongly opposed any change. Two months previously, after another request, Land had separately asked Nigel Barron and Terry Cooper, General Manager of the Bar Division, to review the sales structure and assess whether the firm should move to selling by product divisions. Alternatively, if the existing structure were to be kept, he asked them to consider closing the regional sales offices and using the regional sales managers for product sales. Now, as before, there was a fundamental disagreement as to what the outcome of a change would be.

The Existing Sales Organisation

Arthur Lee & Sons Ltd was an old-established family company based in Sheffield, processing specialist steels. Basic materials were bought in from outside suppliers, principally the British Steel Corporation, and processed in Arthur Lee's works. Unlike BSC, however, Arthur Lee had recorded steady growth and reasonable profits, although the latter took a nose-dive from time to time when the economy slowed down.

There were four principal product divisions: Strip and Wire, Bar, Rope, and Stockholding. Descriptions of the activities and product ranges of Strip and Wire and Bar, which both accounted for about 100,000 tons per annum, are set out in Exhibit 1. General managers of the four divisions reported directly to the Group Managing Director, as did the executives responsible for central group services: finance, commercial, sales, technical and personnel.

The Group Commercial Director, who was also General Manager of the Stockholding Division, was responsible for administration of group commercial policies, pricing, trade associations, and purchasing and market research departments.

The Group Sales Director, Nigel Barron, aged 55, was currently in charge of the United Kingdom external sales organisation representing Strip and Wire, and Bars, and responsible for Central Sales Records, the Export Sales Department, Advertising and Public Relations. Stockholding operated an entirely separate sales force. Sales were usually in smaller quantities and often cut to order; moreover, the Division had been acquired as a separate ongoing organisation. The Rope Division also operated its own sales force, but it was a very small operation with markedly different products going to quite different customer industries.

The United Kingdom was divided into three sales territories. The Northern Region was the largest and covered the country north of a line stretching from Boston (Lincs) to Derby, to Crewe, and West into Caernarvon, plus Northern Ireland. The Midland and South West Region lay to the south of this line and included territory right down to the South Coast west of a line from Bournemouth to Swindon, Banbury, Bedford, Cambridge and thence to Kings Lynn. Southern Region covered the remainder.

In each region a regional manager controlled several representatives. The Northern Region had five representatives, the Midlands and South West four, and

Exhibit 1 *Arthur Lee & Sons Ltd Product Divisions*

Strip and Wire

PRODUCTS
a) Mild, Carbon and Stainless Cold Rolled Strip in a comprehensive range of qualities and tempers.
b) Copper Plated Strip.
c) High Grade Wire in Carbon, Alloy and Stainless Steels.
d) Precision Rolled Flat Wire.

PRODUCT USES
Aerospace equipment; agricultural machinery; ball, needle and roller bearings; ball point pens; beds and mattresses; boat fittings; bicycles; business machines; brewery machinery; cables; chains; conveyor belts; circlips; chemical plant; cutlery and flat ware; electrical appliances and motors; flexible tubing; food handling equipment; garden tools; hospital equipment; tubes; hydraulic equipment; household goods; motor car fittings and accessories; office furniture; pollution control; radar systems; radios; rivets; springs; shop fittings; telephones, and many others.

WORKS
Strip — Meadow Hall, Sheffield
Wire — Ecclesfield nr. Sheffield

BASIC PROCESSES

Mild and Carbon Strip
Sheet slitting (where appropriate), pickling, followed by one or more cold rolling operations and heat treatments (annealing) depending on the quality and temper required, final rolling and slitting, inspection, warehousing and despatch. If thinner than 0.020", extra heat treatment, recoiling and rolling is required.

Stainless Strip
Sheet Slitting, softening and descaling and then splitting or further rollings and softening and descalings, depending on the thickness and temper required. The material is inspected at every stage.

Copper Plated Strip
Electrolytic copper plating followed by annealing and slitting.

Carbon and Alloy Wire
Descaling, heat treatment, multi-hole machine wire drawing, intermediate heat treatment supplied as required.

Flat Wire (Raw material Round or Flat Rod)
Descaling, heat treatment as necessary, rolled to size supplied in hard bright, finally annealed and intermediate tempers, coil or cut length.

Bar

PRODUCTS
A wide range of Mild, Freecutting, Carbon and Alloy Steel Bars, Drawn, Turned or Ground: Hardened and Tempered or otherwise heat treated.

Special Sections: A large range of shapes available and will produce to customer's own drawings.

PRODUCT USES
Business machines; agricultural machinery; aircraft engineering; axle shafts; ball, needle and roller bearings; bicycles; chains; drill chucks; clocks; electric appliances; engineering steel; household equipment; hydraulic equipment; mining equipment; motor car components and accessories; screws and fasteners; telephones; tools and many others.

WORKS
Meadow Hall, Sheffield.
Warrington.
Glasgow.

BASIC PROCESSES
Raw material inspection, scale removal by acid pickling or shot blasting, drawing on single or multiple draw benches or continuous coil fed machines, shearing, straightening, centreless turning, centreless precision grinding, heat treatment (annealing, normalising or hardening and tempering).

Southern three. Northern and Midlands had areas of great industrial concentration, as well as tracts of less intensive activity, such as the South West, parts of Wales, North East England and Scotland. In consequence, representatives' territories tended to vary in size, although the numbers of accounts were not necessarily dissimilar. A man servicing a large area made about eighteen calls per week, whereas the norm was nearer twenty-two. Customers were classified according to turnover and potential, with the largest requiring visits once a month or even more frequently.

Annual sales were currently running at £3.5 m per representative with everyone selling products from each of the three product ranges, and there were no substantial differences between the regional structures. Out of approximately 1500 live accounts, about one-sixth bought from more than one product range.

The three regional offices acted as pillar-boxes for the representatives in the region, as 'watering holes' for visitors to the regions, and as venues for regional meetings. Files were kept at each regional office, but generally duplicated those carried by the representative at home and also maintained at head office where representatives' sales reports were typed.

The sales representatives were managerially responsible to the regional managers and via them to the sales director, but decisions concerning prices and other marketing variables were made by the Divisions. Strip and Wire, and Bars both had commercial managers reporting to their general manager and had recently added marketing managers to assist them in analysing market and customer demand trends and changes.

The current sales force personnel numbered 50, as follows:

Internal Sales — 25 Personnel	*External Sales — 25 Personnel*
Mr. N. Barron	3 Regional Sales Managers
2 Sales Administrators	12 Representatives
12 Invoice & Typing Pool Personnel	6 London & Birmingham Office Staff
7 Telex & Mailing Staff	3 Sheffield-based Secretaries
1 P.R. Assistant	
2 Secretaries	

The Sales Director's Comments

Nigel Barron was not at all happy with the renewed possibility of a change as can be seen from his report:

Selling by Product Divisions

The present system works effectively from the point of flexibility and customer orientation and, in my view, so as to maximise sales. Nothing stands in the way of restructuring the selling activity by splitting it into product divisions, but whether this will benefit volume or cost effectiveness is quite another matter. These, after all, are the main criteria.

a) There is no doubt that if we wished to sell by products, without a substantial increase in the establishment, this would involve each representative in having to cover a considerably larger territory — three times the present size.

b) In doing so, we would greatly increase the mileage each man has to travel. This in turn would mean less time to face the customer in actual selling. Let us remember that for more than 80% of customers, the representative is the sole Lee presence. He is the 'Arthur Lee Group' in the customer's eyes.

c) I don't wish to labour the additional cost of the mileage which will have to be travelled and the hotel accommodation that has to be paid. I would, though, stress the additional wear and tear on representatives' health through long hours spent in the saddle. This cost should not be under-rated, nor can one minimise the effect of temporarily losing one man out of a complement of four, as against a man out of twelve as at present. Moreover, it is physically easier to cover for someone in a more densely serviced area, as at present.

d) By splitting sales into individual products, between two hundred and three hundred customers would be receiving calls from more than one representative — possibly from all three — and possibly on successive days. The buyer would not be too excited by this prospect, especially as he is handling all our products himself. Nor will our left hand know what the right one is doing and, when faced with a complaint, a representative might have to say that it wasn't any of his business but that he would pass on the message!

e) One of the points put forward in favour of a product split is a greater product knowledge if the salesmen were made to specialise. This argument would be more cogent if we were selling vastly disparate products. As it is, our products are inter-related, and the expertise built up by representatives in one area benefits the spread of applications. Very often they can deal with complaints on the spot, and only problems requiring a technician have to be referred to HQ. No one so far has suggested that representatives should cope with all technical matters.

f) Far from being a disadvantage, selling our whole product range keeps the representatives' interest fully engaged. They also obtain a wider viewpoint, with better knowledge of the overall problems facing industry. If job satisfaction is one of our criteria, then to narrow their field of activity is counter productive.

I have tried to keep an open mind and have endeavoured to look for advantages under the above heading. The fact that I have failed to do so may be my fault and perhaps someone else can enlighten me.

Maintaining the present selling strategy but closing the regional sales offices and using the regional managers for product sales

Again there is no problem in doing what has been suggested, but I am not sure what this is supposed to achieve. A minute saving certainly, but at what cost?

a) Regional offices are a focal point of our selling activity. It is true to say, though, that more customers are now on telex so that we receive a greater number of messages direct. Nevertheless, there is great merit in customers being able to make what is, in essence, very often a local call and speak directly to someone from our organisation. Someone, moreover, who is usually enthusiastic to provide an answer to the customer's problem. We have long been accused of being works-orientated. Today, we are probably more so than ever since we have severed the sales office link with customers on matters of progress (something we ought to take a serious look at in order to effect an improvement or a change). Closure of regional offices — whatever amenity we choose to put in their place — is unlikely to be a meaningful public relations exercise.

b) Three regional offices are a better focal point than one centralised head office. Messages are more easily received and, where necessary, passed on to the man in the field; it is easier to keep tabs on a salesman's daily movements through a regional manager at his regional office, than to demand a daily roster from representatives who are situated all over the country. It can be done the other way, but what would be the gain, and what our loss?

c) Regional offices play no part in receiving customers. Only very few call on us in person. However, people make good use of our regional facilities to communicate with us. Again, we could centralise, but would this be as satisfactory from the customer's point of view?

d) Regional offices serve, of course, as the centre for regular meetings of the sales force. They are also the place where records are kept, where sales activities are planned, and where common problems are discussed and, hopefully, dealt with. Records could, of course, be housed elsewhere and meetings held at suitable hotels or suchlike. On the other hand, without the present regional structure, everyone would have to travel to Sheffield for meetings, which would be more time consuming and costly (extra mileage and overnight stays for some).

e) As to the regional managers becoming product salesmen, this would add three representatives to the present twelve or, if regional managers are not to be demoted, $3 \times \frac{1}{2}$ a representative. They already fulfil a hybrid role in their back-up of the representatives.

I would welcome views and arguments in favour of these points. Despite much thought and heart-searching, I can only see a minimal cost saving coupled with the possibility of weakening our customer links.

In trying to summarise this exercise let me make my own attitude quite clear. I believe in questioning regularly the validity of what we do and how we do it, especially within the context of changing circumstances. To do otherwise would be to assist in the hardening of our commercial arteries. This credo is not, however, in sympathy with change for the sake of change, or in support of some kind of empire building.

With this in mind and after due consideration of the salient points, I believe that we would damage our interests by scrapping the existing selling mechanism. Our customers would lose out on the easy access they have to our representatives, we would impair our representatives' swift reaction to customers' problems (which we can maintain at present without undue dislocation of the day-to-day selling effort), we would reduce the maximum selling time face-to-face with the customer, we would lose out on the detailed knowledge of a more concentrated sales territory, we would lose the more effective control of three separate regions in exchange for one larger one (we are all familiar with the proportionately less effective and less constructive decision making in meetings of fifteen people compared with meetings of only five people).

To make these points is not to equate them with perfection, there is always room for improvement and I hope that 'improvement' is an ongoing situation which I keep firmly in my sights. But, regardless of any other benefit, it is easier to exert pressure quickly and in the right spot within the present set-up because weaknesses are more easily discernible. To borrow from military jargon, the problems of extending one's supply lines can be applied if one stretches lines of communication too far.

For all these reasons, I don't believe that the postulated variants would serve us as well in our desired objectives which I still take to include maximum per capita sales for maximum profit.

Bar Division General Manager's Comments

Terry Cooper saw several disadvantages to the existing sales organisation:

a) The territories were formed before the main development of the motorway system in the UK and little recognition is made of the system in the present regional and territory boundaries. Nor do the present sales regions and territories reflect the usage of bright bar in the UK. They were based mainly on wire and strip usage, which are sold to industries not necessarily compatible with those using bars.

b) Direction by the product division is not so easy. Urgent calls required by a bar customer may have to be dovetailed into calling-cycles for other products, although it must be said there are few, if any, instances of this having happened.

c) At present the representative has to determine his own priorities and a small bar account may suffer because of a larger strip account or vice versa. At least, if all his time is occupied with one product unit, there will be no conflict of loyalties.

d) The representatives have a multitude of products to sell and the range is ever increasing. This means that the product knowledge of the representative must be limited. Of our competitors, I know of only one where a representative may sell other than bars and that is in the case of British Rolling Mills who also produce steel strip. In the rest of the cases, our representatives have to operate in competition with specialist bar representatives employed by bar producers. Even our smallest competitor operates his own selling organisation.

e) Because of the multitude of products, the amount of product training received by each representative is limited as the time must be spent on all products, not just bars.

f) Again, selling many products to a multitude of industries does not encourage a detailed knowledge of the bar market and bar user industries to be gained.

g) Whilst every effort is made to keep representatives informed of developments within each division, it is difficult to justify taking them off the road for more than a couple of days a year to see any development in one division, when this means neglecting the products produced by the other divisions.

h) Because the representatives are selling a wide range of products and their efforts are spread over a number of profit centres, it is difficult for them to relate to the success or failure of a particular operation. I feel that if they were selling only Bar Division products, they would become closely involved and instead of being on the outside, in both senses of the word, they would become part of the 'team'.

On the other hand, he did see some advantages to the existing system:

From the Bar Division's point of view, the *advantages of the present system* are as follows:

a) Planning calls should be easier because of the relatively small territories of each representative and this should increase face-to-face selling time. This is very relevant in thinly populated areas such as Scotland, the North East and South West England.

b) There is a limited amount of spin-off from strip and wire calls which can lead to our discovering a bar user.

c) Regional events can be arranged to which bar customers are invited. There are sufficient bar, strip and wire customers in the present regions to arrange such things as luncheons, golf matches etc.

d) As travelling time is relatively low, expenses are low also.

Terry Cooper's Proposal for the Bar Division

His comments having made it amply clear that he favoured a change, Terry Cooper laid out his alternative for the Bar Division as follows:

1. We have estimated that the total number of bar-using customers in the UK purchasing over 100 tonnes per annum is approximately 380. These 380 accounts have an estimated usage of 440,000 tonnes out of a national usage of 546,000 tonnes. The majority of stockholder purchases will ultimately be sold to small accounts whom we are not too interested in supplying.

2. As 40% of their present time is spent on bar, we have assumed we would utilise 40% of the personnel in the existing sales force. This means one regional manager and five representatives.

3. We have tried to allocate territories fairly to each representative so that they each contain a similar tonnage potential and also a reasonable number of existing sales outlets. We have also taken into account the motorway system which can now be used to greater effect to gain access to various parts of the country.

4. We have assumed that the regional manager would become sales manager and be responsible for a number of main accounts which, at the present time, are dealt with by Head Office personnel or regional managers. These number 30, with an annual potential of 190,000 tonnes of which we get 33,000.

5. This leaves approximately 350 large user accounts to be divided into five Sales Regions. The proposed geographical regions are in Exhibit 2 and a summary of the customers and usage in these Regions is as follows:

Area	No. of Present Customers Buying Over 50 Tonnes p.a.	No. of Total Region Customers With Potential Above 100 Tonnes p.a.	Current Tonnage Potential
A	29	51	60,734
B	43	75	53,766
C	10	80	41,305
D	22	48	32,110
E	2	96	61,620
TOTAL	106	350	249,535

6. No system can be perfect, given the multitude of variables and considerations affecting an exercise such as this. One drawback with this proposal is that Area E has a high proportion of potential customers numerically, but in view of the geographical position it is less likely that these people will deal with our Works in the North of England and will be more inclined to use Southern-based stockholders. Area D has a comparatively low number of potential accounts but this area is widespread and one would not expect as many calls per day.

7. The Regions suggested have a span of approximately 160 miles which is roughly double the present representative's area span. But, if the representative is suitably sited, somewhere near the centre of the Region, his farthest point should be within two hours' driving. It would probably be necessary for the representatives to spend more nights away from home in the extremities of their area. This proposed scheme must assume a reduction in calls because of the larger areas covered and must be counter-balanced by a greater effectiveness of calls. This can be done by visiting only accounts with a minimum potential of say 100 tonnes.

8. We would expect the representatives to have effectively 44 working weeks, with 220 working days, to cover an average of 70 customers, plus say a further 20% potentials, total 84. Calls per day should amount to 4 compared with the present target of 5, giving a total number of calls of 880 per representative per year. On this basis, each customer should get 10 calls per year, or approximately 1 every 5 weeks. The sales manager making only 1 call per day for the 30 special accounts should be able to call on these 8 or 9 times per year.

Exhibit 2   *Proposed Sales Regions for Bar Division*

9. Contrasting these calculations with the number of calls in which bars were *mentioned* last year (5053), and the year before (6206), very little is lost in the new system.

10. The product sales manager would be responsible for his field sales force. I see his job as looking after a limited number of very large accounts, spending time in the areas with his representatives and co-ordinating the field sales effort with the commercial manager, sales office staff and the works personnel. He would be directly responsible to the divisional general manager and I feel that ideally he should be based at Head Office as perhaps one-third of his time would be spent in the Office.

It is assumed that under the proposed set-up, the allocated cost of the 25 internal staff would remain as at present and that Bar Division would continue to use the typing and telex services, public relations services, sales administration etc., provided by the Group. There would, however, be a saving of about £10,000 from the 40% allocated cost of external staff and another £4,000 from the present 40% allocated for Birmingham and London Office expenses. Even if an additional sum of an extra £1,000 per annum per man = £6,000 to cover extra travelling and accommodation was allowed for, a net saving of say £8,000 per annum could be envisaged.

The Strip and Wire Division's Viewpoint

Whichever way he moved, John Land could see difficulties arising. He felt it only right at this point to ask Paul Dane, General Manager of the Strip and Wire Division, for his comments as well. Paul was also very much in favour of the change:

1. Our representation system is old hat; the days of the very respectable (and in former days whisky smelling) salesman have gone. Customers want sharp information direct from source, and when they see salesmen they want them to bring real knowledge of the progress of their orders, the manufacturing ability of the works and the current lead time situation with them.

2. Our sales base is very narrow. I suggest it is too narrow because reps. cling on to old contacts and aren't in a position to open up new accounts. Whilst divisions can close off longstanding accounts which are unprofitable, we can't open new ones. We do not have sufficient control of sales.

The commercial manager, with his marketing manager and an existing regional manager changed to a product sales manager, would be charged with this responsibility AND be in a position to do something about it. This may sound a top-heavy team, but between them they would be equivalent to an additional representative and they would be able to support reps. where necessary. Instead of the man from Head Office being a nuisance, they would form a composite team with their four product salesmen.

3. Our narrow sales base frightens me. We are not doing enough to reduce our dependence on 30 customers who take over 50% of sales, who might be producing products with no future; who might turn against us for many reasons, including being taken over by a competitor; who might go bust. I feel our split of sales responsibilities is the root cause.

Conversely with this narrow sales base, product selling is anything but difficult.

4. In strip, we have 244 customers buying over £2,000 p.a. from us. At 15 calls per week with the larger sales areas, as against the current 20, a rep. can call on 60 customers each and every month. Thus 244 customers can be visited very month by 4 reps.

Of course, reps. must call on prospective and former customers as well as live accounts, but equally they needn't call 12 times per annum on customers buying under £20,000 of goods from us.

Once a month down to: £100,000
Once every 2 months down to: £20,000
Once every 3 months down to: £2,000
Then the calls reduce from 244 to 211

Add the visits from Head Office and surely 4 reps. can adequately cover strip (probably 3 if we have a sales manager).

5. The figures for wire are quite similar:

Category	Size of Large Customer Above:	No. of Large Customers
Stainless Wire	1 ton	97
Alloy Wire	5 tonnes	34
Carbon Wire	5 tonnes	49
Flat Wire	5 tonnes	130
		310

Allowing for overlap, these represent about 270 accounts. This is little more than the 244 strip accounts and probably the same call pattern will emerge and be handlable by three or four reps.

6. In no way am I suggesting we should not have a group sales chief. There is a vital co-ordinating role; there is the P.R. role and clearly we should continue to benefit from Nigel Barron's high-level customer involvement.

Whether reps.' salaries, succession, cars, expenses should come directly under Nigel Barron or not, needs decision. Certainly, we must ensure the rep. remains Lee minded and reports customer activities on other than 'his' product.

Despite this need for a degree of central guidance, supervision or control, I feel that product selling has a lot going for it.

This case was prepared by Martin Flash, under the direction of Kenneth Simmonds and Dean Berry of the London Business School. © London Business School, 1980.

CASE D10
TEKSID

In September 1975 Ferdinando Palazzo took up his appointment as head of FIAT's steel division. A man with a reputation for turning companies around, he was previously a director of the ailing Italian private steel company, Breda. He had joined FIAT to take up the challenge of turning the steel division into an independent profit centre and from a totally captive supplier to FIAT into a unit capable of selling 50% of its output on the open market.

The figure of 50% had been Palazzo's idea as a target and Gianni Agnelli, president of FIAT, had accepted it without seeking to analyse it. Before accepting the appointment, Palazzo had first argued with Agnelli that such a drastic change in policy was not required to make the division profitable, though the division had been the source of some serious losses to the group. But this may have been a tactical ploy to protect himself should his 'new broom' not work.

Palazzo had decided subsequently that given suitable emphasis on the division's principal expertise, the making of special steels, an independent profitable existence was possible while still providing a service to FIAT. The problems confronting him were three-fold. What were the markets in which the division could make money and what were the markets to get out of, both in Italy and outside? What was the rate at which he should aim to capture sales in these markets? And, most important of all, what were the changes required in the present organisation to carry out the new policy? One decision at least was already made. To distinguish itself from FIAT for its non-captive role, the steel division was to rename itself Teksid.

The Teksid Businesses

Teksid employed some 37,000 people, of whom 7,000 were in the steel-making units. The rest were employed in a variety of steel-consuming units which manufactured springs, tubes and other extruded products, tools, fasteners, a range of forged parts, ferrous and non-ferrous castings and refactories. A listing of product categories is shown in Exhibit 1. Nearly 85% of the production of these units found its way back into other parts of the FIAT group, where it was absorbed into end products.

The steel-making units had a hybrid combination of approaches for supplying FIAT's steel requirements. A diagram of the production flow is shown in Exhibit 2. About 800,000 tons of ordinary steel were purchased as hot coils from Italsider, the state-owned basic steel plant in Genoa, and re-rolled as sheet by Teksid, primarily for the automobile divisions. Some ordinary steel was made by Teksid rather than re-rolled, but the volume had been falling every year and stood at about 250,000 tons in 1975. Steel was produced from scrap in a series of 100 ton arc furnaces and made into bars, billets and rods primarily for the other units of the division. Production of special steels was about 550,000 tons per year. Stainless steel production represented a further 60,000 tons per year, mostly in the form of sheet, but unlike the other steels much was sold outside FIAT.

The principal customer for the re-rolled coil was the car division, which bought the sheet for body panels. The leader of the car division had always kept his coil prices as low as possible, resisting strongly any moves by the steel division to raise them. The re-rolling equipment was not very modern and the quality was poor — with expensive consequences. As the buyer of the car division pointed out:

> In the past there has been large variation in thickness compared with other producers. Teksid is working on this and their current aim is to save the Auto Sector 15,000 tons

Exhibit 1 *Teksid Products, 1975*

Steelworks:

Semi-finished products, bars, wire, rods, in alloyed and non-alloyed special steels
Hot rolled and cold rolled strips
Hot rolled and cold rolled sheets made in quality steels for hulls, boilers, pressure vessels, for general use, for pressing
Sheets and strips in stainless and heat-resistant steels
Drawn and ground bars
Standard and special sections.

Hot and Cold Forming Units:

Forged and pressed pieces for automotive and mechanical industry
Axles and shafts for engines and compressors
Pieces, in general, of complex shape and large dimensions
Cold upsetting pieces: screws, medium and high-resistance nuts, special bolts and nuts for important uses in the automotive field
Cold extruded components, having high characteristics regarding quality and precision; also suitable for the hardest working solicitations: joints, bushing for chains, gears for differentials, ball-and-socket joints for steering gears
Special components for automotive use and others, i.e. fasteners, connecting rods, elements folded by wire.

Foundries:

Grey iron castings, nodular graphite iron castings having high mechanical characteristics, aluminium permanent mould and pressure die castings
Small and large series castings for use in the automotive and tractor sectors as well as in household appliances
Light-alloy sand castings for special uses (aeronautical and nuclear industry etc.)

Mechanical and Diversified Units:

Equipment for foundries and forging workshops
Half-elliptic and spiral springs, stabilising bars, torsion bars
Welded and drawn tubes in carbon and light alloyed steels, for special automotive and mechanical uses and for oleodynamic and pneumatic cylinders; and in stainless for industrial installations, for heating uses, etc.
Chromium-plated steel bars
Shaped and unshaped refractories used for steel manufacturing, and in the ceramics, cement, glass and petro-chemical industry.

Exhibit 2 *FIAT Steel Division: Production Flow*

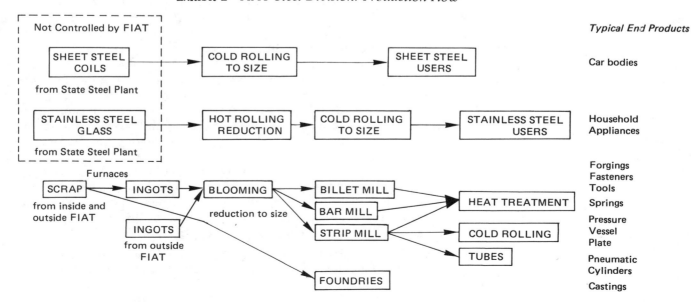

a year through more uniform thickness. We ask 0.75 to 0.78 millimetres, but we are now getting 0.75 to 0.81. This represents a difference of 200 million lire per year.

The special steel making was both modern and integrated. Investment had been based on achieving maximum melting efficiency and adequate capacity. The rolling lines producing the bars, billets and rods were reasonably adapted to production, but there was one potential bottle-neck. The heat treatment facilities were small and new facilities might cost 20 billion lire. FIAT, however, had managed to adapt its heat treatment requirements so that the volume constraint had no effect on the steel producing efficiency. The stainless steel facility sometimes bought in ingots from outside, but its sheet-rolling operation was efficient and its sales were profitable.

The production facilities of Teksid's steel-consuming units were also up-to-date. The foundry units had new facilities which were reputedly the biggest and the best in the world. The foundries took billet and ingot from the steel-making units, which it then converted into castings such as engine blocks. Facilities existed for very sophisticated castings in special alloys and aluminium, which were sold outside FIAT to the aircraft and petrochemical industries among others. The forging units also took billet, wire and rod from the steel makers, and produced items like crank-shafts, springs and steering rods. These were hot forgings, of which Teksid was the second largest producer in Europe. Cold forging, for which higher quality steel was usually required, produced items such as fasteners (nuts and bolts). Tubes were produced by hot and cold extrusion processes, for which again steel quality was quite important, and which was supplied by the steel making units.

Even the 15% of Teksid's production that was sold outside FIAT was not unaffected by the rhythm of group consumption of intermediate products, as this remark by a car division manager indicates:

> It is also important that so many of the smaller mechanical companies are linked to our car production. Of the suppliers I would say 70% are really captive. So when there is some kind of variation in our production, this creates a big change to the whole system and really affects more of the steel business than what they supply directly to us. Other producers have a wider spread in their portfolios.

As a set of cost centres in FIAT with profits and losses passed onto end products, the steel division had had no clear picture of where profits were made. The component factories were probably quite profitable. They were demonstrably as efficient and as good as, or better than, similar factories in Italy. They were probably as good as the best component companies in other countries, most of which did not operate outside their national boundaries. Despite their dependence on FIAT, they had little to fear should they be required to operate on a less direct basis with the group than at present. With steel making, the picture was more confused. Steel making had been a source of large losses in 1975, but exactly where the losses were incurred was not evident.

Teksid Sales Organisation

When part of FIAT, the bulk of the steel division had had no marketing force, no real stock control, and no R & D. Its relationship with the end-product divisions were such that these functions were normally carried out by them. In particular, the division responded to whatever the automotive sector wanted. FIAT, however, had not been a demanding customer, nor the steel division a diligent supplier.

Some sales functions did exist. The component factories had small sales forces that sold about 15% of production to companies outside FIAT, although these companies were often themselves sub-contractors to FIAT. On the steel-making side, two sales organisations existed. One was Coffermet which sold stainless steel inside and outside Italy and had sales offices in France and Germany. In France, Coffermet had 5% of the overall market but had captured 70% of the escalator covering market, having helped a manufacturer with some problems with finishes, and subsequently grown with that manufacturer's sales inside and outside France. Coffermet also had 20% of the French tableware market, a consequence of French tableware producers' need to meet Italian competition in stainless tableware. In Germany, Coffermet had a 3% market share overall, but much more in the sinks sector, where again this was the result of closely following a new development (deep drawing) in the market.

The second steel sales company was called Prosidea. It sold second quality steels and small quantities of ordinary steels that were surplus to needs. Compared with Japanese companies, for example, the scrap rate in FIAT was at least 15—20% higher, indicating a weakness in the quality control in the steel-making activities. The sales of Prosidea did not necessarily reinforce the image of FIAT on the open market, as a senior executive observed:

> We have a reputation for being unreliable in the market. This is because in the past we used steel outside FIAT as a kind of buffer. When auto production was down we sold, and when we needed steel we didn't. We used price as the mechanism for controlling this. So the FIAT image is poor.

The Italian Steel Industry

The bulk steel market in Italy was dominated by the Italian State company Finsider and its principal off-shoot Italsider, which produced nearly 60% of all Italian steel although little of the special steels. Many of the investments were made in the South for social reasons, but the enterprise had over-extended itself on the basis of optimistic demand forecasts in the early seventies. The private sector accounted for the remaining 40% of production and generally did not compete with the state sector. Much of the production was based on scrap and geared towards particular requirements as in Teksid's case, or to particular market areas, as was the case for the Bresciani. Italian steel production was roughly equivalent to French or British output and half that of Germany, as shown in Exhibit 3.

In 1962, with some 14% of its steel production in special steels, Italy had been in advance of its neighbours in emphasising these steels; but by 1974 France and Germany had caught up and overtaken Italy, as shown in Exhibit 4. On the trade front, the Italians had again been less successful than their European partners, with more imports than exports of special steels (Exhibit 5). Although some of the companies exporting into Italy had their own subsidiaries, the majority of imported sales in Italy were made through distributors, who also sometimes carried steel from Italian companies.

Within the special steels sector, the four companies who accounted for the greater part of the production were Teksid, Piombino, Cogne and Breda (Exhibit 6).

Exhibit 3 *National Crude Steel Production, 1974*

Country	Tons (millions)	Producers	Tons (millions)
Germany	53.2	Krupp	4.5
		Thyssen	16.0
		Klockner	3.5
		Röchling	3.3
France	27.0	Usinor	9.0
		Creusot-Loire	1.4
		Sacilor	8.0
UK	22.3		
Italy	23.8	Italsider	23.8
Sweden	6.0	Domnarvet	1.2
		Granger	1.0
		Norbutten	0.7

Exhibit 4 *Special Steel Production, 1974*

Country	All special steels (million tons)	Stainless steel (million tons)
Belgium	0.6	0.1
France	3.4	0.6
Germany	7.8	0.7
Italy	3.1	0.3
UK	2.9	0.2
Spain	1.7	0.1
Sweden	1.5	0.5

Exhibit 5 *Special Steels, 1975*

Country	Exports ('000 tons)	Imports ('000 tons)
Germany	678	323
France	459	411
Italy	190	217
UK	389	150

Exhibit 6 *Italian Production of Special Steel*

	1974 Output ('000 tons)	Proportion of Total Company Output (excluding re-rolling) (%)
Teksid	610	70
Acciairerie di Piombino	400	30
Nazionale Cogne	360	100
Breda	310	75
Acciairerie de Bolzano	200	100
Redaelli	190	85
Italsider	130	1
Idssa-Viola	60	100
Aveg	30	65

Each had its own speciality. Teksid was much the biggest, but was notable for its lack of presence in the market as its sales were internal to FIAT. Piombino was basically a bulk steel company, but had 80% of the high carbon steel market of about 400,000 tons. Of the low alloy market (63,000 tons) Teksid had 40%, with Breda and Cogne each holding 20%. Of the medium and high alloy market (280,000 tons) Teksid held 75% and Cogne 20%; and of the bearing steel market (57,000 tons) Breda and Teksid each had 45%. Finally, in the stainless market of 100,000 tons, Teksid had about 70% and Cogne 30%.

A particular feature of the Italian special steel sector were the Bresciani — small producers of steel for special purposes and markets. By careful selection of markets with tightly integrated mini-mills, these producers were able to supply particular products, like reinforcing bars, at very low prices. Because of abundant hydro-electric power in the Alps, there was extensive use of electricity for steel making in Italy. Low-cost electricity permitted smaller scale activity than was possible in Germany, where coal was the predominant power source. These small Italian mills, however, had little tradition of high technology and individually were not commercially strong.

The special steel market in 1975 was weak, partly as a reflection of general low demand for steel and partly because Cogne, Breda and Piombino were all in financial difficulties and were cutting prices to maintain cash flow.

The European Steel Industry

Special steel production in Europe was almost uniformly in private hands, but the state was found in varying degrees in the ordinary steel sector; and this sector was facing a deepening drama over excess capacity. The markets for both special and ordinary steels had very different characteristics outside Italy.

The UK market was dominated on the production side by the British Steel Corporation producing all the bulk and some special steels, and on the distribution side by distributors who were generally independent and situated nearer the users than the producing plants. The market was effectively controlled by the distributors, despite BSC's attempts to gain power through its restructuring. The smaller producers (of which GKN was the most notable) had generally integrated their business into engineering. Imports of special steels, mostly from Scandinavia, represented about 20% of consumption.

In Germany forward integration by the steel makers into mechanical and electrical engineering was common, and the industry was generally situated near the end user. The special steel producers were linked to the bulk producers and so were the distributors. The result was a market well defended by the steel producer, which showed in the low penetration of imports — about 5% versus the UK's 20%.

The French market was geographically fragmented, with little integration between bulk and special steel producers and a complex distribution system. Unlike Germany, prices were generally weak and import penetration of special steels higher at 15% of consumption. Compared with the other two countries, France was felt to be relatively weaker in producing special steels, and some evidence for this is given by the ratio of imports to exports of special steels shown in Exhibit 4.

The smaller European countries of Belgium, The Netherlands, Switzerland and Austria, were generally specialists only in certain types of steels, and with businesses strongly oriented externally, might be easier to enter. On the other hand, any position achieved might be correspondingly difficult to defend.

Teksid did not know much about the principal competitors in Europe, because of its low sales outside Italy which were concentrated in stainless steel.

In the UK the most well-known special steel company was GKN. They were strong in fastenings, forgings and most car components. The UK fastenings market was about 140,000 tons and 7,000 tons of wire rod were imported for it. In spring manufacture there were a number of small companies, using at least 500 tons of imported wire rod. Tube Investments dominated the tube market, about 75,000 tons, and little steel was imported for tube. In stainless steel BSC was an important operator, as were the Scandinavian companies, and nearly 40% of the sheets were imported.

In Germany the large forgings' market of 700,000 tons was tied in with the steel and car producers. Openings here were not obvious. Fasteners came from three main producers and amounted to 200,000 tons, half of which went to the automotive sector. In spring manufacture nearly 10,000 tons of wire rod were imported out of a total production of 100,000 tons, divided among several manufacturers. Germany was the leader in tool steels, using 435,000 tons in tool manufacture, but there were again few imports. In stainless steel about equal quantities were exported and imported (160,000 tons), about 60% from France in the case of imports. About 15% of the bearing steel market of 145,000 tons was also imported.

In France there were no figures readily available. Two important companies were Albert and Duval, which produced a whole range of high quality steels, and Creusot-Loire which, while specialising in one area, heavy plant, produced a number of forging steels. The forging industry itself was fragmented, but consumed about 200,000 tons of steel.

The information on international production was thus fragmentary, although (over the past decade) there was a clear trend of a rising proportion of special steel to ordinary steel produced in every EEC country except Italy. The market growth in special steels in Italy appeared to have come to an end, although this might just reflect the general economic situation.

Successful Business Strategies

Despite the prevailing gloom in Western steel markets, Palazzo knew that there were companies with a successful and profitable existence as the result of carefully chosen market strategies. One such company was Sandvik. A Swedish special steel producer, Sandvik had had considerable success developing steels that were used in cutting, grinding and abrasive applications. The emphasis in the company was on customer problem solving, and customer demand in effect determined both the R & D and product programmes. This orientation was accompanied by the ownership and tight control of the distribution system, again to provide optimal customer service.

Creusot-Loire, the French company, had taken a different line. They had decided to specialise narrowly in heavy plate, wire, industrial instruments and special welding electrodes, and to avoid direct competition with larger steel companies. The company also concentrated very heavily on certain specific steel qualities. As the fabrication process involved the use of scrap, they had used the financial resources of the Emapin group, of which they were part, to enter scrap merchanting and guarantee raw material supply. Their merchanting capacity was reputedly 200% of their melting capacity. They also bought small foreign steel companies to ensure a presence in important markets and to protect their niche. Customers were supplied from service centres and management control was achieved using decentralised profit centres.

GKN, the British group, ran fully integrated steel-making plants producing only long products (bars and billets), for the group companies. These companies, generally automotive component makers, bought 60% of the output (classified by GKN as high volume, high quality). The companies were independent profit centres, but their relationship with the steel-making capacity of GKN was close and tightly co-ordinated.

Another example of the benefits of tight integration was Willi Korf of Germany. Korf operated small steel mills based largely on scrap or directly reduced ore. These mills produced a small range of not very sophisticated steels which were sold to particular local markets. The operations were highly flexible, with stock held to a minimum. The small Bresciani steel makers in Italy operated on a similar principle and had achieved unbeatable prices in certain markets — for example, reinforcing bar.

Lessons could also be taken from the performance in the USA of Japanese and European steel makers. Price was generally felt to be only part of the reason why foreign suppliers had been able to obtain market share from even such nationalistic buyers as the car companies. The Japanese and, subsequently, the Europeans had been very skilful in developing new marketing approaches based on problem solving and better servicing, to the point where their service was clearly better than that provided locally.

Buyer Requirements

The requirements of buyers of steel components such as Teksid made in its forging, casting and extruding operations were generally conventional. Consistent quality, low price and quick delivery put a premium on internal efficiency of production, and manufacture was often to client specification, leaving small room for product innovations by Teksid.

In steel making the buyer requirements were more varied. Buyers like the car division made large orders, but looked for corresponding discounts on volume. They needed reliable tolerances, regular delivery and loyalty through business cycles. Distributors, who sold to a broad range of users, would normally handle the more common products, but would be concerned with the range a steel company could provide, as well as its prices. Special relationships meant relatively little to them, although they might be important to their own customers and they were often big importers. Customers like Teksid's components companies were often looking for problem solutions as the basis for an order. Buyers would place their orders as a consequence of some technical co-operation over a problem, initially in small test quantities, but followed by regular orders of standard quantities. Finally, buyers in the steel-using companies that manufactured either small runs or custom-built items would be interested in immediate delivery of small and varied quality amounts. Although Teksid had no precise idea of the size of each market segment, each was large enough to be considered as a possible outlet for large tonnages.

Inside Teksid thinking about sales tended to be in terms of products. Thus the producers of sheet steel saw themselves selling to sheet steel users, without defining much who they were. The same was the case for bar production, rod and wire production and billet production. In addition, the whole production philosophy within Teksid was based on supplying FIAT's requirements. Other buyer types were practically unknown.

The Strategy Choice Palazzo had to marry his vision of Teksid as an independent provider of service to FIAT, while developing as a major outside force in special steels, within the market possibilities and the constraints of Teksid's present organisation and past experience. There was no certainty that all of Teksid's activities were suitable for the future; and decisions could not be postponed on activities to be encouraged, encouraged only to support others, or phased out. Above all, Teksid had to be profitable — something never asked of it so directly before. The choices before Palazzo were many.

This case was prepared by Kenneth Simmonds of the London Business School.
© Kenneth Simmonds, 1978.

CASE D11
Household Distributors Ltd

Household Distributors Limited was founded by George Grange in 1960 as a builders' merchant to supply building, plumbing and heating items to local builders and tradesmen. The warehouse was located in an industrial sector of Watford on the outskirts of London on its northern rim. Change came suddenly in 1974. The building trade suffered a severe setback as a result of the poor management of the economy, the firm incurred substantial losses, and in October George died of a stroke at the early age of 52. The firm's shares passed equally to Stephen Grange and his sister. Stephen, aged 25, who had been working with his father, immediately took over as Managing Director. Christopher Malden, his brother-in-law, then left his commercial post with an importing agency and joined Household as Finance Director.

George Grange had been fairly conservative financially. With some pruning of excess stocks and a close watch on credit, Stephen and Christopher Malden were able to bring the firm back into profit by the Spring of 1975, while avoiding any major refinancing. Sales recommenced their climb more steeply than before and by the end of 1976 were being hampered by the lack of storage space for the expanding stocks. Stephen found it necessary to rent additional space in a building half a mile away.

This arrangement was complicated and expensive, so Grange and Malden decided to extend their warehouse. It could be easily extended onto the remaining part of their own land, which until this time had been occupied by a makeshift store for roofing materials, an unplanned scrap corner and a convenient place for employees to leave their cars. There was sufficient street parking, however, for these vehicles.

The new extension would permit storage of a larger stock and also leave room for a display area for a completely equipped kitchen and several bathroom layouts. These displays would encourage further direct retail sales, which had begun to grow more common over the past few years. Kitchen renovation had been a major factor in building retail sales, as fitted layouts were sought to replace individual cupboards, tables and sink units. The increased display was also needed because more and more builders and tradesmen were sending customers along to decide on the style and colour of the kitchen or bathroom suite that they wanted.

Shortly after the draft accounts for the year 1976 were drawn up in the last week of January 1977, Grange and Malden visited the Provincial Bank to seek an increase in their overdraft limit. Household Distributors had banked with the Provincial since 1960, but had hardly used the £10,000 facility arranged many years previously. Mr John Vreeland, the Provincial branch manager, was shown the 1976 accounts and the forecast statements for the year 1977, reproduced in Exhibit 1, which included estimates for the cost of the new building. Grange and Malden pointed out that their existing cash resources and earnings over the next year would easily cover the building extension. However, they would have to meet a sudden drain on resources for the seasonal increase in sales of builders' merchandise during the spring and early summer, combined with the new extension and income tax payments. After some discussion about the business generally and the rising value of land in the Watford area, Mr Vreeland readily agreed to an overdraft limit of

Exhibit 1 *Household Distributors Ltd*

Balance Sheet as at 31st December	Actual 1976	Forecast 1977
Assets		
Cash	£ 111,400	£ 82,400
Sundry Debtors	124,000	142,400
Stock[1]	332,000	366,800
Payments in Advance	14,400	15,600
Current assets	£ 581,800	£ 607,200
Fixed assets (at cost)	115,400	195,400
Less provision for depreciation	64,400	71,000
Net fixed assets	£ 51,000	£ 124,400
Total assets	£ 632,800	£ 731,600
Liabilities		
Sundry Creditors	£ 43,800	£ 41,800
Miscellaneous accruals	8,200	7,000
Provision for income tax	51,600	79,600
Provision for dividend	56,000	86,000
Current liabilities	£ 159,600	£ 214,400
Shareholders' Funds		
Share capital	200,000	200,000
Retained profits	273,200	317,200
Total liabilities	£ 632,800	£ 731,600

Profit and Loss Account for Year Ended 31st December

	Actual 1976	Forecast 1977
Net Sales	£1,940,800	£2,329,000
Cost of Sales[2]	1,261,600	1,467,200
Gross profit	£ 679,200	£ 861,800
Operating expenses[3]	543,400	652,200
Operating profit	£ 135,800	£ 209,600
Income tax	51,600	79,600
Net profit after tax	£ 84,200	£ 130,000
Dividends paid	56,000	86,000
Retained profit	£ 28,200	£ 44,000

1. Stock as of December 31, 1975 was £279,600.
2. Purchases during 1976 were £1,314,000. The estimate for 1977 was £1,502,000.
3. Expenses include depreciation of £3,200 in 1976 and £7,000 estimated for 1977.

£100,000. It would be secured as a floating charge over the company's assets. As the extension would be in operation by the end of May, Mr Vreeland specified that the overdraft be reduced to no more than £30,000 by 31st January 1978.

Christopher Malden stopped in to see Mr Vreeland every few months during 1977. Construction of the new extension was completed in May as planned and Malden reported that each month's sales were up on the previous year. Minimum lending rates had fallen from 14.25% in the last quarter of 1976 to 6.5% in October 1977, and housing starts had begun to creep up to an annual rate of 170,000 from the previous year's 158,000.

On 10th February 1978 Mr Vreeland finally received the 1977 accounts shown in Exhibit 2, with an invitation from Malden to visit the completed warehouse:

It gives me great pleasure to enclose our annual accounts for the year ended 31st December 1977. You will be interested to learn that sales so far this year are again running ahead of those of a year ago.

I believe you have not seen our warehouse extension since it was completed last May. I hope you can find time in the near future to pay us a visit and see around our premises.

Exhibit 2   *Household Distributors Ltd*
Profit and Loss Account for Year ended 31st December 1977

Net sales	£3,166,400
Cost of sales[1]	2,105,600
Gross profit	£1,060,800
Operating expenses[2]	839,000
Operating profit	221,800
Income tax	84,200
Net profit after tax	£ 137,600
Dividends	86,000
Retained profit	£ 51,600

Balance Sheet as at 31st December 1977

Cash	£ 400	Sundry creditors	£260,200
Sundry debtors	173,600	Miscellaneous accruals	11,200
Stock	628,800	Provision for income tax	84,200
Payments in advance	15,200	Provision for dividend	86,000
		Bank overdraft	11,000
Current assets	£818,000		
Fixed assets	231,200	Current liabilities	£452,600
Less Provision for depreciation	71,800	Shareholders funds	
		Share capital	200,000
	£159,400	Retained profits	324,800
Total assets	£977,400	Total liabilities	£977,400

1. Purchases during the year were £2,402,400.
2. Includes depreciation of £7,400.

This case was prepared by Kenneth Simmonds of the London Business School. © Kenneth Simmonds, 1971

CASE D12
Meridian Electric

Early in 1963 Mr Donald Bennett was appointed general manager of Meridian Electric. Meridian was the fully owned British subsidiary of International Electric Corporation and distributed International products in Britain along with a number of lines from other manufacturers. Mr Bennett's appointment had been made by Mr G.C. Sakuda who, as Vice President International of International Electric, was responsible to the board of directors for all foreign subsidiaries. The previous general manager had retired early for health reasons and Sakuda had persuaded Bennett to transfer to Meridian Electric from an engineering supply firm in which he held the position of assistant to the managing director.

Sakuda pointed out to Bennett that the past results of Meridian were poor and the board did not want to see the company continuing with lines which had an after tax return on the assets held, below the company minimum target of 10%.

Meridian was organised into four product lines as shown in Exhibit 1. Small appliances covered radios, television sets, record players, tape recorders, and hand appliances such as mixers, electric irons and hair dryers. Large appliances covered domestic refrigerators, washing machines, etc. Industrial appliances were sold to hotels, hospitals, restaurants and works canteens, and covered larger and more substantial appliances than those sold for domestic use. The parts and replacements line covered all replacements for the other three lines.

The sales staff were responsible directly to the sales manager, not to the four product line managers, and worked through wholesalers or, in the case of industrial appliances, direct with the potential customer. Each salesman had a specific territory to cover.

Bennett began his appointment by requesting the product line managers to prepare a full-scale report on their product lines and their plans for the future. Three weeks later Mr Grey, the manager of the small appliances line, presented the report set out in Exhibit 2. The small appliances line had been showing the lowest return of the four lines and accounted for 35% of Meridian's total sales.

Exhibit 1 *Meridian Electric Organisation Chart*

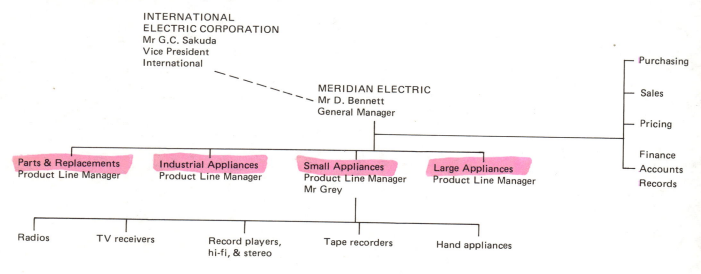

312

Exhibit 2 *Meridian Electric Internal Memorandum*

TO: Bennett
FROM: Grey
SUBJECT: Small Appliances Line Plan

Analysis of sales volume and gross margin for the period 1960—63 shown in Table 1 points up the following facts.

1   The decrease in sales has been most noticeable since the peak year 1961. In 1961 gross margins were cut and longer credit terms were extended to distributors. In addition, many distributors bought more goods during this period than they were able to move and consequently went into 1962 with large overstocks.
    Other factors hindering sales in 1962 were higher prices and shortened credit terms. These moves were taken with a view to increasing gross margins, reducing receivables, and thereby increasing profits.
    Despite the lower sales, figures show that this move was successful and profits have increased.

2   In mid-year 1962, large appliances were transferred out of the line, but the figures for the two lines are shown together until December 31st. After that date figures include only small appliances. This change, of course, affects the validity of trend-line figures.

3   Television sales reached a peak in 1961, but the market is becoming saturated.

4   International radios have decreased in volume, mainly because of increased competition from foreign producers. Other brand radios were successful until foreign manufacturers moved into the market with similar, lower-priced goods.

5   Tape recorder sales were hurt critically because poor products were shipped in 1961—62. With this problem now out of the way, there should be no difficulty in making up lost ground.

6   Record player and hi-fi volume has increased since 1960 and has remained fairly constant. There has been some hesitancy to purchase, because of the advent of stereo. However, orders are coming in now and we may exceed last year's figures.

Table 2 shows the overall operation for the years 1960 through 1962 and estimates for 1963—64.

1   Gross margins are improving and will continue upward. Low grosses were taken in 1961. Since then they have improved measurably, despite sizeable mark-downs and write-offs due to defective tape recorders and slow-moving other-brand radio stocks.

2   Expenses have been cut appreciably; where there were seventeen people engaged in the marketing function a year ago, we now have only seven. Mechanisation of order handling has also helped cut expenses.

3   Net profit, which was in the red in 1961 and broke even in 1962, will be well in the black in 1963, despite lower volume. With the expenses further pared down, lower inventories and the write-offs on tape-recorders and mark-downs on other-brand radio receivers behind us, we can expect a greatly improved net profit in 1964.

4   Total assets peaked in 1961—62 due to large debtors and other-brand radio inventory. Here again good progress has been made and the assets will be brought down to a point more consistent with volume and profit potential.

5   Great progress will be made as far as the sundry debtors picture is concerned. This will be due in great measure to having shortened our terms and eliminated large appliances. There still remains a problem so far as overdue debts are concerned. An estimated £100,000 will be difficult to collect.

6   Return on assets will show great improvement this year and the 2.9% return is conservative, as we see a good possibility of 7.0% for 1964. With continued progress on inventories, gross margins, expenses and receivables, we should, within the next few years, realise 10% return on assets.

    Mr Grey had received an International Electric Group circular noting that the central office had imposed a 10% minimum return on assets for lines of activity to be continued, and in commenting on his report he said that Mr Bennett should be careful in interpreting the figures shown because they tended to make his line look worse than it really was. Grey claimed:

Table 1 Small Appliances Line Sales and Gross Margins

Sales (£'000s)

		1960	1961	1962	Budget 1963	Budget 1964
				GM (%)		
Radios: International Electric Brand	Sales	231	296	159	117	107
	GM	N.A.	14.8	14.6	14.0	13.6
Other Brands	Sales	176	228	322	89	—
	GM	N.A.	20.0	14.2	10.1	—
T.V. Receivers	Sales	433	1053 *estimated*	610	537	556
	GM	N.A.	14.6	18.2	18.2	18.4
Record Players & Hi-Fi	Sales	143	254	241	228	236
	GM	N.A.	14.3	17.6	23.8	26.8
Tape Recorders	Sales	121	154	95	101	128
	GM	N.A.	16.4	16.2	16.8	19.8
Hand Appliances (Large Appliances until end of 1962)	Sales	634	729	553	62	43
	GM	N.A.	13.8	15.0	20.0	24.8
Product Line Total	Sales	1738	2714	1980	1134	1070

Table 2 Small Appliance Line Selected Operating Figures

(£'000s)

	1960	1961	1962	Budget 1963	Budget 1964
Sales	1738	2714	1980	1134	1070
Cost of Sales	1464	2307	1659	928	857
Gross Margin	274	407	321	206	213
% to Sales	15.8	15.0	16.2	18.2	20.0
Expenses	229	418	321	159	126
% to Sales	13.3	15.4	16.2	14.0	11.8
Net Profit (after taxes of 50%)	22	(5)	—	24	44
% to Sales	1.3	(0.2)	—	2.1	4.1
Average Inventories	338	669	594	192	132
Sundry Debtors	654	1122	1152	645	478
Total Assets	1022	1809	1801	872	629
Current Liabilities	N.A.	N.A.	509	289	270
Asset Turnover	1.7	1.5	1.1	1.3	1.7
Return on Assets (%)	2.1	(0.3)	0	2.9	7.0

Approximately 85% of the costs in my profit and loss are allocated costs rather than direct costs. The accounting practice has been simply to total all the expenses for the company — advertising, sales promotion, rent, heat, light, warehousing, provisions for bad debts and inventory losses, allocated corporate overhead, and so on — and to allocate these expenses to the product lines on the basis of their sales budgets. Only sales, inventory and gross margin are broken out by specific product lines. The way the accounts are set up, it is impossible to find out what the small appliances line is actually spending. It also seems to be that pro-rating the costs among product lines on the basis of sales budgets is wrong. If a manager has budgeted low and has a good year, this method of allocating makes him look doubly good because he is charged with less than his proper share of expenses. Likewise, if he has been too optimistic with his sales projections, he looks doubly bad because he's carrying more than his load of costs.

Another problem concerns sundry debtors. The acounting practice has been to report sundry debtors for the firm as a whole, by customer and by type of account — such as special terms account, regular open account, instalment contract account, and so on. For purposes of calculating the return on assets of the various product lines, the accountants first compute the ratio that total debtors bear to total sales. They then apply this ratio to the sales of each product line, and come up with an allocated debtors figure for each. The same sort of formula has been used to allocate cash and fixed assets to the product lines, although these items aren't quite as large as debtors and therefore not as important. I would say that the actual overall sundry debtors for small appliances does not exceed 120 days' sales and is probably closer to 90 days' sales. Yet my allocated debtors are reflecting the experience of the other product lines. Also some of the products within the line are doing much better than others on asset return. Some may be doing 10% or more. But because I can't get exact or detailed debtors figures, the whole product line is made to look bad.

Bennett decided that he should discuss some of these points with other Meridian executives, to help him in his interpretation of Grey's report. He discovered that a number of these executives had strong reservations about the validity or usefulness of the product line studies, particularly about the return on investment as a measure of a product line's performance. One product line manager said:

We're merchandisers, not accountants. You can't tell just from looking at figures what makes a good product mix, and you certainly cannot expect every product to turn the same profit. What about the loss leaders? They're as old as the history of merchandise. I'm not saying we should carry a line that shows a steady loss, but neither do I think we should consider dropping it just because its profit doesn't come up to some arbitrarily established level. The small appliances line helps us to sell other lines. I think that, especially in going into new markets, we should regard consumer products as the calling cards of our business. They're a way of getting the International Electric trademark known and respected so that later, when we try and sell industrial lines and International's other products, people will know who we are.

When asked what value he thought carried over from his line to the others, Grey observed that, while it was difficult for him to assess the role that small appliances played in cultivating markets for other Meridian product lines, he had found that a given product frequently helped generate consumer preference for other products in his own line. He pointed to the relation between radioreceivers and television receivers as a case in point. In areas where Meridian radio receivers enjoyed popularity, they had paved the way with the beginning of television broadcasting, for the introduction of Meridian television receivers. He added that possessing a full line of consumer products was important in establishing and maintaining Meridian's position with distributors and dealers.

Another of the product line managers, who had been with Meridian for many years, told Bennett that within the firm the size of gross margins had traditionally been the measure of the value of a product line and that, in his opinion, gross margins were still the soundest index. He thought this was particularly true since gross margins were based entirely on *actual* figures, completely avoiding the question of allocated costs or assets. He pointed out that the average gross margin on small appliances had risen from 15% in 1961 to 16.2% in 1962 and that it would probably exceed 18% in 1963.

Yet another product line manager expressed the view that while return on assets might be a valid measure of a product line's performance in some business organisations, it was not a valid measure at Meridian because product line managers did not have complete control of either the assets for which they were responsible or of certain cost elements which affected profits. He pointed out, for example, that the purchasing function was not under the direction of the product line manager:

I have no complaint against our purchasing people and I know that they make purchases only on orders from the product line managers. But anyone knows that a purchasing agent who's got his heart in it can save a lot of money and help keep inventory levels down. The problem is that the purchasing people aren't on the product manager's team. They aren't under the manager's control. Since the product manager doesn't have purchasing under his administrative control, I don't see how he can be held responsible for asset management.

More important though, is the fact that the sales operation isn't under the product line manager's control. While sales aren't as removed from the product managers as purchasing, still the sales people don't share the product managers profit-and-loss responsibility; with the result that they may not try as hard on a sale, or press for terms, the way they might if they were on the marketing team. This matter of credit terms also affects the manager's performance in asset management. We all know that the product manager has the right of final approval on variations from established credit terms, but he has to rely largely on the sales organisation's appraisal of what terms it's going to take to close a deal. If a salesman is a little too liberal in his estimate, the product managers get tied down to higher debtors which, of course, reduces return on assets. I think if the salesmen were on the product manager's team and shared his profit responsibility, they'd be more hard headed about credit terms. Finally, the fact that sales aren't under the product manager's control means he may not have the sales force he would like to have representing his line, or that the sales force isn't administered in the way he thinks best.

These are all factors that affect a product line's return on assets, and they're outside the manager's control. So I don't see how you can consider return on assets an accurate measure of a product line's performance.

Meridian's controller expressed the view that return on assets, though a useful financial yardstick in determining the effectiveness of a given product line, was not the only measure to be considered.

I think that before you drop a line you have to take into account how much it contributes to the total sales volume and how much overhead it may be carrying, especially if you don't have any other product to replace it. Small appliances provide the second largest sales volume among Meridian's product lines and accounted for 35 per cent of 1962 sales. At this level, small appliances absorb significant amounts of Meridian's administrative expenses, of corporate administrative expenses allocated by International Electric, and of the manufacturing division's factory overhead and product engineering expenses. If one were to estimate these figures, which is perfectly possible, it would be seen that the small appliances line is making an important corporate-wide contribution to fixed expenses. If the line were dropped, these expenses would continue and would simply have to be reallocated.

Since this argument called for estimates of overhead that would not be eliminated if the product line was dropped, Bennett asked the controller to obtain for him the appropriate figures for 1962 to 1964. These estimates are shown in Exhibit 3.

Exhibit 3 *Controller's estimate of Overhead that would not be Eliminated by Dropping the Small Appliance Line*

	(£'000s)		
	1962	1963	1964
Included in Cost of Sales			
Manufacturing Divisions' Overhead			
Including Depreciation	55	23	21
Amortisation of Product Engineering Expenses	15	6	6
Included in Product Line Expenses			
International Electric's Allocated Corporate			
Expense	13	7	7
Meridian Electric's Fixed Administrative Expenses	62	26	25
	145	62	59

(Based on Actual 1962 Volume and Budgeted
1963 and 1964 Volume)

based on sales

This case was prepared by Kenneth Simmonds of the London Business School.
© *Kenneth Simmonds, 1977.*

CASE D13
Construction Industries Ltd

The board of Construction Industries Limited customarily devoted special attention at its February meeting to a review of the group's marketing performance and prospects. The usual accounts and commercial statistics had been circulated with the February 1977 board papers, together with a special five-year forecast by the Commercial Director, Preston Smythe. These are shown in Exhibits 1, 2 and 3. Smythe opened the discussion:

> On the commercial side the group has weathered the deepest recession since the 1930's. The worst is now behind us, however, and I am confident that this year will see us back into profit — provided we keep our production costs under control and restrain overheads. The market is looking a lot healthier than it did two years ago, and we will get the work the production side needs. The commercial side has made its own contribution to efficiency, as can be seen from the comparative statistics, and we intend to keep our staff down to these levels.

Exhibit 1 *Construction Industries Ltd: Group Trading Accounts (£m)*

	1973	1974	1975	1976
Sales	54	56	58	59
Cost of Invoiced Work	49.1	51.2	53.9	55.3
Gross Margin	4.9	4.8	4.1	3.7
Overheads	3.6	4.2	4.8	4.8
Profit before tax	1.2	0.6	(0.7)	(1.1)

Exhibit 2 *Comparative Annual Commercial Statistics (£m)*

	1973	1974	1975	1976
Order Book at End of Year	35	38	25	20
Orders Received				
Estimated Invoice Value	59.4	58.6	44.9	54.2
Estimated Markup	5.7	5.2	3.0	4.9
Bids Submitted				
Value	331	293	187	285
Estimated Markup Included	33	26	12	26
Enquiries Received				
Estimated Cost of Work	420	338	192	305
Commercial Staff (No. of Employees)				
Sales Representatives	11	11	12	10
Estimators	25	24	22	20

Exhibit 3 *Commercial Five-Year Forecast*

Market Conditions   Economic forecasts suggest a very small percentage real growth until 1979, and continued control of government expenditure on new public buildings. Nevertheless, there are some signs of an increase in demand in the sectors in which we operate. Even taking a conservative view we expect a steady growth in the market open to us, as capital expenditure generally rebounds from the small level of orders placed in 1975. Measured in contract cost before margin we estimate the volume of orders that will be placed as follows:

	Last 4 years (actual prices £m)		Next 5 years (1976 prices £m)
1973	780	1977	540
1974	600	1978	650
1975	320	1979	725
1976	425	1980	825
		1981	900

Competitive Conditions   There has been a noticeable increase in the average number of firms bidding against us over the past two years:

Year	1973	1974	1975	1976
Average No. of Competitors	4.0	4.0	4.5	4.6

In our opinion this is a reflection of the smaller volume of new work and we expect that by next year the number will return to its traditional level. As part of our monitoring of competitive conditions, we commissioned a study of competitor prices over the last four years. As far as we can gather there has been only minor variation from year to year in the dispersion of competitor prices on the work we have tendered for. The standard deviation of all bid prices around the average price is around 9.3%. We believe that competitor prices veered downwards by 2 or 3% in 1975, as did ours, but that the competitive lessons have been learned and margins have returned to the old levels. With the hard lessons of recession behind the industry, we predict that margins will gradually creep upwards over the next five years.

Sales and Profit Forecast   Assuming that the economy can be kept on a steady recovery path, the group should be well able to react with a steady increase in orders. Provided that proper precautions are taken to control overhead expenditure, the group should move into substantial profit by 1978. Sales and profit estimates are as follows:

	1977	1978	1979	1980	1981
Orders	75	100	125	150	175
Markup	7.0	11.0	13.0	17.0	20.0
Overheads	5.2	5.5	5.8	6.0	6.5
Profit before Tax	1.8	5.5	7.2	11.0	13.5

CASE D14
The Widget

The 'Widget' was an important component in the electronics industry: its two major uses were in *Product A*, a consumer end-item, and in *Product B*, an industrial end-item. Seven European companies made the widget, which was well standardised in design. There were no duties on the widget and shipping costs were a negligible proportion of its selling price.

The largest European widget maker was Lamar Electronics, which made nearly 50 percent of the total European annual volume of 98 million units. One of the smallest widget makers was Electronic Products Incorporated (EPI), one of four European subsidiaries of Western Electronics (WE). Each of the WE houses maintained a separate profit and loss statement and balance sheet and had decentralised profit responsibility. (See Table 1 for a partial organisation chart of WE and its subsidiaries.)

All four WE subsidiaries made *Product A* and three made *Product B*, but EPI was the only WE subsidiary that made the widget. The WE policy on intercompany transfers stated that the subsidiaries were free to purchase their component needs from outside the WE System if they could obtain a lower price commensurate with good quality and dependable supply. (See Table 2 for excerpts from WE's transfer policy.)

EPI had offered to supply each of the three other WE subsidiaries with their annual widget requirements, but its sister houses claimed that they could purchase their requirements more cheaply from Lamar, and in fact they all bought from Lamar. Each of the subsidiaries admitted that EPI's quality was comparable with Lamar's.

EPI made three million widgets a year, using one million for its own production of *Product A* (these were transferred to the *Product A* division at an intrahouse price of $0.66) and selling the remainder to a variety of small manufacturers at prices averaging $0.68 per unit.

The annual widget requirements of the WE subsidiaries, the prices at which they purchased from Lamar, and the prices offered to them by EPI were as follows:

Subsidiary	Annual Purchases	Lamar Unit Price	EPI Price Offer
WE X	1 million units	$0.49	$0.55
WE Y	2 million units	0.44	0.50
WE Z	3 million units	0.42	0.49

EPI's manufacturing costs at various volumes were as follows:

Annual Volume (million units)	Total Fixed Manufacturing Cost (million dollars)	Fixed Cost/Unit ($)	Variable Cost/Unit ($)	Total Cost/Unit ($)
3	1	0.33	0.27	0.60
4	1	0.25	0.26	0.51
5	1	0.20	0.25	0.45
6	1.5	0.25	0.24	0.49
7	1.5	0.21	0.22	0.43
8	1.5	0.19	0.21	0.40
9	1.5	0.17	0.20	0.37
10	1.5	0.15	0.18	0.33

Total widget sales for the year were $2.02 million of which $1.36 million were to customers outside the WE system. EPI's marketing expenses for the year were 14 percent of widget sales to outside customers. General and administrative overhead was charged at 4 percent of total sales. Thus, the widget line operated at a before tax loss of about $60,000.

Table 1 WE Partial Organisation Chart

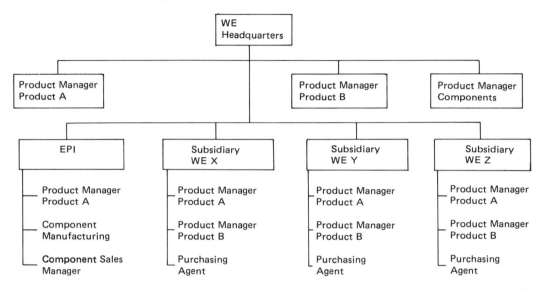

Table 2 Excerpts from WE's Inter-Company Transfer Policy

1. Purchases should be made from other system houses rather than from outside competitors if price, quality, delivery, and service are competitive. . . .
2. Where the parts in question are of standard design, are obtainable from outside the system, and are being used in manufacture by the buying company, they should be transferred at cost plus 10 percent, but not to exceed the lesser of market or most favoured customer trade price for like quality, . . . less discount for sales and advertising expense not incurred in interhouse business.
3. As used in paragraph 2, cost is to include material, labour, and manufacturing overhead, but not administrative or marketing expenses.